BESSIE QUINN: SURVIVOR SPIRIT

From Galashiels Mills to Gardens Cities

The Story of an Irish Family in Scotland 1845-1922

Ursula Howard

Published by:

The Endless Bookcase

Suite 14, STANTA Business Centre, 3 Soothouse Spring, St Albans, Hertfordshire, UK, AL3 6PF.

Available from:

www.theendlessbookcase.com

Paperback edition:

Also available in multiple ebook formats.

ISBN: 978-1-914151-33-0

Half the author's royalties from this book will go to the Glasgow Care Foundation, a small Glasgow charity established in 1874. Today their aim of alleviating poverty is still the same. They provide assistance to some of the poorest individuals and families who are experiencing financial and emotional hardship and cannot get help from any other source. They receive no Government funding and all royalties will go directly to people in need. For more information visit the website: https://glasgowcarefoundation.org

For my father, his mother,
and all the descendants of
Mary Lyons and Owen Quinn

Bessie Quinn's Family Tree

Arthur Quinn
b. Leitrim, Ireland
m. Mary Smith

Mary Smith
b. Leitrim, Ireland
m. Arthur Quinn

Owen Quinn
b. ca 1831, Leitrim, Ireland
m. Mary Lyons
d. 1901, Newington, Edinburgh

James Lyons
b. Sligo, Ireland
m. Betsy Commons

Betsy Commons
b. Sligo, Ireland
m. James Lyons

Mary Lyons
b. 1844, Heapstown, Sligo
m. Owen Quinn
d. 1922, Kirkpatrick Durham

Peter Lyons
b. Heapstown, Sligo, Ireland
d. 1868, Haddington

Betsy (Bridget) Lyons
b. Heapstown, Sligo, Ireland
d. Haddington

Owen Quinn
b. 1864, Bowland House, Stow
m. Alice Butler
d. Unknown

Patrick (Peter) Quinn
b. 1866, Galashiels
m. Ellen Brooks
d. 1928, Edinburgh

Arthur Quinn
b. 1868, Haddington
m. Jane Tocher
d. 1893, Newington

James Quinn
b. 1870, Galashiels
m. Mary Rehill
d. 1934, Melrose

Mary Quinn
b. 1872, Galashiels
d. 1905, Dalmuir

Peter Quinn
b. 1874, Galashiels
m. Susan Boyle
d. 1959, Duntocher

Alexander Quinn
b. 1876, Galashiels
d. 1903, Clydebank

Bessie (Betsy) Quinn
b. 1879, Galashiels
m. Arthur Cecil Howard
d. 1919, Hendon, London

Thomas Quinn
b. 1881, Galashiels
d. 1909, Dumbarton

Augustine Quinn
b. 1884. Galashiels
m. Annie Robertson Innes
d. 1930, East Lothian

Owen Quinn
b. 1889, Edinburgh
d. 1907, Clydebank

Key
b.= Born
m. = Married
d.= Died

James Quinn
b. 1894 d. 1951

Ellen May Quinn
b. 1897 d. 1994

Barbara Quinn
b. 1902 d. 1980

David Quinn
b. 1907 d. 1985

David Forbes Quinn
b. 1936

Arthur George Quinn
b. 1892, Galashiels
d. 1965, Galashiels

John Quinn

James Quinn

Mary Quinn

Thomas Quinn

Frances Howard
b. 1939

Joy Bernardine Howard
b. 1941

Ursula Howard
b. 1946

Cecil Geoffrey Howard
b. 1909, Hendon, London
m. Nora LePlastrier
d. 2002, Gloucestershire

Rosalind Mary Howard
b. 1948

Donald Gordon Howard
b. 1911, Hendon, London
m. Mary, née Gallinger
d. 1984, Surrey

Mary Julie Howard
b. 1936

Gail Annette Howard
b. 1940 d. 2016

William Lennox Quinn
b. 1917 d. 1979

Elizabeth 'Bessie' Quinn
b. 1920 d. 2001
m. William Herning

Kenneth J Herning
b. 1949

Menzies Herning
b. Selkirk, 1973

"This is the stuff of real history - atmospheric, emotional and acutely well observed. Bessie is a captivating figure. From the moment you see her wonderful, knowing smile on the cover, she has your attention and affection. This is a superb piece of patient and loving work."

Alistair Moffat, author

"A book that shows why family history matters so much. A moving story about a grand-daughter's quest for her grandmother's origins in famine-ravaged Ireland, a granular evocation of industrialised Scotland, a social history of early 20th century Bohemianism, and an examination of the damage done to families by pandemics and silence. Bessie Quinn, Survivor Spirit, deserves the widest possible readership."

Ian Marchant, writer and broadcaster

"In a trajectory one can only describe as miraculous, Bessie Quinn leads a transformed life in Hampstead Garden Suburb... Rich historical detail is woven with memories and vivid imagining of the losses and gains that Bessie's rise to the middle class inevitably entails. An innovative contribution to histories of migration, class mobility, and family relations."

Lyn Thomas, Professor Emerita, Centre for Life History and Life Writing Research, Sussex University

"A marvel of dedicated research, energy, presentation and imagination - with lucid writing holding it all together."

Grey Hen Press: www.greyhenpress.com - publishing poetry by older women

"A journey of Irish and Scottish roots ending in a garden suburb, cut short by Spanish Flu. Drawing on archive sources, fascinatingly illustrated with contemporaneous photographs, the book retrieves the untold story of life on the other side of a family that produced Ebenezer Howard and the Garden City movement. Ursula Howard searches for answers to questions about lives hidden among fragments of evidence, and in so doing brings to life not just Bessie Quinn as a resourceful, resilient woman, but the hard grind of family emigration in difficult circumstances at a time in which urbanism was remade in remarkable ways... An absorbing social history from below, in which Bessie Quinn's life is both remarkable in itself and illuminates themes of poverty, class, social change and the transformative remaking of place."

Susan Parham, Academic Director, International Garden Cities Institute

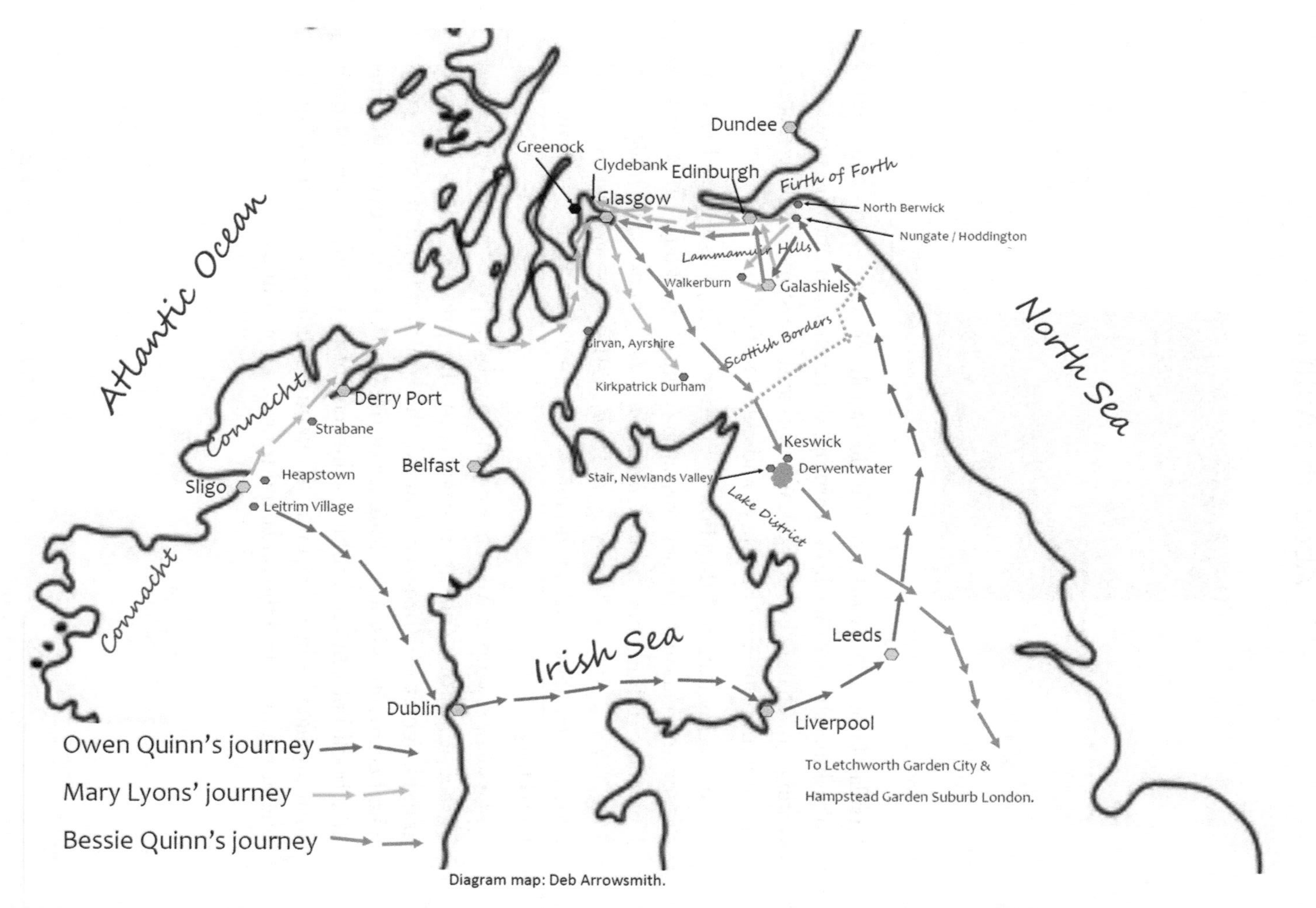

Diagram map: Deb Arrowsmith.

About the Author

photo: Tom Pilston

Ursula Howard's working life in adult literacy and community publishing showed her how learning, determination and the power of writing can change lives. Names, voices and life stories replace silences and assumptions about the lives and culture of others.

At the Institute of Education in London (UCL) Ursula was Director of an international literacy research centre. Building on a Sussex University DPhil, her book *Literacy and the Practice of Writing in the 19th Century: a Strange Blossoming of Spirit*, (2012) was well received and widely cited. She has an honorary doctorate from Wolverhampton University.

Ursula grew up in Manchester, and has been preoccupied ever since by social history and its relevance to the present. She is a great-granddaughter of Ebenezer Howard, the son of a London pastry-cook who became the visionary founder of the Garden City movement. This new book links his astonishing achievement to the life stories of poor Irish immigrants in 19th-century Scotland – the forgotten Quinn family, one of whom defied the odds and found her own life.

CONTENTS

Family Tree

The Quinns' journeys through Ireland and Britain

About the Author.....ii

List of Illustrations.....vi

Thanks.....ix

PART ONE

1 Hampstead Garden Suburb, London
December 1919.....1

2 Hampstead Garden Suburb, London
1914–1917: Family Photos.....6

3 Galashiels: Grounding Ghosts.....14

PART TWO

4 Leitrim and Sligo
1845–1860: The Ireland They Left Behind.....26

5 Leitrim, Leeds, and Lothian
Late 1840s–1851: Owen Quinn's Journey.....41

6 Sligo to Scotland
Late 1850s: Mary Lyons Emigrates.....50

7 Prestonkirk, Haddington, and Nungate
1850s: On the Wild Side.....55

8 Walkerburn, The Whin, and Galashiels
1862–1864: Old Places, New Communities: Wool, Stone, Water.....64

9 Stow and Galashiels
1863–1865: Owen and Mary.....74

10 Nungate
1860s–1890s: Life with the Lyons Family.....84

11 Galashiels: Comelybank Mill

1870s: Family Life, Fluctuating Fortunes 91

12 Galashiels

Late 1880s–1895: The Best of Times? 108

13 Edinburgh and Galashiels

1880s: Young Owen Quinn and Alice Butler 112

14 Galashiels

1892–1895: Arthur Quinn and Jane Tocher 118

15 Galashiels and Clydebank

Late 1890s: Those Who Found their Way, and Those Who Lost It 123

16 Newington, Edinburgh

1897–1900: The Worst of Times 128

17 Clydebank and Newington

1900–1903: Under the Singer's Clock 139

18 Causewayside, Newington

1900–1901: Owen Quinn's Last Years 149

19 Clydebank

1901–2: The Tenement by the Canal 153

20 Galashiels

1879–1901: Springs of Change: Bessie's Girlhood 158

21 Clydebank and the Dalmuir Shipyards

1902–3: Bessie and Alexander 162

22 Clydebank, Girvan, and Edinburgh

1904: Inside the System 166

23 Scotland and France

Other Brothers: Roads Taken and Roads Home 175

24 Radnor Park and Kirkcudbrightshire

1904–1906: Granny Quinn and Her Daughter Mary 193

25 Clydebank, Govan, and the Road to Nowhere

1904–1909: Poor Tom 199

PART THREE

26 Cumberland

1904: A New Life 208

27 Keswick

1904–1906: Significant Strangers 218

28 Keswick and the Newlands Valley

1905–1906: A Working-Class 'New Woman' 226

29 Stair: The Newlands Guest House

1905: Jolly Holidays: 'All for one and one for all' 235

30 Newlands Guest House

1905 or 1906: A Meeting 241

31 Keswick, London, Letchworth, Cornwall

Catherine Howard: Emancipated Eccentric 255

32 Letchworth and Keswick

1906–1907: Four Weddings 264

33 Kirkpatrick Durham, Kirkcudbrightshire

Mary Lyons Quinn 275

34 London: Hampstead Garden Suburb

1907: At Home Alone 280

35 Hampstead Garden Suburb

1909–1919: Modern Mother 285

36 Hampstead Garden Suburb

1919: 'We Had Not Known Illness' 298

37 London and Letchworth

1934: Return to Golders Green 303

POSTSCRIPT: A LONG AFTERWARDS 309

Notes and Resources 318

Index 329

List of Illustrations

Figure 1: 22 Asmuns Hill with December roses, 2021 5

Figure 2: Langfier's studio portrait of Bessie and her children 6

Figure 3: Tea in the garden at Asmuns Hill, Hampstead Garden Suburb 7

Figure 4: Bessie and the boys in their garden.. 10

Figure 5: Bessie, on the right in the Egg & Spoon race? Social Council Sports Day in the Suburb, 1913................................. 12

Figure 6: HGS Children's Garden Association: first nursery class 13

Figure 7: High Street, Galashiels and the 1888 Co-op tower: Mary Quinn's daily run?.. 21

Figure 8: Winter sunset at Greenock harbour ca. 1850s (P. Downie)..51

Figure 9: Carters crossing the Tyne at Nungate 57

Figure 10: Tannery workers by Old Nungate Bridge............................. 58

Figure 11: Brownrigg Farm, East Lothian: Mary Lyons' farm cottage 60

Figure 12: Owen's grandson Geoffrey's wedding to Nora, 1935 - looking more a Quinn than a Howard? 63

Figure 13: 'The Whin', Owen's lodging, north of Galashiels 65

Figure 14: First houses for mill workers at Walkerburn......................... 66

Figure 15: Bowland House Lodge, Stow, Galashiels 77

Figure 16: Our Lady & St Andrew Church, Galashiels 81

Figure 17: Comelybank Mill, Low Buckholmside, Ladhope with allotments: Bessie's birthplace... 82

Figure 18: The New Schoolhouse, built 1879 next to Our Lady and St Andrew.. 96

Figure 19: Galashiels Library and Reading Room (opened 1873) & Cornmill.. 98

Figure 20: 4 Chapel Street, Ladhope, with allotment gardens.............102

Figure 21: Halliburton Place, 1890: street scene, including Bessie and younger siblings, ca.11 years old? 109

Figure 22: 20 Mowat Place, 198 Causewayside – the Quinns' late-1890s home 129

Figure 23: Causewayside with shops, tenements up the hill 129

Figure 24: Middlemass biscuit factory, Causewayside/Salisbury Place, 1890s 131

Figure 25: Galashiels Poorhouse, Kirkbrae (foreground), the Eildon Hills beyond 132

Figure 26: Forth and Clyde Canal, Clydebank towards Kilbowie Road, Victoria Street tenement third left 140

Figure 27: Singer's four-faced, 200-foot factory clock 142

Figure 28: Singer Hire Purchase Agreement & Sewing Machine 162

Figure 29: Edinburgh Catholic Working Boys' Home, 52 Lauriston Place, 1913 171

Figure 30: Augustine's Army Discharge Certificate, 1919 176

Figure 31: Ellen 'Nellie' May Quinn 189

Figure 32: James Quinn of the Royal Scots 9th Battalion: the kilted 'Dandy Ninths' 190

Figure 33: Dumbarton Combination Poorhouse, Townend Road (image 1966) 200

Figure 34: Marion Twelves, at her spinning wheel, Porch Cottage, Keswick 210

Figure 35: Canon Hardwicke Rawnsley in 1907, the year he conducted Bessie and Cecil's wedding at Crosthwaite Church, Keswick 213

Figure 36: Edith Rawnsley, artist and co-founder, KSIA 213

Figure 37: One of Bessie's Ruskinian-lace edged linen smocks 216

Figure 38: T.A Leonard, founder of the Co-operative Holiday Association 219

Figure 39: Ebenezer Howard in his fifties, the time of his Keswick Lecture 221

Figure 40: Newlands Guest House – the Old Mill, Stair, 1907 230

Figure 41: Women cyclists' outing, 1900s 231

Figure 42: Mr Pape's waggon taking Newlands holiday-makers to Keswick Station 236

Figure 43: Women dipping in the mill pond, Newlands (1930s) 238

Figure 44: Up Scafell, 1907 238

Figure 45: Walkers' tea party al fresco, Newlands Valley 239

Figure 46: Hikers resting on Grange Bridge, Borrowdale 240

Figure 47: Arthur Cecil Howard in his twenties 242

Figure 48: The Dining Room, Newlands 1907 243

Figure 49: Motorcycling pioneers at a Keswick rally 244

Figure 50: Lizzie Howard, Ebenezer's wife, Cecil's mother, Garden City advocate 246

Figure 51: From Ruskin's Memorial, Friars Crag over Derwentwater to Catbells 253

Figure 52: Manor Farm, Norton, Letchworth Grange, William Ratcliffe's 1912 painting of Roger Parker and Catherine Howard's farm. The figures could be Catherine and Roger, with family or friends. 260

Figure 53: Letchworth Railway Halt, 1912. F. Spencer Gore (1878-1914) 266

Figure 54: 'Mother's Hall', Letchworth's first public building, 1906 .. 269

Figure 55: Living on a building site: Hampstead 'model village' under construction,1908 280

Figure 56: KSIA Copper Kettle set and Bessie's handwritten order. So Dad's trademark 'd' upstrokes copied hers 281

Figure 57: The Maypole Dancing at the top of Asmuns Hill 2814

Figure 58: Family Outing, Herne Bay pier, 1920s – photo by Bessie 295

Figure 59: Geoffrey and Donald on Cecil's motor-tricycle by Homesgarth, Letchworth, Ebenezer Howard's communal flat, 1921 305

Thanks...

To archivists, librarians and experts: Vicky Axell, Letchworth Study Centre and Garden City Collection, and Josh Tidy, Letchworth International Garden Cities Exhibition; Chris Cassells and Jo Sherington, West Dunbartonshire Council Archives; Erica Johnson, Dumfries and Galloway; Hanita Ritchie at the John Gray Centre, Haddington, East Lothian; Paul Barrett and Iain Duffus, Edinburgh City Library; Marion Lynch, Ayrshire Archives; Nerys Tunnicliffe, Mitchell Library, for insights on Scottish Poor Law. Clydebank Central Library staff; Anna Elzbieta Kulwicka, Mount Vernon Cemetery, Liberton, Edinburgh; Elma Fleming and Christine Nichol at Borders Family History Society; Bill Stewart, who drove me to Bowland House, where Mary and Owen spent their first year of married life; Jared Squirrel for precious information on the Borders wool industry and living conditions; Hawick Heritage Hub; Karen Lawson and Murray Dickson, Old Gala Club, Galashiels; Debbie Beament, Newlands Activity Centre; Sue Mackay, Keswick Museum and Art Gallery; Ruskin linen experts Louise Pullen at the Guild of St George, Sheffield, and Rachel Dickinson, Manchester Metropolitan University; Gillian Lonergan, National Cooperative Archive; staff at Golders Green Crematorium. At every archive and library I've had unfailing help, including Lothian Health Services Archive, U. of Edinburgh; Carlisle Archive Centre; Hampstead Garden Suburb Trust; London Metropolitan Archives; National Archives, Kew; Hertfordshire Archives and Local Studies and the Bodleian Library, Oxford.

To family: My sisters will remember things differently, but you've stayed interested, perceptive, and patient for so long, adding your memories to mine. That's mattered a lot: Bessie was grandmother to all of us. Thank you. Nancy and Ben, her great-grandchildren, have been patient as ever with my preoccupation. I hope this new set of ancestors will make even richer connections to the past for you and my beloved grandchildren. Rob Kenmir first spotted Bessie in Galashiels: his lock-picking opened her world. Aunt Betty Rowlands described Cecil Howard's life after Bessie; cousin Dorothy Jenner added more. My cousin Julie Rudkin, another granddaughter, found the images of Bessie and children in the garden and shared memories of her father

Donald Howard. Rudi Paul investigated 19th-century Scottish railways and designed the Family Tree, which amazingly fits so many Quinns into a two-page spread. Tom Pilston improved old photos and took new ones. David Quinn is my happily new-found cousin, touchstone and support. He's gathered information on the Quinns, and it's been great to know that I'm not alone. Menzies Herning, another discovered cousin and Borders man, found David for me. Thank you both. COVID-19 has stopped us meeting yet. But we will, and I can't wait.

To critical friends: Kieran Hardy, much missed, talked for hours about life in large Irish families. Sean Gibson read early chapters: his knowledge of Ireland and Scotland past and present, acutely attuned to people's experience, stories and motivations, kept me anchored to the Quinns. Jenny Litster read drafts as a Scottish critical reader, alert to language, culture and facts, from schooling to sweeties. Cilla Ross challenged me to search for Bessie's feelings among the facts. Alison Light was constantly supportive, while asking incisive questions. Timothy Ashplant offered advice as a historian steeped in life-writing from below, but also accessed texts with wizardry when the Covid pandemic closed libraries. Many more friends have supported me through thick and thin.

To teachers, fellow-writers, readers and everyone in the editing and publishing process: Julie Summers, Ian Marchant and Lois Pryce, Arvon Foundation tutors, saw this book as a reality when I had little to show beyond sketchy ideas and a few scribbled paragraphs. Since 2016, Ann Kelcey and the 'WriteStuff' Group have been staunch fellow-writers, as has the 2018 Arvon writing retreat group, including Andrew Hill's wizardry in finding elusive Ruskin references. The Literary Consultancy offered invaluable critical feedback. Stephen Carver, literary historian, inspired me to reshape the text. Catherine Robinson copy-edited and Gillian Lonergan provided the index – each of them meticulous and supportive in equal measure. I can't thank Carl French and Morgana Evans at The Endless Bookcase enough for their superb professional service. To everyone else who has generously shared knowledge, insights and solidarity: thank you. The mistakes are mine, not yours.

Stephen Yeo, who knows more about the period and subjects that this book covers than I ever will, brought critical, creative, narrative-changing ideas and insights to my father and me. You've lived with the Quinns patiently and attentively, for more years than any book should take. Without your essential love, and belief in me and our life, there would be no book.

Credits

Texts: Leontia Flynn's 'Mangles' reproduced by kind permission of the author. Lines from Lemn Sissay's 'Before We Get Into This' reproduced with permission of Canongate Books. Extract from Karen Brodine's *Woman Sitting at the Machine, Thinking* reproduced with permission of Red Letter Press: www.RedLetterPress.org.

Images: Galashiels: The Old Gala Club, Galashiels & District Local History Association. Nungate: East Lothian Council, John Gray Centre. David Cox, Innerleithen textile manufacturer and mine of local knowledge provided the Walkerburn image. The Whin: Robert Fogarity, Urban Explorer, @robertfogarity. Edinburgh: Edinburgh City Library Capital Collections, City of Edinburgh Council. Middlemass Factory, EDINA project, University of Edinburgh. Clydebank: West-Dunbartonshire Council Arts and Heritage and the Singer Archive. Lake District: Marion Twelves, John Marsh collection, Keswick. Newlands Adventure Centre Archive. Hardwicke & Edith Rawnsley: https://www.hdrawnsley.com/index.php/photographs/hardwicke-s-family/edith-and-the-fletcher-family. Cyclists: Nottingham City Museums/Galleries. F. Spencer Gore 'Letchworth Station': NRM Pictorial Collection/Science & Society Picture Library. Mid-Quay, Greenock (Patrick Downie): McLean Museum & Art Gallery, Inverclyde Council. London: Hampstead Garden Suburb Archives Trust. William Ratcliffe (1870-1955) 'Manor Farm, Norton, Letchworth' reproduced by kind permission of North Hertfordshire Museum. Other images by author and family. Every effort has been made to trace copyright holders and minimise errors or omissions.

A Note on Sources

Official family records, including censuses, births, marriages, deaths, Catholic ceremonies, military and passenger records: Scotland's People; Ancestry.co.uk and UKCensus online. Poor Law records for the Glasgow area: Mitchell Library; Galashiels area: Borders Family History Society. Other local records as credited in the pages above.

PART ONE

Before we get to know each other
And sing for tomorrow
And unearth yesterday,
So that we can prepare our joint grave,
You should know that I have no family,
Neither disowned nor distanced – none.

Lemn Sissay
(from 'Before We Get Into This', in *Gold from the Stone*, Canongate Books, 2017)

1 Hampstead Garden Suburb, London December 1919

On a drizzly December morning, her body was lifted away, light as a sparrow, from 22 Asmuns Hill in Hampstead Garden Suburb. The signs of her struggle to hold on to life were plain. Her husband, Arthur Cecil Howard – Cecil to her – had stayed beside her through three days of sickness and churning fear. That's how my father remembered it. He was ten, his brother was eight, and they hadn't been allowed to see their mother since she fell ill. Huddled in each other's arms like babes in the wood, they'd lain awake in the next room, frightened by forest noises, murmurings, thuds, gurgling coughs, and eerie moans. They slept long into the watery light that morning, heard the silence, and asked each other as they sat up: was she better now?

Three days later, on 18th December, the undertakers carried Bessie Howard, née Quinn, to Golders Green crematorium, the first in London, a short walk away from their home for the past twelve years. The low red-brick reception building sat at the edge of a wide-open space by the entrance on Hoop Lane, close to the Jewish cemetery, designed in the fashionable Italianate, Lombardic style. It was only a few years since the opening of the crematorium after years of campaigning for a more hygienic, space-saving way of dealing with the city's dead than overcrowded cemeteries. The gardens were still being landscaped, and a few scattered plaques commemorating the first people to be cremated – many of them social reformers – were mounted on the walls, including the family's friend, the socialist artist Walter Crane. The secular pioneers of modern burial rites had been joined by much larger numbers of soldiers, fatally wounded in the First World War. The remains of many victims of Spanish Flu were the latest casualties. After a small funeral attended by Cecil's family and their close friends, Bessie was cremated, her ashes carefully picked over, prepared for the urn, and returned to Cecil. Modernity in death, as in life.[1]

Changing attitudes to burial included the early 20th-century idea, fast becoming the norm, that it was emotionally harmful for children to participate in funerals or other rites of death. The children of the Victorian era had lived openly with death. Dolls had black mourning costumes and coffins, and children joined funeral processions. Infant mortality and death in childbirth were then so common that they could not be avoided, especially for people who lived at close quarters. But in the early 20th century as these twin blights on families receded, forward-thinking people, inclined to agnosticism or a secular view of life on earth, thought that children's exclusion from the rituals of death would help to protect them from grief and its imagined emotional harm. Death was silenced, and speaking of grief and loss was shunned for decades, not only for children. Geoffrey and Donald were not allowed to attend their mother's funeral. They stood together, my father Geoffrey remembered, at the end of their street and knew that whatever was happening to their mother, it was something to do with the tall chimney near the Heath. The sight of a crematorium was distressing to my father for the rest of his life.

Scattering ashes in a beloved place was a custom not yet imaginable. In those early years of cremation, people in mourning must have wondered what on earth to do with the ashes in their little urn – so they just kept them. So it was that for years Bessie stayed on my grandfather Cecil's living-room mantelpiece – or was it in the sideboard? The presence of her ashes in my grandfather's subsequent homes was undisputed: first of all in the communal flat of his father, Ebenezer Howard, in Letchworth Garden City, the utopia that he had invented. Ebenezer had attended my grandparents' tiny, discreet wedding in Cumberland, and now he was the comforter at Bessie's public funeral, a subdued, warm presence in the stricken lives of his children and grandchildren. Within days of her death, plans were laid and her husband set about systematically dismantling the family home, distributing and discarding their possessions – furniture, letters, photographs – all the evidence of their passionately shared life. Then he piled his two boys into the side-car of his juddering motorbike and rode away from Hampstead Garden Suburb.

My father didn't see his childhood home again until 2001, one year before he died. Yet the presence of his mother's ashes throughout his childhood was seared on his memory, and he always held to his story. The ashes must finally have been disposed of, but no-one except her husband, and perhaps Ebenezer, his father, knew when or where – until now. Bessie dropped into a well of silence, unbroken for a century. This is the end of the life story of my grandmother, never to know her grandchildren, who was reduced to dust and splinters and actively disappeared from collective memory by the very person who loved her most.

Perhaps Cecil and Bessie both wanted an obscure ending. The evidence has gone. All her belongings were lost, apart from three photos, a few home-sewn children's clothes, linen expertly edged with embroidered Ruskinian Greek lace, an Everyman volume of Browning's poems which my father thought was hers, and a beaten-copper kettle from the Keswick School of Industrial Arts – squatting on a stand with a jug, a sugar bowl, and a dented spirit-warmer. Arthur Cecil Howard kept to himself the facts known only to himself, and perhaps to his father, Ebenezer. He locked away every single memory of beloved Bessie, her secret stories and their life together, and carried them silently through his troubled life to his grave 46 years later, in June 1965. All he knew about her, that is. It was almost the perfect cover-up. The grief of three people was smothered, left for dead, trampled by the pace of change, their long lives obliquely shadowed by a trauma which had never been worked through, and so never softened.

The twitch of a smile in two of three surviving photographs of Bessie is self-conscious, controlled, wistful. Of course, photos were more composed in that era: the primitive technology of exposure times limited facial expressions. But there is still a tangible sense of enjoyment, of relaxed amusement even at her children's tantrums: she's the stray cat that got the cream, surrounded by comforting domestic belongings in a pretty surburban garden. She gives little away, but I don't feel she has locked the door to the place where she keeps her secrets. She didn't choose to die in 1919, a month before she became 41, two or three years after these pictures were taken, although wispy anxieties about the state of her health, her underlying frailty, may sometimes have invaded her as she touched wood about her improbably happy life with the man she had fallen for, hook, line and sinker. Over the decades, embellishing and smoothing uncomfortable memories of the poverty and the troubles of her childhood and youth, far away from London, she might have told her own stories as her thinning plaits turned grey. That might have been possible, once the feelings of guilt had receded and the anticipated prejudices against her class, nationality, and religion felt less threatening. It is because of how she looks out at me that I feel spurred on to know her story, to picture the patterns of her childhood struggles and rising hopes. I hope I can get her blood pumping again, hear her respond to question after question. I can imagine her talking, her chary smile slowly broadening without exposing her poor teeth – and I begin to understand all that she lost, and what she found, before she herself, among millions of others that year, was lost.

Figure 1: 22 Asmuns Hill with December roses, 2021. Photo Nancy Rohde

2 Hampstead Garden Suburb, London 1914–1917: Family Photos

Bessie Howard looks out at the world from three photos with her two sons: Cecil Geoffrey, my father, who was born in 1909, is aged 7–9 in the pictures; and his brother Donald, born in 1911, aged 5–7. The first image is a formal signed composition, taken in Langfier's studio round the corner at 343 Finchley Road. Langfiers was a well-known photography company, established in Glasgow, then in Edinburgh, and then in London; Finchley Road was their second London studio, established in 1895. The Langfiers – Louis Saul, Adolph, and other family members – were early celebrity photographers specialising in images of actors, including Ellen Terry, Charles Wyndham, and the music-hall stars Dan Leno and Marie Lloyd. They had royal patronage: a picture of the young George V is among the National Portrait Gallery's collection of 76 Langfier portraits. Some of the studio's soft-focused images of dancers reflect the modern free-movement dance trend pioneered by Isadora Duncan. The photographer in Finchley Road is 'R. W. Langfier'. Bessie and Cecil's choice reflects the Howard family's long-standing passion for photography – choosing the best artist they could find for their only family portrait. Perhaps Langfier's Scottish pedigree appealed to Bessie. She herself must have taken a few family photos, like the one of Cecil and the boys on Herne Bay pier (Figure 58).

Figure 2: Langfier's studio portrait of Bessie and her children

I've long been aware of the studio image, but without ever studying it before. Bessie is elegant and enigmatic, with the hint of a smile playing at the corners of her mouth, her large, slightly hooded eyes looking straight at the camera. Her linen blouse has a lace border to its square neckline, embroidered with a Ruskin-inspired rose motif. The skirt is short enough to reveal bony ankles. Medium height, slim, solid-necked, leaning slightly forward towards Donald. The boys are washed and combed, dressed in classic sailor suits with neat whiter-than-white socks and patent leather shoes: being shown off in their best outfits. Dad's hands already have the beginnings of their square, Picasso-like, solidity.

There are two more images of Bessie, informal but still staged. They were unearthed by my cousin Julie Rudkin, née Howard, another of Bessie's granddaughters. In both of them, Bessie's sleek, healthy boys are dressed for a special occasion, with shiny well-cut hair and home-sewn matching outfits. It is evident that someone took care to set up and take these pictures because – despite long exposure times – spontaneity and emotional drama escaped into the negative.

Figure 3: Tea in the garden at Asmuns Hill, Hampstead Garden Suburb

It is teatime in the garden at Hampstead Garden Suburb in one picture, with tablecloth, best china, and scones. The home-baked cake, quart-sized milk-bottle, and Bessie's bare ankles give the occasion a picnic atmosphere. She is paying attention to her boys. Geoffrey is in his smart sailor suit again, and his brother Donald in a loose linen tunic. Dangling legs and sandals suggest that the family is relaxing on a warm summer day. Bessie is in looser clothing – a floppy *crêpe de chine* shirt. The colour might be cream. She looks as if she's flourishing, enjoying life. She and a grumpy-looking Geoffrey are looking straight at the person behind the camera. The boy looks pained, as if he's been told, please, look at the birdcage sitting on the grass. It's stylish, with a big ring on top, enthroned on a base draped with a damask cloth. Donald also looks unimpressed. A little bird is just visible on the floor of the cage. It's too dark for a canary: perhaps it is a linnet, or one of the hybrid finches or 'mules', bred as caged birds for their song. Or a whinchat with a red-tinged breast and a sweet song, common in the Scottish borders then. Like other household pets, caged birds became hugely popular in Victorian and Edwardian middle-class Britain. Perhaps too common to be a memorable possession for a child – they are not treating it like a novelty that a guest had brought along. My father never mentioned its existence.

The battered chest, a makeshift seat that afternoon, could be a toy box, but more likely it was about to store motorcycle parts, which, at about this time of year, Cecil carefully cleaned, oiled, and put away for the winter. According to my father, the parts were unpacked year after year in Spring so that Cecil could reassemble his treasured motorbike and side-car for weekend outings to Letchworth or the Chilterns, or family holidays in the Lake District, Kent, or Heacham on the north Norfolk coast. The torn labels on the trunk are a give-away. The chest must have been Ebenezer's, carrying his prototype inventions, and among his clothes letters from his wife Lizzie, received on his voyages to America to sell his machines, promote his Garden City ideas, and meet up with friends, reformers, and fellow Spiritualists.

Despite a relaxed, fond smile, Bessie's lips are barely parted; her teeth are not on display. She looks her age, and there's a weariness about her: her face is slightly puffy, her eyes half-closed. Her hands – too work-worn to show? – are hidden under the table. Is Bessie still not quite middle-class and English enough – or still too Keswick-Letchworth-Bohemian – to know or care that a milk jug and silk stockings are essential to uphold middle-class tea-party standards, even in the garden? There are no guests visible in either garden picture, although the laid table and sailor suits point to a special occasion.

Bessie's husband Cecil, my grandfather, is probably behind the camera, an avid photographer, like all the men of the family. His uncle Frederick Harrison, married to Ebenezer Howard's sister Elizabeth, was a thriving professional photographer. Many of the family photos which survive were taken at his studio in Norwood, south London. And Cecil's favourite uncle, Ebenezer's long-lost radical socialist brother, Harry Caswell Howard, had been an avid photographer and camera expert.

What were they celebrating with a tea party that warm afternoon? The slightly ragged, overgrown hedges, long dry grass, and lilies – day-lilies? – suggest high or late summer. If this is September 1917, it was a warm dry month in London. September 1916 had been too cold for such outdoor treats. All four of their birthdays, and Grandfather Ben's, were in the winter, so perhaps the little party is the tenth anniversary of Bessie and Cecil's wedding – September 5th 1907; or were they marking the date they'd first met in Keswick?

It feels a happy afternoon. Perhaps Cecil's sister Kathleen Daisy (Kitty) brought her children across the road from number 7, Asmuns Hill. I remember her making any gathering cheerful, well into her old age. Maybe Grandfather Ben had brought one of his friends, fellow peace-lovers, social reformers, architects, literary giants, and advisers to his Garden City project. George Bernard Shaw and H.G. Wells were trusted friends of Ebenezer and visitors to the Suburb – in which Shaw held shares, just as he did in Letchworth. He and Ben held similar views about the war: that both sides were to blame for causing it, and that the working men of Germany, Britain, and its empire were the hapless victims of powerful elites. Ben's music-hall idol Marie Lloyd, who lived the other side of Finchley Road in Golders Green, was a friend and Garden City supporter who might have been there; if not, tales of her exploits and the singing of her songs were staples of parties given by Grandfather Ben. The dynamic, exacting 'benevolent tyrant' Henrietta Barnett, founder of Hampstead Garden Suburb as well as Toynbee Hall in Whitechapel, was another possible guest, but I don't think so. Bessie is probably too relaxed for that, and the children are not on their best behaviour. It's more likely they were put out by too much adult talk and were making their presence felt.

In the second garden picture, taken in the same season, probably the same year, Bessie is wearing a new outfit, similar to the one in the tea-party photo, but this time a thicker white cotton blouse, probably lined poplin, has replaced the *crêpe de chine*.

Figure 4: Bessie and the boys in their garden

The boys are both in sailor suits, open sandals replaced by patent leather pumps and white socks. It feels like a deliberate photo occasion, and the mood is altogether more tense. Bessie is indulgent, breaking into a smile as if she is amused by something mischievous that one of the boys has said. Or she is trying to cajole Geoffrey out of a strop. She is in profile, and the nose, which looks so straight full-face, looks longer, more pointed, slightly beaky. She's amused by something, and it feels as if a storm is just passing. Geoffrey is smouldering, perched on the arm of the bench, square hands clasped, and looking away. I know that clasp; it was exactly the same when he was 90. Two model ships lie beached on the grass – hurled in fury? – below Donald, who snuggles up next to his mother, in pride of place, a triumphant smile playing at the corners of his mouth. She has one arm round him, and you can see tips of – swollen? – fingers holding the handkerchief that she has used to wipe his tears and snot away. She feels like a kind onlooker and comforter, not a stern nor even a very firm parent of rather wayward boys. Her fingers betray a hard-working life. Her bony ankles, straight high forehead, long legs, solid neck above a slim body, and solid clasped hands (partly concealed) are Quinn family features which reappear among her descendants.

The two model steamships in the garden have either just arrived as gifts, or have emerged from Cecil's workshop. He was a skilled carpenter, chiselling Arts and Crafts motifs on useful objects such as trays and pot stands. Perhaps he made the ships for outings to the Round Pond in Kensington Gardens, which my father remembered as a favourite place for sailing model boats. They could be souvenirs from Grandfather Ben, who'd always brought back presents for his own children from trips to America in the 1880s, heralded in newsy love letters to his wife Lizzie – boats and balls for Arthur Cecil, 'dollies' for the girls. Eighty-five years later, Ellen May Quinn remembered the excitement of great ships launching on the Clyde near her aunt Bessie's home. And Alex Quinn could have hammered in the rivets of the world's then largest passenger liner or polished its miles of woodwork. Grandfather Ebenezer may well have crossed to America on the Lusitania in its heyday. But the luxury steamship lay at the bottom of the North Atlantic. Requisitioned as an armed merchant ship for the war effort, it was torpedoed by a German submarine off the coast of Cork on 7 May 1915. 1,198 people lost their lives. Ebenezer Howard, lover of ships, compulsive traveller, a man opposed to any war on land or sea, may have been dismayed by these reminders of deadly destruction lying on the grass.

The war may have featured in their conversations during those afternoons: September 1917 was three years into its horror. Cecil worked directly for ministers at the Ministry of Munitions – and there were already Quinn family casualties at the Front (which Bessie may have heard about). There had been German 'Gotha' airship attacks on London in June, killing 162 civilians. Yet like much of English life in the war years, this family scene feels far removed from battlefields and trenches. The Battle of Passchendaele – the Third Battle of Ypres – had been raging since July. In 1917 the whole world was in turmoil. Russia was embroiled in the war, and in the midst of revolution. The Tsar had abdicated, and two months later the Bolsheviks overthrew the interim government, set up the Soviets, and pulled Russia out of the war at the Treaty of Brest-Litovsk. Germany had launched unlimited submarine action, and America joined forces with the allies.

If they did talk of the war in the garden that afternoon, Ebenezer might well have changed the subject to lighten the mood, always preferring talk of peace to talk of war, or perking up the children with practical jokes, and always avoiding the subject of his miserable marriage. He would mimic his hero 'Buffalo Bill' Cody, who'd died earlier that year. He'd seen his Wild West Show in Chicago and taken Geoffrey to see it in London. If talking politics was unavoidable, he'd look to the future as cheerfully as he could manage.

There are hundreds of photos of Hampstead Garden Suburb (HGS) in the London Metropolitan Archive and the archives of the HGS Trust on Finchley Road. Images include Asmuns Hill being built in 1907, just before Bessie and Cecil moved in. Emerging from a building site, the generous green spaces and trees quickly made the Suburb beautiful: houses on wide streets which would merge on to the extension of Hampstead Heath; the area alive with sporting events, tennis courts, mothers out with prams, schools and nurseries, residents working on shared allotments, festivals and royal ribbon-cutting. This was urban life modelled on a country village, lived as much outdoors as the climate allowed. The Suburb was designed by Raymond Unwin, one of Letchworth's architects, and the Garden City ethos is unmistakable. I've found just one photo of Bessie in public – running in the egg-and-spoon race at the August sports day in 1913. I swear it's her. I know her well enough by now.

Figure 5: Bessie, on the right in the Egg & Spoon race? Social Council Sports Day in the Suburb, 1913

Figure 6: HGS Children's Garden Association: first nursery class

In the search for answers to questions about the lives hidden among these fragments of evidence, every clue brings more questions. No more pictures have come to light, and four years later Bessie was dead, a host of memories lost or buried with her. Bessie Quinn's officially recorded life and death give us bare facts about her and her birth family. Otherwise, the real-life snapshots and hundreds of mental images suggested by the official records are the only other glimpses into her all-too-human-ness, the historical presence which hovers below the surface of documents. Her slight figure steps lightly in and out of the public record, offering minimal information, or withholding altogether – at least in words – critical elements of the formative years which fashioned her striking resilience. What richness there must be in writing about a subject who wrote letters or postcards – even just one or two – kept a journal or inscribed precious books. I have to imagine much of Bessie's life, covering long distances between one official record and the next, some of them ten years apart. Apart from my father's vital memories, sparse, ambivalent and selective as they are, and five pictures and five artefacts, the choreography and the music of her life between censuses and official records of events went without a single recorded performance, lost for ever as primary evidence for a factual account. Luckily, much has been written and interpreted historically about the places, times, contexts and circumstances in which Bessie lived. That richness helps my efforts to imagine and reconstruct the possible patterns of her life and the lives of her birth family: the Quinns and the Lyonses.

3 Galashiels: Grounding Ghosts

My first glimpse of Bessie Quinn's early life came from the 1881 Scottish census. The enumerator must have crossed the Quinns' threshold in April (officials generally felt no need to knock on the door of a working-class home). Bessie was just over two years old, still the baby of the family, though not for much longer. She was living in Galashiels in the Scottish Borders with her mother and father, Owen and Mary Quinn (born Lyons), six older brothers and one older sister. Her parents were both born in Ireland. Bessie herself, sometimes known as Betsy, was born on 20 January 1879 in one of two rooms in a row of terraced cottages, built in 1852 for the workers of Comelybank woollen mill, on Buckholmside in Ladhope, at the northern end of Galashiels. 'Gala', as it is locally known, was a small but fast-growing industrial town in Roxburghshire and already the epicentre of Scotland's wool industry. Comelybank was one of several large woollen mills which were built on the banks of Gala Water in the middle of the 19th century as the global wool industry boomed, and the Cheviot sheep, providers of the raw material, grazed so close by that the people of Gala could hear them bleating.

Holding in my hand a print-out of the online 1881 census record rekindled the embers of a long quest to find Bessie Quinn the child, adult, and mother who would have been my grandmother. The tiny yield of facts from snail-paced searches – in person and by post – that I'd made with my father Geoffrey, Bessie's oldest son, had dried up when he died in 2002. The census entry may have been a basic find, but I felt triumphant, as if I'd solved a maddeningly obscure but significant clue in a nearly abandoned crossword. It might be possible to assemble some fragments of Bessie's life story after all. The 1881 entry named nine other people and smashed one of my father's treasured myths, which was that his orphaned mother had no family and came from who knows where, a mystery to him and all of us. Looking for one displaced Irish orphan-girl, I'd found a family of twelve living together, far away from Ireland, in factory dwellings in Galashiels on the Scottish Borders. As there are Quinns alive today, Bessie's direct descendants and her brothers' children's children, a large cast of characters makes up my suddenly much-extended, flesh-and-blood family.

Getting to know two generations of my Quinn and Lyons ancestors and where they came from gripped me more than trying to locate previous generations in Ireland, a formidably difficult quest. Without indisputable or even approximate information about Irish birth dates and places, from tiny townlands to villages to parishes, I was unlikely to find a soul, let alone a gravestone. My great-great-grandparents died in the Great Famine, when victims were hurriedly buried in mass graves. Surviving records are patchy, and many have been destroyed. In my case, the strong attraction of investigating contemporaries rather than centuries-old antecedents was that they were part of Bessie's life: people who hadn't existed in the mythical account of Bessie's life. Now, a hundred years after her death, she had walked back into my family, with a cast of twenty Quinns and Lyonses in tow: a group of blood relatives who, until that moment, I hadn't a clue existed, apart from her father's name on her marriage certificate. Gathering some sense of each of them, especially her immediate birth family, has helped to summon Bessie's elusive spirit. They all start their lives on sheets of black and white documents, but the faded lines suggest brushstrokes to help create shape and colour, and bring to life the Scottish landscapes and communities which held them.

Sibling relationships matter in real life, if not so much in family trees. Parent–child relationships dominate, not only in family records, but in the social construction of families and in psychoanalyses of how lives are affected by the nature of attachments, by personalities, and by emotional, physical, and mental states. But the importance of sibling position and relationships is increasingly recognised, and in Bessie's formation as eighth child and youngest daughter in a working-class family, her brothers and sisters may have mattered nearly as much as her overworked, distracted parents. Poverty meant having no room of your own, no individual retreat, no gendered spaces, few if any personal possessions, eked-out food rations; nursing younger siblings, at the beck and call of older ones; constant comings and goings; sleeping bunched-up, all in one bed; learning inner self-containment among a noisy crowd, and every sibling fully occupied with the unceasing daily struggle to get by.

Bessie's life story is also the story of her parents, siblings, aunts, uncles, nephews, nieces, and friends, who lived and died in her lifetime. She and her Quinn–Lyons tribe now have a historical, material reality: some are almost within touching distance, others elusive or absent altogether. Knowledge of her extended family begins to explain her life, and her actions illuminate theirs. The presence of all my working-class, Catholic, Irish immigrant family in Scotland had been as forgotten as was Bessie herself, always a name but never a life, and absent from my generation's consciousness, absent from the elaborate tapestry of my solid other-side-of-the-family's middle-class past. Clues to understanding myself more fully had long ago melted away in the smoky 19th-century air.

The Quinn family is no longer lost to the present or future, not even the ones with no direct descendants. The official records are richer than mere recorded facts, the raw materials of life history. The inky markings offer pointers towards paths through a dark forest. For any particular life there are precise times, dates, places, beliefs; and spouses, children, friends and acquaintances, attendant officials, priests, experts and authority figures; skills, work, living conditions, health, sickness, travel, and death. They are the springboard for reconstructing how people lived their daily lives, as alive and visible at the time as the illustrious, memorialised, and well remembered – but no-one was looking. They shared that invisibility with millions of others. I wanted to make them part of the human story: in this case, part of working-class, Irish, and Scottish history. The Quinns and their social group – poor, Irish, Catholic immigrants, illiterate and without documents to leave behind – have until recent decades been mostly voiceless, usually anonymised: a spoken-for people, clumped together to illustrate class characteristics or add to evidence for an argument in social or economic history. They are still neatly classified to suit professional typologies: skilled or unskilled; toilers or idlers; respectable or dissolute; craft-skilled masters, aristocrats of labour, or '*lumpen*', unskilled slum-dwellers and paupers.

Over the past forty years, the writing of history has become more inclusive. Social, cultural, and oral-history movements, working-class autobiography, and community writing, family history and life-writing 'from below' have earthed narratives and arguments and drawn millions more names, individuals, and groups into published histories and biographies of 'ordinary lives' and the imaginative explorations of fictionalised history. Boundaries between genres have become more porous. Previously voiceless people speak and write from their point of view, as well as through sympathetic proxies or versions of Antonio Gramsci's 'organic intellectuals'.

Like millions of others, the recovered lives of the Quinns are more than dry-as-dust statistics, just unadorned names of distant ancestors or one-dimensional, 'ordinary' people without psychological depth. One after the other, Bessie and her big family emerge as complex characters, agents of change as well as oppressed victims, living in communities, actors as well as victims in an unequal society. They are a close-knit, resourceful people, as different from one another as ten children's life journeys must be. There were things they shared, good and bad, and things they didn't. The Quinns turned their hands to whatever offered survival, bobbing and weaving to preserve their independence and stability. Every one of them dealt with their precarious place in the world, dodging some of the rules of the powerful, complying with others. Surviving independently was everything. They grew up, loved, had sex, married, bore disappointments, lost their way, struggled with ill health, disappearances, and death, and managed misfortune with more or less dignity, humour, and stoicism. Their communities were local: tenements, lodging houses, workplaces, pubs, clubs, and sports fields. Every working day their time and energy was consumed by the labour, paid or domestic, necessary for survival. Occasionally a day dealt daunting or tragic events. The Quinns were both distinctive and typical of their time. As immigrant workers, they created a momentum of their own as essential contributors to Scotland's economic, social, cultural, and religious history. It was Irish people who built, and maintained, the 19th-century urban Scottish and English environments – houses, public buildings, factories, hotels, railway lines, ships – creating the linked-up towns and cities on which we still rely. They laboured in fields, quarries, and building sites: blasting tunnels, breaking stones, and laying bricks. They mined coal, worked textile-mill looms, peddled goods door-to-door, joined the army and fought and died for their new country. As it is for millions of others, the labour of the Quinns and

Lyonses is the anchoring fact of their lives and ours. And while social, cultural, and economic historians have paid detailed attention to crafts, few interest themselves in the processes of manual labour, the interaction of humans and their tools with raw material. That has been captured by poets, painters and novelists. On the pages of Walt Whitman's *Leaves of Grass,* long rhythmic lists of tools, machines, and the motions of human labour are lined up. Romeo Mancini's image of an Umbrian stone-breaker spoke to me of Owen Quinn's life, as Millet's gleaners spoke of Mary's.

The discovery of a new fact about the Quinns triggered shockwaves through my mind and body: delight, sadness, curiosity, anger, grief, and a peculiarly protective love. I had been prepared for strong feelings when I encountered my grandmother Bessie, but not heady elation or dismay at the fate of her parents, grandparents; aunts, uncles; her brothers, their wives and children, and sister. It may all be projection on my part: in what sense are feelings for dead unknown others really about them, rather than one's own emotional response to the 'material'? Yet this project feels the nearest I've ever come to a visceral sense of connection to the meaning of poverty. A blood-bond. It was also a romance, from light to lurid to dark. In the archives, I unwrapped surprise gifts, like a child: delightful treats and disappointing duds. Curious and intrigued, I fell in love with buoyant, steady, and tragic figures, elaborating their characters as I learned their fates. The sudden arrival on paper of disturbing or rewarding relatives was profound in its effect. Gradually I got used to them. They became normal, giving me a deeper sense of myself and people to love vicariously across time, standing back for a proper view of their stories – my past – to analyse and connect.

The Quinns' lives and deaths are visible now and cannot disappear again, even if they gather dust until someone else wants to know more. Working-class life is better known than it ever was, even though the lives of millions of migrants and their forebears remain hidden, apart from those who wrote autobiographies or caught the attention of social investigators. History still excludes millions of names, and being forgotten has been their scandalous status. The debate about the legitimacy of speculation and imagination in historical writing feels relevant. If history is not to be forever dominated by middle- and upper-class perspectives, because written 'evidence' is plentiful, how best to go about life history from below, where facts are sparse to vanishing? This book is primarily based on official records, written and oral memories, then connected to what is known about comparable lives, events, and movements. The Quinns are contextualised in time and place. But imagination, signposted and historically informed, I hope helps to illuminate their lives more clearly.

The name Betsy, as Bessie was also known as a small girl, had previously cropped up on the Lyons side of the family (her mother's). Bessie was referred to only twice as Elizabeth: once at her church confirmation, and more than a decade later by a Clydebank Poor Law inspector. It's not rare, in this or other families, for names to slip and slide. Their identity was still partly in their control, despite the attempts of the State to pin down in writing precisely who they were. The Quinns were not policed by official literacy: it was new to them, and illiteracy carried little shame before the era of universal state education. Indeed, their lack of it offered a certain freedom to use their own currency, oral memory, to suit the needs of the moment or to comply with official demands. Subject to daily anti-Irish prejudice, and with Church and State authorities breathing down their necks, telling them who they were and how they should behave, changing a name, a place, or a date expressed a wish or a practical need to define their own lives. At its most extreme, a change of name also helped people to disappear from view if need be.

Bessie's first home was two rooms (each with one window) in Comelybank Mill workers' terraces, Low Buckholmside, Ladhope, Galashiels. It was a tied dwelling: no work, no home. One room served as kitchen, living room, and parents' bedroom combined, with two set-in beds – one for the latest baby alongside theirs. When Bessie was born, the second room was the bedroom for seven older children. Close-up living bred in many a self-protective reserve, tough skins thickened through bodies living and sleeping together, regardless of gender; tacit acceptance of shared sights and smells, and when to turn away; things known and felt, but not spoken about: intimacy, wanted or not. And chariness: a none-of-your-business, keep-out message to the outside world.

Life was hard. Pumping cold water, lighting fires to heat it. Sharing amenities with other tenants: pumps, laundries, washing lines, and nooks and crannies for storing coal. Inside, a shared bucket was filled with excrement and put out for sewage collections twice a week. No lavatories in the factory either, and a sweaty twelve-hour working day. Gala citizens weren't despised by other Borders towns as 'pail merks' for nothing. Overpowering stenches inside and outside, twenty-four hours a day. The tannery which processed thousands of sheepskins every week stank. The whole town stank.[2]

Owen Quin(n) and Mary, née Lyons, were Irish immigrants to Scotland, both recorded as orphans, refugees from the hunger and hardship of the Irish Famine (1845–1852) and its aftermath. Bessie was the eighth of their ten children, and all but two were born at home in Galashiels. The Quinn children were born every two years or so, and every one born alive survived into adulthood. Perhaps there were miscarriages or stillbirths, but no official written record was required for these. The children's survival is striking evidence of their mother's good health, her attention to their well-being, a reasonable diet, and undoubtedly long periods of breastfeeding, the usual and easily the safest baby food which (for a while) also offered her some protection against pregnancy. The Quinn children, in order of birth, were Owen (1864); Patrick (1866); Arthur (1868); James (1870); Mary (1872); Peter (1874); Alexander (Alex) (1876); and Bessie (1879). Two more brothers followed: Thomas (Tom) in 1881 and the youngest, Augustine, in 1884.

In 1881, when Bessie was a two-year-old bushy-haired toddler, still the youngest, she would have walked hand in hand with her mother Mary over Gala Water to the shops or stalls along the bustling main streets of Galashiels. Oatmeal porridge, or a pap of stale bread with milk-and-water, warmed her belly, now that her mother's milk was drying up. The family had moved from the mill site at Buckholmside to two rooms in a cottage in Chapel Street, Ladhope, still sharing a front door with other tenants. I imagine her running down the pathway in front of their new home, a typical toddler stopping to peer around, running into alleyways, and on wintry mornings wading through snow, mud and stinking manure in hand-me-down boots, cracking icy puddles, stooping to pick up the stones, feathers, and debris from the squelchy ground.

Figure 7: High Street, Galashiels and the 1888 Co-op tower: Mary Quinn's daily run?

As a working-class girl in a large, poor family, Bessie would have started housework young, even before she went to school at the age of four or five. She trailed alongside her mother and older sister – the two Marys. She'd have learned early how to clean, help with the washing, cook, sew, and mend clothes. Much of a young girl's time, every day, was spent tackling a task, then the next, and the next, so that the whole family was fed, clothed, and able to work.

At school, educational materials weren't confined to sand, blackboard and chalk. The Catholic church school, Our Lady and St Andrew, provided catechisms, primers, grammars, a ration of paper and a pencil to clutch between chapped fingers. Given the size of Gala's Catholic population, this would have been a mixed-sex school and, as in most schools, teachers were lay Catholic women or Religious (nuns), helped by pupil teachers (recent school-leavers). Inspection reports suggest that Catholic schools were mostly good, despite the poverty of the children's homes. Each morning, Bessie would have trotted behind a noisy group of older brothers, dressed in the winter months in a patched and mended coat, chilblained fingers exposed, woollen stockings, a pinny over a prickly woollen skirt, and old buttoned boots so tight that hammer toes were already forming. They walked through Ladhope to the school on Stirling Street and disappeared for the day. The provision of Catholic elementary schools like theirs was patchy in 1880s Presbyterian Scotland, and the schools were not integrated into Scottish state education until 1918. The church organised its own schools in the big cities, but too few for the growing population. The Galashiels school was built unusually early, thanks to the heirs of Walter Scott – a local hero of the Borders, as well as a literary giant. His granddaughter Charlotte and her husband Robert Hope-Scott, converted Catholics, inherited Scott's money, his estate, and his patrician concern for people's welfare. The two philanthropists donated the money for the building of the Catholic chapel in 1853 and its 1870s extension into an imposing church with a schoolroom attached, close to the centre of Galashiels. The church still stands, solid and imposing, beside the Bus Station. The Quinn children were luckier than many other Irish immigrant children in Scotland without friends in high places, who either had no schooling, or attended Protestant establishments or the industrial 'Ragged' schools.[3]

I picture Bessie at the age of 12 running back from school after classes, wavy brown hair bouncing as she pushed open the front door and sat down to bread and milky tea. From 10 or 11 she'd have been half-time at school, half-time at work: on alternate weeks three days or two days at school and the other days among the machinery at the mill, or helping her mother at home, leaving education altogether on her thirteenth birthday at the latest. Her housework might have run as follows. She'd tie a pinny round her and start scrubbing and washing, then stitching and darning to help her mother. Working-class women, officially described as 'wife' or 'housewife' on the census, in reality took in work to supplement the wages of men like Owen, labouring on precarious contracts. It's highly likely that Mary, a former woollen millworker from an Irish hand-spinning and weaving culture, sewed for money as well as altering and mending her family's home-sewn and second-hand clothes. Her output could double if she and both daughters mended, patched, altered, and darned. Once her daughter Mary reached the age of 12 and worked full-time at the mill, Bessie would also be peeling potatoes and chopping vegetables for a soup or stew on the kitchen range, ready for her father and siblings coming home from their various shifts. She would be keeping an eye on her two younger brothers, Tom and Augustine, and, after 1890, Owen, a live-in nephew who was still too young to go to school. More of the youngest Owen later. She'd have stopped their squabbles, brushed tears from dirt-streaked faces, wiped their noses, and cleaned their bottoms with rags and scraps of paper after they'd squatted over the family pail. If she did all this, she was typical of multitudes of girls in similar circumstances.

Any free time for Bessie would be on Sundays, after Mass and Sunday School. Attached to their church was a library, built in 1872, also funded by the Hope-Scotts, initially filled with books and valued at £500 – nearly £60,000 today, so either the valuation included the costs of creating and furnishing it, or some very valuable books were lodged there. Either way, the sum suggests ambitious investment in the Catholic population's cultural life. There is no record of what happened to the library or its contents.[4] Bessie could have borrowed books to read stories to Tom, Augustine, and later her nephews Owen and Arthur George – if they could hear a word of it: evenings must have been noisy. Shouting, joking, banter, quarrels, and fights. She had no sway over the mood and tumult in their rooms as she wove her way to the sink between the sweat, steam, and jabber of jostling older brothers, carrying piles of plates and spoons. If and when they ate together: many families didn't, as limited space and varied shifts made communal eating almost impossible. The water that had been lugged from an outside tap and heated over the fire for tea and washing wouldn't stay hot for long, especially in winter.

Their father Owen, certainly exhausted and probably wheezing from debilitating bouts of bronchitis, would have been picking out rich loam stuck under his finger-nails with a splinter of wood from the pile. Splinters were also used to pick teeth clean, helped along with soot or salt. He may already have been working on their shared allotment. And on paydays, called in at the Ladhope Inn or another regular haunt with workmates and his oldest boys. There was a lively pub culture in Galashiels and all the Borders towns, and Saturday sometimes stretched to Tuesday or even Wednesday.[5] These were the years when six or seven pairs of cracked work-boots and stiff, reeking trousers and underwear littered the floor that Bessie had probably just cleaned, and the mud-streaked tiles were as slippery as melting ice. She, her mother, and her sister were left to mop up.

Here is one scene, typical of families like theirs. On Saturday afternoons their living room – kitchen, dining room, parents' bedroom, and sewing workshop – became a bathroom. That was when families took a bath, scrubbing away the week's work with carbolic soap. Girls would disappear while men and boys took turns. A traditional line-up would start with Owen, as head of the family, then the brothers immersed themselves in order of age. Little Augustine would have needed a wash-down after a quick dip into tepid greasy water with scum and sediment from the drifts of fibres which thickened the woollen mill's vaporous air. When Mary and her girls bathed is unknown: another time, when they were by themselves. But the girls would have prepared the Saturday afternoon bath for the men and boys, making a roaring fire, helping their mother to bring up the tub – shared with other tenants – and emptying kettle after kettle and every pot and pan full of hot water into the tub. Their job done, Mary and Bessie might set off through Gala, arms steaming-pink, poking out of soggy rolled-up sleeves, soon cold and shivery from the damp. For Saturday's evening meal, they might have brought home weak beer, slopping over the sides of an enormous pitcher.

As she grew up, the family would have depended on Bessie more and more to run the household and care for the youngest ones, taking responsibility and hard-pressed from daybreak to dusk. Her sister Mary was often sick and her mother couldn't manage everything. Little more than a decade later her mother would be officially reported as unable to manage anything much at all. Aged 10, Bessie would have started work as a half-time mill-piecer, crawling under the big looms all day. She was lucky to survive unscathed.

PART TWO

… we sell ourselves in fractions, they don't want us all
at once, but hour by hour, piece by piece. our hands mainly
and our backs. and chunks of our brains. and veiled expressions
on our faces, they buy. though they can't know what actual
thoughts stand behind our eyes.

Karen Brodine
(from 'Woman Sitting at the Machine, Thinking', in the book of the same name, Red Letter Press, 1990)

4 Leitrim and Sligo
1845–1860: The Ireland They Left Behind

My great-grandfather was Owen Quinn; his parents were Arthur and Mary Quinn, née Smith. My great-grandmother Mary Lyons's parents were James Lyons and his wife Betsy, née Commons/Montgomery/Creamer/Mac an Iomaire – variants of her maiden name entered on Scottish certificates. Who minded then what these discrepancies meant? They reflected different oral usages of Irish-language names; or the officiating scribe's interpretation of the voices of information-givers, his patience, and how seriously he cared about the minutiae of records for working-class immigrants who couldn't read or write themselves. The exercise was concerned with numbers, not names or stories. Bessie's parents both grew up in the west of Ireland during the Great Famine of 1845–48: *An Górta Mor*. Owen was 14 in 1845, give or take a year. Mary was between five and seven years old when the deadly sequence of potato-crop failures ended in 1849. Both of them lived through the aftermath – the Quinns in Leitrim, and the Lyons family in Heapstown, Co. Sligo, near the Leitrim border. Marriage certificates show that the fathers of both Mary and Owen, my great-great-grandfathers, were agricultural labourers. Their mothers had no named occupations, although in Leitrim and Sligo they are likely to have spun flax into linen at home, tended animals and poultry, and helped to farm the small patch of land they rented, usually through a middleman, from a landowner. Alternatively, they may have been landless seasonal or day labourers, with only a makeshift roof over their head, earning money for food. Landless labourers were the most vulnerable of all to the effects of the Famine.

Quinn, Ó'Coinn in Irish, is one of the 20 most common surnames in Ireland. It is found in every county, but associated most strongly with the west, the counties of Clare, Longford, Mayo, and Roscommon, although it is also widespread in Dublin and some of the Ulster counties. Quinn is also a Traveller name. And the name Lyons turns up frequently among Irish hawkers and pedlars in Scotland, and among common Irish Traveller names. Bessie's father Owen Quinn was born in County Leitrim around 1831; I can't be precise about the year, but this is my best estimate, taking into account discrepancies on certificates and triangulating the data across different records. My great-grandfather's name was usually spelt Owen Quinn, although a Protestant spelling was Quin: it appears without the second 'n' in many Scottish documents. Bessie's mother, Mary Lyons, was born in County Sligo in 1844, or a year either side of it, most likely in the townland of Heapstown, a tiny rural settlement close to the Leitrim border. Both Mary and Owen were born before the Great Famine, when the potato crop failed three times in four years. They grew up in this poorest, most westerly of Ireland's provinces in the thick of those catastrophic events, Owen through his mid–late teens and Mary as a little child.

Young survivors of the Famine and unbeknown to each other, Owen and Mary left Ireland, Owen travelling with friends or family in the late 1840s. By 1851 he was in Yorkshire with a group of other Irish refugees. Mary had left Sligo, with two of her siblings, by the late 1850s. Neither of them had any money or possessions, but they'd survived the worst of the hungry years, leaving behind a hollowed-out country with bleak prospects for the poorest fraction of the population who survived and stayed.

Scotland offered a better life: they'd already have known that. Census records show hundreds of Quinn and Lyons families settling in 19th-century Scotland, and many thousands of other emigrant-refugees. Since the first decades of the 19th century, Irish workers had travelled in growing numbers to Scotland as seasonal 'economic' migrants, mainly to work on the harvests. In these early 19th-century decades, they were among Ireland's poorest people, with nothing to do between sowing and harvesting the potatoes. But by the time Owen and Mary arrived, Irish people were crossing the sea in tens of thousands, permanent immigrants, refugees from sickness and starvation, but essential to Scotland's economy as all-year-round cheap labour for the burgeoning industrial and mining country that Scotland was becoming. They were British subjects, although they felt like outsiders and were treated as such.

Census documents, at least the few in which the far right-hand column '*born in…*' wasn't left blank by Scottish officials, confirm that Mary Lyons was born in Sligo, and Owen Quinn in Leitrim. The two counties sat next to each other in the north of Connacht, where the population depended for survival almost wholly on potatoes, the only crop which for several centuries had flourished sufficiently in the province's thin soil to feed poor peasant farmers and labouring families like the Quinns and the Lyonses. Potato country stretched across Connacht from the boggy, windswept lower slopes of the hills and mountains of Galway, Mayo, and the fields of Roscommon to the south, and eastwards to their home turf of Sligo and Leitrim. Beside the long lochs of Connacht, long low ridges of abandoned potato beds can still be seen stretching up steep hillsides from the water's edge. The soil was poor across the province. In his memoir, John McGahern wrote of the soil of Leitrim, where he grew up, as 'no more than an inch deep. Underneath is daub, a blue-grey modeling clay, or channel, a compacted gravel. Neither can absorb the heavy rainfall. Rich crops of rushes and wiry grasses keep the thin clay from being washed away.'[6] Growing potatoes and grazing a patch of land were possible ways of farming in the small fields between the many small lakes of Leitrim. Sligo was hard hit by the Famine, but had a coastline to comb, a harbour, and a growing shipping business.

Not that potatoes had been a poor subsistence diet. The population of Ireland had grown from one million people in 1600 to eight million in 1841. Farms and small-holdings made up much of the agriculture in the west, which was the most densely populated part of Ireland. Even poor people were not doing too badly. Potatoes had developed from being a supplementary garden crop, 'an spáinneach' – food brought by the Spanish Armada – to constitute the core diet. Potatoes and buttermilk were relatively healthy foods, especially supplemented by grain, as well as foraged and poached food, such as shell-fish and river salmon, gathered by gleaning, not fishing, which would have required boats.[7]

But gradually, from the start of the 18th century, the diet of the poor was hollowed out by the export of meat, butter, and grain, although as output expanded, those with means went on eating a broad diet. By 1845, the near-total dependence on potatoes, without milk, however plentiful, would prove disastrous in the west and elsewhere. The first year in which the blight struck and the crop failed, potatoes formed the staple diet of over 45 per cent of the Irish population, and one third of farming land was dedicated to growing potatoes. Using an ancient ridge-and-furrow system, rows of seed potatoes placed on their ridges were topped with a mix of earth, shells, sand, and seaweed: *dulesk* and *flukern*, harvested by women. This arduous method, using natural nutrients, was disdained by the British as a system of 'lazy beds', encapsulating landowners' opinion of their tenants.

People ate a lot of potatoes: some estimates claim up to 70 a day each; others between 12 and 14 pounds a day. An 1839 survey found a similar pattern: labourers' intake was 5 pounds twice a day for men, and 4 pounds for women, with no evening meal in down months like November, December, and January. And they drank a lot of tea. This was the likely diet of James and Betsy Lyons or Arthur and Mary Quinn. Herring or milk might supplement their diet, providing some Vitamin A and D, and calcium protection against soft-bone diseases like rickets, pellagra, and typhus, fractures and ophthalmia, which caused weeping eyes and blindness – to become a major disease in Poorhouses.

In Ireland, ownership and uses of land were grossly unequal. At the apex of society were absentee landlords, often living in England or in the castles and manor-houses of Ireland. The Protestant Anglo-Irish 'Ascendancy' dominated Ireland politically, economically, and socially from the 17th to the 20th centuries. Between the Protestant Ascendancy and the tenants and labourers at the bottom of the heap were land-agents and farmers, some Catholics as well as Protestants, in whose hands the fate of the poor rested. To produce enough to survive well, a family needed at least three acres, for tillage and grazing for a cow. Better-off tenant farmers who had ten acres often sublet them, taking a share of produce. Many survived on as little as a quarter of an acre, helped by gathering and spinning wild flax, used in Leitrim to supply the Ulster linen industry.

Preparing and spinning flax into yarn brought money into the subsistence-farming households of Connacht. Domestic linen production had long contributed to family incomes. Flax and potatoes were complementary rotation crops. But over the 1820s and 1830s, Ulster's machine-spun yarn had all but destroyed this additional source of income and swelled seasonal migration, especially to Scotland and especially among young people like Owen Quinn. The population of Leitrim was already plummeting before the effects of the Famine. In

Scotland, as well as harvesting there was work on the railways, and still some handloom weaving. Labourers roamed from place to place in search of seasonal work: 57,000 people aged 16–35 in 1841. Migration to Scotland helped the poorest to stay in Ireland. Emigration was for ever.

Those with less than a quarter of an acre to farm had barely enough to survive, even in good years. In bad years, they were done for. The very poorest lived from hand-to-mouth as landless labourers, selling their strength and energy by the day. Owen and Mary's parents were among this poorest social group.[8]

The Great Famine and its aftermath of hunger, death, and emigration is still an emotive, nation-defining, and contentious event. The potato blight descended on Ireland from the Americas via mainland Europe, arriving in mid-summer 1845 after a good early harvest. At first, the second crop looked healthy too, but overnight it became a foul-smelling, inedible mass. This was the first disaster of the famine years. Half the year's potato crop was lost. The harvest was devastated twice more in the course of the following three years, and in 1846 the crop was annihilated. Ireland and its people suffered far more than any other country struck by the blight. The scale, intensity, and length of it had a cumulative effect: the aftermath was long-drawn-out.

The consensus among historians is that nearly a million people died from hunger, malnutrition, disease, cold, exposure, and exhaustion caused by the potato blight between 1846 and 1849, with the western counties the worst-affected region. Hunger, unemployment, and sickness lingered on into the 1850s; the population continued to shrink, as death and mass exodus emptied out the island. Those who suffered most were people who already lived in absolute poverty, whose only shelter had been the makeshift hovels that they assembled on a rented patch of land, some with a shed for an animal or two. Official documents dressed up dwellings which were no more than mud-huts as 'cabins'. Most of the poor rural population had never owned winter clothes and often had no shoes: they couldn't have afforded them, but in any case they hadn't needed them. Their outdoor life was seasonal. They ate the potatoes that they grew and tended an animal or two on a small patch. When the Famine came, scavenging and begging for food, and later compulsory work-schemes, replaced working on the land. On a good day, people ate cabbage, and soup made of watercress or nettles gathered from the land. On a bad day, they had grass or nothing. The numbers made homeless swelled as tenants were evicted by landlords' agents from their small parcels of tenanted land. Three unusually cold, wet winters added to the troubles of people forced to take to the road. Theft, violence, and murder stalked highways and villages, as well as the towns, where there was plentiful food for those who could afford it, and sometimes deadly competition for scraps between those who couldn't. Washing, and changing clothes, were next to impossible, so lice which spread typhus had free rein. The youngest and the oldest were sometimes sacrificed to keep those who might work alive. People died on the roadside, left to the rats and to rot.[9] Every day, as hungry people walked, the sight and smell of a baker's shop spelt anguish for starving wanderers and their emaciated children.

Signs of the Famine scar the landscape of the west of Ireland. In remote parts of Galway and Mayo a melancholy still hangs in Connemara's soft, damp air among the fields and dry-stone walls: collapsed, mossed-over stone cottage walls and field markings: a still-living abandonment, where death and flight hover over nettle-smothered banks and peaty streams, bones close by the ridges of old potato fields, tilled by a once populous, close-knit society. A sense of the uncanny: the shivering presence of death and sorrow still haunts the fields, cliffs, and reedy edges of deep black water. The Famine is more prosaically present in plain public works in stone and cement, built by the starving and homeless during the crisis and for years afterwards, policed by well-fed foremen and soldiers. There are the long straight 'famine' roads, harbour walls, and solid bridges which channel foaming brown rivers. There are intended monuments which stand isolated and exposed on the sides of those same roads, memorialising those who walked in search of food and were denied it – as they were at the doors of Delphi Lodge in Mayo – dying after a final false promise of food. One child, on a recent trip with her father to explore her Irish ancestry, wondered aloud why so many signposts point towards graveyards. It sometimes seems, he agreed, as if there are more here than anywhere else on earth. There are sculptures paying homage to lost children, like one I came across perched on a cliff-top on the Renvyle peninsula in Galway, half-hidden in long wet grass and protected by giant hogweed and thick brambles hung with luscious berries. The people of the Famine were the last inhabitants of thousands of ruined cabins, crumbling piles of stones in overgrown fields, beside footpaths on the edges of streams, or hunkering beside sea-inlets – still a productive source of seaweed. My ancestors lived among these ruins.[10]

The first comprehensive history of the Famine was commissioned in 1946 by Éamon de Valera, Taoiseach (Prime Minister) of Ireland. In the intervening century, anger, myths and a reluctance to address awkward issues proliferated. For decades, the English and the Protestant Ascendancy bore the entire blame in popular consciousness and among historians and, some suggested, even caused the potato blight itself, although the disease was first discovered in the Netherlands. The Famine has been described as genocide, even a holocaust, because so much food in Ireland which could have been made available by the Government to halt starvation was knowingly withheld. Intentionality is a bone of contention about what precisely the Famine can be called. De Valera's action triggered scholarship, debate, and imaginative accounts of the disaster.

By 1845, Ireland had been ruled by the Westminster government for nearly 700 years. Serving commercial interests, the laws of the market dictated that millions of pounds' worth of grain was exported from Ireland to England during the Famine years, while men, women, and children starved. Robert Peel's Tory government took small faltering steps towards a humanitarian response to the first crop failure, but emergency provisions were slow to arrive and woefully inadequate. Quakers stepped in as the practical leaders of early relief efforts, preparing great cauldrons of soup to serve to the hungry. There were 3,000 Quakers in Ireland, among a population of more than eight million, but, patchy as their efforts to import goods were, with their well-developed networks in Ireland and links to Quakers in England (some travelled across to join them), they often made the difference between life and death, giving the equivalent of £11 million today, and establishing employment schemes, model farms, and training, such as the Ellis family's settlement in Letterfrack. At Colmanstown in Galway, Quakers distributed seed when they could be sure it wouldn't be purloined by landlords in lieu of rent. They helped struggling fisheries, including the Claddagh, and established new ones, as at Ring in Waterford. In rural Sligo, home to the Lyons family, Quakers persuaded landlords to offer free use of land to improve agricultural methods. They paid fares for emigration to North America, Scotland, and England, and helped newcomers at quaysides as passengers disembarked. But in their 1852 report, Quakers felt their efforts had been a failure with a terrible toll. The Ellises, for example, went home to Leeds defeated by the magnitude of the suffering they were trying to alleviate. But Quaker famine work is still respected in Irish memory and history.

The Peel government offered starving people grain – at a price. Oatmeal was out of reach for most and 'Indian meal' (maize flour) was a cheap substitute, imported from America. 'You could almost eat it yourself!' was the response of one wealthy benefactor. For a time, the story circulated that it was kindly American 'Indians' who had taken pity on the Irish and donated the cornmeal to ease their plight. Over the Famine years, without one good potato harvest and with demand for grain outstripping supply, exacerbated by grain exports, food was desperately scarce. The price of oatmeal and other grains sky-rocketed. Oatmeal cost Poorhouses alone £2 a ton in 1845; a little over a year later, it cost £20. Beyond the government's small, ineffective measures, only charitable alms, Quakers' efforts, and Poorhouse soup-kitchens briefly offered pockets of relief.

If the Peel government's help to the hungry in 1845–47 was feeble, it had at least ostensibly been designed to relieve suffering. A Whig Government led by Lord John Russell replaced Peel's Tories in early 1847, after which these gestures were replaced by new measures. Change for the worse came in 'Black 47', as folk-memory labels the year in which 66,000 people died in Irish workhouses alone. The soup kitchens were closed down in June, barely a year after they were established, for fear of encouraging the three million people who flocked to them into dependency on the State. The new rulers were fervent believers in free-market, *laissez-faire* ideology, although the State intervened when it suited them: soldiers were deployed, paid out of tax revenues to protect grain exports from Ireland. And the Poor Law's underlying purpose was to warn against the hardship, homelessness, and hunger that it was created to address. No-one, certainly not the Irish peasantry and labouring poor, should be given food, or anything else, for nothing. The punitive and convoluted system directly caused death, destitution, and dispersal. Food, work, and shelter were made available for some, with conditions which included forced labour and eviction. Over six years, just £9.5 million was spent, most of it before mid-1847. £4 million was spent on the Irish Constabulary, and £10 million on an increased military presence to keep order. And Irish, not English, taxpayers would pay for the Famine. Yet by the end, one third of Irish taxpayers had paid anything at all, and they stood to gain a lot. The shame of asking for relief clung to poor emigrants like the Quinns and Lyons families as they built new lives in Scotland.

In 1847 Parliament had passed the Irish Poor Law Amendment Act, including new Poorhouses for 'indoor relief' for the infirm, the old, and children. Outdoor relief came in the form of a meagre wage in return for compulsory work, often the construction of roads, harbours, and bridges. At the core of the new Poor Law legislation, which was the last straw for Quakers and other charities, was the notorious 'Gregory Clause', designed by Sir William Gregory, husband of Lady Gregory who decades later became associated with the poet W. B. Yeats and the Irish nationalist cause. An assiduous, kindly landowner, she nevertheless saw poor working people as a species apart: there were 'people who use a toothbrush and those who don't'. Her husband wouldn't have got close enough to know. The Gregory Clause forbade anyone from receiving relief, whether in the workhouse or on outside work schemes, until they relinquished any rented land in excess of a quarter of an acre. At the stroke of a pen, destitute families were forced to abandon any prospect of continuing to harvest meagre crops from poor soil to keep themselves and their children alive. Tenants were evicted in tens of thousands and their 'cabins' or 'hovels' burned to stop them returning home.[11] The numbers affected vary. The number of evictions counts heads of households, not families, and recent studies estimate that nearly 600,000 people were evicted between 1846 and 1848.

The Famine conveniently paved the way for agricultural rationalisation, offering prosperity for large landowners, stability and security for middle-sized farms. The 'Gregory Clause' signposted the future for Irish agriculture which politicians and landowners had wanted to bring about long before the blight struck. The huge numbers of evictions after 1847 signified the start of consolidating much agricultural land into larger, more profitable tenant farms. The Irish economy surged, freed from the deadweight of looking after the wellbeing of the whole population. For the poor, destitution, forced labour or emigration were the options. Colm Tóibín has described the Famine starkly as 'thinning out the fabric of Irish society', managing emigration for profit.[12]

Historical studies now extend the charge of callous, catastrophic, criminal neglect and ideological blindness beyond British governments and landowners to local officials and others in Ireland who did well in those years: farmers, millers, bakers, and shopkeepers. Irish Catholics, it is now acknowledged, as well as Protestants, continued to make a tidy living from trade in food and other essentials, almost as if times were normal. If responsibility for the Irish Famine lies overwhelmingly at the door of England, with centuries-long oppression, brutal military actions and callous absentee landowners, some of their work was done by local people on the ground. The Famine was an Irish disaster and a colonial outrage. At its heart, enabled by the Russell government, was the unequal struggle between social classes in Ireland itself. The rural poor, the tenant farmers, the near-landless peasantry, and – right at the bottom – the landless agricultural labourers hiring themselves out by the day, all suffered and died at the hands of the English, under the noses of those in Ireland who lived well above the breadline, lived close to and knew the victims: as customers, neighbours, hired hands, fellow worshippers, local parents and grandparents.

What of those real people who died, or managed to survive: labourers like the Quinns and the Lyons families? Since so many are buried in mass and unmarked graves, and official records are top–down and uneven, little is known about the hungry people who walked miles a day, slept in the open, fought for food and very rarely, in desperation, scavenged corpses; who broke stones on public-works schemes and built the Poorhouses, bridges, harbours, roads, and walls which still stand today. There is no shortage of numerical data about the famine years, but few stories survive, apart from some evocative emigrants' letters. Novelists and poets have filled the gaps with imagined experience. First-hand stories are absent, but official statistics are not. The numbers labouring on public works grew from 26,000 in September 1846 to 714,000 by March 1847. Agricultural workers, seasonal or day-labourers, small-holders, weakened by hunger and lack of shelter, died on compulsory work schemes through those winter months, especially during the unusually hard winter of 1846–1847. Clothed in thin rags and barefoot, many died of cold as much as malnourishment.

Labouring on public works, or wandering in search of food, marked a total break from the traditional winter-time life patterns of potato growers. Once the last crop was dug out in November, there had always been fallow time through to the next planting season in February and March. What did people like Arthur and Mary Quinn, or James Lyons and Betsy and their children, do then? They harvested winter vegetables if they had a patch, gathered free fuel, spun dried flax stalks; poached fish from rivers; gathered shellfish and seaweed if they were near the sea; staunched roof leaks, mended their cabins, repaired and sharpened tools, tended any livestock, cooked and washed and mended clothes. It was a neighbourhood life, with social gatherings and attendance at church, unless the embarrassment of having nothing to put in collections for the priest deterred them. They told and sang stories in Irish, danced, and on mental maps gave still-surviving names to places around them: fields, coves, creeks, strands, streams, hills, and settlements. Their stories died with them, though not the talent for telling them. Winter brought slowdown: a bit of rest and ease. This, some argue, is the origin of the persistent English idea that the Irish are indolent, feckless, improvident, and disorderly. Catholicism was central to their alien character, and destitution the consequence of an improvident lifestyle. The Famine was the hard lesson they were taught by rulers and moral judges.

Until the early 1850s, famine survivors lived by the skin of their teeth in a wild, unstable world. Hard graft and seasonal labour for some, but also widespread begging and robbery. In the mass emigration, the majority sailed to the USA, and some to Canada or Australia. Those who couldn't find the fare for long voyages crossed the Irish Sea to Scotland or England, my great-grandparents Owen and Mary among them. There is no evidence that they ever returned. In

Scotland, they carried their stories of the Famine to the grave. Like many who live through the brutality of war, famine, and flight, they probably didn't tell their own children what they had endured. For those who left Ireland to create a new future, the past was too painful to tell, and illiterate, Gaelic speakers couldn't write it down. And who would have wanted to hear and write down their accounts? Immigrants carried the long wake of their collective shock across the sea. But what would it have served to relive horrors and reawaken sleeping memories when there was a living to make?

Arthur and Mary Quinn, and James and Betsy Lyons, my great-great-grandparents, were recorded 'deceased' when Mary married Owen in Scotland in 1864. Even if they had survived the Famine years, they were too old to benefit from better times, and well below the status of those who did. On Scottish records, they were agricultural labourers, which generally meant landless, living on potatoes and foraged food. Their last years would have been spent trying to keep dependants alive. They would have died in middle-age, during or after the Famine, of hunger or its side-effects. Births and deaths were recorded in townlands, the smallest local unit, then incorporated at village and parish levels. But the missing documents among patchy records of that time suggest they were buried in mass, unmarked graves, or singly, by their own families. Arthur and Mary Quinn and James and Betsy Lyons were lost, along with younger children they would undoubtedly have been raising between the 1830s and 1850s. As young people, Mary and Owen would have seen siblings die, and lost contact with others, who stayed in Leitrim and Sligo, emigrated or disappeared like them to English and Scottish cities. The Griffiths Valuation (conducted between 1848 and 1864 to determine liability to pay the Poor Rate) records one Lyons farming seven acres in the 1850s in Heapstown, Sligo, Mary's likely birthplace. That would be an indicator of economic recovery: a benefit of agricultural restructuring. There are no signs that Mary or Owen's parents left for Scotland. Mary and Owen were orphaned by the time they left, typical emigrants: young people seeking survival. But Arthur, Mary, James and Betsy are not wholly lost to history despite the absence of records. Mary and Owen's choice of their parents' names for their children memorialised their lives.

Names matter. They claim a place in history. Colm Tóibín and Diarmaid Ferriter address the almost total silence, in historical writing about the Famine, of voices of the people who lived or died during it: the absence of accounts by them, or directly about them, even second-hand reports. Simply recounting the names of victims from official reports changes our relationship to what happened:

> Mrs Kilkenny and child, after several applications for relief in vain; Mary Connell, found dead by a rick of turf; Philip McGowan's wife and daughters; Bryan Flanagan, found dead by the road side; Andrew Davy…. John Healy's two daughters.

The names and places are 'enough to allow you to imagine them, to think you may have known them'. Tóibín argues that 'pondering the names makes you wonder about the whole enterprise of historical writing itself, how little it tells us, how brittle are the analyses of administrative systems in the face of what we can imagine for ourselves just by seeing a name with a fact beside it'.[13] Millions of 19th-century English and Scottish working-class people taught themselves and each other to read and write, many motivated by names and dates inscribed in public places like churchyard graves: their open-air schools. Pip, the orphan boy in Dickens's *Great Expectations,* reflected real-life examples. Marianne Farningham, a girl from a Kent village, was denied school and learned to read and write from tombstones.[14] Without the tools to excavate people's stories and broadcast them, the pattern of forgetting 'ordinary' pasts starts to set. Diverse stories decompose into a midden, and history often simplifies complex bonds between different human lives. There is another side to this. For the person who wants to slip out of sight, cut ties and start afresh, a change of name offers cover and hides the past life they want to bury.

Leitrim and Sligo, the home counties of my Quinn and Lyons ancestors, were among the most famine-affected places – and already poor, as this story by Phelim Roneen, tenant of a small Leitrim farm, illustrates:

> We generally reckon on a coat once in two years, and that costs 15s and as for the wife and children, their little rags do not come to 10s a year. It's seldom we buy anything for the young ones.

The middle-class commentator James Nixon words it differently:

> There is a great deal of nakedness … a man has perhaps one good suit, which he wears on the 52 Sundays, and on a few holidays, but all the rest of his time he is in rags, both summer and winter.

Nixon put this down to 'sloth' but, grudgingly, also to 'necessity'. A Sunday suit was commonly shared with others: worn for early Mass by one person and then handed to someone going to Mass later in the day. Then it was back to the threadbare, torn clothes, commentators dubbed 'rags'. Some had battered shoes, others tied tatters round their feet. In Mohill, Leitrim, in the early 1840s, there were fewer shoes than in the time of the Napoleonic Wars in the 1800s. Over the famine years, Leitrim lost 28 per cent of its population and Sligo 29 per cent, including those lost to emigration. In Sligo, excess mortality – the number of deaths above normal expectations for the period – was 52.1 per cent; in Leitrim it was 42.9 per cent. In Cork, also hard-hit, the toll of excess deaths was 32 per cent, a level similar to most other counties. Quakers ran soup kitchens in Leitrim and Sligo from 1845. Perhaps the Quinn and Lyons families benefited. There was also profiteering, theft, and murder, the criminal demi-monde flourished, and corruption in awarding contracts was the norm.[15]

Knowledge of the millions who lived through the Irish Famine, including Owen and Mary's parents, is irretrievably lost, apart from a few terse notes in Poor Law records and land transactions. But among the Irish diaspora, their culture has been kept alive by the people who settled, some perpetually unsettled, in other countries. Those who survived and even thrived in new countries tell stories of belonging and not belonging; of tight-knit communities, bound by a strong collective identity. Whether in countries which made room for Irish Catholics to help create a new immigrant nation, or in England and Scotland, where the hostility of the host country drove immigrant people to cling closer together as they built the new 'industrial inferno', Irish identity and allegiance survived through work, myth, music, political drive, sports, literature, art, and a sense of historical injustice that still has life in it.[16]

When Owen left Ireland in the late 1840s and Mary in the mid-late 1850s, what choices did they have without work or prospects? Those who were strong enough and found the fare emigrated, many to north America. Ships sailed from several ports, including Sligo, although far and away the greatest numbers of passengers to the new world left from Cork – out along the Cobh to Boston and New York. Those who were too poor to pay their passage to America, or were not 'assisted' by landlords like Lord Palmerston to leave their land and emigrate, or who already had relatives in Scotland or England – or just nurtured hope, based on rumours of available work – made the shorter journey across the Irish Sea. Owen and Mary were part of that exodus to Scotland, their chosen place to start a new life. Large numbers of poor families emigrated even before the Famine hit. In 1840, 656,145 from a population of 8.2 millon left Ireland. In 1850, it was 1,029,486 out of 6.6 million; in 1860, 427,419 of 5.8 million.[17] 'Emigrant' and 'migrant' are euphemisms for refugees. Penniless, unschooled labourers and domestic servants, a few peasant farmers, carpenters, bootmakers, blacksmiths, stonemasons and a handful of teachers. Hungry for a new life, work, and hope. Most of all, hungry.

5 Leitrim, Leeds, and Lothian
Late 1840s–1851: Owen Quinn's Journey

About how old were my great-grandparents Owen and Mary when they each left for Scotland? By my calculation, Owen was born around 1831, although isolated records show him up to ten years younger. As he aged, with no prospect of giving up work, he'd have had good reason to make himself out to be younger, a vigorous man seeking manual work. Mary was born around 1844, as her death certificate and most documents indicate, although one source states her birth year as 1838. Marriage certificates and censuses of the time are inconsistent for many reasons, influenced by social, gender, and employment factors, as well as literacy levels. Additionally, people like Owen and Mary were reliant on fading memory, if they even knew. Like so many others, if they did know when they were born, there was often good reason to lie to the authorities and hope that their story would go unchallenged – easier to achieve without birth certificates to disprove them.

Owen and Mary didn't read or write, growing up in an oral, pre-literate culture with no schooling on offer. Irish, or Gaelic, was their likely first language, like most people from their part of Ireland in the first half of the 19th century. The decline of Gaelic was precipitated by the Famine, which disproportionately hit Gaelic-speaking areas like Sligo and Leitrim. After that, as the grip of Britain's National Schools on Ireland tightened, English was forced on children and adults, and Gaelic was ruthlessly suppressed, leaving their contested traditional language to survive only in westerly corners of the country. If any documents – unlikely – had been handed to the families at the births of Owen or Mary in Ireland, they were long lost. They couldn't check enumerators' elaborately handwritten entries in English, with their abstruse abbreviations, couched in the technical codes of the census. To calculate accurate-enough dates, I've taken account of discrepancies in documents over time, working backwards from death certificates. The informants reporting a death are often from the next, more literate, generation; but their understanding of a parent's age is based on inherited family wisdom, so death certificates won't do on their own. To estimate the most likely birth dates, I correlated death certificates with earlier information, such as censuses, Poor Law records, marriage and other certificates: all information taken from oral statements to officials who didn't know the family. Marriage certificates are notoriously unreliable, subject as they are to wishful thinking, social ideals for brides to be not many years older (or more literate) than their grooms – and initial fibs to reassure a partner. In oral societies or those, like 19th-century Britain, still in the process of becoming literate, hovering between oral and written cultures, some of the historical testimony of working-class people was in their own hands, reflecting their experience, memory, and self-interest at any given moment. The bureaucracies of State and Church engaged in power struggles over information, and not all the cards were stacked against the poor.

Owen Quinn was 14 when the Irish potato crop first failed. Mary, probably born around 1844, was still wriggling in Betsy Lyons's arms in rural County Sligo, taking her first faltering steps. By the time they met in the late 1850s or early 1860s, Owen already had fifteen or so years of working life behind him, mostly in present-day East Lothian. He was a mature man with a variety of skills, not to mention years of labour as a child and young man in rural Leitrim, scratching for survival during and after the Famine. It is possible that he left Ireland in the late 1840s as either an emigrant or a seasonal farm labourer, travelling to and fro under the wing of older labourers from his neighbourhood.

Before 1850, Owen set out from Leitrim for good. What would have held him back for longer? 1847 was a hopeless year. His parents and many people he knew would have been starving, or dead, or had already left for good. 1848 was worse. He'd have to find the fare and walk to Sligo town, a distance of 35–40 miles, to travel by sail or steamship to the British mainland. There, he'd have seen the other, affluent side of society. The Glasgow and Liverpool Steam Shipping Company already ran steamships from Sligo's port to both cities. A newly constructed harbour had been built in the early 19th century, and shipping was buoyant, controlled by powerful Sligo families, not least William Polloxfen, who co-owned the Middleton and Polloxfen Milling Company. William married into the Middleton family of merchants and smugglers and founded The Sligo Steam Navigation Company, merging two powerful Protestant families whose trades – ships and grain – assured them an ideal place to gain from the Famine. Polloxfen's daughter Susan was to marry John Butler Yeats, father of the poet W. B. Yeats and the painter Jack B. Yeats.

Lord Palmerston, who owned large tracts of land in Sligo, was among the wealthy landlords who organised the systematic emigration of starving tenants, the coercive Assisted Emigration Scheme that emptied lands of small-holdings, speeding up agricultural rationalisation in the interests of big landowners. Frequent sailings crossed to Glasgow and Liverpool. And in 1846 alone, 11,000 emigrants left Sligo for destinations that included Canada and the USA. There was a packet boat from Sligo to Liverpool via Derry and on to Greenock at the mouth of the Clyde. But very few migrants to Scotland took that route, especially after the tragedy of the most infamous 'coffin ship', the 'Londonderry', in December 1848 – a Scottish paddle-steamer with a crew of 26. Their cargo was 180 Sligo peasant farmers and labourers emigrating to Liverpool via Derry. A violent storm broke and, as towering Atlantic waves broke over the deck, passengers were ordered below and trapped there to steady the ship and, it was said, to save lives. Hatches were locked down, despite mounting clamour and screams from below, which gradually grew quieter. Seventy-two passengers perished in their dark hole, including 18 children and 32 women. The captain and crew blamed robbers and cut-throats among the victims, until the truth came out. Even then, piles of unburied coffins were later discovered. No-one wanted to take responsibility. It's possible that Owen took this boat, aged 17, and survived. The dates fit.[18] More likely he walked 100–120 miles from home in Leitrim to Dublin, where the steam packet embarked from Eden Quay on the River Liffey; or took the new-fangled iron paddle steamer from Drogheda, a shorter walk across Ireland. Either way, Liverpool was his likely destination: the first port of call for countless Irish emigrants to Britain.

Raised to labour on the land, Owen must have been physically strong and resilient enough for the kinds of work on offer in the towns and cities of England and Scotland, which were common knowledge among intending emigrants. In the 1840s and 1850s, there was navvying for Irish workers in all the big cities and building the railways connecting them. He may not have travelled with other Quinn family members, if any survived: there's no trace of any family interaction. But on Owen's home turf, Leitrim, as well as in Sligo, Roscommon, Mayo, or Cavan, he will have had friends, fellow workers and seasonal migrants, along with thousands of strangers heading in the same direction. Nearly three quarters of those leaving for England and Scotland in those years came from Mayo and Sligo.

If Owen did land in Liverpool, he did not stay long. The first surviving written reference to his life anywhere locates him in Leeds, Yorkshire. In spring 1851, aged 20, he was working there as a labourer, the only Owen Quin (sic) recorded in Britain on that census. He was a lodger with John and Catherine Moran and their family at 8 Williams Court, Sovereign Street, off Swinegate. There were twelve people in the household. The eldest was John Moran, aged 40, and the youngest was 15-year-old James Clifford. Michael Hegarty and Martin Devany were about Owen's age. Every detail fits my great-grandfather: born in Leitrim in 1831, aged 20 and a labourer. Indeed, everyone in the household was a labourer, including the only woman, Catherine Moran, all of them born in Ireland.

8 Williams Court was a courtyard dwelling, one of several small buildings down an alley at the back of No 6 Sovereign Street, near the railway, and the mills and warehouses on the bank of the river Aire. Owen would have been tipped off about work on the railways or nearby building sites or in the textile and engineering mills. Leeds was known then as 'the city where everything is made': woollen textiles, ready-made clothing, flax, hemp, jute, and heavy machinery. In nearby Swinegate, the flax, hemp, and jute yarn merchants Boyle and Son flourished. Holgate, just south of the river from Williams Court, was the engineering quarter, where jute-spinning machinery was manufactured to service the great mills of Dundee. Word of mouth was the force that moved hungry, poor people to more promising places, and the story of the Quinns in Britain revolves round textiles. They were drawn to places where flax and wool were spun and woven: materials and processes they were familiar with. It's also possible that another Owen Quin, who had kept a shop not far away at Quarry Hill, at least until the mid-1840s, was an older relative whose existence drew young Owen to Leeds. In the town that year, the architecture and plans

of the famous Leeds Town Hall had been agreed, and construction work started soon afterwards: thousands more immigrants were needed to realise that vast project, let alone the ever-increasing mills and speculative housing for workers and their families. Ireland was the source of that labour. In Britain, labourers might earn 11–15 shillings a week (ca. 55p to 75p) and pay a fifth of that in rent. It left barely enough to live on. Only better-off workers could save for hard times, send money home, or join the Friendly Societies founded by working-class communities to help with sick pay, medical treatment, or funeral expenses. Life was hand-to-mouth for people like Owen and his housemates.[19]

Neither Owen's dwelling place, nor Leeds itself, is likely to have felt like home to a young man from rural Leitrim. The city was a muddy, malodorous sprawl, pulsating energy, fast moving, smoky, and near the mills that deafened by day and night. Its working-class streets and yards were steeped in soggy filth: heaped in excrement and rotting waste. This was squalor worse than rural destitution, but there was work and food, for which mid-19th-century cities attracted young immigrants. It was not all about reluctantly leaving the bad and the impossible behind. They must have felt shockwaves, nevertheless. In this predominantly Protestant town, incoming Catholic Irish workers were met with suspicion and hostility, which could escalate into violence. The city's need for labour to realise its grand civic and commercial ambitions did not translate into a warm welcome to the people whose toil was making its dreams a reality. Cheap speculative housing was springing up across the city. Irish workers, most of them young single men, lived in the town's cramped quarters in places like Williams Court, sited as close as possible to their work. A 'court house' was an early back-to-back, a working-class dwelling which ran down the side of the houses that faced on to the main street. Rents for court houses and the next generation of back-to-backs were cheap, and they were popular: one rung above the Common Lodging Houses and cellar dwellings, they were all that many people could afford. By 1847, it was calculated that 30,000 Irish migrants lived in court houses. They were built hastily and haphazardly, filling the yards behind the better-built, larger, street-facing houses, lining the walls of the rear yard or 'court'. The space in the middle was a midden, where every kind of waste was dumped.

Court houses backed on to their mirror opposites in the adjoining yard, so by definition they were 'blind backs', with no rear light or ventilation: the back walls faced each other, bang up together. They were 'blind alleys', or 'cul de sacs', accessed only through a side passage, or a tunnel under the first floor of the front house.

There was usually one room per floor in Leeds court houses at this time, with one outside privy shared between several houses, open to view from all sides, always foul and stinking. When they were cleaned up every six months, up to 75 cartloads were filled. There was one shared outdoor tap. Williams Court was typical. Owen lived there with 11 other people, also typical. In 1842, even before the numbers of Irish immigrants in England swelled, the northern and Scottish cities were growing exponentially, with monumental public buildings constructed alongside the mills and factories; many court houses already housed 10 people, sometimes 20. Numbers can only have increased by the time of the 1851 census. By 1866 improvements were made to court houses in Leeds, and by 1872 'blind alley' dwellings, which fitted no regulation or bye law, were banned. Ironically, 'cul de sacs' were first legislated into being in 1906 to allow Hampstead Garden Suburb to build a salubrious, even utopian, version, in the place where the sweet home of Owen's daughter, as will be seen later in this book, can be found.[20]

Owen's head of household, John Moran, was the tenant, not owner, of the tiny dwelling in Williams Court. The other tenants, all classed as lodgers, were John's wife Catherine, 43; William Walsh, 20; Michael Walsh, 18; Anthony Moran, 25; Owen Moran, 18; James Clifford, 15; Michael Hegarty, 21; Anthony Hogan, 18; Thomas Hart, 16; and Martin Devany, 20. Among the twelve, Owen Quinn had company in his age group and he's likely to have travelled from Ireland or across from Liverpool with some of them. How long he lived in Leeds is not known. The household scattered, and most of Owen's house-mates disappeared out of sight of history. I traced just two of them and will tell their stories here, since their lives closely touched his. They'd have looked for work together, shared meals, slept in the same crowded room, taken turns on the privy, and lined up by the cold-water tap in the yard.

Intimate, close-connected living among strangers and familiars created friendships, enmities, trust, and betrayal, the strong meat of emotional, visceral, and faith-based attachment experienced by millions of working-class people, and intensely so among Irish immigrants. For some, the grounding force was to stay with their own people; others wanted to leave them behind. Their impulses must have been informed by ingrained memories and feelings: the long aftershock of the Famine.

The stories of those closely linked lives and deaths reverberate through Irish immigrant history. In 1852, aged just 19, and illiterate, Anthony Hogan married Mary Fenighty, a 'charwoman' born in Ireland. By 1861 the couple were living with her parents and others in another Leeds backyard court house, Wellington Yard, on the other side of the railway tracks. In 1871 they still lived with Mary's mother, now a widow, and Mary had become a mill hand, either in the linen or woollen industries or in Holbeck, where jute-spinning machinery was manufactured. Anthony was, apparently, only 24 in 1861, although he was recorded as 36 in 1871. Perhaps he was still a child when he first arrived from Ireland, younger than he'd dared to tell the census enumerator, in case he was thought too young to survive on his own. As an unemployed orphan, he could have been dispatched to the lonely miseries of the Leeds Moral and Industrial Training School in Beckett Street, set up under the 1834 Poor Law for orphans and poor children; or returned to unemployment and hunger back in Ireland. Anthony died of tuberculosis in 1878, his age 'calculated' to be 44.

James Clifford, the son of handloom weavers Douglas Clifford and Sarah Coulter, was only 15 when he was living in Leeds in 1851, and then possibly travelled north to Scotland with Owen. The two may have parted in Glasgow, already the most Irish city in Scotland. James headed for the coalmines of Rutherglen in Lanarkshire, but Owen did not choose mining and instead walked east. James then returned to Ireland, where he married Matilda Dunne, and their first daughter, Maria, was born in 1860. They returned to the Lanark mines, and a second child, Elizabeth, was born. As was common, James and Matilda took in boarders: an elderly widow, Janet Jackson, native of Rutherglen; and William McIntryre, 18, and Robert Brown, 19 – both local-born coal miners. Among manual workers, miners were relatively well paid, but lodgers helped families get by and join a Friendly Society to pay for sickness and funerals. They lived among other Irish families, including James's brother Robert. There are plenty of mining widows in the censuses, and Matilda become one of these sad statistics. James Clifford was a bottomer at Stonelaw Colliery in Rutherglen, one of the people who loaded and unloaded the cages at the bottom of the shaft or at intermediate stations. One day he fell down the deep shaft. He lived on for 25 minutes after the accident, attended by a surgeon, but died of his injuries. He was 37. His brother, a full-time worker from childhood without a single day's schooling, marked the death certificate with an 'x'. There was an inquest into James's fatal accident, as the entry is marked as 'corrected' in 1875. As widows quickly had to conjure another livelihood, Matilda, like others later in the Quinns' story, took in lodgers to keep herself and her children afloat.

Arriving in East Lothian by 1861, Owen already probably knew his way round farm work from spells of seasonal planting or harvesting. He seems to have known where to aim for when he settled in Haddingtonshire, probably in the late 1850s. Decades later he was to live, work, and die in Edinburgh, but for now he was drawn to the land, or to the new railways connecting towns and cities. The 1850s saw a railway boom, and on the Edinburgh–Hawick line of the Northern British Railways a third of the navvies were Irish.[21] Haddington must have suited him: he had choices, yet he stayed put. The swathes of rolling, rich arable and potato-growing land south-east of Edinburgh were a relatively rare destination for immigrants, compared with the mines and mills in the west; but farm work, despite worse wages, matched Owen's skills and background and – the clincher perhaps – he seems to have known Irish workers who were already settled there.

The 1841 season saw 57,651 Irish people, mainly men, migrate to England and Scotland to work on the land, but relatively few stayed on. All that changed from the late 1840s, not only in farming. Rules were relaxed, and Irish workers settled in Scotland permanently, met with a welcome which ranged from warm to grudging to outright hostile. Cheap labour was in demand in the coalmines, the mills, and many vast building projects. Scotland needed navvies and skilled construction workers for every building trade and occupation, as well as spinners and weavers, working by hand and machine, to service the textile mills around Dundee and in the Scottish Borders. In the 1830s, the mechanisation of the Ulster linen industry had destroyed spinning and weaving as the second-string economy of poor families in north-western Irish counties; but now their skills were relevant. There was also boundless work in the Lanarkshire and Ayrshire and Midlothian coalmines. But work wasn't everything. People had lives to lead within their own culture and community and wanted their children to have the schooling which they had been denied. But Scotland did not happily absorb the stream of Irish Catholics who arrived on the packet boats into Greenock and Glasgow in the post-Famine decades: hostility was the set face of Scotland which met the incomers: coldly civil at best and violent at worst. The human impact of emigration was profound. Seasonal migration had helped people to stay in their own country. Emigration was to be permanently in exile. How to make the best of the rest of life in a new country, however cold the welcome?[22]

6 Sligo to Scotland
Late 1850s: Mary Lyons Emigrates

Mary Lyons left Ireland in the late 1850s, even as late as 1860. She was 16 years old or thereabouts, and she had her younger brother Peter and her sister Betsy (also known as Bridget) in tow. Although some Lyons relatives struggled on in places like Heapstown in rural Sligo, the siblings' immediate family was dead, disappeared, or scattered elsewhere. They were orphans. Sligo life was unforgiving: families living hand to mouth in a quest for basic food and shelter. Vast numbers of destitute children without family support – orphans, foundlings, and abandoned children – were subject to the harsh operations of the Poor Law or the regimes of religious orders.

By 1861 the young Lyons siblings had changed their lives utterly. They were employed as farm labourers in the parish of Prestonkirk, 25 miles east of Edinburgh along the Firth of Forth, living in a row of farm cottages attached to Brownrigg Farm ('Broonrigg' to locals), near the village of Athelstaneford in the then county of Haddington. Brownrigg is a handsome building. With solid labourers' cottages and outbuildings, it has the look of a prosperous Victorian model farm. There were other individuals named Lyons already in Haddingtonshire, probably members of their extended family – and the siblings met other Irish people who earned their livelihood nearby as farm labourers, distillery workers, hawkers or pedlars, making and gathering useful objects to sell on doorsteps or along urban streets: encounters which must have offered comfort and company. They could be part of a small Irish Catholic community in this distant rural corner of lowland Scotland.

What sort of journey had it been for the Lyons orphans, setting out from Heapstown via Leitrim, over the Irish Sea to western Scotland and then all the way across to the North Sea on the other side? It is possible that Mary walked to Sligo, the closest port, as Owen might have done years earlier. But for Mary, walking north-eastwards to Derry port was by far the quickest, cheapest option.

The vast majority of emigrants or refugees heading for Scotland from the north-western counties of Connacht sailed from Derry Pier on the 'Scotch Boat' to Greenock, 'across the Sheuch' ('the ditch' – slang at the time for the narrow North Channel of the Irish Sea). Smaller numbers embarked from Belfast, so they most likely took the *Derry and Glasgow Steam Packet* for the short crossing to Greenock at the mouth of the Clyde, round the Mull of Kintyre. Before 1840, a passage from Ireland to Greenock at the mouth of the Clyde on Scotland's west coast cost six pennies (6d – about £2 today), and the fare stayed low for decades – much too low, in the opinion of many people in Scotland. When immigrants fell on the mercy of the Poor Law, and efforts to send people back were considered, the costs were prohibitive: from 2 shillings and 6 pence to 5 shillings, plus food, per person. Irish newcomers were in Scotland to stay. Greenock was the main point of arrival, where most immigrants disembarked, although a few ships sailed on to the Broomielaw, Glasgow's central port, made possible once the river was dredged in the early 1800s.

Figure 8: Winter sunset at Greenock harbour ca. 1850s (Patrick Downie)

Mary's walk to Derry with her siblings, a three-day trek, was made in the company of hundreds of other emigrants. They might have been picked up by a carter for some stretches of the way, possibly in exchange for labour, or stopped for a few hours or days to work in the fields and earn money for food or the ferry. Using today's non-motorway roads, the walk from Heapstown, Sligo to Derry measures 103 miles. Hungry and wet, their journey would have been made longer and more strenuous by stony lanes and meandering footpaths. It was a painful three-day walk if they had no boots or shoes, or if any of them were sick.

Mary, Bridget, and Peter would have carried their bundles on their shoulders, rested under haystacks and slept under hedgerows, or in abandoned hovels, heads cushioned on damp belongings. In the unlikely event that travellers like them had coins to spare beyond the sixpenny ferry fare and basic food, they could have boarded the steam-train that ran from Strabane to Derry from 1847. From 1854, trains even ran from Enniskillen to Derry, so the young orphans' walk could have been even shorter. But trains were for other people. Groups of walkers putting one sore foot in front of the other would have included acquaintances and total strangers, from tiny children to the old and feeble. In the 1820s, at 97 years old, Mary Barber set off to walk from the west of Ireland to London to see her daughter. She couldn't read or write a word, but was helped along by carters and scribes. Later, she dictated her life story to a scribe who had it published.[23]

The majority of emigrants were young, nurturing hopes and fantasies, keeping themselves going on conversations and Gaelic song. Later accounts of navvy life speak of raucous drinking, falling out and falling into brawls, fist-fights, gambling, weeping, laughter. And the subdued hours, as exhausted walkers made their way along dirt roads, some with gaping holes in the wet rags wound round their feet, some women with babies at the breast, and some helping the old along. Others wore second-hand boots, including the heavy half-boots that navvies called 'Bluchers' (after the Prussian general who came to Wellington's rescue at Waterloo), but few owned a matching pair, nor a size which fitted. There was a brisk market in single boots across Ireland and Scotland.[24]

Not everyone completed the journey. Those who died along the way had to be buried by fellow walkers; others struggled along in a mess of wet clothes, contending with diarrhea, fever, running blisters, and the breathlessness brought on by constant hunger. They cooked potatoes and meal over fires, drank water from streams, and slept under hedgerows – unless they were ill enough to qualify for the Poorhouse. They would have been hungry before and after meals, and, unless they were very lucky, their wet clothes – no more than rags – would have clung to them at night. Wool was prized, because it stayed warm even when it was wet; linen and cotton offered cold comfort. They could not really know what was in store for them in Scotland, but along with memories of the last few years, a concoction of fear, nightmare memories, and hope must have kept them going. There was no turning back to the hopelessness of home. Connacht offered no future, and Scotland, so they'd heard and believed, offered a decent life in exchange for hard work. Despite the legacy of the Famine, these were, mostly, physically and mentally strong and resilient people.

Migrants were packed tight into the steam packet at Derry port, succumbing to seasickness as the boat dipped and rolled across the choppy Irish Sea. On landing at Greenock, the first priority was food. Then some means of getting dry, mending clothes, and finding a place to sleep. Philanthropists, Quakers, and Catholic priests waited at the quayside with improvised soup kitchens, essentials, and advice for penniless newcomers about where to find shelter, food, and work. They offered some protection from regular gatherings of hostile crowds, overwhelmed and angry at the arrival of huge numbers of Irish, with their alien religion and way of life. Prejudice began at the docks, violence sometimes erupted, and it was not unusual for stones to be thrown at the newcomers. The *Glasgow Courier* reported regular complaints about the cheapness of the steamboat ferries, which allowed these 'most miserable of beings in the lowest state of wretchedness and want' to overwhelm the west of Scotland. The most likely help for Mary, Peter, and Bridget would have come from one of the priests. Catholic networks across Scotland yielded information to direct newcomers towards places where they could put their experience and skills to use.[25]

Irish people may not have been welcome, but the cheap labour that they offered undoubtedly was. There was abundant work in the industrial west, and the majority of Irish immigrants stayed in or near to Glasgow and the industrial west, or travelled on to the burgeoning mining settlements in Lanark and Ayrshire and along a belt which stretched east to Lothian and Fife. Many settled around Greenock, the entry point to Scotland, and became the majority in some workplaces. The town's sugar refineries became dependent on Irish workers, who proved adaptable and resilient in the face of excessive heat. They reportedly worked with more heart and civility than their Highland, lowland Scottish or English counterparts. Although conditions were still harsh in an industry dependent on slavery for its success, word of mouth brought more and more friends and relatives from Ireland to 'Billy Conn's sugar house', welcomed with open arms. Irish workers could also be found in quarries and rope-making workshops round Greenock. Along the Clyde, traditional skills that immigrants brought as boatmen and boat-builders were adapted for the dockyards. And not all Irish immigrants took so-called unskilled work: by 1851, when Owen Quinn was working in Leeds, a third of Greenock's shoemakers were Irish. Others were sawyers, masons, and tailors.[26]

The Irish immigrants who travelled eastwards went mainly to Edinburgh, where all the building trades were in high demand; or to Dundee, where the large number of women established a strong Irish community; or to Forfarshire, where there was plentiful work in the jute mills and linen industry, weaving sails for tall ships on the Tay. Everywhere in Scotland, anyone strong enough to break stones or lay bricks was in demand: stone-breakers, masons, bricklayers, carpenters, blacksmiths, navvies, and plate-layers or 'surfacemen' on the network of railway lines spreading its tentacles across Scotland. In the lowland cities and Scottish Border towns, factories and mills sprang up like mushrooms, and alongside them tenement blocks and multiply occupied houses with rooms to rent in new neighbourhoods. Mary, Peter, and Betsy Lyons did not stop for long in the west of Scotland, although they would have known people in the mills, building sites and workshops of Greenock, Gourock, or Glasgow. From the 1840s, Lyons family members settled there, and in the Lanarkshire coalfields. Our Lyons orphans took a less-trodden path, but their story illustrates the diversity of immigrants' destinations and experiences.

7 Prestonkirk, Haddington, and Nungate 1850s: On the Wild Side

The Lyons siblings travelled to East Lothian and familiar ways of life: farm labouring, spinning, brewing, hawking, and peddling. And it seems they had relatives living close by. In 1861, John Lyons, a 52-year-old hawker and his wife Nelley (Helen), aged 50, lived in two rooms at 7 Church Street, Haddington with their three adult sons: the whole family were immigrants from Ireland. They had arrived at least ten years earlier and by 1851 had moved no further than the other end of their street. Hugh and Patrick were in their late twenties, Miles was 20, and Peter 19: the older two were farm workers, the youngest a porter. Miles had inherited the hawker's trade and he will reappear as part of the family story.

In 1861, Mary, Betsy, and Peter were working as agricultural labourers, six miles north of Haddington, once one of Scotland's biggest and most important towns. It was grand, well connected, influential, and elegant. In the 1740s, the mason William Adam (father of Robert Adam) had risen to prominence as Scotland's foremost architect; he designed the neo-classical Town House with adjacent jail, steepled courthouse, and assembly rooms, which dominated its wide main street. Pavements had replaced cobblestones early, and there was a large triangular market square. The town is still proud of its influential inhabitants, like the Protestant preacher John Knox, who was born in Nungate, and the naturalist John Muir. Haddington was Samuel Smiles's childhood home, where his widowed mother ran a shop so that her son could study medicine. Instead he devoted his life to the railways and wrote a life of George and Robert Stephenson, inventors of the world's first passenger locomotives: Smilesian heroes, self-educated from scratch. Smiles espoused radical causes, including Chartism, women's suffrage, and co-operation, and he found enduring fame as a writer with *Self Help* (1859). As a handbook for individualism and the free market in 1980s Britain, Smiles's view of 'improvidence' as a main cause of poverty, and his promotion of thrift, were misused to justify punitive social policies which ignored his belief in mutuality.

But away from its imposing centre, along the Hardgate and on towards the river, Haddington's houses grew more huddled and ramshackle. In 1861, Owen Quinn was working as a 'general labourer' in the hamlet of Nungate, separated from Haddington by the 16th-century red sandstone Nungate Bridge, which spans the Scottish River Tyne, and by the newer Waterloo Bridge, which replaced a rickety ancient wooden one after the Napoleonic Wars. Today, Nungate is part of Haddington, a pretty place with neat, affluent-looking cottages, and a smart riverside pub. On the Haddington side, close to the river, are two ancient churches. St Mary's is surrounded by beautiful gardens; the modest Catholic church, also St Mary's, is a few yards away, built as a chapel after a design by E. W. Pugin. Walking along the grassy path beside dark, languid water, past a tree planted in 1838 for Queen Victoria's coronation day, I saw a kingfisher dart from its nest in the wall of the riverbank. Nungate was not so tranquil in Owen and Mary's time. It was Haddington's poor relation. The streets where the Irish community lived, including Owen and Mary's extended family, housed the poorest families, prey to outbreaks of cholera and smallpox. It was busy, with public washhouses, crowded lodging-houses, and plenty of employment on local farms and at the distillery. Across the bridge, the women of Nungate and Hardgate used the Sands, a former bowling green, to dry linen laundered in the river.

Nungate, a long-established centre for weaving as well as distilling, had become a gathering place for Irish immigrants, Travellers, and members of the Roma community. Some established residents took a dim view of this. Once a place for 'respectable families, many of them farm tenants', it had become an 'Irish colony, very unlike the Nungate of former days'.[27] By the 1850s, Nungate was the heart of a community of hawkers (sellers with a horse and cart) and pedlars (those who tramped from door to door). Mary (and possibly Owen) may have had Irish Traveller roots: many Nungate dwellers did. Others named Lyons and some Quinns in the area were hawkers or pedlars and quite likely to have been Irish Travellers by origin. It is more likely true of Mary, and, if so, her identity placed her even further from respectable Protestant Scotland than her Irish Catholic identity – enough in itself to attract prejudice. Travellers had long existed in Scotland as well as Ireland. Whatever their genetic make-up, they were looked down on as 'pikeys' – a term much resented by the Roma, the people thought to have crossed to Europe from India. Travellers also had their own languages in addition to English: Gaelic, Shelta (a secret language or cant, which was deliberately unintelligible to outsiders), and Gamin. After long campaigns in the Republic of Ireland, Travellers were recognised as a distinct ethnic group as recently as 2017: the two-edged gain of separate status long experienced in England and Scotland.

Figure 9: Carters crossing the Tyne at Nungate

As well as hawkers and pedlars, the Irish in Nungate were a community of immigrant workers, itinerant day-labourers, seasonal farm-workers, forestry workers, distillery hands, and keepers of labourers' lodging houses and inns. There were single men as well as families with children, and widows. Many were settled permanently. The Nungate Irish formed a fiercely close-knit group, in which people spoke the evolved mixed language of the Scottish Lowland and Borders Travellers, whose roots were Roma, although there is much debate about their origins. The Nungate cant included some Gaelic, and had its local variants. It was a community language which developed, like 'rhyming slangs', into a code which was useful precisely because it was not understood by outsiders, especially enforcing authorities. Scottish Lowland cant is not to be confused with the entirely separate Highland cant. It is a Romani-derived language, elaborated further with the arrival of Irish immigrants. Gaelic words included 'shain' (bad); 'caint' (talk), and 'cluishes' (ears). An Irishman was a 'yerrackan', and a 'stardie' a policeman. If outsiders couldn't understand the cant, then it was a successful counter-language designed to protect a precarious people in a hostile host society.

Figure 10: Tannery workers by Old Nungate Bridge

Nungate had its own drinking places, entertainments, and local employment. The distillery, founded by James Cummings in 1825, turned locally grown barley into liquor. A few decades later it became a brewery and later a tannery. In 1861, one of the Lyons migrants – another Peter – was a porter in the distillery. All these characteristics made Nungate and the working-class streets of Haddington suspect, although at the time there were several distilleries dotted round the county, right up the coast to North Berwick and Dunbar. Single labourers lived in Nungate's lodging houses – work-toughened, fit, and hard-drinking men from Ireland who struck fear into the hearts of boys and young men from both sides of the Nungate Bridge. As children wandered home from school over the bridge, they would run like wild deer when they got near the lodging houses.[28] In respectable Haddington, Nungate was feared as a wild, lawless place, purely because of its Irishness, and the scraps involving boys and young men from either side of the river were legendary. At the Battle of Nungate Bridge, two gangs fought each other with knives and sticks, hurling stones from either side. The Scottish boys were defending themselves against the blaspheming, name-calling, violent Irish, or so one version went, and the fight stopped only when women onlookers intervened after a child was wounded.[29]

However hard Nungate dwellers toiled on the wide acres of arable land around, and however essential the goods were that hawkers made and sold to local Scottish people, they were looked down on as much as feared. In Haddington's myths and memories, Nungate's despised people were identifiable by their 'tackety' boots, while the Haddington townspeople wore stout shoes. As it happens, Owen was not staying at a terrifying lodging house, at least not in 1861. He lived with an Irish family: Mick and Mary Gilroy, and their children Mick, Catherine, and Thomas – and another Irish lodger, John Reynolds. They occupied no more than two rooms in one of those now-desirable cottages you can see along the Tyne riverbank. All of them, women and men, worked as labourers.

Nungate was not many miles away from Brownrigg Farm, where in 1861 Mary Lyons worked as an agricultural labourer. She said she was aged 21–22, living with her brother Peter Lyons, aged 18, and her sister Betsy (also known as Bridget) Lyons, aged 20. Mary's date of birth on the 1861 census was 'about 1839', and her birthplace was Ireland. In reality she was nearer 17 or 18, born in 1843–4. And (drawing on later records) I calculate that her sister Bridget was 16, a year younger. All three siblings were young to be alone so far from home, although that was hardly unusual for the post-Famine generation. They were all recorded as unmarried, agricultural farm labourers, and their home was in a row of workers' cottages at Brownrigg Farm in the parish of Prestonkirk, a short distance from two villages, East Linton and Athelstaneford, where they could shop. The row of single-storey cottages where the siblings had their room has hardly changed. The farm is still an isolated place in the midst of large fields, surrounded by hedgerows and criss-crossed by straight country roads. When I visited in May, some fields were lush green and some ploughed up, revealing dark vein-red soil. Brownrigg lies west of Prestonpans, where in 1745 the Jacobites crushed the English in the first fierce battle of Bonny Prince Charlie's campaign to be king and restore the old faith to England and Scotland.

Figure 11: Brownrigg Farm, East Lothian: Mary Lyons' farm cottage

Perhaps Mary's childhood malnutrition put years on her appearance, at least enough to fool census enumerators. Nevertheless she was strong and healthy enough to withstand long working days in the fields. As the eldest she would have taken charge of her siblings' migration to Scotland and led their route across Scotland from Greenock, through Glasgow, on to Edinburgh and the final stretch to the Lothian farming country where so many other Irish workers were being taken on gladly by farmers. Agricultural labourers were often paid up to two-thirds of their wages in kind, mainly food – one reason why their presence was begrudged by locals.[30] All three of them survived, at least for a few years. Bridget was a spirited, strong, and determined character, and neither she nor Mary, from the evidence of their later lives, would have easily let others get the better of them. At Brownrigg, they could eat well, survive, and shape the next phase of their lives. Mary would have taken decisions to protect her family, especially Peter, who was nearer to 15 years old than the reported 18, and when infections struck, he struggled through a working day.

Mary had experienced suffering in Ireland at first hand. With no choice but to leave, she must have been homesick to her bones for the fields of Sligo, the hills to the west, the lakes of Leitrim to the east, the peaty Garavogue river – An Gharbhóg to her – fast flowing through Sligo town, and the roaring sea at Strandhill, Rosses Point, and Coney Island, where potato growers gathered shellfish and seaweed for fertiliser. Weeks and months passed. As long as a year could have gone by in the eerily quiet North Berwick landscape, with its wary people and huge open skies; too much time when the three of them only had themselves and neighbouring workers at Brownrigg Farm for company.

Walking four and a half miles north, they would spot North Berwick Law, a worn and weathered old cone, guiding them towards the sea. It wouldn't look out of place in Sligo, squatting above long sands, the fishing harbour, and banks of rocks. Along the south side of the Firth of Forth, herring fishing flourished, and they could have felt connected to home, singing to the seals on the water, shuddering at stories they'd heard of King James VI's witch trials in the town and the women hanged for devilry. There would have been more ordinary walks, to nearby villages; or down to Haddington to shop or go to Mass, passing set faces and greeting friendlier ones as they crossed the Nungate Bridge.

Speaking in Irish mingled with Scottish English, they'd have sat on the rough cottage floor after bread and soup at the end of a long day's toil. They'd have made a fire with scavenged wood and oily, aromatic whin-bush branches to kindle it. With lives lived beyond their years, exiled and still disoriented, I see them re-telling stories of home and family, the dead and the left behind, digging their history into the Scottish soil, so the memory of their own people still flowered. They were teenage children living a tough adult life. They must have let their hair down, larked about, fabricating and embellishing stories to make each other laugh, and singing Irish songs – laments, songs of love and longing for lost or dead lovers, murder ballads, rebellion songs – the music they'd learned from childhood, new tunes from Irish labourers they met on their journey, and even newer ones learned in Nungate.

Somehow, somewhere in the early 1860s, despite a six-day working week, ten hours a day and longer during harvest times, Mary Lyons and Owen Quinn met. In fact the odds of that were favourable. Six miles was a shortish distance to walk, so a tramp from Brownrigg to Nungate to meet Mary Lyons' relatives, known or unknown, was no obstacle. It'd be natural to pay a call – a social gathering is the meaning of *ceilidh* – among an Irish community with dancing, drinking, and singing after work. On a Saturday night during the harvest or on a saint's day, let's say. Nungate's reputation for animated get-togethers with plenty of drink was well known, and a *ceilidh* would have drawn in labourers from the countryside seeking company, revelry, or romance. When the planting season was over, there were weeks of underemployment before the hay harvest of high summer or early autumn, and again after the late potato crops. Alternatively, did Owen, day-labouring on the land, or employed at the distillery or the brewery in Nungate – both in business at the time – come up to Brownrigg to work on the grain and potato harvest? A handful of miles from Nungate – and hawkers and carters plying their patch could offer him a ride.

If word of mouth beckoned Mary, Betsy, and Peter to a ceilidh at Nungate, they'd have washed the week's dust and dried mud from their hair and bodies in a tin bath, washed and hung out their threadworn clothes in the cottage garden, and spit-polished their cracked boots. They'd set out on foot, the girls' shawls wrapped tight against the sharp north-easterly breeze. If it was autumn, the lanes at twilight were tricky to navigate, unless the moon shone. They could be sure of a welcome in Nungate, among their own, in from the cold, plied with food and drink, and dancing to the music of a fiddle by a blazing fire. They would have met Lyons cousins, close and not so close. Perhaps it was on one such occasion that Mary met Owen. If so, imagine what he might look like to her, in fustian trousers, jerkin, collarless shirt, cap tilted back on his head. Jaunty. Probably tall. I'm working backwards from photographs of Owen and Mary's grandson, my father, as a young man. Was it Owen, Mary, or both who had the strong build, full lips, and thick wavy chestnut hair – my father's pride, until daily hair-oil and World War II RAF caps, squashed down on his head, uncoiled it for good? Which of them (or both) had the fair skin and freckled limbs that my father (and all his children) inherited? Did one have his grey-blue eyes, and the other hazel ones? Did they both have the wiry strength and broad, calloused hands characteristic of people who spent years building 19th-century Britain and working its fields, walls, and hedgerows? Did Owen see in Mary a 'clean and tidy little woman', as her sister Bridget was later described in a court of law? Tidy as in good-looking, or just neatly dressed? From which of them did their daughter, my grandmother Bessie – who also looks 'clean and tidy', if not petite – inherit the big hands, long sharp nose, and careful smile? Mary and Owen were both fit, to judge from the decades of hard work ahead of them, though not every Lyons was in robust health. They must have been strong, loose-limbed, at ease in their young bodies, even if they still bore traces of childhood malnutrition: scrawny and bow-legged maybe, but both would have had the will and vitality to sing and dance to the fiddle for a few hours. And undeterred by the prospect of more change, more travel, and more risk as they each sought to shape the next phase of their life.

Figure 12: Owen's grandson Geoffrey's wedding to Nora, 1935 - looking more a Quinn than a Howard?

8 Walkerburn, The Whin, and Galashiels 1862–1864: Old Places, New Communities: Wool, Stone, Water

By the summer of 1863, Mary had left Brownrigg and walked south towards the Borders' textile towns. She had not persuaded Peter or Bridget (Betsy) to go with her. Bridget was evidently growing close to Myles, their Nungate cousin, and Peter depended on her. Mary walked towards Galashiels, the fast-growing wool town, where mills were sprouting like mushrooms and factory owners were hiring domestic servants. All that was common knowledge to the Irish community, who had built the new mills, as well as the villas of their middle-class owners. Mary may have been following Owen, or she'd simply struck out to make a new life for herself without responsibility for her brother and sister – prefiguring the actions of her daughter Bessie four decades later. Mary must have saved enough for food along the way, bought second-hand clothes and boots to replace those worn out in the Brownrigg fields. She must have had to steel herself to leave everyone she knew, but she could earn better money, hope to marry and make a family of her own; and perhaps she already knew that Owen Quinn was working in the Borders. It was a few years before she returned to visit her family.

Mary crossed the moorland slopes of the Lammermuir Hills, dotted with blackface sheep grazing rough grass, and miles of heather as far as she could see. Perhaps she joined the path south from Dunbar taken by fishermen to sell their herrings at Lauder market. If she walked alone, she was unusually brave. Robbers preyed on travellers in the Lammermuirs, and although Mary had nothing to steal, a young woman on foot was vulnerable to violence and rape.[31] The sea to the east and the arc of the sun helped her find her way through Berwickshire. She walked along streams flowing into the Tweed, until she saw the railway – the Waverley route – which ran from Edinburgh to the Borders, and she kept close to the tracks. Eventually she saw smoke rising from tall chimneys in the distance. With spinning and weaving in her blood, she'd have been confident of finding work. Galashiels turned out not to be her destination on this particular journey. Instead of walking straight on, she crossed the railway, followed the Tweed westwards, spotted a tall chimney, and walked towards it.

It's possible that Owen had advised her to head for Walkerburn. At the foot of William Law, rising above Gala Water and the Waverley line, stands the dilapidated ruin of a farmhouse, its peeling whitewash stark against the scrub. The Whin, as it's known, is four miles from Galashiels and close by the lanes that run west along the Tweed to Walkerburn. Owen was still living there in 1864, working as an agricultural labourer or maintaining the Whin railway bridge and the Bowshank tunnel: branch lines to Peebles and the Midlothian coalfields ran through the new tunnel. Mary could have met Owen there for the first time, as she passed, if she had not already arranged to call on him, as an acquaintance from Nungate – possibly more than that. Whatever the truth about their first meeting, they were married within a year.

Figure 13: 'The Whin', Owen's farmhouse lodging, north of Galashiels

Weighed down by her load, stockings soaked and new boots pinching, Mary Lyons arrived in Walkerburn, a small village halfway between Peebles and Galashiels. Perhaps Owen walked along the river with her to Walkerburn, which was no ordinary village. It was brand new, although producing cloth was not new to the valley. In 1846 a liberal landowner and entrepreneur, Henry Ballantyne, bought land to build a new tweed mill where the Walker Burn meets the Tweed. He found a prominent architect, 'Eccentric' (Frederick Thomas) Pilkington to build 11 houses for the new workers and villas for his own family on the north side of the Tweed, and the village grew into a working community by 1854, with tiers of housing on the hillside, facing south to catch the sun, the inhabitants' employment status reflected in how elevated their house was. No doubt Mary Lyons lived with others in a room near the bottom. Yet Walkerburn was also an early model for the pioneering communities Bessie Quinn would later discover.

As in Ireland, spinning and weaving as cottage industries went back hundreds of years in the Borders. Before the enclosures, sheep were kept on common land in Scotland, everyone helped with shearing, women carded and spun, and cloth was woven on handlooms. Now, Henry Ballantyne was making his name as a producer of fine tweed, attracting workers from Galashiels – a viable walk to work. Mary was lucky: she lived in the village, probably in a room at Plora Terrace, one of the first workers' dwellings in this modern settlement, with good sanitation, a school, and a railway station. There was a post office (still there) and several churches – but no Catholic chapel. There were sports clubs, a co-operative society, a public hall, gas street lighting, and a French-style *pissoir* – a public toilet. Shops proliferated, many of them in people's front rooms. Walkerburn was a self-contained industrial community, smaller than New Lanark, Saltaire, or Quarry Bank Mill, which were also created by benevolent employers. It also has the feel of a forerunner of Garden Villages. Mary Lyons, 'woollen-mill worker', still lived there in 1864 when she married Owen Quinn.

Figure 14: Early housing for mill workers at Walkerburn, model mill village

The Borders towns, Galashiels in particular, were well placed to develop Scotland's textile industry. The climate, the rivers, the undulating hills where sheep grazed, and several small towns along the Tweed and Gala Water all combined to produce ideal conditions for the mechanisation of old crafts. The towns were linked to Edinburgh, about 35 miles from Galashiels by road, and from the late 1840s by rail once the Waverley route opened. Good roads connected them to English cities, and the region was benefitting from the influx of Irish immigrants, offering cheap labour for building, railway, and factory work.

By the 1880s, there were 22 mills in Galashiels, a town ideally suited to weaving wool and making clothes. Mills sprang up in strings of other towns along the River Tweed: Selkirk, Hawick, Jedburgh, and Kelso. The Galashiels population boomed from 5,919 in 1851 to 15,330 in 1881, to 17,367 in 1891. The number of mills multiplied: there were 13 in 1851 and 22 in 1891. People born in Ireland numbered 203 in 1851, just 3.4 per cent of the Galashiels population. There were 391 in 1881, 2.6 per cent of a growing population. First- and second-generation Irish families increased. Immigrants' children were registered as Scottish, so fewer were counted as Irish, although their primary loyalty, habits, and faith lay with their own community. Like their parents, the children worked in the mills, on the railways, and on building sites.[32]

Galashiels had a high profile and a lively cultural inheritance long before it became the hub of the Scottish woollen industry and host to a growing Irish community. The town was famous for violent incidents and skirmishes in centuries-long recurring battles between the English and the fiercely independent Borders people. Its people were famously – and respectfully – known as 'Soor Plooms' (Sour Plums) after their role in a 14th-century incident in which some murderous English soldiers, stopping to pick wild plums as they relaxed in victory, were slaughtered by Gala townspeople in a revenge attack. Robert Burns wrote two Galashiels poems, 'Sae Fair Her Hair', and 'Braw Lads', the latter still sung each year at the Braw Lads Gathering to commemorate the event. The novelist Walter Scott and his descendants lived south of the town, across the River Tweed at Abbotsford. The Scott family's influence on the town's development later included offering protection to, and even promotion of, Catholic culture and education.

In 1832, a year before Walter Scott died, J. M. W. Turner came to the Borders to draw and paint – his 'Abbotsford Diary'. His subjects were Melrose Abbey, and views from Buckholmside at the north end of Galashiels towards the Eildon Hills, visible four miles to the south-east, long before Comelybank Mill, where the Quinns would live and work, was built there. Turner's literary executor, John Ruskin, whose lace designs Bessie later learned in Keswick, visited Abbotsford and, later, Galashiels, and catalogued Turner's drawings of the Eildons.

The bare, worn-down outlines of the Eildon Hills rising out of curving fields south of Galashiels are steeped in legend, the fount of wild stories. The enveloping silence of the mysterious old hills is said to be broken by fairy apparitions and uncanny happenings – beliefs alien to the dour rationalist culture of 19th-century Presbyterianism. Connecting the strange to the disturbing, Dingleton Hospital – the 'lunatic asylum' – was built at the foot of the Eildon Hills. Some of the Quinn brothers were bricklayers on the site; at least one family member was a patient.

There are ancient rivalries between the Borders textile towns, especially between Galashiels and (to Gala people) 'Dirty Hawick'. Hawick people called their rivals 'pail merks' – a slur on the inhabitants of Galashiels, the last Border town to be plumbed into mains water and sewage systems. But with or without the latest sanitation, as the 19th century progressed, Gala grew in size and manufacturing muscle. More than 20 mills were built, and both spinning and weaving thrived in the town. Wool had been spun and woven in the town since the 1580s, and the 'weavers' corporation' was formed in 1666. Over the centuries it was mostly a peaceable place. But the French Revolution of 1789 and Tom Paine's ideas about the Rights of Man inspired hope and energy for change among millions – met by a deep fear on the part of the ruling class that the ideas would cross borders. War with France brought high bread prices, unemployment and unrest, resulting in panic and laws to stamp out civil unrest, riots, and Naval mutinies. The 'unstamped' press was criminalised, as were public meetings and the formation of unions, including among textile and farm workers. In 1810, Walter Scott wrote to the poet – and fellow Tory – Robert

Southey from Abbotsford House, sharing his fears of revolutionary activity among local weavers. Scott thought Borders people were being dangerously egged on by the Manchester Weavers' Committee, which raised levies from weavers elsewhere, 'doubtless to sustain them in their revolutionary activity'. Galashiels weavers were already seen as a force powerful enough to threaten the social order.

Unsurprising, then, that 19th-century Galashiels had a lively political culture, which developed into animosity and violence when electoral reform was debated. The Borders was Whig territory with leanings towards liberal reform. But there were Conservative strongholds. The 1837 election in Hawick – five years after the Great Reform Act of 1832 brought votes to groups of people previously excluded because they lacked property or long tenancies – was a typically brutal affair. Large crowds named and shamed anyone voting for the wrong side in the violent theatre of polling days before the advent of secret ballots. Turncoats were assaulted by Whig supporters, who stripped their clothes off their backs, accused them of being paid by the Tories, and threw them over the wall into the river. Their friends hauled them gasping from the water. After two days, the militia were called, but as they didn't show up, local councillors had people arrested for rioting and sentenced to seven years' transportation.[33] Then, for the sake of social peace, a Royal Pardon saw them released as heroes instead. Despite successive electoral reform acts, the Quinns could not have voted until 1918, when suffrage was finally extended to all men over the age of 21 and women over the age of 30, including those with no property to their names. Too late for Owen and Mary, for their daughter Bessie, and many of her generation.

A few miles down-river from Gala, Selkirk was a spinning town. Jedburgh and Kelso were weaving towns, and Hawick, also a weaving town, was the main centre of machine-knitting, stocking-making, and knitted garments. Spinning and weaving were distinct trades, and apprenticeships in each were established from the eighteenth century onwards, covering all aspects of the industry, including design, sketching, copying, and technical drawings, paper pattern making, and drawing up instructions to the producers. Rivalries between the spinners and weavers were fierce, as they were also between weavers and knitwear makers. The knitters saw themselves as top dogs, as did knitwear designers and pattern makers. Hawick's knitting was proudly fully-fashioned, not 'cut and sew', so its garments were all of a piece. Colours were vitally important to the quality: a 'yarn chaser' would go from loom to loom to check that matches from 400 different shades of black were precise.[34]

Mary and Owen came from spinning and weaving country. Leitrim and Sligo had been western outposts of the growing Ulster linen industry since early in the 18th century. Local spinners supplied hand-loom weavers before mechanisation broke the cottage industries. The gruelling, messy process of working flax into linen yarn and then into fabric was a common skill among women in rural communities across the west of Ireland and the Ulster counties. Flax was also grown in Scotland around Dundee and Forfar from the 18th century, and fibres imported from England and Ireland were processed alongside local-grown flax. With jute, flax formed a significant part of the Dundee textile industry, but spinning and weaving cloth was transformed by the change from home-based wheels and looms to machine-based mills. Still, working fabric was second nature to many Irish immigrants, including making and mending garments. Mary is likely to have joined the many dressmakers, clothes repairers, and second-hand clothes dealers in the Borders. Linen and wool were in her genes, and she would have passed on her skills to her daughters, Mary and Bessie. whose contribution to the family economy is likely to have included sewing and mending for well-to-do families, as well as for poorer families without those skills. Clothes had to last. Working-class children like the Quinns wore second-hand clothes, repaired and reshaped to fit, mended and patched again and again, then handed down the line. New clothes were not for people like them. The linen smocks that Bessie left behind are the tangible legacy of the Quinn women's skill with linen.

Two young adults still on separate tracks, Owen Quinn and Mary Lyons went to live in the Borders in the early 1860s. There was plentiful work for Owen: building mills, tenement houses, bridges, roads, walls, and public buildings like schools, churches, libraries, hospitals, and institutions. In the countryside, there were stone walls to build and repair, and employment on the 'Waverley' line from Edinburgh through the Borders, and routes down to Northumberland

and on to Carlisle. This was the age of the navvy, and the Borders offered its share of stone-breaking, masonry, bricklaying, hammering, dynamiting tunnels, plumbing, and building sewage works. It was overwhelmingly Irish labourers who built Britain's infrastructure. Patrick McGill, Donegal navvy-poet and novelist, tells of immigrants' physical strength, resilience, comradeship, mutual enmities, wild habits, violence, and reckless courage. Physically strong or not, they worked their fingers to the bone from dawn to nightfall, poached and fished, ate and drank in camps at night to drown out the day, and drove their bodies to injury, sickness, and an early grave. Some sent money home to Ireland; some hoped to; and others cut loose. Some dreamed of returning home one day, or emigrating to America. But drink, fighting, sex, and gambling beckoned to distract them, soothing the pain and exhaustion of now. Life in Scotland, for most, was permanent and short.

Producing food to help feed a growing population was another source of work for Irish immigrants from the late 1840s, fuelling the demand for year-round farm workers to tend livestock, sow seed, and harvest crops. Supporting trades, such as transport and catering, demanded labour too: in breweries and distilleries, as packers, carters, shop-keepers, costermongers, cooks, and in the refreshment and hotel trades. The need for cheap labour all year round to produce and transport food swept away the old seasonal restrictions on immigration.

For women like Mary, there was no shortage of work. Traditionally, hand-spinning or weaving at home, then on factory power looms; sewing for customers; domestic service; farm labouring, cooking, cleaning, and shop work. Textile mills offered power-loom weaving, spinning, carding, knitting, and associated occupations. Survival was possible, despite low wages and long working hours. For Catholic children, schooling, if any, came to an end at the age of 12, and from 10 many attended school half-time and worked half-time. From 13 at the latest, children were full-time contributors to the family income. For girls, childhood was even shorter. They did hours of domestic work from an early age. They washed and mended fathers' and brothers' clothes, peeled potatoes, boiled cabbage, scrubbed floors and baled out the bath-water.

In Borders towns like Galashiels, and surrounding villages and farms, the numbers of Irish people grew as the mills proliferated and they soon made up a still-small but growing and close-knit community: a minority less threatening than Glasgow felt its millions of Irish immigrants to be. Reports suggest that hostility and prejudice were less pronounced in the Borders than in Glasgow, Edinburgh, or Dundee. As elsewhere, the Irish Catholic community in Galashiels stuck together. Official certificates used for this book reveal a litany of family names linked to the Quinns: Boyle, McAnulty, Gilroy, Moran, McIntyre, Butler, Rehill, Tocher, Connel, O'Brien, McLean, Flynn, Hogan, Devany, McDairmid.... On and on, a list poem of migration. They had good reason to stay close. They were in a Protestant country, with their separate local priests and church networks, facing unrelenting hostility and anti-Irish prejudice as immigrants, labourers, people with little or no literacy, who lived in poverty and the inescapable circumstances of the poor. Their Catholicism was more vilified than their Irishness, as adherents of an alien, long-rejected faith, following a path scorned by many Protestant Scots. The Protestant Irish were accepted more readily, but Catholic Irish stood collectively accused of idleness, fecklessness, drunkenness, criminality, insanity, idolatry, undercutting wages, breaking strikes, and political corruption. But they were needed. No Irish labour, no industrialisation and wealth accumulation, so they were tolerated for their essential work, although they had plenty of other less acknowledged skills and means of getting, spending, and feeding themselves. Ireland was home, its hardships and culture were their shared memories. It's not surprising that they usually married people from their own community. Catholicism, a forceful shaper of communities, was their community life as well as their faith.[35]

There was little stigma attached to illiteracy in England or Ireland in Mary and Owen's generation. Few had had the chance to go to school for many weeks – or at all. The majority of the agricultural population of Ireland was still illiterate in the 1850s, apart from those who attended informal hedge schools. Irish (Gaelic) was the majority first language, as well as a means of subverting power, and the English sought, often brutally, to suppress it. In 1841, three million people spoke Irish, a figure reduced to two million by 1851.[36] Their policy and actions are unflinchingly enacted in Brian Friel's drama *Translations.*

The British offered little or no education to Irish Catholics until the new National Schools were established from the mid-19th century, which were deeply unpopular, on occasion attacked and burned down. In Leitrim and Sligo, Irish was the first language in many areas, and Owen and Mary are both likely to have grown up with it. If English was their second language, it was used outside their home and local community, to bow to pressure to use English in contacts with officialdom, landowners and their agents, schoolteachers – all those more powerful than themselves. Orally, they were bilingual, but the absence of literacy among adult immigrants to Scotland defined the limits of their grasp of their second language and added to the disdain in which they were held in a country which was among the first in Europe to raise literacy levels, long before elementary education was fully established. Schooling became compulsory in Scotland from 1872, based on the existing system of Burgh schools, but education for Catholics on the same terms was not established until 1918. The Catholic Church offered a parallel system for children, as the hierarchy feared that a system grounded in Protestantism would undermine the faith of their flock.[37] Among adults, a culture of self-education had flourished among weavers in Scotland since the 18th century. The first Mechanics Institutes in Britain were established in Scotland to promote technical skills. And apprenticeships were open to Catholics in many trades.[38]

9 Stow and Galashiels 1863–1865: Owen and Mary

The first recorded event in Owen Quinn and Mary Lyons's life together is their wedding at the Catholic Mission Chapel of the Blessed Virgin Mary in Ladhope, Galashiels. The marriage was solemnised on Friday 10th June 1864, after the declaration of banns 'according to the form of the Catholic Chapel'. The Jesuit parish priest Father James Henry Corry officiated. Both of them marked the marriage register with an 'x'. It is possible, though highly unlikely, that Mary could write a little. Throughout the 19th century it was common for brides to spare their grooms the humiliation of signing their name in full when their spouse could not write his. But there is no evidence that Mary could read or write a word, any more than Owen could. On the record, Owen was 24 and Mary was 21, a year younger than she'd said she was on the 1861 census.[39]

Friday was a working day, so the wedding probably took place in the evening. Mary would have set off from Walkerburn, perhaps on one of the carts that regularly took cloth from Walkerburn mill to Galashiels. Their wedding was attended by two friends, witnesses to their mark: Patrick Charles and Mary Connel. It's possible that the Lyons siblings or distant Quinn relatives were there, but unlikely, given the distance and the limited wedding celebrations practised by working people. Without writing skills, Peter or Bridget Lyons could not have been witnesses. Mary would have been visibly pregnant. Afterwards, they could have wandered through Gala and had tea, or walked to the Ladhope Inn, a well-established pub even then, joined by workmates and friends for a drink or two. Afterwards, Owen must have collected his own belongings from The Whin and Mary's from Walkerburn, while Mary found her way to nearby Stow to start their life together at Bowland House: she was to be a domestic servant until the baby was born; he had work on the estate's farms. The arrangement would last a year.

How did Mary and Owen get to this point in their lives? Taking the black and white ink-sketches that official records offer, I've added brush strokes and a colour-wash to documented facts, figures, and reports and correlated them with other narratives of Irish life in Scotland to create my sense of their story.

Mary had fallen on her feet at Walkerburn, with an enlightened employer and a good place to live. Most Sundays, she'd walk to the nearest church, in Galashiels, for Mass, and shopping for essentials. As dawn broke, she'd set off with a group of factory girls for a three-hour tramp through fields and copses and over streams. She may have wondered whether Owen Quinn would be seen in town. He was still at The Whin, sowing, harvesting, and stone-breaking. A restless fly-by-night perhaps, but never short of work and at his age beginning to hanker after someone to look after him.

If they met on Sundays they had plenty in common, especially Nungate people and their Irish language. They could share a path home as far as The Whin, and the west of Ireland was right there among the yellow gorse flowers, the shallow streams, the alder trees, the dewponds, the green slopes, and the rain-squalls. I see them resting on her shawl, as she scrapes soil from under his fingernails with a sharpened twig. And Owen at Mary's doorstep, twirling his fraying cap on a forefinger and easing it on to his head, lop-sided, peak tilted towards heaven, poking in unruly curls. Then he picks his way back through the pitch-black night to the farmhouse, joining his fellow tenants for a drink. Life must have seemed as promising as it ever had been.

By the end of March 1864, Mary must have known she was pregnant and gone to see Father Corry, then told Owen that they should get married that summer, well before the baby was born. Quick thinking, decisiveness and a sense of responsibility seem to have characterised Mary Lyons. Charm, physical attractiveness, dreaming of a better life in the next place, a hard-working, and probably hard-drinking, lifestyle seem to have characterised Owen. There are plenty of stories of people in Owen's shoes then who cursed their luck and all priests and then bolted. Possibly he wanted to flee, find work somewhere else, sail for America, go back to Ireland. But he was of normal marriageable age in his culture, and known from Nungate to Galashiels: he'd already put down roots. Mary was much younger, a common age gap in their generation and culture. There's no reason to suppose they didn't love each other and want to marry.

Their June wedding and the baby's date of birth offer more than the obvious insight into Owen and Mary's intimate lives up to these life-changing events. Although for the moral guardians of society and religious rules, sex before marriage was condemned, it was how many people lived. Marrying after a woman became pregnant was a normal sequence in 19th-century working-class courtship. Couples often lived together or with their wider family without marrying, whether they had children or not. Marriage was undertaken when it was affordable, or essential for a specific family reason, as much as a gesture of obedience to the Church. The records point to the Quinns as actively Catholic, and Mary and Owen were probably undeterred by the priest's fees for their wedding or subsequent baptisms, typically for poor people who also dropped their coins into the collections at Sunday Mass.

Although Catholic people carried their own fears of mortal sin and an eternity in Hell, the church at the local level seems to have turned a blind eye to sex outside marriage. And although couples would have felt the pressures of living in a country presided over by stern Presbyterian morals, marriage in Scotland was legally more open-ended than in England. Twelve was the marriageable age, a marriage did not require banns or licences, and under the law no third parties were required to be present for a wedding to be legally binding: simply a solemn pledge between two people.[40]

Respectability was probably the least of Owen and Mary's concerns. They had no parents to protect from any stigma attaching to illegitimacy. They would have been oblivious to the stark entry of 'illegitimate' on a birth certificate, which might have pushed better-educated lovers into a quick marriage. Pregnancy seems to have been the incentive for them to marry then, and a dip into birth records confirms the large numbers of women who gave birth a few weeks or months after marriage.

Finding an affordable room would have been their most pressing need. A mill-worker like Mary had to move out once she stopped work at Walkerburn, and The Whin was a male labourers' lodging. Their first home together, on the Bowland House estate, five miles north of Galashiels above the village of Stow, was either in the gatehouse lodge or just across the path in a farm-worker's cottage. Their accommodation may have been rudimentary, but the setting at the edge of a mansion's grounds was grand, surrounded by ornamental and vegetable gardens, farmlands, lodges, and farmworkers' cottages. From the outside, it seems to have hardly changed, but I'm told that today's landowner is even more absent than his 19th-century predecessors. He makes appearances to hunt and shoot, while an estate manager breeds the pheasants and other wildlife for the pleasure of his city guests.

Someone at Bowland offered Owen and Mary work and a room, under the protective wing of the owner. Either Mary or Owen was already known to William Walker, or someone on his estate offered Owen a farm-labouring or stone-breaking job and a place to live. Stow lies just a few miles north of The Whin farmhouse, so perhaps Owen was known to local land agents. Mary had only four months to offer as a domestic servant before she gave birth. If she was a well-regarded employee, Henry Ballantyne at Walkerburn probably vouched for her character. Local Borders landowners operated in a social network of shared self-interest and political affiliations, whether liberal-leaning or conservative. In a city, with no identification documents to show to landlords, setting up their first home close to work might have been far tougher. So although it is unlikely to have been a wholly charitable arrangement, Bowland Lodge offered the couple a year's refuge.

Figure 15: Bowland House Lodge, Stow, Galashiels

To some extent, landlords and mill-owners in the mid-19th-century Borders still operated elements of a paternalistic 'moral economy', which did not exclude Catholics. Labourers were still seen by some employers and agents as people rather than the mere wage-earning 'hands' – whether factory hands or farm hands – of the new 'political economy', which was fast gathering pace in an increasingly brutal and anonymous industrial labour market. Bowland's owner, William Stuart Walker, belonged to the pattern of land-owning life in the Borders: intermittently in residence, and preoccupied with professional and social concerns. The Walkers were a wealthy Edinburgh society family. William's father, Alexander, a Brigadier in the Indian army, had bought Bowland House and retired there with his collection of Arabic and Persian manuscripts, which his Oxford-educated son eventually donated to the Bodleian Library. William's wife, Eliza, née Loch, was known for her fashionable salons at 7, Colme Street in the New Town. On fleeting visits to Bowland she would stay a few nights, making inventories of linen, furnishings, and furniture before ordering the carriage to whisk her back to Edinburgh society. Walker was a lawyer and prominent local landlord, known for his engagement in poor relief. A liberal-minded conservative, he had an influential role in the Episcopal Church in Scotland, serving as a member of the Poor Board and engaged in schemes for working-class self-improvement. He was a founding director of the mutual Scottish Equitable Life Assurance Society and of the insurance company Standard Life. Walker liked to shoot and fish on his large tracts of land at Bowland House. He was also deeply embroiled in one corruption scandal, the sale of tenancies on his land (so-called 'life-rentals'), which bolstered the numbers of those eligible to vote, for example at the fiercely contested 1837 election. A Parliamentary Select Committee undertook a major investigation into 'Fictitious Votes (Scotland)' in 1838 in which Walker's dealings and those of other local landlords (not, it seems, Henry Ballantyne of Walkerburn) feature prominently. Walker did not appear in person at the Westminster inquiry: he left that to his agent. Apart from these facts, there is almost as little known about this wealthy Edinburgh family as there is about the Quinns, whose lives touched theirs so closely in the 1860s.[41]

Four months after moving to Bowland Lodge, Mary Quinn went into labour. There would have been a fellow-servant, possibly even a nurse, provided by the Walkers, to prepare the room and assist with the birth. On 19th October at four in the afternoon her first child was born. A few days later, when John F. Walker, the Stow Registrar, probably a relative of the land-owner, came to record the birth, he would have explained to Owen, as he handed him the certificate, that the words written beside his 'x' were 'Father, present': present to record the birth of his son, but not to witness it: a father's attendance was not expected, although cramped living sometimes made it impossible to avoid.

As was customary, they named the baby Owen after his father, and he was doubtless baptised at the Galashiels Catholic chapel. The Catholic Church in Scotland offered support and sacraments to the faithful. For a socially excluded group, local parishes were at their best a cultural, recreational, and educational hub, as well as the spiritual home and guardian of morals for Irish communities in Scotland. Irish parishioners were regulated and controlled as well as supported by the parish, which organised a raft of activities: schools, libraries, devotional associations, Friendly Societies, and football clubs. Catholic culture was part of the fabric which held people together and was particularly active in Galashiels, where two churches and a school were endowed and built within two decades. Secular associations outside the church's control also proliferated, however, and secret political 'ribbon' societies were still active among the Irish diaspora.[42]

Before 1853, a visiting priest, Father Taggart, had travelled to Galashiels from Hawick to celebrate Mass, first in someone's home, then in an assembly room. In that year, the first Mission Chapel of the Blessed Virgin Mary, where Mary and Owen married, was built to accommodate the expanding Irish population of the town, and a decade later a schoolroom was built. The Chapel was a plain, red brick building with an unpainted wooden interior and one big square window. Makeshift matting covered the yellow brick floor. The couple would have walked in through a side door and taken three steps up to the altar, which was covered in a claret cloth. As Catholicism had been largely wiped out before Irish immigrants arrived, Scotland became a 'mission' land after the Relief Acts. The first missionaries, the Oblates of Mary Immaculate (their headquarters then, as now, in Leith), had decided that the chapel was much too small for the growing Irish community: it held only two hundred people, sitting and standing. This was the intended base for spreading Catholicism across the Borders, to be led by the next 'mission', the Jesuits. It had far more pew-space than Owen and Mary's small wedding group needed, but puny compared with the second church that Robert and Charlotte Hope-Scott endowed in the 1870s.

As the Irish population grew, the Hope-Scotts considered the arrangements for worship inadequate. Charlotte was the granddaughter and heir of the novelist Walter Scott and lived at Abbotsford, the vast manor-house that he built at Tweedbank in the 1820s. Her husband was a parliamentary lawyer, accomplished linguist, and, stemming from his Oxford days, a friend of John Henry Newman, leader of the Oxford Movement. When Hope-Scott converted to Catholicism, Charlotte followed him into the faith.

The Hope-Scotts bought a piece of land close to the railway, and work started on a much larger Catholic church. Our Lady and St Andrew's Church was the biggest gift that Robert, already praised for a lifetime of philanthropic projects, had ever made. He lived to see it finished, but died not long before the ceremonial opening in 1873. It is still the parish church, a Gothic Revival building which looms over the Galashiels Bus Station next door. As for many Catholic churches built after the Roman Catholic Relief Acts, bells and steeples were not permitted, and architectural styles developed accordingly. It's an unmissable landmark, evidence of an unusual story of Irish life in Scotland, among a handful of other examples of aristocratic Catholics endowing schools and teacher-training colleges in the period after the 1872 Education Act, including the Benedictine Abbey and school founded at Fort Augustus in the Highlands. The Irish Catholic Borders communities may not have been a large, Irish Catholic presence comparable to those in Glasgow, Edinburgh, Dundee, or the coalmining districts. But they received an unusual degree of protective help, symbolised by the imposing new church, a school and a library, at a time when Catholic children were kept outside the post-1872 Scottish school system by the Catholic hierarchy, and access to education was patchy at best. Influential Catholic sympathisers like the Hope-Scotts contributed to the extent to which the Borders towns accepted the close-knit minority community in their midst.

Figure 16: Our Lady & St Andrew Church, Galashiels

By autumn 1865, Owen and Mary had moved from Stow to Ladhope at the northern edge of Galashiels, which would be their neighbourhood for the next fifteen years. As a couple with a baby, they would live in one room in the Comelybank Mill workers' dwellings at Shepherd's Place, Magdala Terrace. Their next move was metres away, into two rooms in Old Buckholmside, another terrace beside the mill. They then spent a few months in Selkirk, before returning to Galashiels. Owen, always an outdoor labourer, had to follow the work until the children were old enough to work at the mill.

The mill at Buckholmside was demolished in 1996. The one-storey, metal and plastic buildings of Comely Bank Retail Park squat there now on a stretch of tarmac between road and water: Matalan, Carpetright, and Currys feature, with a car park wrapped around. It feels as if a strong gust of wind could blow the whole lot away, unlike the solid built-for-ever old woollen mill. No archaeological fragment survives of its long history of making essential goods: textiles, and clothes, from plain, homely work-wear to the full array of tartans, those Scottish traditions completely reinvented for an eager international market.[43]

Figure 17: Comelybank Mill, Low Buckholmside, Ladhope with allotments: Bessie's birthplace

At Buckholmside, Owen worked at the mill and Mary worked from home. If she was typical of women in her circumstances, she lost no time taking in sewing from better-off parishioners and townspeople. Their budget and their diet would have been rich in vegetables that they could grow on the allotments around Comelybank's mills: better workers' dwellings than the infamous slums of Manchester's textile factories, nearer to, if not quite, a model company settlement, even without a sewage system. The Quinn family grew. Their second child, Patrick, was born on 18th May 1866, the first to be born in Buckholmside. Following his birth, Mary gave birth to a child more or less every two years. As was the practice, she would clean the house as she neared full-term and made sure there was a clean sheet to lay over the bed in the kitchen and paper spread over that to soak up the waters, blood, afterbirth, and mess. The floor would be covered with paper or rags. She would have water containers and clean rags ready by the fire, and made sure her chosen friend or neighbour, the informal midwife, was close by when Owen or a neighbour ran to call her. Without expert medical help, Mary would have been unlikely to survive many long labours with complications or heavy bleeding. A doctor was out of the question unless her life was acutely at risk, but there were no fatal complications for Mary and no recorded infant deaths. Stillbirths and miscarriages were in any case not recorded, but perhaps there weren't any. So every two years, Mary gave birth to a baby who survived. All being well, breast-feeding usually continued for well over a year, the sole source of food for her babies. Breast-feeding offered some (if not fail-safe) protection from conceiving another child before the family could cope with the latest addition.

10 Nungate
1860s–1890s: Life with the Lyons Family

Mary's third child, Arthur, was born on 18th July 1868 in Nungate, when she and Owen returned there for a visit. There's no sign that the Quinns had moved back to Haddingtonshire, but Mary's sister Betsy Lyons (from now on called by her usual name, Bridget) lived in Nungate with her new family, and Peter Lyons had moved there from Brownrigg. Mary would not have seen her two siblings for five years. Now she could introduce her children to her siblings before her imminent third baby made travel more unmanageable. She was at least seven months pregnant, so if they had spare cash – unlikely – they might have travelled some of the way by train, and the rest on foot. It's more likely that they set out to walk the 30 miles to Nungate, hoping for a lift in a passing hawker's cart. Two lively boys under four were a handful for such a trek.

The timing seems curious. But there was a pressing reason for Mary to return to Nungate that summer, despite advanced pregnancy and Owen's undoubted fear of losing earnings. Word must have reached Mary from Bridget in early July that their brother Peter was desperately ill, too weak to work. Perhaps the priest at St Mary's Nungate had alerted Father Corry, or Bridget managed to send a message via hawker friends travelling the country, or even via the penny post. Mary would already have known about his tuberculosis – 'phthisis', as it was then termed. Brownrigg's bracing air, in reach of the sea, had been a good place to hold at bay a disease usually associated with cramped urban living and factory conditions. Peter was unlucky. By 1868 he'd moved to lodgings in Nungate, still working as a farm labourer, when his illness flared up and laid waste to his energy. Bridget then took him in, juggling her home-based spinning or weaving work with nursing her brother. The arrival of Mary must have been an emotional reunion. Mary could talk and he could listen to memories of their Sligo childhood, how they'd made their way to Scotland and life in Galashiels. Peter could watch his two little nephews play. Mary stayed close to Peter in Bridget's two rooms and gave birth to Arthur there. Perhaps Arthur was premature when he was born in Nungate. If so, one benefit was Bridget's presence as makeshift midwife. In her own home, already looking after Peter, she was well placed to bring hot water, sheets, scalded scissors, and clean rags. In a few years' time, Bridget would show that she was equal to bigger challenges than this.

Mary recovered by the fire as Peter sank. The pattern of TB's final stages meant spasms of coughing and spitting blood, then he would be quiet for hours, eyes burning. Sometimes he was agitated, knowing he was dying. If hopelessness overwhelmed Mary, she probably wouldn't have let it show. A week after Arthur was born, Peter died, in the early hours of 26th July. He'd witnessed a lot in his last week of life. Mary would have been wakeful, alert to the baby's rhythms, and witnessed his death while she breast-fed close by. There was no time or money to call the priest. Bridget wrote her 'x' on his certificate, the simplest mark of finality. Their links with Ireland, their shared memories, were fraying. Peter Lyons was 26 years old, or thereabouts. The priest arranged his Catholic funeral in St Mary's Chapel across the River Tyne, and the Irish community would have turned out for a procession. The size of Nungate's Catholic funerals, and the presence of women and children at funeral gatherings, was astonishing enough to onlookers, peeping from cottage windows, to be reported in the local press. Perhaps the unhappy circumstances of little Arthur Quinn's birth cast a long shadow over his own short life. Like Peter, he struggled with chronic ill health as a young man: perhaps he'd been frail from the start.

Mary's sister Bridget had married Myles Lyons in 1865 at St Mary's and settled in Nungate. Myles was a 24-year-old hawker, born in Ireland; and at the time they married Bridget was a 26-year-old wool-industry 'out-worker', either spinning or weaving. They both marked their 'x's on the register. Their family histories were intertwined, and Myles Lyons was surely a cousin, close or distant, of Bridget. Peter Lyons's death certificate says that his (and Mary's and Bridget's) deceased father James Lyons had been a 'linen weaver' in Ireland, although elsewhere he is reported as being a labourer. In the Irish rural economy of the previous generation, it is highly likely that James Lyons was a home-based linen weaver alongside casual employment as a farm labourer in the growing and harvesting seasons. He may have emigrated soon after the Famine to the east coast of Scotland north of Dundee. The linen industry thrived in the 19th century around Forfar, manufacturing sail-cloth for the tall ships which embarked from the Tay estuary across the world. Lyons family members are recorded in the area from the 1840s. So an alterative migration story is just possible: that the Lyons children migrated with their father to Dundee, travelling down to Haddingtonshire after he died. Both the given and family names – and trades – for each of their parents differ between documents, but Miles (or Myles), Myles Lyons' father, had also been a hawker, and records show several individuals with the name Lyons living as lodgers, plying their trade as hawkers in Edinburgh, Fife St Andrews, and across lowland Scotland. One, Mary Ann Lyons, a hawker just a few years older than our Mary Lyons-Quinn, turned up again in 1891, by then a pauper, living next door to Bridget in Nungate. The Lyons family, scattered immigrants, were still loosely tied together, surviving by their wits and willingness to help each other as they moved around, travellers by trade and cultural tradition, labourers only by necessity.

After Peter's death, Mary, Owen, and three children walked back home to Galashiels to their life at the factory, poor but stable enough for the time being. The Lyons family members who stayed in Nungate had a different story. In the census year of 1871 and for a few years after that, all went well enough for Bridget and Myles: they had two children, John and Peter. They lived in a stone cottage in Goodall's Place, Nungate, more than surviving on what Myles could sell from his own horse and cart: he was clearly an effective salesman, and Bridget's subsequent life showed that she too had a head for business.

One winter's night in 1877, Myles went missing. Days later, after a long search in bitter winds, his wife found him at 7.30 in the morning on March 4th. He was lying stone-cold on 'Frasers Land' in Nungate. Bridget called for help, but the doctor could only confirm that her husband was dead, the cause 'supposedly, starvation after heavy drinking', and that 'no medical attention' was needed. The beer and whisky had done for him. Bridget wrote her 'x', as the informant present. The death was unusual enough to raise suspicion. Was any foul play suggested? How long had he been lying there? Long enough to starve and dehydrate, and probably to develop hypothermia, which might have been a quicker killer in prolonged icy weather. The cause of death was baffling, and a Coroner's investigation took place. The death certificate has been 'corrected', with the Coroner's report confirming that a 'Precognition', or interviewing of witnesses, had taken place. No further action was taken. But the Lyons family were clearly conspicuous enough among Nungate's Irish community to attract wider interest in Myles's fate. A few days later, on 9th March 1877, the Haddingtonshire *Courier*, the main broadsheet for the county, reported his 'sudden death':

> On Sunday morning, an Irishman, named Myles Lyons, died very suddenly near his own house in the Nungate. Deceased was of rather intemperate habits, and had been drinking heavily previous to his death. The interment, which took place on Tuesday presented certain aspects of an unusual character, from the large number of mourners in their ordinary apparel, and the presence of two or three females in the procession.

At the time, women and children in Scotland did not normally attend funerals. So it was noteworthy that Bridget was there, and perhaps her sister Mary came up from Gala, and, if so, with four-month-old Alexander on her arm. They were the likely 'females in the procession'. Clearly, dressing up for funerals was not *de rigueur* for Irish workers, any more than it is today for working people in Italian and other European rural communities. The untimely end of a Nungate character would have made for a raucous get-together after the burial.

The Lyons family had form. Other reports point to Bridget and Myles as well-known local figures, even notorious to the powers-that-be. Five years earlier, in October 1872, the *Courier* had reported the following court case in detail:

> **JUSTICE OF THE PEACE COURT**
>
> *Held in the County Buildings, Haddington on Tuesday, the Right Hon R.C. Nisbet Hamilton; A Trevelyan Esq., of Tyneholm; and W Dodd Esq., Haddington, on the bench.*
>
> **FURIOUS DRIVING UNDER DUBIOUS CIRCUMSTANCES**
>
> Bridget Lyon [sic], the wife of a hawker, in Nungate, was accused of driving a horse and cart from Easter Bearford to Nungate in a

furious manner to the danger of the lieges. The panel, a clean and tidy little woman, with one child in her arms and another at her foot, denied the charge, and was defended by Mr James Stobie, writer.

A constable was examined in support of the charge, and said that he had cried after the woman when she was galloping the horse along the road, but the louder he cried the faster she drove. He kept her in sight till she got to the south-west corner of Charteris Dykes, but she did not slacken her pace.

In defence, Mr Stobie interrogated defendant's oldest child, a sharp boy of five years, whose precocity was put to a severe test by Mr Hamilton, asking him if he could read his Bible or ever had it read to him, to both of which questions the child gave a dubious negative. Although not up in his letters, the boy remembered what occurred on the occasion of the alleged furious driving. The horse, he said, was only "trotting" and could not gallop at all. The cart was loaded with crockery dishes, and contained, besides himself, his 'wee sister and wee brother'.

Myles Lyons, the panel's husband, stated that the constable came into the House shortly after his wife's arrival. The constable asked the woman why she had not waited on him when he cried after her, and he added – "It would have been better if you had waited, because I wanted a lift and I will now report you for furious driving". The wife replied that she was not in the habit of giving men "lifts", and that as for the reporting, he could (do) his worst. The witness added – "He is in the habit of doing that". The horse, he further said, was eighteen years old, and was not in very high condition. (A laugh). It would require very hard whipping to make it go at the rate of six miles an hour. (A laugh)

Mr Gemmell said it was quite a common excuse of parties accused of furious driving, that their horses could not gallop. The constable had distinctly spoken to the facts, and he claimed the verdict on his evidence.

Mr Stobie urged the improbable character of the circumstances under which the furious driving was said to have taken place. The age and infirmities of the horse put the idea of galloping out of the question, besides which the safety of her load of crockery, as well as of her children would prevent the woman going fast, even if the animal had the pace in him. The constable also appeared to have been able to keep up with the cart a distance of over a mile and a half, which showed that the speed of the horse was either very moderate, or the constable's running powers somewhat unusual.

Mr Hamilton (on behalf of the bench), said: 'There is a certain doubt about this case, of which we will give you the benefit. We will not, therefore, convict you, but be more careful in future'.[44]

Despite strong anti-Irish feeling among many middle-class and working-class inhabitants of Haddington towards the Nungate community, the newspaper's columnist, for one, felt some pleasure in the spirit of those impoverished and socially insignificant Irish neighbours, as well as respect for the quick-wittedness and fearless ingenuity of the Lyons family – including their five-year-old star witness. The boy may not have learned to read, but he knew his lines. The family's defence brief, James Stobie, a 'writer' – meaning lawyer – from Haddington, was quite a catch, given the family's low social standing. Together they had trounced the bullying constable. And the Magistrates – land-owning bigwigs and establishment worthies – had been forced to bow to a good argument and offer justice even to a hawker family, beyond the bounds of respectable society. Years later, one of those 'wee brothers', Bridget's son Peter Lyons, became a police constable himself – a 'stardie' in the Cant – and could have witnessed the Battle of Nungate Bridge between the Nungate Boys and the Haddington Boys in the 1890s. 'Sharp' five-year-old John followed in his parents' footsteps and became a hawker.

Myles and Bridget Lyons had five children. The youngest, Bridget (sometimes called Bessie), was born around 1876, so she was less than a year old when her father died. His spirited wife recovered over time from his death. She never remarried and in 1881, aged now about 36, had become 'head of house' in the census, and had taken over the hawking business to support her growing family. Perhaps she'd always been the driving force. The eldest, John, was already a hawker; three other children, including little Bridget, were at school.

By 1891, life had tipped Bridget back into serious hardship, and the rest of her family faced mixed fortunes. By then she lived at 63 Hardgate Street over the Nungate bridge and worked as a washerwoman. Her daughter Katie was an unemployed, unmarried servant, but the younger daughter Bessie (Bridget) was on the up as an apprentice milliner. Myles junior was a 'cellarman brewer', probably in Nungate, where a new brewery had replaced the old distillery. Bridget's son Peter Lyons was away on the night of the census, perhaps out patrolling the streets to keep the precarious peace. In 1892, the 'valuation rolls' show that he had become a police constable, living with his mother. The family was see-sawing between just-about surviving and acquiring new skills to improve their earning power. By 1895, Bridget seems to have been living with a group of people with several different family names; her younger children have flown the nest, and the house is full of lodgers. Bridget Lyons was expert at bobbing and weaving to make ends meet. And seemingly still a wayward spirit in her fifties. In 1897 'Elizabeth Lyons', aka Bridget or Betsy, was convicted of breach of the peace, at the Temperance Hotel of all places. Not so lucky this time.

11 Galashiels: Comelybank Mill 1870s: Family Life, Fluctuating Fortunes

Galashiels lies at the heart of this story: the town was Bessie Quinn's only childhood home, before she left for Edinburgh and Glasgow and moved south to England. Nearly half her life was spent in Galashiels, where she learned everything which, against all odds, helped her to knead her adult life into a different mould. Bessie was born in Gala in 1879 and left in the late 1890s. When English people, listening to her speak, asked her where her home was, her instinct must have been to reply 'Gala'. Whatever she decided to reply, and however hard she may have worked to anglicise her vowels, drop Scottish words, and flatten the notes of her Scottish Borders lilt, her voice was one thing she couldn't suppress. She may have been proud to carry this living legacy into her London life. As music, my grandfather's reedy London twang would not compare well.

Six Quinn boys and one girl were born before Bessie came into the world. Mary and Owen's fourth boy, James, was born on 4th August 1870, the second child to be born at Comelybank Terrace. Their first daughter, Mary, was born there, on 2nd November 1872; Peter, their sixth baby, followed on 1st July 1874. That year, Owen fell ill. Their income dried up, they had nothing to fall back on, and they were forced to make their first application for relief under the Poor Law. An inspector from the Melrose Parochial Board called at 7.30 in the evening on 16th October 1874. He noted all the particulars as relayed to him by Mary. Once again they differ significantly from other records. Owen's age, as on several occasions, is minimised, no doubt to talk up his credentials for exacting manual work. He's reported as '35', born in Ireland, and Mary as '30' (which at least chimes with most of the other data). For the first time, Mary's birth name is given as 'Johnston', the name she'd continue to give to authorities in moments of crisis. It may have helped that 'Johnston' could pass for Protestant. As was the norm, all their prior residences since marriage were listed. Owen was certified 'very poorly' and 'wholly disabled' from work. As a result, ten-year-old Owen was keeping the whole family afloat. He was working half-time at the mill, half-time at school, earning 2 shillings and 6 pence a week (12p) as a mill-piecer – the sole income to feed all of them. His father was 'in need of all sorts of nourishing food'. The family had barely enough to eat. The inspector recommended financial relief, and temporary help may have been forthcoming before the Parochial Board overrode his judgement and refused the application.

Alexander Quinn, the seventh child, was born on 10th November 1876. The family was struggling on, but two years later, in February 1878, their circumstances nosedived again and they made a second application for relief to the Melrose Board. Owen's age jumped to '45', and he was again 'wholly disabled', 'laid up with bronchitis for about a fortnight'. Perhaps he was delirious, or they decided that an older age would help his case. Mary is down as 40, and named as 'Mary Lines' by birth. Young Owen, now 13, is keeping them all again, working full-time and more to bring home 10 shillings (50p) a week. The inspector's recommendation to approve their application was refused for a second time. Perhaps they were lucky not to be 'relieved'. That year, another Lyons family in town, probably relatives, applied for Poor Relief. This homeless married couple was 'on the tramp' with two teenage children because the husband 'says he can't find work', and his wife (another Mary) was lying ill in an outhouse. Their application was successful. 'Relieved', the wife was 'removed' to the Poorhouse for several days before the dubious help was withdrawn, although their situation was unchanged. Working-class Irish Catholics did well to be careful what they asked for.

Bessie, the Quinns' second daughter, was the last child born at Buckholmside – on 20th January 1879 – in the depths of one of the most ferociously cold winters ever recorded. Temperatures that month were on a par with the winter of 1947 or 1962–3, but for poor families then it was freezing indoors as well as out. It would take all their efforts to scour the woods for fuel or scrape pennies together for a coal fire. It was a harsh end to the 1870s, and they survived only because they managed to ward off sickness, the mill work kept coming, and the roof over their heads was secure.

In the spring of 1881 the family moved house, and their ninth child, Thomas, was born on 8th July 1881 in their new home. They had not moved far: still in easy walking distance of Comelybank mill and in earshot of the factory bell. As before, they had two rooms, but now they arranged their cartful of possessions in a small multi-occupied house at 4 Chapel Street, Ladhope. It's tempting to think that this move marked a rise in their fortunes, but it may have been that, in a time of economic depression, Owen had lost his labouring job at the mill and the tie with Comelybank was broken – for now. Other tenants in their house, the Taits, applied for Poor Relief in 1884, suggesting a general downturn in available work. Owen was working somewhere in April 1881, freewheeling, going wherever there were stones to be broken or building workers needed, a day or a week at a time. The Quinns' tenth and last child, Augustine, was born in Chapel Street on 17th January 1884. By now there's the feel of a more stable ménage, which means that Owen managed to stay healthy, and one by one the children left school and headed for the mill: half-time as early as ten, full-time at 12 or 13.

The terrace along Chapel Street is still there, and little changed. It's a short dead-end street. Estate agents now might say a 'quiet cul-de-sac', close to Gala Water at the bottom of the narrow valley. A single row of cottages lines one side of the street, at right angles to the river. A broad pathway runs along the front of the houses, and on the opposite side is a picket fence, punctuated by a gate opposite each front door, opening on to an allotment garden, big enough for the tenants of each sub-divided cottage. In working-class gardens, potatoes, beans, peas, leeks, cabbages, and root vegetables were popular; fruit included currants, raspberries, brambles, and gooseberries. Pansies and violets were universal Victorian favourites.[45] Chapel Lane must have seemed a quiet haven compared with the mill terraces. It was further from the deafening 24-hour din of looms, engines, and generators and the unceasing clatter of shift workers on cobbles. Because of the perpetual glare from the mill's lighting – gas, then electricity – factories were rechristened 'Light Satanic Mills': noise and light polluted workers' dwellings. Chapel Street, where the night was dark along the river bank and the noise was a few streets uphill, was closer to the town centre, but still near enough for the family to walk to work, school, and shops in minutes. Like any halfway-healthy mother in their circumstances who could produce milk, Mary will have breast-fed all her ten children for a year, even 18 months. She provided a solid foundation for their survival, even if ten successive pregnancies, as well as possible miscarriages, and the best part of 20 years' breast-feeding, slowly but relentlessly sapped the strength of her body and mind. Mary's health would have been sacrificed to nurture her children's. She'd have been lucky to have many or any of her teeth left, even on a low-sugar diet. If she did, the cost would have been chronic toothache, soothed slightly by salt-water rinses or cloves if she could afford them, ended only by whisky-dulled do-it-yourself extractions. Mill children's lives were laden with the risks to health that went with their living conditions: fibre-laden air, shared beds in which several children huddled together, all of them exposed nightly to disease and the causes of disease. Common maladies among working-class communities were rickets, scurvy, cholera (until clean water arrived), and smallpox, for which compulsory, monitored vaccination in Scotland came late, in 1863, but, unlike in England, it was detached from association with the Poor Law. There was an outbreak of measles in Gala in 1875, a killer before vaccination; and diarrhea, pneumonia, and tuberculosis were rampant. Nutrition was one vital determinant of health. Safety was another: accidents on machinery caused injury, permanent disabilities, and violent death.

Infant mortality in Scotland was 129 per 1,000 births in the 1890s. Many more children died before reaching the age of five, and the figures were far higher among poor families in tenement rooms and city slums.[46] That all the Quinn children survived into adulthood is testimony to a healthy-enough lifestyle, hard-wrought over decades of precarious, hand-to-mouth living. By their own efforts, Owen and Mary successfully provided a home, however cramped, eked out home-cooked food made from raw ingredients, clothed and healed their growing children, sent them to school and church, and helped them to develop. The Quinns, in these years, and people like them, do not match the stereotype of the feckless, reckless, lazy Irish.

Mary's day would include shopping for bread and ingredients for soups and stews at one of Gala's Co-operative stores, known simply as The Store, or from hawkers, costermongers, and market stalls. Until the late 1930s there was a weekly market in what is now Scott Park, once the 'Gala Policies'. All kinds of foodstuffs and livestock were bought and sold from local farms: horses, cows, and sheep, but also pigeons, rabbits, eggs, grain, fruit, and vegetables. On their plot there was space for a fruit tree or two, currants, and berries. Owen must have become a skilled-enough gardener there, if not at Comelybank: the 1891 census states that he was gardening for a living. Besides housework and minding little brothers, the older brothers and daughters Mary and Bessie could have helped Owen on the plot. The Quinns' diet was probably averagely healthy, even above average, for the country as a whole. The mid-19th century saw more poor children reach adulthood than the late 1880s and 1890s, when cheap sugar brought mass-produced confectionery, sweets, cakes, and biscuits, and tinned and processed meats. The key was fresh food: vegetables, grown or bought; fresh milk; occasionally offal and other cheap cuts of meat; oatmeal and grain for wholemeal bread, although white bread was ubiquitous. The Quinns' diet would have been supplemented by the odd rabbit which labourers caught in fields and woodlands, quickly tucking tonight's supper into a jacket pocket. Trout-tickling was another skill that men like Owen learned, passing on the skills to his sons. There was plentiful wild food in the Borders: fungi, brambles, cloudberries, wild raspberries and strawberries, rosehips, blueberries, hazelnuts, elderflowers, and rowan berries. The Quinns came from rural stock, so foraging would have been second nature to them. Large families had limited portions, which kept people just-about healthy, but in trim: obesity was not the problem. Tea and weak 'small' beer (less contaminated than water) formed part of a typical diet.[47]

When it came to education, Mary and Owen were conscientious parents. All the Quinn children went to school from the age of five to their thirteenth birthday, even when their financial situation was at its most fraught, although they attended half-time for some of the last two or three years. Neither the authorities nor the Church would have insisted on it, but they must have believed in education and harboured hopes for their children's future. School attendance was free from 1872, but parents still had to fork out for exercise books and materials and decent clothes, stretching their means to the limit. If the family needed their earnings when they reached the age of ten, the children could attend half-time, as we saw with first-born Owen in the 1870s, although they could not stretch to enrolling any of them at the technical schools in Galashiels or Hawick.

The Quinns benefited from a longer period of schooling than poor families, especially Catholics, would have been able to afford in

England before 1890, let alone Ireland. How was it possible? The Scottish elementary school system was established earlier than elsewhere in Great Britain and Ireland. Since the 16th century, education had become a pillar of Scottish national identity and literacy, at least for boys. Following the 17th-century Reformation, schools at parish level were supported by Presbyterians and other Protestant churches, and they accommodated most children.

Figure 18: The New Schoolhouse, built 1879 next to Our Lady and St Andrew

Small Catholic Irish communities had settled in the rural south-west from the late 18th century, especially in Kirkcudbrightshire and Wigtownshire, and parts of East Lothian. But after the Napoleonic Wars, Catholic communities from the western Highlands and Ireland began to cluster in towns and cities. The question of migrants' schooling became pressing amid concerns that it was 'far too cheap and easy for people to migrate to Scotland, even if only for seasonal labour' and that the country would be overwhelmed by Irish migration.[48] The Catholic Church was strongly opposed to Catholic children attending Protestant schools, fearful of the inculcation of Protestantism among their flock, although some parents sent their children anyway, especially to Ragged Schools. When the 1872 Education Act made elementary education compulsory and free, handing responsibility to the Burgh (town council) to provide and pay for an elementary school, usually the Parish school renamed and developed, the Catholic Church decided not to participate. Instead, they paid the extra taxes, and paid again to create a patchy network of Catholic schools, in which, apart from religious teaching, they borrowed heavily from the mainstream school curriculum.

In Galashiels, the Quinns were lucky to be able to send their children to a Catholic school. From 1867, a schoolroom was attached to the Catholic chapel in Galashiels, in time for all their children to attend. As the Catholic population grew, another room was added. When the new church opened in 1873, Our Lady and St Andrew's RC School was housed in a schoolroom inside the old chapel, which the younger Quinns attended. In 1879, again in time for the younger siblings, parts of the presbytery were demolished to make way for a whole new school with a playground, opened by the local priest, Father Corry. There has been a Catholic school in Galashiels continuously ever since. It is now St Margaret's RC School and located elsewhere in town.

Elsewhere in Scotland before 1872, the provision of education had been inadequate for working-class children. Yet despite the continuing voluntary nature of Catholic education, there were 65 Catholic schools in Scotland by 1872 and their number was growing, funded and made possible by benefactors, church associations, and the lay community.[49] In places, some Protestant children joined Catholic children at their schools. But the Catholic Church opposed their own children's attendance at Protestant schools, even at the price of many missing out altogether. More widely, working-class attendance for all 5–10 year olds in Glasgow and elsewhere, Protestant as well as Catholic, stuck fast at 50 per cent in the 1850s and 1860s. And throughout the 19th century, there was no secondary education at all for Catholic children – or for many others. The best that a Catholic working-class school-leaver could hope for was an apprenticeship, which a few of the Quinns and their Lyons cousins managed. Schooling was driven by the faith, with the catechism to the fore, yet Catholic schools followed the 1872 curriculum, therefore neglecting Irish history, and reinforcing a British Catholic identity. Their teachers qualified in Catholic training colleges in Liverpool and Glasgow, and pupil teachers assisted them. The Church accepted Scotland's inspection regime, grants for books and a seat for priests on School Boards. Their schools were finally integrated under the Scottish Education Act of 1918.

As well as reading, arithmetic, and religion, sewing was part of the curriculum. Writing was taught at Our Lady and St Andrew's, too, although in most 19th-century schools across Great Britain writing came a poor second to reading, so many children did not learn a skill judged essential only for those who aspired to use it to earn a living. Thomas Paterson, the Galashiels Registrar who had completed Owen and Mary's marriage certificate and all the birth certificates of their Galashiels-born children in elegant handwriting, also founded a writing school in the town and taught there for 28 years. In that era, handwriting and spelling were popular subjects, increasingly a passport to employment in copying and other clerical jobs. The Quinns who later signed official family documents clearly learned to write a neat hand in their Galashiels school.

Galashiels was a progressive and encouraging place in which to grow up, for those who could afford to benefit from improving activities and organisations. Several schools taught arts and science subjects, as well as music. When the new Catholic school was completed in the 1870s, a library was created, endowed by the Hope-Scotts and valued at £500, so plenty of books were available to parishioners and their children. There's no trace of its later history.[50]

Figure 19: Galashiels Library and Reading Room (opened 1873) & Cornmill

From 1837 the Mechanics Institute held public lectures, and the Galashiels technical school later offered working-class people science and art qualifications. A funding campaign established a free Public Library and reading room in the 1870s. The library was an instant success: a librarian was appointed, free lodgings included with his salary; crowds queued, and 13,794 books were lent out in the first year, leading to book rationing. Daily opening hours increased to 9am–10pm as book loans multiplied. A museum followed. From 1892 a 'juvenile' library opened, despite moral disapproval and alarm that children would be distracted from school and would damage books. Bessie, aged 13, could nevertheless have joined.

As Bessie grew up, chinks were beginning to appear in rigid Victorian educational values and practices. In Galashiels, two daughters of a mill-owning family, the Sime sisters, introduced Froebel's educational methods to Borders kindergartens and schools. They had learned new theories and practices in Berlin, studied at the Leipzig conservatorium, and in 1882 founded the Moat House Kindergarten and schools, employing visiting teachers for piano, violin, and dancing. Their school flourished at least till 1898. Bessie may have known nothing about this, let alone participated. Yet their approach to education was reflected in decisions that she later made for her own children.

When Mary and Owen increased the ages of their children on censuses, it may have been an expression of regretful feelings about taking their children out of school at the earliest opportunity. But the size of the family wage was the decisive factor in their collective survival. Therein lay their vulnerability and that of millions in their circumstances, forced to take short-term decisions with long-term consequences. The mills and factories on which they depended for their livelihood were also the cause and accelerator of the chronic sickness and disease that throttled it. The unnatural conditions and patterns of factory work laid waste to human health. Illness and injury stalked the poorest communities, threatening the ability to work or live long into adulthood. Cholera may have been defeated, but work-related and poverty-related TB, bronchitis, and pneumonia engulfed communities, eroding the health of millions.

Scottish censuses show the Quinn children starting one by one in the mills after leaving school. By 1881, young Owen had been a 'woollen factory worker' for nearly eight years. Patrick and Arthur, aged '16' and '14', were also 'woollen mill workers'. Each of the entries makes them out to be a year older than they were, but there was no cross-checking of the census with other records. Children's income from the age of ten trumped learning in the harsh realities of a family economy. I can hear Owen and Mary conferring, offering up numbers, hovering around the earnest middle-class data gatherers, enumerators, and other authorities sitting at their kitchen table, complying with the State's demands, fingers crossed behind their backs, 'forging' if not simply trying to remember. They never dodged the census and they unfailingly produced the required information, although they could neither read the form nor confirm that the document was correct. The Quinns were not the signatories: official enumerators signed off the truth about the population.

The Quinn family were practising Catholics. At least four of their children were confirmed in the Catholic Church, trained and prepared at school for the initiation ceremony. All religious rites carried costs, but confirmation took place in large batches of children, which made it more easily affordable for poor families. Owen, the eldest, was the first to be confirmed, aged 10, at the church of Our Lady and St Andrew on 26th July 1874, just a couple of weeks after Peter, the sixth child, was born. Owen was devout, it seems; he was still with the faith a few years later when he married Alice Butler, a young woman who had been confirmed at the same church. Typically, confirmation ceremonies were held on a saint's day. At that time, it was a rite of passage linked to maturity, usually performed as children approached their teens. In Catholic doctrine, it marked the advent of adulthood when an understanding of church teaching and personal responsibility for sin could be expected. Confirmation was then the second sacrament of initiation into the Church, following baptism. It was not until 1910 that Pope Pius X lowered the age of reason and moral responsibility. Seven became the age for first Holy Communion, following a child's first confession of their sins. Ironically, the new 20th century, dawn of a modern age, saw a heavier moral clampdown on the assumption of a child's innocence compared with 19th-century Catholicism, when children had been theologically exempt from sin until they were adult enough to confirm their faith. New spiritual burdens were placed on children whose freedoms were already pinched by hard work and poverty.

Owen's confirmation record survives. He was young to be confirmed, and his parents must have sanctioned it, as doctrine dictated that they decided when a child accepted the sacrament. According to custom, Owen took a saint's name – Ignatius, after the Jesuits' founder – as did several confirmands that day. It was an unusually grand ceremony, as Owen's godparents were local grandees Mary Monica Maxwell-Scott of Abbotsford, writer, historian, and great-granddaughter of Walter Scott, and her husband Joseph Constable Maxwell-Scott. The couple spiritually 'adopted' 94 godchildren that day. The Scott family's engagement with Galashiels' Catholic faith and culture was now in its fourth generation.

After Owen came Arthur in 1881, aged 13 (he took 'Joseph' as his saint's name); and Mary in 1886, aged 14 (she took 'Anne'). In 1886, the numbers of young Catholics taking confirmation had risen to 172 – perhaps because the Archbishop of St Andrews and Edinburgh, John Strain, presided over the ritual. There was no appearance by the Maxwell-Scotts. Bessie's confirmation record has also survived. In October 1889, she was recorded as Elizabeth, aged ten, and took 'Clare' as her saint's name. She was now deemed to be a responsible adult. Poor Clare, she was certainly doing the work of one.

As the children left school, they were first taken on as mill-piecers or scavengers. Piecing was lethal work, part of the manufacturing process which depended on the small frames of vulnerable children who crawled under enormous throbbing looms to catch and re-tie broken strands of wool into a continuous thread. They spent all day walking up and down the great sheds, through the long rows of spinning frames, or 'billies', and whirling spindles, leaning over the spinning machines. They had to move fast to reach across in the brief moments when the wheel was coming out. Linger a second or two and a limb might be mangled. Scavengers, usually the very youngest ones, crawled beneath the mules, to clean off surplus oil, dust, and dirt. John Fielden, the Manchester factory reformer and MP, watched one girl at work and confirmed reports that mill-piecers walked more than 20 miles a day. Crippling, sometimes fatal, accidents were all too common as hair and limbs were caught in machinery. Several of the Quinns were mill-piecers, bringing home a few essential pennies a week. In 1881, Owen had left to become a 'mason's labourer', and Mary was occupied at home minding Betsy (Bessie), aged two, and her 'scholar' siblings. She washed bodies and clothes; shopped, cleaned, and cooked on a coal-fired kitchen range; gathered and boiled herbs as remedies; made, mended, and altered clothes for the family, and, like so many home-bound women, would also have sewed for customers.

The Quinns' daily life in their sequence of homes may look to us like grinding hardship, but for them it probably felt like getting by and occasionally even getting on. They never occupied more than two rooms with windows. That was the norm. Three rooms was out-of-reach luxury, and many families occupied one 'single end' room. In the mid 19th century, the solidly built cottage that we see today at 4 Chapel Street, which looks like a decent-sized family home, was multiply occupied, rented accommodation. The Quinns shared facilities with other tenants: rubbish tips, laundry, washing lines, and allotments.

Figure 20: 4 Chapel Street, Ladhope, with allotment gardens

How did they organise themselves in their two rooms, whether in the mill cottages or at Chapel Street, when at least ten or even twelve of them lived there at the same time? One room was for living, including cooking, eating, and a weekly hot bath. This was also where the parents slept, with the youngest infant in a small bed next to theirs. Above the entrance, a crucifix was probably the only ornament. The second room was the bedroom for all the children, and if there were proper beds, there was a large one for all the boys, and a smaller one for the two girls. They might sleep in a row across a thin mattress, or top-to-tail, close together either way and breathing over each other as bedbugs bit. Lice, threadworms, and infections would soon spread; coughs, catarrh, and wheezy restlessness made deep sleep difficult. Shared diseases and fitful sleep were part of life. They were used to it. Mary's life was the non-stop toil of working-class mothers, supported by the conscripted labour of her children.

At Comelybank, life had been more complicated than at Chapel Street: noisier, darker, smellier, and unhealthier. Jostling with neighbours along the row, there was more competition for laundry and drying space and a losing battle to keep flying fibres and dust under control as they swirled out of the factory. Lavatories were either a family pail, or a hole in the ground, so the waste flowed or dropped straight down into a shaft, built as part of the mills and workers' terraces. One occupant of a later Hawick tenement talked of lavatories 'breeding spiders the size of elephants'. The shared copper tub was housed in the back yard, one for every three or four tenants. It was filled with cold water, then a fire was built underneath, which each user was responsible for lighting and extinguishing again. Eight out of ten women worked in the mill or took in work, on top of their domestic load, so weary older children looked after younger ones, and the little ones often bore the scars of accidents. This was the pattern, six days a week.

The day started when the mill bell tolled to wake the early shift. With bread and tea for breakfast, sleep in their eyes, they walked towards the mill, caught up in the crush as the crowd jostled along 'wynds' – narrow alleys – towards the glare of the gas light. Electric lights arrived in 1898 at Comelybank, the first mill in the country to be electrified. Candles were followed by gas lighting, which stayed on all day in the winter months, when not a finger of sunlight reached down the steep valley. At the end of the day, the crowd streamed out, walking home faster, exhausted or not. This was the pattern of life for the Quinn boys. Their mother did her sewing at home, paid and unpaid, by hand, helped by her daughters once their skills passed muster. It was not until the 1890s that mass-produced sewing machines became popular in homes, usually bought on the never-never. For his part, Owen set out at dawn to break the dark red and grey stones of Roxburghshire, building and mending stone walls around the fields, or labouring on new mills and tenements to house the growing population.

What time was there for recreation in their lives? They could take leave from work for two–four days per year: a half-day on Christmas Day, New Year's Eve, and New Year's Day, plus a couple more: all unpaid leave. Women often took all of Christmas Day off and weren't always penalised for it. The Factory Act of 1847 limited the working hours of women and young people aged 13–18 to 10 hours a day. For the Quinn children, Saturday afternoons were free after school, and for adults too in some mills, where the working week was rejigged so that they could close altogether on Saturday at 2pm: saving money but demanding the same hours. From 1894 there was a football club with two teams, Gala Fairydean and Gala Rovers FC, which flourished until the First World War, when the deaths of so many young men put paid to sporting life. There were well-subscribed public buildings open in Gala: the library, reading room, halls, and churches. A cycling club formed in Gala in 1884, with headquarters at James Boyd's cycle shop. Bicycles, and soon afterwards motorcycles, gained popularity fast, including among women. Perhaps it was at Boyd's that Bessie learned to ride a bike. One popular racing event in Gala in 1914 was for motorcycles and sidecars – by that time, a feature of Bessie's new family life in England.

Basic wages for mill-workers and labourers were supplemented by piece-work to bolster productivity, and by women's extra earnings at home, or as seamstresses, wet-nurses, cooks, shop-workers. Mill-workers largely looked after themselves, as trade unions were weak until the first decade of the 20th century in this part of Scotland. Many Irish workers were day-labourers or contract workers or worked independently as carters or hawkers. It would have been hard for them to organise, moving from job to job. The Borders was a betwixt-and-between region: rural, but with small towns and local industries. Although union representation increased as the numbers of mills grew, there was prejudice in unions against both Irish and women workers, who made up a large proportion of mill-workers.

Bessie's eldest brother was still only 16 in 1880, when she was a one-year-old toddler. At this time, all 12 of them lived in two rooms at Comelybank, and in the late 1870s only the three eldest, Owen, Patrick, and Arthur, had started work. By 1881, young Owen had left home. He had other plans for his working life and was living independently in Edinburgh: one less mouth to feed, but one less wage coming in. James and the next three siblings, Mary, Peter, and Alex, were all at school. These were the hardest years to keep food coming to the table.

Yet, from the first half of the 1880s, the family's fortunes started to look up, not just financially. By 1881, they had moved to a better place: Chapel Street. The eldest children had left school, able to read and write. Arthur was working as a wool-carder, and during the 1880s, one by one, James, Mary, Peter, and Alexander started work in the woollen mill. Mary soon became a tweed-birler, a more skilled job, checking the quality of woven cloth emerging from the looms, identifying, returning, and discarding lengths with imperfections, and reporting which looms were the most productive. In the late 1880s, Peter and Alexander started half-time as mill-piecers.

Several brothers pursued ambitions to move on from mill work: Owen, Patrick, Peter, and Alex. Ten years on from the 1874 Poor Law application, several more wages were coming in and there were fewer mouths to feed. By the late 1880s Patrick had followed Owen to Edinburgh, Owen to work on the railways and Patrick as an apprentice bricklayer. Perhaps they sent money home as long as they were single and their incomes were stable. This would seem true to Owen's character, but Patrick was more likely to drink away any surplus. Peter and Alex bided their time.

Bessie's two youngest brothers were born in Chapel Street: Thomas in 1881 and Augustine in 1884. Mary's pattern of pregnancy, childbirth, and bringing up babies may have been routine and normal for her class and era, but the toll taken on her body and mind by ten pregnancies within 20 years, the sequence for so many working-class women, would have been severe. She was about 40 when Augustine was born. Perhaps the menopause was setting in. Was this the point at which she began to lose the energy and mental sharpness she'd needed to keep the family fed and thriving for so long? People meeting her for the first time would have seen a worn old woman, not a woman in the prime of life.

More is known now about the impact of pregnancies on women's later physical and mental health, on which multiple pregnancies and poverty all have a negative influence. If women like Mary were physically worn down and prematurely aged, they were also mentally at risk, with now-familiar conditions like post-partum psychosis and post-natal depression. The symptoms then were trapped in moralistic strait-jackets, with high-handed condemnation of socially unacceptable 'behaviours', which sat side-by-side with medical terminology, both slotted into the crude, cruel categories which then defined mental health. The impact of serial pregnancy and large families came later in life: Mary Quinn's life is one example among multitudes of women.[51]

At the end of Mary's childbearing years, the plight of a fellow parishioner and mill-worker illustrates attitudes to and perinatal practices in women's mental health in the 1880s. There was keen medical interest and much debate about the psychotic dimension of post-natal disorders, rather than depression, which remained a neglected condition. But there was little tolerance, subtle understanding, or suitable medication, let alone talking therapies for handling post-natal distress. At home, bewildered men and children could offer little emotional or practical support for new or experienced mothers. At the end of their tether, new fathers reported symptoms which resulted in their wives' enforced admission to an asylum. And although the medical and bureaucratic process of certification, when it came to dealing with psychosis, was meticulous, it was also moralistic. In May 1881, a 23-year-old Catholic woman and probable relative, Elizabeth Quinn, gave birth to her first child at 6 Abbots Place, Galashiels. A few days later, she was taken by force to Dingleton Hospital, the local lunatic asylum, authorised by a 'Certificate of Emergency', signed by the local Board of Lunacy on multiple grounds and certified, as was the law, by two doctors. Her husband, a stonebreaker who worked for the woollen mill, reported that she had not slept more than a few hours since her confinement. She was 'violent', 'behaving outrageously, a danger to herself and others' …. 'screaming and shouting at the pitch of her voice', according to her landlady. At the hospital, her delirium was noted, as well as her habit of 'constantly rhyming incoherently': calling her friend's black dress a 'black gas'. Her refusal to eat and her 'filthy habits' were attributed to 'preoccupation'. Elizabeth Quinn was diagnosed as 'labouring under puerperal mania' and confined from May until October 1881. What happened to her baby over that time is anyone's guess: wet-nursed, fed on pap or still-dangerous bottled milk. The mother recovered and had another child a few years later, but remained fragile for the rest of her life and died young. Women's breaches of all the norms of feminine social behaviour were as much a cause for alarm as their actual suffering. Wealthy women were more likely to be treated at home than women like Elizabeth Quinn, confined in the local asylum. Post-natal conditions, and the impact of pregnancy on women's health, later became reputation-makers as medical science became increasingly specialised. Interestingly, this included the concept of healing not just the woman, but the whole family which was at risk. Poverty and neglected health became, and still are, accepted as contributing to 'puerperal mania'.[52]

12 Galashiels
Late 1880s–1895: The Best of Times?

Not long after Augustine, their last child, was born in 1884, the Quinns moved house again. Chapel Street was close to the river, and damp; in winter months, thick fog from smoke and clammy air blanketed the valley. Perhaps anxiety about Arthur's health had crept in, a reminder of the death of Peter Lyons in the same week he was born. If Arthur was often forced to miss work, the family income suffered. Chest infections would also keep Alexander (Alex) home from school, although the others seem to have sailed into adulthood in reasonable health.

By the mid-late 1880s, there was a stable-enough income for Owen and Mary to rent rooms in a healthier neighbourhood. Halliburton Place was on the flank of the hill east of Gala Water. They needed more room than ever. On a Saturday evening after work, the Quinns would have piled beds, tables, chairs, clothes, and pots and pans on to a borrowed horse-drawn cart belonging to Irish friends. Carting, a business often taken up by Irish immigrants, went with hawking, peddling, and costermongering. Ten of them walked uphill, bundles on their backs. This was the last time they moved house in Galashiels – almost.

47 Halliburton Place was perhaps a small notch upmarket, although Parish Records for the 1880s show several families on the street living in acute poverty. The Quinns occupied two rooms along a terrace of stone cottages, a longer walk from the mill, on the north-east side of town at the edge of the countryside. It's a long, broad street, curving up the hillside, a steep incline up from Gala Water, above Ladhope and the main road through town. Their row of houses is perched half-way up, overlooking rows of rooftops, and beyond them the river valley and the mills. The air is fresher on the hill. They'd have smelt and tasted it as they walked home from town, looking down over the smoke hanging in the valley.

Inside, their new home was light, especially when afternoon sun poured through their west-facing front window, and they could watch deep red-striped sunsets. From their front door today, a Victorian mill can still be seen across town, on the west side of the water: the last one standing, someone told me. Halliburton Place and the parallel streets still have an airy quality – a suburban neighbourhood above the town, leaves rustling in the copse above it, and colourful well-tended front gardens with azaleas, magnolias, heathers, cotoneasters, and bright bedding plants. Lace curtains dress big windows. It's quiet, although, down below, the traffic speeds to and from Edinburgh and down to Hawick along the A7. The only people outdoors on the bright May afternoon when I walked around was a group of Muslim women talking together while their small children circled round on scooters and tugged at their mothers' burkhas. The recently established Borders Islamic Society on Roxburgh Street is not far away for prayers, courses, and support for 21st-century immigrants.

During the 1880s, Owen had started to supplement his stone-breaking wages with gardening work. Opportunities appeared as growing numbers of affluent mill-owners, managers, and middle-class professional families occupied new villas and mansions around Galashiels. They hired both full-time and jobbing gardeners to landscape their gardens, tend flowerbeds, and bring produce to table from kitchen gardens. People taking an evening or Sunday stroll in town could have admired Owen's patch at Chapel Street, and his prospects looked up, as conversations over the garden gate with shoppers in town turned into offers of work. It was probably all the advertising he needed, with gardening contracts settled then and there.

Figure 21: Halliburton Place, 1890: street scene, including Bessie and younger siblings, ca.11 years old?

The later years at Chapel Street, and then at Halliburton Place, seem to have been as secure as the Quinn family ever got. From the 1880s, there is a more regulated feel to their lives. The younger ones, Bessie, Thomas, and later Augustine, could run down the hill to school together, watched by Peter and Alex. There were shortcuts down the cobbled pathways to the parallel roads below Halliburton Place which follow the contours of the hill down to the valley.

Better air at Halliburton Place would have been a tonic for the babies, and soothed Arthur and Alex's susceptible lungs. The move seems to have worked for a while: their health did not deteriorate in these years. Arthur, James, and sister Mary continued to work at the mill, followed by Peter in 1886 and Alex in 1888. Bessie would have been the one to notice any disquieting changes which started in this period, as she was constantly with her mother. Relief at arriving in a place where she could hope to stay for a long time, if not the rest of her life, could have slowed Mary down. But apart from this change for the better, she was overstretched, with much to worry about. Bessie's role as the daughter still at school, doing the daily grind, responsible for the reading, writing, and numeracy tasks, and minding the youngest ones, inevitably escalated as she organised more of her family's home life, a notch up from running home from school to help prepare supper for ten. She'd been doing that since she was five. Bessie was still at school in 1891, but probably half-time or as a pupil-teacher. Her sewing skills may have extended to embroidery and, if so, were perhaps prized by her mother's customers. In 1891, Owen was established as a 'jobbing gardener', the lowest tag in the hierarchy of professional gardeners, employed by those whose budget didn't stretch to a full-timer or by wealthy households needing extra 'hands' in a team of gardeners. Jobbing gardeners were often despised as 'ignorant' (too much tidying up), as were the sellers of forced plants in local markets. It's possible Owen had no choice but to change tack. Perhaps he'd suffered an injury on a building site and needed less back-breaking labour than splitting stones. Or his chest problems may have returned. Fortunately the going rate for jobbing gardeners was higher than for labouring, and he could pay back the investment in tools: jobbing gardeners had to bring their own wheelbarrow, watering can, fork, scythe, shears, spade, trowel, and hoe. They often took a child along with them, so Owen could have benefited from the help of Bessie and her younger brothers.[53]

Gardening was lighter work than stone-breaking, and closer to Owen's roots on the land. Chapel Street had been his first vegetable patch in Scotland, but he would have known in his bones how to grow potatoes, cabbages, and onions. At Chapel Street he could have branched out from vegetables into culinary and healing herbs, which were still prized: patent medicines were unaffordable for many. The gardens at the back of the Halliburton Place houses are a good size, and he would have had access to them with other tenants. Owen's children could also help to grow their food, and Bessie might have learned skills that she practised in adult life. At Halliburton Place Owen could make more compost and grow some of the flowers popular at the time: spring bulbs, sweet peas, roses, calendulas, dahlias, wallflowers, and fuschias, their hanging pink and purple droplets reminiscent of West of Ireland hedgerows. He could sell seedlings at the local market, or save seeds and bulbs and share his produce with fellow workers and drinkers at the local pub.

By the late 1880s, Mary had seen the last of her children learning to walk and talk and starting school, and her family sailing on a more even keel. She had no more babies to bear, breast-feed, wean, feed, and clothe. Despite weariness and growing dependence on Bessie's help, Mary had reason to be optimistic, more in control of each day than she had been for two decades. Then one day in 1889, the pattern of her daily life suddenly changed, bringing a new test of the family's fragile well-being. A newborn baby arrived on their doorstep.

13 Edinburgh and Galashiels 1880s: Young Owen Quinn and Alice Butler

It was events in the life of Bessie's eldest brother Owen that caused the upheaval to the Quinn family's settled ways in Halliburton Place in May 1889. As well as eight children still living at home, Mary Quinn was also now caring for her first grandson, third-generation-Owen, a weeks-old baby. For help, she had only ten-year-old Bessie who could watch over her two youngest, Tom (7) and Augustine (5), before and after school. The older ones were out at work.

Owen Quinn, the eldest son, had lived in Edinburgh since 1880, working as a railway surfaceman (the Scottish term for platelayer), a skilled job laying lines (plates), doing track maintenance, and improving safety. It was dangerous work. Before 1914, more than 600,000 people worked on the railways. In the 1880s and 1890s, there were thousands of accidents annually in Britain, with some 500 fatalities each year. Over the last 25 years of the century, 13,000 railway workers were killed. No action on safety had followed a Parliamentary Enquiry in 1846.[54] From the age of 10, Owen had become a half-time worker, half-time scholar, earning a small wage to supplement his father's wages. Twice, in 1874 and 1878, while his father was sick, the boy's wages as a mill-worker had been the whole family's sole income, and the family sought financial help from the Parish Board. The Board twice refused, although it was clear from reports that the family was on starvation rations. Still hardly more than a child, Owen junior fell in love with Alice McNulty-Butler, a local mill-worker. But she was several years older than him, and he was still too young to marry his childhood sweetheart. His solution was to leave home for Edinburgh around 1880, escaping the burden of supporting the family, aiming to do an apprenticeship, then find better-paid work. He found a cheap room to rent at 3 Howe Street, in workers' dwellings inside the Georgian New Town, some of which serviced the wealthy residents of the new development and housed railway workers and other essential tradespeople. Owen's house is now a Grade I listed building within a World Heritage site, but this was not a grand dwelling then – far from it.

By the 1880s, when Owen arrived in Edinburgh, the Catholic population was growing and seeking a cultural foothold. One example was football. In the 1870s, Cowgate boy Michael Whealan and Canon Edward J. Hannon, the Catholic priest at St Patrick's Church, had founded the Young Catholic Men's Society. Many local boys were football-mad, but Catholics were excluded from existing clubs, and often formally banned. In 1875, Whealan and Hannon formed their own soccer team, the 'Hibernians' – Hibees, Hibs, or 'cabbage and ribs' – a clue to what their opponents thought Catholics lived on. Canon Hannon was the first coach and manager, and Whealan was their captain. In their green and white strip, they were Edinburgh's Irish team, based in Cowgate at the centre of 'Little Ireland'. The Meadows served as a training ground where, in 1875, Hibernians played their first fierce derby with their rivals, Heart of Midlothian. Hibernians' fans were also known for their support for Irish Home Rule, and some went further, seeking total independence from Great Britain, among them James Connolly. Connolly was Cowgate-born, had gone to school at St Patrick's, and spoke on the Meadows at large gatherings of the Scottish Socialist Federation; protests and marches still end in rallies there. Apart from pubs, clubs, and churches, young people like Owen could gather on the Meadows for company.

For years Owen Quinn courted Alice Butler, saving money while she worked on at one of the Galashiels woollen mills, staying with her mother, Alice McNulty, at 4 Park Street. Her father, Peter Butler (sometimes known as Patrick), an Irish-born farm labourer, was already dead. Owen and Alice were married at last on 21st May 1886, when he was 21. She was officially recorded as 20: in fact she was 25. Their wedding was conducted at the Broughton Street Catholic church in Edinburgh. Owen's brother Arthur, still living in the family home in Galashiels, was his brother's witness and the Quinn family's representative. Perhaps Owen and his next-born brother Patrick did not get on so well, which would not be surprising, as later stories of Patrick suggest. Owen, of all his generation of Quinns, seems to have kept the strongest ties to Catholicism. Alice, like him, had been confirmed in Galashiels RC church in 1870, as had her siblings. The local priest was clearly undeterred by her parents' unmarried state or Alice's 'illegitimate' status. Records of marriages, births, and baptisms suggest that many Irish Catholics who had scarcely enough to live on still engaged with the local church, paid their dues when they could, and attended Mass and other sacraments and rituals. Equally, many local priests accepted the reality of parishioners' circumstances, sin or no sin, turning a blind eye to the doctrines and the moral approbation handed down by the hierarchy. They let live, and held off adding fear of eternal damnation to the troubles of parishioners in this world.

Owen and Alice made their home in one room at 2, Leith Street Terrace, along a side-alley behind the busy main street. Their time on Leith Street feels the best of Owen's life, after years of propping up his parents and long hard labour to make this new life possible. After three years, on 25th April 1889, Alice gave birth to their son. They called him Owen, a third-generation Owen Quinn. Their stretch of Leith Street was a busy shopping thoroughfare teeming with pedestrians. Tenants crowded into cheap lodgings. The area has been demolished, replaced by a wide causeway and road junction, dominated by a John Lewis store. Alice's mother was living on Cowgate, close enough to help her daughter with labour and the baby's first weeks. Nothing went awry, and following the birth Alice and her baby Owen did well. But after a few days of recovery from labour, Alice's condition suddenly worsened. Perhaps lung disease lurked dormant from years of exposure to wool fibres as a Gala mill-worker and flared up in a body weakened by childbirth. Owen must have stoked the fire in the chill April air and kept Alice warm, but she was ill enough for him to call out a doctor, a hard decision for people without a penny to spare beyond paying for food and rent. Perhaps Alice's mother prepared trusted remedies like steam inhalation, or honey stirred into herbal brews, recipes from Ireland, scouring the Leith Street shops to find cheap ingredients. But after six days of acute bronchitis, Alice weakened and died in the early hours of 7th May 1889. It feels inevitable. This was nearly 40 years before Alexander Fleming, the doctor from a poor Ayrshire farm-workers' family, made his way into medicine and in 1928 discovered penicillin and the first antibiotics, which could have saved Alice Quinn.

Owen was with Alice when she died and signed her death certificate later the same day. His shaky handwriting bears witness to shock and grief, reverberating down the generations: a distressing story told in one surviving document: 'Owen Quin, widower, present'. Widower, aged 24. This grim task accomplished, Owen registered the birth of his son Owen later the same day, 7th May: 'Owen Quin, father'. In their bewilderment and grief, he and his mother-in-law Alice McNulty must have arranged Alice's funeral, but would have been preoccupied by a more immediate crisis: how to find a way to feed a three-week-old baby boy – within hours. Working-class families faced this crisis all too often: how to keep a motherless baby alive that day and the next. After that, who would care for him? It is clear that Alice McNulty, the baby's grandmother, was not in a position to help bring up a child, even with the help of a wet-nurse if they could afford one. She was living under the wing of the clergy who offered food and shelter in South Gray's Close, steps away from St Patrick's Church, just off Cowgate. By 1891, she had become an 'annuitant', which probably meant that the church was supporting her permanently with money and lodgings, keeping her out of the Poorhouse. Alice McNulty probably suggested that Owen meet the priest at St Patrick's to allay his distress and helplessness, and to organise the burial. They had to find a wet-nurse immediately or, as a last resort, prepare a 'pap'. After the funeral, Owen and his son left immediately for Galashiels to seek his mother's help. He had no choice.

Owen must have taken the train to Galashiels with his baby for a brief handover so he didn't risk losing his job. His father Owen and brother Arthur tried to calm him. Mary held the baby and fed a pap to the scraggy, fractious creature. After that, there would have been a local wet-nurse who'd take on a number of babies at a time, for a sum, if they could afford it. Keeping infant orphans alive was no easy matter. Barely in a fit state to face the world, Owen left within hours to resume his life in Edinburgh. I picture Mary accompanying him unsteadily down the hill to the railway station, carrying his baby son in a blanket. There is no evidence that she ever saw Owen again.

Mary and her daughters fed baby Owen as best they could. Until the mid-19th century, milk substitutes and supplements were concocted at home. Pap was a slurry of flour, bread, or oatmeal, in water or milk. It was fed to babies from 'pap boats' – like small gravy-jugs. Sometimes sugar, beer, or meat broth enriched the mush. Even opium was added to soothe a fretting infant. The Quinns' budget probably didn't stretch to a wet-nurse, unless Owen left his mother money. They certainly couldn't have afforded still-exotic new luxury baby-foods from Nestlé, which were sold to the affluent from the 1880s. Just as well, as up to a third of babies were dying on the novel diet, in which wheat was mixed with sweetened condensed milk without additional vitamins. Baby bottles were also available from the late 19th century. Bottles of animal milk for babies included donkey, sheep, and cows' milk. Their long narrow feeding tubes bred bacteria and caused so much infection that they were banned completely in 1910. Pyrex bottles with wider necks began to replace the primitive early models, and bottle-feeding took off. Whichever method Mary adopted to feed baby Owen, his food and hygiene must have been adequate. He grew up as healthy as any of her own.

Raising Owen's baby would have been a joint effort. Mary, Owen, and their daughters Mary and Bessie brought him up between them, with help from Arthur, his closest brother. They sent him to school and saw him into work. He reached adulthood with his grandparents. Perhaps, hidden from the records, his father did visit him after the tragic events, and sent money for his keep. But his absence seems total: Bessie's eldest brother disappeared for good. There is no trace of him in any records, alive or dead. Unless ... could our Owen Quinn, 'mason', be one of the 250 passengers who sailed from Glasgow to New York in February 1891 on the mail steamship Anchoria? 'Mason' was near enough to the truth. There are no other traces of him, except that between 1904 and 1907, on various occasions, his much younger brother Peter, who was sheltering his nephew Owen in Clydebank, informed the Dumbarton Parish authorities that 'Owen', presumably his eldest brother and the young man's father, was dead. Neither his previous whereabouts, nor dates, were recorded. Perhaps we should trust Peter's version: he's the most reliable of all the Quinn siblings. Without further evidence, I have a strong feeling that Owen did emigrate, unable to overcome his grief, his bitter memories of Edinburgh, and his sweet ones of Gala. His heart was too broken to piece together again in the familiar old places. Either way, for Peter and the others, Owen was as good as dead. If he did emigrate to America, he became, like thousands of other Quinns, part of the Irish diaspora – in New York, Chicago, Philadelphia, or the towns in between growing cities: wherever a skilled builder and railway surfaceman was needed. After fifteen years, his brother Peter had either heard that he was dead, or assumed he was dead, a plausible story to support their mother's application for help from the Parish. Although, if he was alive and well in America, it's likely he outlived his son.

14 Galashiels
1892–1895: Arthur Quinn and Jane Tocher

Mary and Owen's load was to grow heavier. In 1894 Arthur was struck by sudden loss. Two years earlier, he still lived at home in Halliburton Place, working as a wool-carder in one of the Galashiels mills and helping to bring up three-year-old Owen for the sake of his lost brother.

Owen's marriage to Alice Butler could have been the model for Arthur when he met Jane Tocher, a power-loom weaver, working at the same mill. Like Owen and Alice, they'd probably known each other since childhood: Irish Galashiels was a small and closely bonded community. Arthur and Jane were the same age almost to the day. Jane was born in 1868, the daughter of George Tocher, a family friend and Galashiels carter, who ran his business with a brother with whom he managed to scrape together a living. Jane's mother Margaret was the daughter of an Innerleithen saddler. The family lived at Overhaugh Street, always hovering close to poverty, and Jane probably spent more time mucking out the horse than attending school. When George Tocher died in 1879, Jane was ten and her mother Margaret, who had been supplementing the family income as a domestic servant, had to feed and clothe her six children by herself. She started a business, making and selling sweets and cakes, and for a while she did well. Perhaps Margaret knew she was working against time. In 1883 she was stricken with tuberculosis and died within three months, leaving her six children to fend for themselves. They must have inherited Margaret's resourcefulness, managing to stay put in their home, living independently until adulthood, dodging the prying, disapproving eyes of the Poor Law inspectors and others with the power to break up a household of under-age orphaned children – as they regularly did. The Tochers were a close family in a protective community, which helped them resist the forces which, in the name of moral welfare, would have split them up and dispersed them among Poorhouses, orphanages, residential working homes, or, under 'outdoor relief', in distant boarding houses.

When Arthur was courting Jane in the 1880s, she lived with her younger sister Maggie Tocher and other siblings at 204 Gala Park Road. On 16th September 1892, Jane gave birth there to a baby boy. Maggie was on hand to help. The entry on the birth certificate simply states: 'Arthur George Tocher (Illegitimate)'. There is a blank where 'father' should be, but Arthur Quinn and Jane Tocher married on 30th December, at the church of Our Lady and St Andrew, and set up home at 116 Halliburton Place, close to Arthur's family. Arthur and Jane were still working at the wool factory, and Maggie and the Tocher sisters helped to look after the baby, Arthur George. For over a year, life was calm enough.

In early 1894, Jane Tocher-Quinn suddenly fell ill. She was diagnosed with an excruciatingly painful disorder: stricture of the pylorus – 'Pyloric Stenosis' – a rare condition which is almost exclusively suffered by babies under the age of six months, runs in families, usually affects the first born-child and usually boys. There is still no medical explanation for this peculiar susceptibility. The main symptom of the illness is a drastic narrowing of the passage between the stomach and the first part of the small intestine, so that food simply cannot be processed. This baby disease was first described in 1888 – within an era of multiple medical breakthroughs. In Jane Tocher's mysteriously rare adult case it seems more likely that an inexperienced doctor, boning up on new illnesses in medical journals, may have misread both the symptoms and the affected age-group. Either that, or he was simply careless in the diagnosis of a patient who would certainly die and in any case couldn't afford to pay his bill. The likelihood of affliction in adults was rare to vanishing. Any patient with such an acute illness is not likely to live on in agony for six more months. With no cure for the disease he had diagnosed, he left Jane with doses of morphine, tended by a distressed husband with a toddler to look after. Today, Pyloric Stenosis can be cured surgically, but it was fatal then, a horribly painful death. Stomach cancer or a perforated ulcer could be the likelier explanations for the same symptoms and, undiagnosed, either of them could have killed Jane. She died on 20th June 1894 at home. Arthur signed the death certificate: 'Arthur Quinn, Widower, Present'. He was left grieving with his two-year-old son and Maggie. And when he was gripped by symptomatic TB or bronchial episodes and unable to work, he was thrown back into dependency on his parents.

Mary and Owen agreed to help bring up Arthur George, so that Arthur could work and Maggie could return to domestic service. Arthur George was a docile toddler, making slower progress, physically and mentally, than other children of his age. Bessie would have cared for him every day and noticed it, encouraging him to develop and learn words. Her brother Arthur lived close enough to his parents to see, and confirm to his sisters, what he suspected. The family was in trouble, their mother overburdened by the two grandchildren. And perhaps had even greater worries on her mind.

Since the 1870s, the family had surmounted a series of financial crises, and their fortunes had even improved. But by 1895, the mellower years in Halliburton Place turned sour. Peter and Alexander, the middle boys, had left home. The household now included James, who worked locally; grown-up daughter Mary; teenagers Bessie, Tom, and Augustine; and Owen, their grandson. Within a year of Jane Tocher's death, little Arthur George came to live full-time with his grandparents. Their rooms were full to bursting, and conjuring calm out of chaos was beyond any of them.

Whether, in 1894, Bessie was working full-time or part-time at the mill, or at home full-time helping with the grandchildren, is unknown. The latter would have meant a financial sacrifice for the family; the former was more typical for a girl of her age but would have left Mary intolerably overburdened. Bessie would by then have had additional responsibility for family tasks requiring literacy. She was the sapling on which the family leant for support, physically and mentally resilient. She was helping to bring up young Owen and Arthur George, steering their learning, channelling their high spirits, and calming tantrums. Augustine could protect them on a streetful of children, while adolescent Tom was more likely to push them around and pinch food off their plates. Owen learned to read, and could help his grandfather in the garden. But Arthur George needed hours of encouragement and play before a response glimmered in his eyes. Mary was more dependent than ever on Bessie's help to slog through the daily mountain of tasks. Bessie would have fed and washed Arthur George and changed his nappies, with a hawk's eye trained to stop the clumsy toddler falling as he lumbered around, blotched with bruises and scratches. Her burden of duties seems to have been more intense than was typical of working-class daughters in large, poor families.

Mary Quinn was about 51 years old in 1895. Sewing work probably still flowed in, but, as she aged, the strength and stamina that had seen her through the toughest times were inevitably waning. She was reminded daily of her lost son by the presence of little Owen. Perhaps the uncertainty surrounding the absence of his father gnawed its way into Mary's mind. Arthur's child was an additional preoccupation.

Going by similar accounts in autobiographies, the only time when Bessie could occasionally take an hour for herself would be after her shifts at home, at the mill, or out gardening with her father. When the younger ones were asleep, she might have started experimenting with embroidery on roll-ends and scraps of cloth. Or she could tuck herself in a corner and read. She might ease out weeds or prick out vegetable seedlings with delicate fingers, the way her father had taught her. She could name birds and flowers, as I know from my father's reminiscences. At 17, Bessie may have regretted the end of her education, and in daydreams became a teacher in Glasgow, living with Alex. She would open the door of her cage and fly. But there was no real possibility of escape.

It would have been a severe blow to Bessie when Peter and Alex left home in the mid-1890s. Alex had been the companion of her childhood and her link to the outside world. I believe that, left behind in Galashiels, she lost the drive to carry on with the reading, educational quests, and explorations of sunnier futures that they had enjoyed together. Without Alex's quirky spirit and Peter's steady handling of the bills that threatened the family's financial survival, she would have seen no end to the life she knew. Boys could leave; girls could not. The day Alex's train pulled out of Galashiels station, I imagine her crying bitterly and walking past her home, shawl wrapped tight, up to the woods, where she railed at the pair of them for abandoning her.

Bessie's sister Mary could not help her. She was later described by a young niece as a beautiful aunt, but in her early twenties she was already too frail to add housework to her shifts at the mill. She was prone to bronchial infections, and if she couldn't work, she wasn't paid. Her income was essential to the family, as she earned reasonable money as a 'tweed birler'. Protecting Mary's health was critical, especially as.their father's earnings were falling. Later events suggest that the two Marys, mother and daughter, supported each other, sometimes at Bessie's expense – and if she was working only part-time at the mill, or not at all, that was about to change.

It's said of those times and these that it takes only two adverse events in a person or family's circumstances, whether affluent or not, middle-class or working-class, to plunge people down an unstoppable downward spiral into deep poverty, even homelessness. The most common catalyst is the break-up of a relationship. When the Quinn family began to struggle to get food on the table, they were facing three misfortunes at once. First of all, less money was coming in from Owen's work as a jobbing gardener, and he'd gone back to stone-breaking, even though the relentless toll on his ageing body caused back pain and broken nights. He was probably growing more distant and distracted. Secondly, more and more working days were lost through episodes of sickness afflicting Arthur and their daughter Mary. Thirdly, the loss of their son Owen and daughter-in-law Alice meant they had another mouth to feed. Debts would have mounted. And stone-breaking on a gang contract brought temptation for Owen to drink more of his wages – and escape looming realities.

After more than three decades of survival, the Quinns were heading for a precipice. Change was coming for Bessie, and to begin with change was for the worse. By the end of 1895, the household at Halliburton Place had moved back to the housing tied to Comelybank mill where they had started: two rooms at 28 Low Buckholmside. It must have been cheaper than Halliburton Place, closer to work for Arthur, Mary, and Tom. Now Augustine, as well as Bessie, was working at the mill. But the new tenancy did not last long before this tenacious, close-knit family unravelled, left Galashiels, and dispersed across southern Scotland. The exact reasons are invisible in the murky waters that obscure their uncharted life and struggles in the late 1890s, but the records suggest some explanations for their collapsing house of cards.

15 Galashiels and Clydebank
Late 1890s: Those Who Found their Way, and Those Who Lost It

With nearly seven years in the woollen mill behind them, middle-family brothers Peter and Alexander were no greenhorns, but they'd never lived away from home. Both started working life as half-timers and at 14 were still earning a pittance on gruelling shifts as scavengers and mill-piecers. They would have advanced to other occupations once they'd grown out of those roles, but opportunities for skilled work were limited, and the mill environment was damaging Alex's health.

Hearing stories of better-paid work with apprenticeships around Glasgow, Peter may have gone to assess their chances among the new factories and shipyards springing up along the Clyde. By all accounts Peter was the most cautious Quinn brother and probably did his homework, warming up slowly to a big decision, weighing up the pros and cons of quitting the mill and leaving home. In the end, the prospect of a skilled trade must have been irresistible, because by 1895 the two brothers had uprooted themselves and signed up for apprenticeships at the Singer sewing machine factory. My sense of 18-year-old Alex suggests he was lured, too, by Glasgow's burgeoning labour organisations. On Clydeside, the brothers were apprenticed as French polishers and varnishers at the Singer factory at Kilbowie. By then, the Singer Corporation was already large, rapidly growing, and a seemingly benevolent American company. Both brothers were qualified by 1901, still employed by Singer and living together in Clydebank.

For thousands of years, sewing had been done solely by hand. But the industrial revolution in textiles transformed a craft into a mechanised process. Machines took over in homes and factories, turning linen, cotton, and woollen textiles into clothes and household goods. The first machines appeared in the 1840s, initially opposed by tailors, who protested against the disappearance of home and workshop production into factories. From the 1860s, the American Singer Manufacturing Company produced sewing machines *en masse* in

Glasgow and sold them across the world. Russia was their biggest export market, but sales soon reached every corner of the earth, from mansions to mud huts. Women were increasingly working outside the home, with less time for sewing and mending by hand, and the demand for domestic machines rocketed. Sewing machines served both factories and home-based production. Singer dominated one of the fastest-growing industries of the late 19th century, and its Clydebank factory was the heart of a dynamic business.

The company offered good pay and conditions. For Peter Quinn, who'd only ever known the precariousness of his family's mix of self-employment, contract work, day labouring, and mill work from the age of ten, the prospect of a qualification and steady wage was a glittering prize. Singer's also offered unheard-of company benefits like savings clubs, sickness insurance, and a pension scheme. Even promotion prospects looked promising for conscientious workers. Leisure activities were provided for, with clubs to meet every enthusiasm and skill: horticulture, amateur dramatics, and sports, to name three of many. But there was an iron fist in the velvet glove. Total compliance and unquestioning acceptance of Singer's way of work and takeover of employees' lives were the terms of employment. That didn't bother Peter, who was content to knuckle down, but it seems that Alex was less drawn to the Singer culture, where he may have felt like a fish out of water, drawn more to the large, vibrant Irish community, clubs, trade unions, and socialist associations.

Once he qualified, perhaps Singer's trenchantly anti-union stance pointed Alex towards the door. Health considerations may have played a part, as fumes from varnish, paint, and polish in the Wood Department, as well as swirling wood dust and flying metal shards, would have inflamed fragile lungs as much as the wool fibres at Comelybank. Sickness and injury were no more tolerated than discontent: both were judged as carelessness, with pay docked. Alex stuck it out at Singer's until 1901, then left or was pushed, and went to work on the shipyards.

The brothers' departure in the mid-1890s depleted the Galashiels household income: two lost wages. But the sinkhole which opened up under the Quinns' feet had deeper causes. One explanation, on the evidence of their diverse characters and material situation, is that over the next year or two the family was sinking into a sea of debt. It's likely that rent arrears on Halliburton Place were mounting irretrievably. Once Peter had left, unpaid bills, reminders, and outright threats would have accumulated on the kitchen table, ignored until the most literate member of the family – Bessie – spelled them out. This was an emotionally awkward responsibility. In the late 19th century, literacy became an emblem of generational role-reversal: illiterate parents relied on the children they'd sent to school to guide them through the new and unfathomable world.

It was another dimension of the outsider status of Irish parents, whose children were Scottish-born and literate. Scotland was their children's home country, even if their parents' origins, allegiances, faith, and community tied them all to Ireland. Still seen as outsiders, the Scottish-born generation lived their lives poised between two cultures. The contents of many written communications were humiliating enough, but parents' embarrassment at their dependency on children to read them added to their shame. Bessie knew about her parents' money troubles and she wrote the necessary notes in reply. Arthur was living down the road, preoccupied with his disabled son. James was good-natured and dutiful, but away working in Edinburgh. Bessie's elder sister Mary walked home from the mill each evening exhausted and breathless. Adding to their troubles was a mood of threat: footsteps on the threshold, knocks at the door, even raised voices demanding entry. If they couldn't pay the rent, the Quinns couldn't stay at Halliburton Place, the home that represented a step up in the world.

The Quinns were among many facing hardship in Galashiels during those years. A sharp economic downturn in the mid-1890s, caused mainly by a slump in the US export trade, hit the woollen mills, putting many people out of work in the Borders towns. There was belt-tightening among the middle classes, but destitution for many working-class families.[55] In the second half of the 1890s, Owen's gardening work must have declined and there would have been little else on offer. In his mid-fifties, he was gradually losing the strength and stamina for full-time stone-breaking, suffering back pain, his arthritic fingers crooked and callused knuckles swollen. Gardening work plummets through the winter months. By 1895, as Valuation Rolls show, the family had moved back down to the mill, at 28 Low Buckholmside. There would have been some outdoor jobbing for Owen there, including repairs to the bridges over Gala Water. His daughter Mary still worked at the mill, so the family were eligible to live there. At sixteen Bessie would have worked full shifts, so their mother lost her domestic mainstay just as the younger children's demands grew. In fact, Bessie may already have started as a mill-piecer from 1892, one year after the census showed her still at school, aged 12. Perhaps it's wishful thinking that this bright girl could have stayed on as a pupil teacher, which fits her later interest in educational methods. Either way, the family was desperate for wages, so women on Buckholmside must have helped Mary cope with her grandchildren.

With their move back to Buckholmside, the Quinns' life in Galashiels had come full circle. The respite was brief. They were one of many families hit badly enough by hard times to be forced to leave. By 1901 the town's population had fallen by more than 4,000, marking the beginning of the long, slow, terminal decline of the wool industry over the next half-century.

It was a full-blown crisis. Some of the family must have lost their jobs in the woollen mill, but their decision to move away was complicated by the children in their care. Perhaps it was Bessie who suggested Peter come over from Clydebank to help James and Arthur as they sat perplexed at the kitchen table in the evenings, turning over pieces of paper. None of them was sure what to do, but they knew the price of destitution. Their mother must have been distracted and exhausted. I see her dragging her feet across the floor as if they were pulled down by a giant magnet. Barely restored by a cup of tea and a minute's rest. Perhaps Owen was out of the house even longer, turning his back on their troubles with friends in the pub, still working hard but helpless to put things right. The family could no longer keep their heads above water. When Peter visited from Glasgow, he and James must have taken charge, finding a practical solution to a calamitous situation.

Tip-offs from James and Patrick would have told Owen about work available all year round in Edinburgh, where factories and residential streets were eating up the surrounding countryside. The family could move to Newington, on Edinburgh's south side, live more cheaply and pay off debts. James found a place to live on Causewayside, which runs south from the Meadows through Newington. There was work for everyone. For seven-year-old Owen, there was a schoolroom at St Columba's RC Church, recently built just round the corner from their new place. Mary and Bessie could help keep house, look after the nephews, and work in one of the local factories on Causewayside. They might have consoled themselves that the arrangement was only to tide them over until debt collectors calmed down or lost track of them. The waters would close over the crisis. They could even pay money back, take the heat off family members left behind in Galashiels and, who knows, even return there one day.

16 Newington, Edinburgh 1897–1900: The Worst of Times

On an autumn day in 1897 the family left Buckholmside and took the train to Newington, where Owen and James were already working. Only Arthur, his son Arthur George, and Augustine remained in Galashiels.

Imagine their journey. Peter would have accompanied the women and children to Newington, carrying his mother's belongings. Bessie clutched her linen bag tight to her chest. Mary could have seen The Whin squatting by the track as their train rumbled past. The hillsides were dotted with yellow whin: still in flower, always in flower. Thirty-five years earlier, Mary could walk home from here to Walkerburn. When she turned to face her children, they probably saw resignation rather than distress.

Despite his waning strength, Owen had cleaned his pick and shovel and started general labouring work again. They were to live in a two-room single-storey courtyard house down a side alley, behind a tenement block: 20 Mowat Place, 198 Causewayside, Newington. James had already moved in. It was uncannily like Owen's back-to-back lodging in Leeds, fifty years earlier. The sight of their new home must have been a shock: small and dark, with powerful smells from the courtyard, where communal waste was dumped. They were six at first (seven whenever Tom turned up): Owen, Mary, James, daughters Mary and Bessie, grandson Owen. Within weeks Arthur arrived with Arthur George, too ill to cope without respite. From 1897 to 1900 the family was crammed together inside two poky damp rooms with no outside space. Seeking corners of privacy like crabs in crevices, the young women ventured out into the light to their jobs over the road, possibly on different shifts to take turns minding their mother and nephews. Comelybank, even with its chimneys belching smoke and fog, must have seemed a light and airy heaven. They must have dreaded coming home.

Figure 22: 20 Mowat Place, 198 Causewayside – the Quinns' late-1890s home

Figure 23: Causewayside with shops, tenements up the hill

The rent was affordable as long as the Quinns held off debt collectors and everyone found work. There was a shared outside toilet and cold running water inside, for a rent of less than 3 shillings a week. Newington was lively, with building sites everywhere and a growing Irish community. It was a stop-gap measure, Owen might have told himself and his family – until their troubles blew over. He would keep himself to himself, change his name, earn some money, and, before long, things would steady. Heeding Peter's advice, he called himself James Quinn, and to officialdom his wife was once again Mary Johnstone, born in Jedburgh – suggesting good Scottish stock. The whole family were briefed, but occasionally forgot their lines when speaking to officials. Even Peter, James, and Patrick, seeking steady above-board lives, made mistakes. Family records of these years are more than usually inconsistent.

Factory work for Mary and Bessie was a stone's throw from their new home. The Middlemass Biscuit works on Causewayside made digestive biscuits, an exotic new treat which Robert Middlemass insisted he had invented – hotly disputed by McVitie, another Edinburgh biscuit maker, who claimed the recipe was his. Biscuits were all the rage, and Middlemass's other novel treats included the *Balmoral* and the *Albert* (sold in patriotic tins), followed by elaborate chocolate-coated 'melbas'. While the textile economy of Galashiels suffered from the collapse of its US export trade, Newington was booming as Edinburgh became the headquarters of changing domestic tastes. The city was the epicentre of cheap sugar in Scotland, and probably in all Great Britain. Sugar's unstoppable commercial strength was growing exponentially, unhampered by its unrepentant (and then unacknowledged) reliance on the transatlantic slave trade. In 2019, an exhibition at the Glasgow Botanical Gardens entitled 'It Wisnae Us' powerfully exposed the city's long denial of complicity. Processed and sugar-based food industries flourished, with damaging effects on working-class Victorian diets. Middlemass, McVitie's, and Crawford's dominated manufacture, adapting and elaborating the plain old ship's biscuit into luxuries for all. The tradition endures: Burton's Biscuits still makes Jammie Dodgers and Wagon Wheels in Edinburgh. The true human cost of simple, cheap luxuries was kept out of sight.

Figure 24: Middlemass biscuit factory, Causewayside/ Salisbury Place, 1890s

Biscuits were followed by sweets. Local entrepreneurs fast turned their back-of-shop kitchens into factories to mass-produce confectionery to meet an escalating, insatiable popular passion for sugar, refined in Greenock, Scotland's 'sugaropolis' and shipped across to Edinburgh. Starting in Leith, John Millar then opened a second shop at 176 Causewayside. Iconic Scottish products included pan drops, bright-green soor plooms, chocolate éclairs, and a range of brightly coloured boiled sweets. W & M Duncan, famous for Walnut Whips, started making cakes in the 1860s, opening a sweet factory in the 1880s. The escalating confectionery industry offered employment primarily for women, who were entering the workforce in rapidly growing numbers, in manual and clerical work. For Mary, making biscuits in the baking heat would be as tough a shift as birling at the woollen mill; for Bessie, perhaps easier than weaving on the power-looms. For Owen, James, and Tom, there was building work close by, for example bricklaying on the new extension to the Middlemass factory on the corner of Causewayside and Salisbury Place.

Arthur worked on at the woollen mill in Galashiels. At first, six-year-old Arthur George stayed with him at 116 Halliburton Place, missing Bessie and cousin Owen and probably minded by lay teachers at the Catholic school. He'd have trailed behind other children, but at least he was safe. More often, Arthur was too weak to work, forced to apply for help from the Parish. Father and son had spells in the Poorhouse infirmary between November 1897 and January 1898, lodged in separate quarters. The juggling became unsustainable. Maggie Tocher was in domestic service and couldn't help. In January 1898, Arthur took his son to the family in Newington. There were three women there to rescue them.

Figure 25: Galashiels Poorhouse, Kirkbrae (foreground), the Eildon Hills beyond

Arthur visited Causewayside, bringing money and basic necessities to help the cash-strapped household look after his son. Owen had as much labouring as his ageing body could stand. Mary (sister) and Bessie might have hoped Arthur George could attend school with Owen, but he would never make much headway with reading or arithmetic. Between Mary and her daughters' shifts, some sort of solution was probably found with lay religious women at St Columba's church. Whatever arrangement they made was short-lived.

On a March weekend in 1898, Arthur fell acutely ill at Causewayside. Probably all Mary could do was administer affordable cures for TB used in Leitrim, among which were whiskey, lamb's blood, inhaling coal gas, patent medicine – and mullein, but wild flowers would be hard to find in Newington. Tuberculosis had held Arthur in its grip for years. He'd stayed well enough to work, managing occasional bouts of coughing, spitting blood, nausea, and pain in his lungs. He'd have been drained, too, by anxiety about his son. On 25th March he went to bed, no doubt with his son squeezed between him and his brother James. There was no other space. At 5.30 the following morning, Arthur died. He was 30. The two would have found him dead, if his last hours hadn't kept them all awake.

Perhaps Arthur had never recovered from the loss of Jane Tocher, but 'phthisis' was the official cause of death. It had turned his lungs to mush. James, who signed his brother's death certificate, arranged his funeral two days later at Mount Vernon Catholic cemetery at Liberton, paying the small fee for Arthur to be buried in a common grave. His memorial is the location of his burial site: Number 417 in the 'L' section. I've paced the grassy patch beneath which Arthur's bones lie, with many others for company and a sweeping view north across the city. The common graves are wedged between the inscribed gravestones and ornate masonry of successions of immigrant Catholics: Irish, Italian, Polish, and Ukrainian people with the means to commemorate a person with a name, carved angels, and the bones of a recognisable life story.

Mary was no stranger to death, but this was the first time she'd lost and buried her own child. She'd given birth to Arthur in Nungate, a place of shared connections and memories for her and Owen. Peter Lyons died beside her and Bridget that same July week in 1868, until now the only one lost to their family since Ireland, apart from her missing son Owen. Arthur's birth had brought hope in the midst of mourning. Now he'd died in a dank corner of a soulless city. Mary would not have ignored years of symptoms and knew that the TB that took him was not the last wave of a destructive force which bore down on her spirit. The disease was lodged among the Quinn siblings and it was starting to wreak havoc. Phthisis, tuberculosis, more precisely Pulmonary Tuberculosis, was the everyday killer-at-large in the late nineteenth and early twentieth centuries, and it was most prolific in the poorest working-class communities. The disease ate into the structure of the lungs, attacking millions who lived much as the Quinns did.

Over the 19th century 'phthisis' became better known as 'consumption', especially in popular, quasi-medical, and cultural discourses, acquiring a romantic, even fashionable, aura. The term accentuated an alluringly frail and vulnerable femininity, extending to fragile, sensitive men, poets in particular. The most hideous symptoms were edited out, cutting to delicate coughs, spotting a lace handkerchief, to indicate impending early death and the romantic allure of elegaic helplessness. The reality of the painful, long-drawn-out condition belies the remembered deaths of famous 'consumption' victims, among them Elizabeth Barrett Browning, all three Brontë sisters and their brother Branwell, and the poets John Keats and Robbie Burns. Delicate, nobly self-sacrificing romantic heroines like Dumas' *La Dame aux Camélias* added to the feminisation of the illness, cleansed of ugliness and pain. Wealthy inmates of the sanatoria that dotted healthy European mountain and seaside areas from the late 19th century were offered fresh air as a cure – like Thomas Mann's Hans Castorp in *The Magic Mountain* – or sun and sea breezes on the Côte d'Azur. It was usually a stay of execution.

'Consumption' was the euphemistic cultural trope which veiled the inescapable truth that, although TB numbered the rich and famous among its victims, those worst affected by far were millions who lived with poverty in working-class communities, sleeping cheek by jowl in cold, damp conditions, several to a bed. Workers in textile mills lived in peril, breathing in micro-fibres for long hours every day. Workers in coalmining, steel mills, heavy manufacturing, and paint works were other stricken groups, inhaling clouds of fumes, dust, and metal filings which flew about enclosed factory floors. Ill health reduced stable families to penury as the number of wage earners dropped and their nutrition and living conditions deteriorated. There was no unemployment or sickness benefit and no free health service. Anxiety and fear must have been the chronic condition of poor communities. The Quinns slept together in shared beds for two decades. Parents and baby in one bed; boys together in another, and girls in a third, allowing the bacillus to ride out on the breath of one and alight only to infect another. They were oblivious to their fate.

The excavation of bodies from Neolithic burial sites has made clear that the spread of tuberculosis is usually linked to urbanisation.

Emigrants like the Quinns left Ireland after the collapse of seasonal patterns of outdoor work, becoming part of an accelerating migration to Scotland at the height of its industrial development, unaware of the lethal hazards of town life.

No-one knew how tuberculosis spread until 1882, when Robert Koch, a German bacteriologist, discovered that the cause was a bacillus: the 'tubercle'. With the help of Louis Pasteur's research, Koch showed that it wasn't a patient's internal weakness which caused TB: it was contagion. Spitting and breathing over others spread the disease. Whatever the medical name and its causes, the most common symptoms of pulmonary tuberculosis were coughing, which produced sputum, low-grade fever, night-sweats, weight loss, nausea, wasting even when the appetite is healthy, difficult or laboured breathing, and bleeding: spitting and coughing up blood, from traces on a handkerchief to spurting haemorrhages which laid sufferers out cold. The wracking cough that victims experience is exhausting, causing soreness in and around the rib-cage. Infected pleura around the lungs are painful, with 'haemoptysis', the coughing up of haemorrhaged blood, sometimes by the cupful. The lungs bleed because gradually their granulomas break down, and infected pus develops in growing cavities which fill with dead tissue, fostering further infection of the lungs and penetrating blood vessels and airways. The lungs, it is said, become like cottage cheese. Unless the patient has a very strong immune system, the disease progresses and the chances of recovery fade or vanish.

When he was uncovering the causes of TB in the 1880s, Koch estimated that one in every seven people was dying of it. Once his radical discovery was made, TB soon became a public-health issue. At times of depression, and when low wages, unemployment, poor working conditions, and closely confined working and living spaces fostered the disease, the plight of the urban poor became a public emergency. The period from the 1870s to the 1890s was such a time. The impact of TB among working-class communities was stronger because the disease intermingled with other conditions such as bronchitis, pneumonia, intestinal diseases, measles, and influenza. Each disease weakened TB sufferers. Treatments are nearly as old as the disease itself. But in 1887, the first British public dispensary for TB patients in crisis opened in Edinburgh in the midst of the tenement slums of the old town. Cough medicine with or without opiates was given out, and the worst cases were referred to charitable hospitals. Public education followed, especially about the dangers of the (then acceptable) practice of spitting in public, to try and prevent TB patients freely spreading the disease around families and fellow workers. Dried dollops of spittle sent bacteria floating through the air and landing on surfaces, so it was thought. Scalded and sawdust-lined bowls were recommended. Paper cups, tissues, reclining chairs, and revolving summerhouses all had their origins in treating TB.

A new idea for curing, or at least caring for, TB sufferers took off in the 1900s: the healing properties of nature. The first purpose-built sanatorium for children was built in 1907 at Stannington in Northumberland, funded by the Poor Children's Holiday Association and the local Poor Law Guardians. Another was opened at Threlkeld in the Lake District. The first sanatorium in Scotland was created at Banchory on the river Dee, partly because of its dry climate and the supposed healing vapours of surrounding pine trees. The curative properties of life in the open air for the sick reflected a mounting British preoccupation with the benefits of fresh air, especially for city dwellers and the poor: holidays, hiking, rest, and respite from crowded living conditions. This zeal for healthier living would move centre-stage in Bessie's life in the coming years.

A spell in a TB sanatorium became an organic element of the growing culture and belief in natural cures during the late 19th and early 20th centuries. Rest in the depths of the countryside offered respite from the inevitable grim progress towards early death. For those who were destitute as well as sick, Poorhouse dormitories were the precursors of sanatoria. Well into the 20th century, Parochial Boards in Scotland, and English Poor Law Guardians, were in no hurry to isolate TB sufferers from other inmates. Eventually, separate sanatoria were attached to Poorhouses. Examples are Craiglockhart in Edinburgh and Dumbarton Combination Poorhouse, each of which took in a Quinn brother.[56]

Two Quinn siblings are unaccounted for in the family's move to Edinburgh. Augustine was only 13 in 1897. He'd left school and lodged with Arthur at Halliburton Place, close to where he would live out his life, breaking stones on building sites around Roxburghshire. As the family drama unfolded, Bessie's 16-year-old younger brother Tom had already left home, wandering, rootless, seemingly unsure of what to do or where to be. He was freewheeling between Edinburgh, Glasgow, and Galashiels, from one family berth to another. There was hardly room at his parents' new place to beg a bed, meal, or maternal comfort. So he was reliant on the goodwill of his brothers. Tom was drinking heavily, Poor Law reports suggest, scarcely remembering where he spent the previous night. If he was like others of his age and social class, he was also smoking: cigarettes were catching on fast, soon viewed as essential rather than a luxury, thanks to the mechanisation of production and mass marketing. Cigarettes were handed out free to soldiers in the first world war, a comfort shared among comrades – with devastating long-term results for those who survived the trenches.

Tom dreamed of wandering beyond the streets of Scotland's cities, across the world, and thought that the military was his best road to adventure. He later tried to make that happen; but for now he drifted, ricocheting between short-term contracts and unemployment. Encouraged by the brothers who'd finished their bricklaying apprenticeships, he managed to get a contract as an apprentice bricklayer, but he was still restless for adventure, and there's no evidence that he finished it. James was best placed to take care of him. Respected for his skill and speed on Edinburgh's building sites, if he sometimes brought his brother along, no-one was going to quibble, despite Tom's poor work-rate. Piece-work carried benefits for dependable grafters like James.

After three years together at 20 Mowat Place, the Quinn family fell apart. In September 1900, Bessie and her mother went to live with Peter in the two rooms he shared with Alex in Clydebank. Bessie would take care of their mother and the housework. He and Alex would bring in wages. Separation was a drastic solution, but it would keep the family independent. The alternative, Peter must have reasoned, was to seek help from the Edinburgh Poor Board and risk their confinement in the Poorhouse, the shame of which the family had always managed to avoid – apart from Arthur, in his final months. Peter was too young to experience his parents' applications for assistance in Galashiels two decades earlier, but would since have witnessed the humiliation of Irish families in Glasgow. Now, his sons may have warned their ailing father to lie low in Edinburgh and keep accounts of himself consistent: the welfare of young Owen and Arthur George – all their independent futures – was at stake. Arthur's death had pushed them closer to ruin. But what tipped them into family breakdown?

17 Clydebank and Newington 1900–1903: Under the Singer's Clock

When Bessie took her mother from Edinburgh to Clydebank in September 1900, she left the small boys with her father, sister Mary, and brother James. What had happened? The Quinns' troubles had stalked them down the hill from Halliburton Place, blighted their last two Galashiels years on Low Buckholmside, which ended in unemployment, and pursued them to Edinburgh's south side in 1897, where they started a new life together, tough as it was, only to be stricken by Arthur's death. The latest crisis was profound. Mary had separated from Owen, at least for now. Was her move to Clydebank a release from unbearable stress, signalling the breakdown of their relationship? Either they had lost the art of juggling and making do, and with it the ability to get along together, keep the family afloat, and grow old together; or their break-up was the unwanted end of nearly forty years together, a surrender of Mary's independence, bending to the will of her children, a misfortune orchestrated by Peter, James, and Bessie. Perhaps Bessie had threatened to go to Clydebank, and taking her mother was the price for leaving the wretchedness of Mowat Place. For Owen and Mary, the music was over, and the reasons are lost in silence. Little sense of hope for either of them is apparent in the separation. But their parting was one way to deal with Owen's failing health, their slum conditions, and the need for Mary to lay down the unmanageable demands and anxieties of child-rearing in old age. The responsibility for all that now fell on Bessie's sister Mary.

Peter and Alex lived at 1 Victoria Street, a tenement block beside the Forth and Clyde Canal, along the north bank of the Clyde. After the crush at Mowat Place, it must have seemed spacious to Mary and Bessie, with just four inhabitants, except on the nights when Tom appeared. There was a view across the canal. And at last Bessie was reunited with Alex: compensation for looking after her mother. Factory work behind her, housekeeping was now Bessie's full-time job: mother and daughter roles were now fully reversed. For another year, sister Mary would bear the Edinburgh household alongside factory work, and visit them when she could.

Figure 26: Forth and Clyde Canal, Clydebank towards Kilbowie Road, Victoria Street tenement third left

Clydebank was in the parish of Old Kilpatrick, a few miles down the web of railway lines that run westwards from Glasgow to the towns along the Clyde and on to Dumbarton, the Vale of Leven, Alexandria, and Loch Lomond. The Victoria Street tenement was pulled down in the 1980s during a decades-long sweep of demolitions across Britain, replacing solid Victorian buildings with poorly built housing estates. The Clydebank tenements were replaced by an indoor shopping centre, which by the flimsy feel of it is unlikely to last a fraction as long as the Victorian buildings that it replaced. It is light and warm, though, and a café offers a good breakfast and *barista*-made cappuccino. But the precinct feels down-at-heel, its energies deflated, as if mean-minded modern responses to poverty offer no more hope than the relentless struggle to survive in the late 19th century, when families worked long shifts to live hand-to-mouth, like the Quinns. Jobs, livelihoods, and welfare benefits now are different, but still precarious, failing to reduce the hardship, inequality, and substance abuse so glaringly visible in post-industrial British cities. At nine o'clock on a weekday morning, homeless people are asleep in shop doorways: it's warmer in the mall. Some emerge from sleeping bags, and others wander around among early shoppers, lighting up, dealing drugs, and emptying bottles. Betting shops, pawnbrokers, and pound shops promise short-term survival. Out again among the rush-hour buses, the huge Victorian Co-operative store and a string of High Street shops connect two eras, a hundred years apart, and a 19th-century Salvation Army centre nestles among them, still energetically helping out.

Bessie and her mother tried to settle in their corner of Peter's rooms and get used to a dauntingly alien environment: the rain-lashed, red-sandstone townscape of Clydebank, the rows of hulking tenement blocks, building sites, factories and shipyards, cranes, department stores, throngs of people, and hard-drinking navvies on street corners. Perhaps Mary's solace was to look across the canal to the vivid green of the south bank of the Clyde, and let her imagination fly to familiar places: the chimneys, terraces, and shops by Gala Water and the rolling countryside beyond.

Alex and Peter were Singer-trained, qualified French Polishers and Varnishers. Working life at the Singer factory suited Peter down to the ground, but American-style, corporatist, carrot-and-stick conveyor-belt capitalism seems not to have worked for Alex. The Singer Sewing Machine Company had arrived in Scotland in 1867, expanding from their US headquarters in New Jersey to meet the soaring international demand for industrial and domestic sewing machines. Glasgow port was well positioned to service the export market. Singer first opened a small factory in John Street, Glasgow, then moved to a larger one in Bridgton, east of the city centre. Demand grew dramatically, and by 1882 the company had bought 46 acres of farmland at Kilbowie on the north bank of the Clyde and built a gigantic factory. The Singer name, emblazoned across a 200-foot-high clock tower, could be seen for miles, a boast to the world and a sharp reminder to workers. Kilbowie railway station was moved along to the Singer factory gates on a specially extended line – renamed 'Singer Station'. The factory is long gone, but Singer Station is still there. Nearly three miles of railway lines threaded their way through the length of the factory site, bringing raw materials and supplies, and shipping out finished machines. The new station brought in thousands of extra labourers from the Gorbals and Govan and across Glasgow. This was an intimidating display of the power of Clydeside's industrial giants.

Figure 27: Singer's four-faced, 200-foot factory clock

By 1884 Singer employed 5,000 workers at Kilbowie, producing 8,000 sewing machines a week. Within six years the company had bagged 80 per cent of the world's sales, Kilbowie was the biggest sewing-machine factory on earth, and Irish workers made up the majority of the employees. For Singer, the lower the labour costs, the higher the profits, and they could attract large numbers of Irish

Catholic factory-floor workers at lower rates than Scottish Protestants. Three thousand of their 12,000 employees in 1911 were women, mainly unmarried.

Peter and Alex finished their apprenticeships as French Polishers and Varnishers in Department 21: the Wood Department was one of 41, plus an on-site foundry, railways system, and timber workshop. Wood and iron were central to production. The sewing machines were ornate, solid pieces: machines doubling as pieces of furniture, housed in cabinets made of pine and gumwood with walnut and other fine wood veneers. Or placed on elaborate wrought-iron stands with foot pedals. It is claimed that Singer's invented plywood, though they didn't call it that. Department 21 was said to be one of the cleanest in the whole factory, although the fumes from glue and varnish swirled round the workshop. Singer workers also remembered how bad the wood workers smelled: oils and lubricants seeped into their skin. Worse still, people who worked with the cast iron which formed the ornate legs and bases were affected by the 'haze of fine cast-iron particles' which floated in the atmosphere, penetrated the skin, and entered the lungs of workers who emerged from a shift as blackened as coal miners. The environment was as lethal as the Galashiels textile mills.[57]

As part of its modern methods, health and safety was top of the Singer list of priorities. Notices were posted everywhere, and warnings littered the works newsletters. The message was clear: the workers, not the employers, were held responsible for their own wellbeing, taking every possible precaution to avoid days off due to accidents. More than three days off sick meant their wages were cut and their jobs at risk. Productivity before people was the Singer way.

Alex set out for Glasgow with Peter, the sensible brother who would have slept beside him and protected him against school and street bullies. But Bessie and Alex grew up together close in age, and in their shared life they could have formed the strong roots that later fed her determination to be independent. In the history of working-class self-improvement, there was almost always a significant companion who nurtured a person's desire for change. It would not have been Bessie's parents or eldest brothers. The two were at school together in a town with cultural networks endowed by benefactors, with libraries, a Mechanics' Institute, and social and church associations intended for people like them. It is my hunch that Alex and Bessie were early companions in curiosity.

For his part, Peter would have known that his brother might not survive at the woollen mill, and that the family's future in Galashiels was in doubt. Woodwork and varnishing skills could also attract after-hours jobs. But soon after qualifying, Alex left Singer's and went to work as a shipyard labourer. Why would he make the change, when he had a secure job? Health fears, as well as hostile company culture, are likely causes. Alex's lungs were highly susceptible to the fumes from the varnishes and polishes used for finishes on sewing machines, as well as the iron filings and wood shavings which choked the air. He escaped. Perhaps the controlling corporate life stifled him, just as the security it offered comforted Peter's cautious nature. Either Alex was disaffected or he was pushed because he lost too many days to ill health. That was Singer's way. Maybe Peter, knuckling down to all the Singer benefits, was relieved when his brother left.

Nearby shipyards were John Brown's at Clydebank and William Beardmore's at Dalmuir. In 1900, Beardmore bought a large tract of land in Dalmuir and established an extensive, modern Naval Construction Yard, building battleships for the Royal Navy. Britain was fiercely competing with imperial Germany to remain the world's dominant naval power, and the drive for more warships was good business. By 1914, naval rivalry between the two nations would boil over, a prime cause of the outbreak of the First World War. At Beardmore's, Alex could have worked on their first battleship, the Agamemnon, which was launched in 1906. There were 13,000 workers at the peak of Beardmore's success.

Alex could have been a waged worker for either shipyard, but was probably hired by the day, by both. It's possible that he still worked with wood, practising French polishing and varnishing inside ocean-going steamships, including passenger liners, where miles of wooden fittings and furnishings lined the interior walls. French polishing was used on the ships to create a high gloss on mahogany, the Victorians' favourite wood for domestic as well as public settings. Alternatively, he reverted to outdoor building work, like most of the Quinn men. However tough and precarious, it was healthier for the lungs. And it was closer to a rural way of life, which still drew people like the Quinns and Lyonses, who for generations had lived and worked on the land. Owen and Mary had gravitated slowly towards town life, but Galashiels was small, and beyond the smoke and clanking din of the mills were fields, hills, and streams. As adults, most of their children chose outdoor labouring over factory work. And they witnessed the dismal effects of their parents' moves to big cities late in life.

For the rest of Alex's short life, he was a shipyard worker, either lifting, heaving, hammering, joining, and riveting; or polishing and varnishing wood installations. He struck lucky. Catholics didn't find it easy to get work at the shipyards. Much employment was controlled by Protestants, including Irish Orangemen, and recruitment practices were strongly biased, especially for skilled craftsmen or labourers seeking promotion. Alex had specialist skills which were in short supply. He was knowledgeable and hard working, or he would not have survived the Singer years. He can't have been blacklisted from the shipyard as a troublemaker, as some workers were when Singer's tipped off shipyard bosses about unionised workers whom they'd fired. Perhaps fellow ex-Singer workers spoke up for him. Extrapolating from the little on record, I believe it suited Alex to work in an environment where workers were organising, talking justice and politics on Clydeside, and ready to fight employers for better pay and working conditions. It's possible he associated with workers planning to found the British Advocates of Industrial Unionism (BAIU), which became the Industrial Workers of Great Britain (IWGB). They included Tom Bell, who went on to work, and agitate, at Singer's, one of the key targets of the IWGB, along with the Argyll Motor Works at Alexandria and the Albion Motor Works in nearby Scotstoun. Alex might have joined the Socialist Labour Party, officially formed in 1903, of which James Connolly was an instigator and leader. Alex, I believe, could have been in his element. All too briefly.

Singer, Brown, and Beardmore dominated employment along the Clyde, along with whisky distillers Yoker and a few smaller distilleries, legal and illegal. Singer, in particular, grew at a dizzying pace, in the forefront of the innovative manufacturing methods which became known as Taylorism. Mass production Singer-style was characterised by hard-nosed management techniques imported from the USA, including piecework, the implementation of time-and-motion studies, and relentless efficiency drives, pushing productivity to the limit and summarily discarding underperforming workers and anyone deemed surplus to requirements. Singer's refused to recognise any union, except for the long-established guild unions, tolerated for highly skilled crafts and trades. Unions for general workers were a working-class movement, a threat to company discipline, and banned. Divide and rule techniques were in Singer's corporate genes.

One later episode in Singer's history which involved Peter Quinn encapsulates the company's culture: the Singer Strike of 1911. It has been written about and analysed, so only Peter's position in the industrial dispute is relevant to this story. He had been working at Singer for well over a decade when the factory's management provoked a strike, which broke out in Department 21, the wood department where he worked. To cut costs, three 'defect repairers' were withdrawn at no notice from a team of 15 women working as cabinet polishers. Their workload was distributed among the remaining 12 women, with a cut in pay for doing more work faster. The 'speeding up' now demanded of them was impossible to achieve. They were doomed to fail. And the women stood to lose around 2 shillings (10p) from their weekly wage packets. They walked out – and were joined immediately by 380 of their 400 colleagues in Department 21.

Was Peter among the 380? He wasn't yet close to promotion to foreman, so as yet had little status to lose, and (from what I know of his character) he was honest, generous, and fair-minded. The women in the cabinet-polishing department, including those who lost their jobs, were his close colleagues. His wife Susan and Alex had both worked for Singer. But by 1911, the loss of wages and the risk to his job would have been hard for Peter's family, with Susan at home full-time with their two small children, John and James. Putting food on the table was the overwhelming priority for Irish workers, still living in absolute hardship and socially shunned. Undercutting wages was the price of survival.

Whichever side Peter chose, it must have been a tough decision. He knew the stakes were high. He must have been revisited by family conflicts. It seems likely that Peter was a supporter of the strike, but equally likely he was not a strike leader and would have known that the company was out to penalise them. The day after the walk-out, 10,000 of Singer's 11,500 employees were on strike, joined on 23rd March by 300 artisans and the following day by 5–600 craftsmen. Like Peter, some were better-paid members of craft unions, with a lot to lose. I doubt Peter wanted to be among the small minority of strike breakers, or wanted to let down his team of women.

The strike was remarkable for its unity, especially given that the majority were Irish workers, who were routinely subject to employers' prejudice and exploitation, and to trade unions' attacks for undercutting wages. Much the same was true for women workers. But this was a community event, including local brass bands and parades. Nearly every family had someone in the strike. It lasted three weeks, until the leaders and supporters from the IWGB and the Socialist Labour Party were outmanoeuvred by Singer's divisive tactics. An unconditional return to work was followed by ruthless victimisation, sackings, and blocking pacts with local employers, who issued 'No Singer Members Need Apply' notices. People were forced to leave the west of Scotland. It amounted to social cleansing, a dispersal of all those deemed troublemakers. Singer had positioned itself on the front line against socialism, and not far behind came militant women, whose suffrage actions were gathering pace in 1911.[58]

There must have been good reason why Peter and so many like him stayed with Singer, in his case for nearly 50 years. After the strike, the company changed tack. Still refusing to recognise unions, they reworked their management techniques, replacing naked threats with a python-grip paternalism which provided an all-inclusive parallel universe away from the local streets, community life, and the religious beliefs of its workers. They were well placed. For decades, there was hardly a family in Clydebank and the surrounding area which did not have at least one family member working at Singer's. The system known as 'Singerisation' delivered real rewards in a Faustian pact which offered a world within a world, driven by institutionalised threat. Welfare measures tethered the workforce and their families to the company, including the pension scheme promised before the strike, and savings and insurance schemes which aped the Friendly Societies – but without the mutual ownership of co-operative or church societies. They offered bursaries for employees' children to attend school longer, and even university grants. Activities took place in top-notch facilities:

sports halls, playing fields, a theatre, galleries. There was football (international games were played with Singer's European factories); hockey, cricket, golf; a horticultural society with an annual display which filled their vast sports hall; photography, pipe bands, an orchestra; pageants, including an annual Gala; outings for current employees; boys' and girls' clubs. The 'veterans' club' organised steam-boat outings 'doon the watter', and along the Ayrshire coast in pleasure craft like the new 'Prince Edward'. Activities like these were otherwise unaffordable for most people.

Company magazines emphasised hard work, with articles, homilies, jokey stories and rhymes warning against carelessness, slackness, and sick leave. One cartoon depicts a young woman tottering at the top of a wobbly ladder: 'You may be a star worker, but don't be a falling star'. Lurid accounts depict careless women machinists who forgot their hairnets and suffered the painful consequences. Naming and shaming was part of the culture. The 'Activities' magazine, while celebrating the Gala Queen and footballing victories, also listed 'Lost Time Accidents', lauding those Departments that avoided absences. More than three days' leave after an accident meant docked pay or the sack. Yet Singer employed married women, creating crèches with dormitories for night-shift workers' children. The Singer life was Peter's family's life.

Controversy dogged Singer's for years. In 1914, there was trenchant opposition to their decision to make munitions for the war effort. Some workers left to work for other Clydeside companies not involved in arms, including Yarrow's, who pioneered the making of artificial limbs, which one young Quinn – Patrick's son Jimmy – would need after he lost his leg on the Somme. Perhaps strong local feeling penetrated the Singer company's carapace and led them to change their minds. Now they are famous for forging a million horseshoes for the First World War, during which thousands of their employees were killed or wounded. But in 1926, the year of the General Strike in Britain, the Singer Company was using tactics which echoed the quashing of the 1911 strike. This was Peter Quinn's working world until he died a 'veteran' in 1959.

18 Causewayside, Newington 1900–1901: Owen Quinn's Last Years

By Autumn 1900, when Mary left him, Owen was in his late sixties. He was still breaking stones, but bronchitis, the old enemy, was back. Owen's ailments went undiagnosed. He couldn't afford a doctor, and, as he knew from his brushes with the Melrose Parish 25 years earlier, official help came with harsh conditions. Back then, the Inspector had reported: 'very poorly with bronchitis, needs nourishing food'. Easily said. After Mary left with Bessie, his daughter Mary and James cared for him and the two little boys as best they could, juggling chores with jobs. The children could wander free round the neighbourhood, past the biscuit factory, rummaging on building sites, climbing the Mowat Place rubbish heap, or running to the Meadows to play football. Perhaps Aunt Mary would slip young Owen a few pennies for Pan Drops or Soor Plooms, or bring them broken biscuits from Middlemass. Young Owen was in charge of Arthur George. At 12, Owen was quick and adaptable, as his later years show: reading, writing, and surviving playground squalls. Arthur George was bewildered by the alphabet, and, ignored or taunted by other children, sat mostly, solid and solitary. He would have been disoriented by changes, especially the disappearance of Bessie, who'd been beside him longest. His father was a fainter memory.

At 70, Owen was still working enough days to pay the rent and buy coal. James earned enough from bricklaying to buy food and save for his hoped-for future. He could still walk the boys to the Meadows, but James would've noticed that his father was no longer strong enough for hard physical work: exhausted by a permanent cough, he sometimes struggled for breath. A good worker, he still seemed well enough to be taken on: weather-beaten, tough, and stringy as an old cabbage stalk – and still with a full head of wavy grey hair? But he'd become melancholy, uncharacteristically quiet. There's no sign that his other children came to visit. Although the Newington and Clydebank families remained in contact, there is no plan on record to reunite Owen with Mary. Irish friends and colleagues would be unlikely to betray their whereabouts to unwelcome enquirers. Deeper trouble threatened to engulf them.

In 1901, when Spring arrived, Owen had withstood a freezing winter of north-easterly winds, probably with Patrick and James to keep an eye out for him, perhaps on the new hotel site at Princes Street station, and perhaps still keeping a wistful eye out for his son Owen, last seen 12 years earlier. Off the record, I assume that the company of Patrick and workmates kept him going. A few whiskeys offered warmth and comfort, and Patrick was no doubt a drinking companion. Owen surely missed Mary, especially when he tried to sleep without the herbal potions she'd brewed to banish fevers, chest pain, wheezing, and coughs: the mullein she'd pulled from hedgerows and hillsides and swore by. Owen was weakening by the day, dependent on his daughter Mary. His wife didn't come. Owen's sober self knew she wouldn't. He'd have thought of Bessie and wondered if she'd remember his hopes for her. He must have been overcome by regret at leaving Galashiels worse off than they started. It was second only to Leitrim in his soul.

Owen Quinn was hiding behind his flimsy new identity: 'James Quinn', married to Mary, whose maiden name was 'Johnstone', born in Jedburgh. This curiously half-hearted concoction of names which the family had conjured up for officialdom must have been intended to protect them from the law, the landlord, and any traders he owed money to. He could parrot the new names, but he wasn't going to learn his letters now. And in the face of official documents to sign, even his well-versed children sometimes forgot they were supposed to be 'Johnstone' on their mother's 'Scottish' side.

Spring turned to summer. On 5th June 1901 Owen struggled through the night. Perhaps he tried to leave the house, picking his way towards the door, before he crumpled. James, Mary, and Owen would have hauled him on to the bed, still a heavy, muscular man. His breathing crunched like boots on gravel. James must have telegraphed Peter in Clydebank, because he came quickly across: compassionate, but unpaid, leave of absence? Owen died at 4.30 in the afternoon. Two days later, Peter signed his father's death certificate: more at home with paperwork than his brothers, with no qualms about falsifying his mother's maiden name, and spelling it right. The name of Owen's dead father in Ireland, Peter's grandfather Arthur, slipped his mind. Instead, he wrote Owen Quinn. Surely just a slip: worn memories and old stories transmogrify over generations. The cause of Owen's death, the official doctor wrote, noting his sons' account of symptoms, was 'apparently, chronic bronchitis'. His age – 70 – tallies with other records. Some repeated narratives stuck. James arranged the funeral at Mount Vernon cemetery, where Owen was buried a few yards from Arthur on the patch allocated to common, paupers', graves. Owen's Plot is L314: some sort of memorial for the people gathered round his anonymous grave. Patrick was doubtless there with his wife Ellen and two children, Jimmy and Ellen May; James, Mary, Peter, Augustine, young Owen, Arthur George, and perhaps Bessie walked in procession up the hill to section L. It is doubtful they located Tom; Alex was working; and someone had to look after Mary. But neighbours and workmates would doubtless have turned out to pay their respects to one of their own – and embellish their stories about him over a few drinks.

James paid off the rent on 20 Mowat Place, and within a few days they'd given away their bits and pieces and all left Newington: James straight to Galashiels with Augustine and the prospect of a simpler, freer life with his beloved, Mary Rehill. There was work on the new railway near Melrose. Peter, his sister Mary, and the boys, bundles on backs, walked to Newington station. Peter was taking them to join the others at Clydebank.

Imagine Peter, putting one foot slowly in front of the other, struggling to contain panic. How was he going to cope, make bed-space, find schools for the young ones and a job for his sister Mary, and still hold his head above water at Singer's? He couldn't remember when he hadn't felt responsible for everyone, but this situation was the most daunting yet. He clung on to the fading dream of having his own family, his front door quietly closed behind the clamorous voices which threatened to break his ordered life apart. While Peter put his hopes on hold, Singer's was his refuge from chaos, emotional conflict, and a mountain of responsibility. It would have taken an angel not to envy Patrick, walking jauntily away from Mount Vernon with his wife, back to Jamaica Street in Edinburgh's New Town, living on his own terms, putting on the charm, and downing a few more drinks. He didn't put himself out much for family. Ellen did that work, not least taking in Tom when he turned up in New Town. Not long after Owen died, Patrick joined James and Augustine on a contract to build a hospital extension in Melrose, which the two had tipped him off about, perhaps at the funeral. Patrick suggested that Tom could join them, and he did – a good-enough bricklayer when he paid attention.

19 Clydebank
1901–2: The Tenement by the Canal

The reunited family was to live at 1 Victoria Street, Clydebank, a tenement block on a 'close': a pathway along the canal. There were two outside stairways and a shared entry. Some tenants had two rooms, others just a 'single end'. Lavatories were at the bottom of the stairways, as were the laundry and water taps, and waste heaps – all shared with others on the same entry.

On the Edinburgh to Glasgow train, Peter took refuge in practical matters: despite the thick fog clouding his head, he began to hatch plans which could work for all seven of them: how much money they needed to survive, how long they could all cram together. He hoped his sister Mary would become a domestic servant, fed and housed elsewhere. He and Alex would support the others between them. Owen would soon be 13, starting an apprenticeship at Singer's. There was a schoolroom at the Catholic chapel in Clydebank run by nuns and lay helpers, where Arthur George could attend without having to meet any expectations. Next to it was a building site, where a grand red sandstone church, Our Holy Redeemer, would open in 1903: the first RC church in Clydebank. It was designed by Peter Paul Pugin and funded entirely by the growing Catholic community working in the dockyards and factories, determined to express their own identity in the city. A few years later, Peter would finally get married there.

Once Arthur reached 13, there was no suitable institution for him, and it was unlikely he'd ever find work to pay for his keep. Bessie could not both earn and look after the growing boy, a responsibility that was now beyond her mother. She was housekeeper-cum-teacher. As ever, she would shop, cook, wash, iron, and coax Arthur George into learning a few more words while she kept him company. When Tom appeared, he'd be comforted by his mother, then sent on to stay with James, or Patrick and generous-hearted Ellen. It was the least his older brothers could do.

The plan worked for one relatively calm year. The rent was paid and there was food on the table: for families like them, porridge, a daily soup, bread, potatoes, vegetables, and a Sunday stew. Peter's priority was to keep his head down at Singer's. He was at full stretch, meeting the Company's exacting standards, but holding his own and unaware of a new storm gathering force. He probably thought it was natural that his mother, at her age, was becoming absent-minded.

Mary Quinn was 57: merely middle-aged, seen through a 21st century lens. Her mental and physical condition might now be called premature ageing. But in 1900 she was an old woman, already ten years above women's average life expectancy (although 12 per cent did live to be 65; and 4 per cent even to 85). Her body was worn, her face lined and hollow-cheeked; and at least a few teeth were certainly missing. Her eating habits and hard life would have kept her thin: obesity was rare among poor people before the age of cheap sugar and manufactured food. She'd suffered the double trauma of losing two sons: one dead and one disappeared. Tom was veering off the rails: she'd be aware of that. She'd struggled to absorb further shocks: losing Galashiels and now her independence. Her family had broken up, and her husband was dead. The life-force of the girl who had overcome a childhood marked by hunger and death, who had led her siblings to Scotland to start a new life, was evaporating. She'd given birth to ten children, nurturing every one into adulthood. Then she'd reared two of her children's children. If, now, she sometimes lost her way back to Peter's rooms from the centre of a town where she knew no-one, it would be unsurprising. Mary must have felt lost. The tenement block was a massive, alien dwelling-place in a strange setting. If she felt her way down the iron stairs at night to look up at the stars, she'd be longing for what was familiar: dew on grass, her own people, her home country: probably an imagined place which fused the whin-dotted Borders with the wet fields of Sligo. If the Irish language laced its way back into conversations, and she began to sing as she once did ... if she wept in bewilderment or wondered why Owen was so late home ... it would hardly be surprising. Whatever her exact patterns of behaviour were, her family was growing anxious about her. She may not have understood that she was in Clydebank for good. That might have consoled her: until recently, she had so often moved from one home to the next, acting in her family's interests, never a helpless victim.

The arrangement became unworkable. Peter wanted to marry Susan Boyle, the young woman he might have first spotted in Department 21, at a Singer's dance, or music-hall evening – or at Sunday Mass at the chapel on Kilbowie Road. Susan came from an Irish Catholic family and she was doing well as a machinist who tested finished sewing machines as they emerged, ready for sale, from Peter's department. In character, he'd have proceeded cautiously. She was friendly, but he bided his time. He was in no position to court anyone as things stood.

Tom's appearances made a strained situation impossible. Always on the move, always engaging, he turned up, drunk or sober, wheedling a meal from Bessie, reeling off his dreams of a better life, talking, talking: fantasy and reality circling, merging, dispersing. He couldn't take the imposed disciplines of regular work for long. The open road caught his imagination, but the military even more so, offering a freer life, with tartan uniforms and exotic travel. Tom's volatile mental and physical state was perhaps one prompt for Peter to start conjuring with a change in living arrangements.

In 1898, aged 17, Thomas Quinn had been living mainly in Edinburgh. He had become an apprentice bricklayer and pitched up at 28 Wardlaw Place, where his brother Patrick sometimes took him in. Or he stayed with James, occasionally joining his father Owen and everyone else at Mowat Place. That was the current address he gave to the military authorities when, in May 1899, he had successfully applied to join the 3rd Battalion of the Royal Scots, the Regiment of Foot, and was sworn in for a period of five years. His nephew, Patrick's son Jimmy Quinn, ten years younger, would later join the Royal Scots, possibly inspired by a childhood romance with the regiment when he'd played war-games with hero-uncle Tommy. Soldiering offered a safe billet, with regular food and quarters. That appealed to Tom's canny side, but the army also fuelled fantasies of foreign wars and colonial adventures, talked about around the bars of Glasgow, where the idea of 'joining up' attracted young men with little to lose. Tensions were mounting again in South Africa, and the second Boer War broke out in October that year. There was a scramble across Britain to sign up half-way healthy young men; but recruitment drives revealed the shocking state of health of working-class boys and young men. Thomas Quinn was judged healthy enough at his attestation to be accepted for call-up. I imagine him as a scrawny, wheezy young man, but he must have been strong enough for bricklaying and he withstood the nights of rough sleeping. He clearly had a gift for talking himself up, dismissing doubts. He'd passed the medical. But Tom soon cut loose from Edinburgh, where the Quinns on Causewayside were struggling, Patrick's family was growing too big to shelter him, and James was often in Melrose. He went to seek a berth with Peter at Clydebank and comforting love from his indulgent mother.

Perhaps Tom did go to war in South Africa, but I can find no record of it. The Royal Scots 3rd Battalion joined other troops in the Boer War, carrying out raids and patrols, but if Tom was posted overseas, he was home by 1901, still bricklaying on and (more often) off, in Edinburgh, Melrose, and Govan – a Glasgow district on the south bank of the Clyde. Once a village, it was now a shipbuilding hub, a working-class area which housed the overspilling population of the Gorbals. Peter couldn't bring himself to turn Tom away to spend another night in the Common Lodging House, although Bessie, who was probably Peter's straightest-talking confidante and the one who reciprocated his kindnesses, might have advised him not to let Tom in: he'd drag them all down. Patrick, James, and Augustine had all sheltered him before, and they could do so again.

Was Bessie beginning to despair of her whole family, not only her wayward younger brother? At some point she must have hardened her heart and believed in her day-dreams of leaving Glasgow. If so, she was one of thousands, as opportunities for working-class women were broadening beyond the straight choice of factory work or domestic service. Hundreds of 19th- and 20th-century working-class auto-biographies express such dreams of change, recalling the discovery of a way to change the course of life. Acts of human agency are social processes. The help, friendship, or influence of a motivating other person is essential when the will to change meets so many obstacles. An attentive teacher, a benefactor, the out-of-the-blue appearance of a beneficent stranger, and sometimes a brother or sister ignited a longing and propelled life in a different direction. A different source of Bessie's energy – as for many young women trapped in servitude – could have been the sight of smartly dressed young women emerging from Glasgow's Charing Cross Station, laughing and talking, arm in arm as they swung down Sauchiehall Street to the heart of the city. Clydebank librarians may have encouraged her if she was the reader I imagine, and other women's stories could have forced a buried seed of rebellion into the light. At some point Bessie saw a life for herself beyond drudgery and compliance with others' needs. Cautionary factors would also be at work: what might happen to her if she didn't break out? The sight of Tom swaying at the door, cigarette in hand, always needing help; the question of care for Arthur George; and the evident truth that Peter couldn't afford to keep her much longer. Bessie was 22 in 1901. The question may have become not if, but how, to make the radical changes that she longed for?

20 Galashiels
1879–1901: Springs of Change: Bessie's Girlhood

1901, a point of profound change for Bessie, saw her precariously poised on a narrow ridge, looking out across the hard monotonous landscape of her expected future in one direction, and unknown, unfathomable territory on the other side. That year offers a moment to stop and wind the reel back to her life as a growing girl. She steps out of the shadows to hint at what led to her decision to break her ties and opt for adventure: rare action for a young woman in her circumstances.

Bessie lived her childhood in the midst of her family and other born-in-Scotland peers from the Irish Catholic community, church, and school. She was confirmed at ten years old. She attended school for seven years from 1884 to 1891, leaving when she reached her 13th birthday, probably after working half-time from the age of ten. This point of transition to adulthood was marked by full-time paid work, and the expectation of reasoning, moral responsibility, with the prospect of heaven, or hell as a consequence of transgression. Bessie, like all her contemporaries, would have confessed her sins regularly once she was confirmed. As far as work was concerned, this diminutive girl was well suited to work as a scavenger, mill-piecer, and power-loom operative, working at Comelybank until the late 1890s, when her family left for Edinburgh.

Unless, that is, Bessie's life had already turned upside down in 1894, when the toll on her mother of looking after two grandsons kept her second daughter at home. Bessie's contribution to the family's viability was not only a mill-girl's wage. She had other ways of bringing in money. Later evidence of her sewing, mending, and embroidering skills suggests she helped Mary sew for customers. If Bessie was at home full-time from 1894, day-long domestic drudgery replaced toiling at the mill. Without the company of other mill-girls, this was a more isolated life, subservient to the needs of the family's men and boys. The daily tasks piled up as her mother passed more of them to her. She'd make sure the men's moleskins were hung out by the fire in the evening and dry by morning. Like many educated children with illiterate parents, she'd have helped with the family's paperwork, especially after Peter and Alex left home. Knowledge of the uneven flows of income and spending, always threatening their way of life, would have brought anxiety and fear to a young girl.

For Bessie, working in the allotment gardens with her father at Chapel Street and Halliburton Place, or joining him on gardening jobs in town and country, was probably closest to play. She reportedly knew about gardening as an adult. Middle-class observers of working life at that time noted that it was fathers, more than mothers, who spent recreational time with their children.[59] Perhaps the quiet, attentive ways she was remembered for as a mother were learned from Owen. She would have seen his calloused hands kneading, softening, and re-stitching leather, patching up boot soles with off-cuts from the Galashiels tannery. She could help to rub mended boots with grease or blacking, spitting and breathing on the polishing cloth. I have no hard evidence that she was close to her father, or watched him at his tasks, or that she resented her mother's demands. My inkling of their daughter–father relationship has only one written indicator: Owen is the only name she ever wrote on any form, certificate, marriage banns, or press notice. But the loosening of ties with her birth family started soon after Owen died. Their affinity is a hunch which helps to make sense of her later attachments. Bessie acknowledged his existence, and practised some of his skills, habits, and, perhaps, charm. I had always thought that the extreme neatness of my methodical father (Bessie's first child) – everything sorted, tucked away in the smallest possible place – was learned at sea in wartime. Now it feels like the inheritance of small living spaces, where precious tools and trinkets were guarded, mended and protected against marauders.

By 1891, when Bessie was twelve, her eldest brothers Owen and Patrick had long ago left; the middle brothers and her sister Mary were still at home. Care for the youngest ones would have fallen to Bessie, as it fell to millions of growing working-class girls in the 19th century. She was ten when Owen arrived as a baby, and she'd have helped to make pap, fill baby bottles, feed him and change nappies. Five years later, she did the same when Arthur George arrived. Who else could have shepherded younger brothers and nephews to school, holding toddlers' hands while Tom jumped all over the street?

My mother read aloud to me, as a child, an old edition of John Ruskin's chilling, fantastical morality tale *The King of the Golden River* (1850), with drawings by Richard Doyle, the illustrator of *Punch* magazine and many Dickens' stories. The grotesque fairy-tale images were as eerie as the story, which was written for 12-year-old Effie Gray, later to be Ruskin's wife in an ill-fated marriage. It fits if this book belonged to Bessie: a copy was likely to be in Galashiels Library, because of Ruskin's connection to Scotland. She could have read it to her brothers and nephews, along with Robert Browning (there was a book of his poems in my childhood home said to be hers, but it has disappeared). She might have bought a copy years later, in the Lake District, when she was surrounded by Ruskinian influences, and read it to my father.

From all that my father remembered of Bessie as a mother, she'd have sung with her nephews and made up rhymes for them to entertain the family. She could have shown them how to make pies and suet puddings from windfalls and let them pummel spare bits of pastry into greasy-grey lumps. Her older siblings might have mocked her 'airy-fairy' ways and her passion for clean bed linen, but the family depended on her to keep them afloat. The above is retrospective conjecture, based on the character later described by children who knew her as a mother, reconstructing her apprenticeship as the young carer of her birth family's children, her allotted role before she chose a different life. It is unusual and tenuous evidence, but it helps to make meaning of her later development. When otherwise did she learn her skills as a creative, attentive parent if not during those years in Galashiels? It's not plausible that she learned everything when she arrived as an adult in a middle-class world. Neither the stereotype of cultural barrenness in poor working-class families, nor the classic hierarchy of working-class types – from 'lumpen' squalor to aspirational respectability – works for Bessie, nor for many others.

Bessie and Alex grew up in each other's pockets: they were middle children, perhaps mutually protective, barely noticed among a clamorous crowd. They'd have walked to school together, and I imagine them playing make-believe, whispering secrets, telling far-fetched night-time stories, sharing in-jokes and lines from poems and novels: 'ever the best of friends'. Like so many others, they'd borrow library books, read by candlelight, returned unread if daily tasks took too long.[60] This is an imagined sibling romance, a way of surviving adopted by millions of working people to develop their intellect beyond elementary education, a bond forged within a fissiparous tribe. Both clever, feeling different, sure that they could achieve something if they ever had a chance. When Alex left home and their shared life abruptly ended, Bessie must have felt the loss acutely. In their way of life, and her rooted place in domestic routines, home visits were unheard of; and uncertainty about when and if a reunion might ever happen would add weight to a sense of abandonment.

One interpretation of the Quinns' last Galashiels years is that week by week Bessie took charge. They all needed her, even if they barely noticed her. When they did, she'd have been justified in feeling more resentment than gratitude. She wasn't their mother. Bessie was clever: she wrote confidently. At the mill she had to pay close attention to the looms or risk terrible injury, but at home she could let her mind rip. As she scrubbed floors, scraped vegetables, washed work-clothes, bed-clothes, rags, and dusters, she elaborated another life, glimpsed at talks that she and Alex perhaps heard at the Galashiels Literary Society or gleaned from magazines and books. All fuel for daydreams: how she would assemble a bundle of clothes, creep out quietly, and set off down the main road which ran through the Borders and which she knew led to Carlisle. She'd reach England on foot, drenched by rain unless kindly strangers offered a ride. It was no more than her mother had done all those years ago, arriving at Walkerburn. Hours would pass in shaping her future, while avoiding mishaps with boiling water in the wash tub or fingers in the wringer – as far as one can tell from later photographs. In those, her guarded looks suggest a careful person. Quiet hours were best for dreaming, when her mother slept and she could plunge a needle in and out of worn garments and turn sheets sides-to-middle without mental effort.

21 Clydebank and the Dalmuir Shipyards 1902–3: Bessie and Alexander

Although Peter brought home a good wage from Singer's, his sister Mary was in and out of work, and when Alex was off sick it was a struggle to feed everyone. Bessie would have worked at home for perhaps sixteen hours till she fell into bed. Damp tenements aggravated colds and coughs, and her lungs probably suffered. She'd have been seen walking along Clydebank's streets, face down, pitted against slanting rain, south-westerly winds, and, in winter, thick yellow fog. Feverish in her makeshift bed in the corner of the living room, she'd have panicked about washing dirty clothes and cooking the next meal. On shopping trips she might have sneaked off her beaten track, walking from the big Co-Op store to the library which opened in the new Clydebank Town Hall in 1902, where she could borrow books for herself and Alex, who was too weak to go out to evening talks or meetings and often fell asleep while she read aloud. The fiction and poetry shelves in the Co-Op library would have satisfied her romantic imagination.

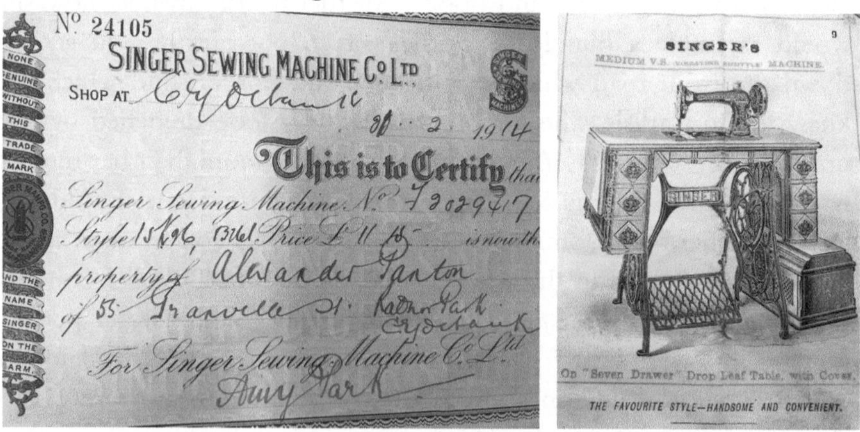

Figure 28: Singer Hire Purchase Agreement & Sewing Machine

Peter found one way to help Bessie improve their fortunes. He had access to Singer's system of providing discounted sewing-machines for employees, a down-payment followed by regular repayments on 'easy terms'. The hand-cranked, vibrating-shuttle, lockstitch machine was hers if she could make and mend the family's clothes. The ornamental black-and-gold designs and highly polished wood surrounds were finished in Peter's department. He'd have warned Bessie of Company policy: if they missed a single repayment, the machine would be taken from them. For the rest of the time Bessie lived at 1 Victoria Street, the sewing machine would have lived in the corner of the kitchen/living room/bedroom, offering her a rare fusion of work and pleasure: piles of tasks but the magic of doing them at untold speed.[61]

At first, the intensity of feeling against Irish Catholics in Glasgow would have shocked Bessie. She'd been used to some of it in Gala, but not the regular foul-mouthed attackers who appeared round street corners and jostled her, or pushed ahead of her in the queue. But she was resilient, and there was also warm friendliness among the people who thronged the local streets. For a time, Patrick had a bricklaying contract in Renfrew, and he and Ellen lived at Scotstoun, four miles away from Clydebank towards the city. Patrick and Ellen's younger daughter Barbara was born there in 1902, and Bessie would have cradled her niece. She experienced the kindness that Ellen showed to the Quinn family, as charmed by her poise and 'gentility' as others reportedly were. Sometimes Ellen and her children Jimmy and Ellen May ('Nellie') visited 1, Victoria Street. Among her earliest memories of Glasgow, written down in her 90s, Nellie May remembered seeing ships launched on the Clyde, and being taken to see 'Granny Quinn' (Mary, her father Patrick's mother). She noted that there was a whole family there, but no grandfather. Her two aunts, Mary and Bessie, were 'very good-looking'. The Quinn daughters must have been striking for her memory of them to stay with her for nearly 90 years. After that, memories of the Clydebank Quinns vanish, apart from one, crucial detail about Bessie to which I'll return.[62] Bessie and Mary would have walked down to Scotstoun, and Ellen, however straightened her circumstances, would have served them tea on an embroidered tablecloth. Walking to Patrick and Ellen's tenement, Bessie would have passed pretty English-style cottages with hedges, on tree-lined streets in grid formation, a newly built, early example of Ebenezer Howard's Garden City vision.[63]

In summer 1902, Alexander fell seriously ill with tuberculosis. As the episodes recurred ever more frequently, Peter was left as the sole reliable wage earner, his income supplemented only by Owen's pennyweight wage as a 13-year-old Singer apprentice. Peter may have paid for a doctor, but they knew there was no cure. Rest and fresh air might stave off a crisis, but the outlook was bleak. Until the summer of 1903, Alexander would have clocked in to the shipyard whenever there was a lull in the coughing and pain that wracked his lungs. But heavy lifting, hammering, and long hours wore him down.

Alex was the first victim of the Quinns' Clydebank years. The family had hauled themselves along until the autumn of 1903, but, as the weather turned moody and wet winds bit, Alex began to miss more working days. Soaked to the skin one too many times as he walked home from work, Alex took to his narrow bed by the kitchen fire, nursed by Bessie. Grey-faced and thin as a paper silhouette, he struggled to breathe, on some days filling dishes with blood. It's safe to assume Bessie cleaned and washed him, fed him soups, kept the fire in all day, whatever the cost, and listened to his fevered stories and hopes. Alex would have read everything there was to know about TB and known it was too late for him. His impulse to work in the open air had been right, but he couldn't avoid the wear and tear of shipyard labour. He survived to mark his birthday on November 10th.

On 20th December, Bessie must have been close at hand when Alex stopped breathing. I imagine her lighting a candle, her back to the wall, hunched head in hands while their mother sat distraught on Alex's bed. Owen fetched Peter from his shift. He would see to the death certificate and burial. It was 8.30 in the evening when Alex died, 'after an 18-month illness'. Officials demanded precise details. Alexander Quinn was a typical case among the grim statistics: 1,000 people a year died of TB in Glasgow alone in that period, nearly all of them young working-class people. Statistics mask stories. Alex was the second of Mary's children to die of TB. And her daughter Mary was growing frailer. Peter and Bessie must have contemplated their own chances of survival.[64]

The two mourned Alex differently: Peter was stoic, although he'd lost the companion of his childhood; Bessie was inconsolable. But they were each making plans. Peter knew Bessie would have to work or leave, preferably for part-time domestic service nearby. Bessie must have told him she'd rather look for work in northern England. She'd be only a day's journey away, should he and Mary need urgent help with their mother and Arthur George. She'd send money back as soon as she could. Even if Peter did not spell out the inevitable consequences of her plan, she must have guessed at them. It didn't change her mind. Within a month or two of Alex's funeral Bessie was gone.

22 Clydebank, Girvan, and Edinburgh 1904: Inside the System

Bessie would not witness the changes that Peter faced as soon as her train pulled out of Clydebank Station. The family formation was unsustainable without her. His sister Mary worked only intermittently, took responsibility for her mother and Arthur George, and kept house. But Peter knew her strength was waning. Her cough was more persistent and the bouts more frequent. The crisis was not just about money: Peter's wage was steady, and there was demand for Owen's painting and decorating skills. But without Bessie, Arthur George's presence at Victoria Street was untenable.

In today's terminology, the boy had learning difficulties. At that time, mental disabilities were defined as a spectrum: *unteachable* at one end, through *feeble-minded, imbecile, moral imbecile* (those who were violent), all the way to *idiot* at the other. These were the terms of the Idiots Act, 1886 until it was reformed in 1913 as the 'Mental Deficiency' Act. Those in the two last categories were usually dispatched to an institution. Arthur George was categorised as 'feeble-minded', so his upbringing was left to the family. He would soon reach 12, but he was not fit for work: not at Singer's, or on the shipyards, or in a store. At first, he probably asked after Bessie, then grew morose without a trusted teacher-companion and nurse. Living in each moment, the concept of future was beyond his grasp, so at least he wouldn't understand that Bessie was not coming back. Arthur George's body was uncoordinated and his mind was impenetrable to the people left to look after him. Initially, any alternative eluded them.

Peter juggled the budget for food and essential medication, but until Bessie sent money home from England, he couldn't make ends meet. No-one else could help. James was in America; Patrick had three children, and he was travelling round the country in search of work – and drinking too much of his wages to keep his own family in much comfort. Tom was back in the Borders staying with Augustine at St Boswells. Augustine, a loyal brother, could break enough stones to keep them both. According to family legend, he eked out his income poaching rabbits, pheasants, and fish, selling some to close friends who could be relied on to keep quiet. Tom worked on and off, between disappearances from which he took days to recover.

The walls of Victoria Street closed in around Peter. Arriving for his working day in the wood workshop brought relief, and different anxieties: how to finish his expected quota to the required standard while industrial discontent rumbled around him, pamphlets circulated, and public meetings were held. By May 1904 records show that Peter knew Bessie was in Keswick, Cumberland and had found work, so Peter could hope for a little money. He was still courting Susan Boyle, doubtless afraid he'd lose her: if he didn't propose soon, someone else would. Every evening he'd walk her home to Second Avenue, Kilbowie, the Singer-owned street which ran the length of the works. Peter had problems to solve before he could commit, and he pushed on slowly towards the fork in the road.

Irish families edging towards applying for poor relief dreaded ignominy and disdain and internalised the 'here comes another' attitude, however well-meaning individual Parochial Board inspectors might be.[65] Owen and Mary's failed applications to the Melrose Parochial Board in the 1870s were lodged in family memory, even though they had managed, despite continuous hardship, to stay independent for decades – and even since their separation. The brother they had leant on was snapping under the pressure. If Owen couldn't work, or Mary was sick, they faced destitution.

On 24th May 1904 Peter Quinn applied to the Old Kilpatrick Parochial Board for Poor Law relief for Arthur George on medical grounds: financial support for his care. The choice was between supporting him within the family or finding a placement elsewhere. The help granted to Peter may not have been what he hoped for. Arthur George's life story to this point was confirmed in meticulous detail by the Poor Law inspector. Six years earlier, in 1898, around the time his father Arthur died of tuberculosis in Edinburgh, he'd lived for two months with his grandfather on Causewayside. Before that, his home had been with his father in Galashiels, including short spells in the Poorhouse during his father's last months. Occasionally Aunt Maggie Tocher at Gala Park Road took him in. After Arthur's death, he'd stayed on at Causewayside with Aunt Mary until his grandfather died. The last move was to Clydebank. Motherless, then orphaned, the boy had grown up under the protective wing of Quinns and Tochers. One by one, he'd lost them.

Poor Law inspectors were dispatched by Parochial Boards to applicants' homes to assess a case: the middle-men between the powerful and the powerless. Inspectors had to pass exams to qualify, yet their pay was low, sometimes less than labourers'. They were expendable, although their task involved the complex human interaction essential to the system: to investigate applications and report to the Board within 24 hours, recommending approval or refusal, and to keep case records updated, sometimes for decades. In this inspector's assessment, Arthur had 'congenital mental weakness'. The grounds for a 'congenital' element may have been suggested by Peter, perhaps because of his own mother's state of mind; or by a doctor's assessment, if one was called. If the diagnosis was correct, no wonder local schools struggled to help a child with learning difficulties to progress through the standard curricula without specialist support.

The decisions of Parochial Boards were invariably driven as much by money as by the good of families or society. The costs to the parish, the city, and the State were paramount, driven by an ideology deeply rooted in the belief that families were responsible for their own poverty. No individual or family should be encouraged to seek parish support simply to ease lives or reward unemployment. So the case for help relied on illness and incapacity. The system was stronger and more punitive than the wishes of many individual Parochial Board members (in England, 'Guardians'), who were often liberal minded and philanthropic, like William Walker of Stow. Some were working people who'd felt hardship themselves, but had earned a public role. But Boards were elected by those with an interest in keeping the lid on expenditure: people whose land and property made them liable for poor rates. Although the system evolved, holding down the costs of Poorhouses and 'outdoor relief' remained the priority.

The inspector recommended Peter's application to the Parochial Board for approval, with a proposed solution. Help was immediately refused on cost grounds. However, after two weeks it was confirmed that Melrose Parish had 'admitted liability' for Arthur George, based on his and Arthur's admissions to the Poorhouse in Kirkbrae, Galashiels. They would foot the bill. By order of Old Kilpatrick board,

Arthur George was to be removed from the family with immediate effect, as was the practice. If 'indoor relief' in the Poorhouse was usual in England, in Scotland 'outdoor relief' was routine, and the boarding out of 'children and harmless lunatics' was common.[66] If this was Peter's hoped-for solution, it was drastic, but no gentler solution was offered.

Arthur George's destination was not a residential institution or family in Old Kilpatrick parish, where his family ties could continue. He was boarded out with Mrs Isabella MacLean at 164 Dalrymple Street in Girvan, on the south Ayrshire coast, 61 miles from Clydebank. Peter must have accompanied him on the train. There were papers to be signed. Once they arrived at Girvan station, they walked to Dalrymple Street, a long street running north to south from the Water of Girvan through the middle of the town. When they arrived at the small house and met Isabella MacLean, Peter would have handed her the parish paperwork: she was obliged to write periodic reports to the Parochial Board and inform them of any changes to the arrangement. Peter left for Clydebank, and Arthur George carried his bundle of belongings upstairs to the attic. His life with his family was over. The Galashiels authorities continued to pay the weekly three-shillings allowance, which would have risen over his six years in Girvan.

In his vulnerable mental and emotional state, the child must have felt bewildered and traumatised to find himself suddenly without any familiar people, places, sights, and smells. Did he understand what had happened to him? Were his memories a solace or a stab in the belly, and how quickly did they disappear into the depths of his unconscious? The ability of a child to be content alone, psychologists have emphasised, depends on the quality of an attachment with a trusted, loved person. It seems he'd experienced that with his father and Bessie, but had been twice abandoned.

A few facts about Arthur George's living conditions in Girvan provide the stage-set and cast-list for the plot of this sad drama. Isabella McLean was a widow, born in Ireland. In 1904 she was a tenant in this single-storey house with attics above, renting one room and an attic. The minutes of Girvan Parish Council for February 1904 show Mrs McLean to be in serious arrears with her rates, but the

Council couldn't enforce repayment because she was on their list of people too poor to pay. Like many women in straightened circumstances, she turned to providing 'outdoor relief' to keep herself from the same fate. The Old Kilpatrick Parochial Board sent her Arthur George, and paid her three shillings a week, about £50 in today's values. In 1907 Isabella McLean moved out, and a Mrs Baillie took over the tenancy and the pauper lodger in the attic.

Mrs MacLean doubtless put Arthur George to work, like Smike in Dickens' *Nicholas Nickleby*, hopefully without the brutality and starvation diet, but also without a hero-saviour. He was among countless paupers, living and working in domestic and commercial settings in exchange for meagre, or at best plain, rations: it was a kind of slavery. He could not leave, he was too old to start school and he might have been expected to work outside his new 'home'. There was no State system by which a boy nearing 13, considered mentally deficient, would be given supported work or training. Any help would come voluntarily from the community or church.

Further details of Arthur George's disability are not recorded. But conditions like his didn't exclude all manual work, and it wasn't the way of the Poor Law system to keep anyone 'idle' if they could do something useful. Girvan was prospering, so perhaps he helped the fishermen on the harbour – hopefully not a Peter Grimes – or swept the seafront. Fishing flourished in the 1900s, the harbour was busy, and there were boat-repair workshops. Once the railway reached Girvan in 1855, the village grew into a popular seaside resort, with cliffs and a long sandy beach, entertainments, and boat trips to the uninhabited Ailsa Craig island. Girvan was a destination for day and weekend trippers from Glasgow, the mining communities and the industrial towns of Northern Ayrshire and Lanarkshire. Under supervision, Arthur George could have cleaned or washed-up in a hotel or café.

Whether Arthur George could roam through the town to the green slopes where the River Girvan meets the sea, whether he was ever befriended, what cap-tipping acknowledgement he met with from passing townspeople, cannot be known. The life-patterns of six years have been obscured, like graphic images smothered under a layer of brown oil-paint: events, places, the passing of time, and feelings: all invisible for lack of witnesses to history.

In a strange twist, Girvan became a popular spot for day trips by Singer workers and retired 'veterans'. If Peter Quinn ever took such a trip, it must have brought back awkward memories.

In February 1910, when Arthur George had lived in Girvan for nearly six years, he was removed, presumably by the joint agreement of the Old Kilpatrick and Galashiels authorities and the Church. Peter Quinn and his brother James may have chosen his next home: the Roman Catholic Home for Working Boys in Edinburgh at 50–52 Lauriston Place. In the census of April 1911, Arthur is listed as an 'inmate', 'aged 16'. Either he wasn't sure of his age, or his uncles so badly needed a berth for him they lowered it, and the clergy in charge didn't bother to check. In fact he was 18. Arthur was one of 60 boys whom the home was certified to accommodate, probably all of them orphans or abandoned young adults who would otherwise, from the authorities' point of view, be dangerously adrift in the city. The Boys' Home inmates were apprenticed to plumbers, tailors, wire-workers, bakers, grocers, fishmongers, ironmongers, creameries, furniture makers, and chemists.

Figure 29: Edinburgh Catholic Working Boys' Home, 52 Lauriston Place, 1913

They also attended institutions like this for board and lodging, 'on licence' from industrial schools such as St Joseph's in Tranent, near Prestonpans in East Lothian – a town near to Mary Lyons's first Scottish home, fifty years earlier. 'Inmates' of St Joseph's Industrial School, for example, learned tailoring, teaching, upholstery, and gardening, worked in kitchens and laundries and did the housework. When industrial schools placed their Catholic charges with employers, mostly on apprenticeships, they transferred them to the Edinburgh Boys' Home.

Was this a break-through for Arthur George? It seems not. The Edinburgh Roman Catholic Home for Working Boys allocated him 'no occupation', on the grounds that he was 'feeble-minded' – the only boarder listed as such. They presumably took him in as part of their charitable purpose to help the poor. Such practices, as I remember from my convent education, continued well into the second half of the twentieth century. Young men like Arthur, who were regarded as unemployable, mopped floors and worked in the kitchens and laundries of places like the Edinburgh Boys' Home to justify their free keep and ensure every young person was spared the temptations of idleness. As Arthur George was denied the status of an occupation, I can only hope, although there must be doubt, that the boys' home was less cruel and abusive than recent investigations have unearthed about 'historical' malpractices in comparable 'homes' – even in recent times. There were military-style drills, and hygiene was upheld by cold 'plunge baths'. The core diet seems to have been mainly bread and milk. There were recreational activities, however, including 'drum and fife' bands as well as Highland, and Irish, dancing.

I have no record of a visit by a Quinn family member to Arthur George in Girvan or Edinburgh, although some establishments allowed home visits once a month. The Quinn family knew where he was, and I cannot imagine that Peter didn't take the train to visit him, reluctantly or not; or that James, still living in Galashiels, who'd been so close to his brother Arthur, would have neglected his nephew entirely: he may have had a hand in Arthur George's transfer to Edinburgh and, as will be clear, James played a part in the boy's future life.

On 14th June 1904, three weeks after Arthur's application, Peter and his mother Mary made another application to the Parochial Board for 'Medical Relief', and the inspector's visit quickly followed. The family's circumstances were recorded meticulously, with a note on Mary's state of mind. The family still gave her maiden name as 'Johnston', born in Jedburgh, the fiction which belonged to Owen's adopted identity in Newington. But it was not unusual, an archivist at Glasgow's Mitchell Library told me, for Irish people trying to get parish relief to conceal their Irish birth and thus avoid the disapproval they repeatedly met. Hopeless ruses, usually, but destitute people, *in extremis,* would try anything, however flimsy, that might reduce the likelihood of an application being rejected on the basis of prejudice.

The Poor Law reports of Mary Lyons Quinn's 1904 applications for medical relief, initiated by Peter, set out chapter and verse of the family's predicament and illuminate the ideology and workings of the system. The family's circumstances and whereabouts over decades are detailed. Mary had been separated from her husband Owen, the notes confirm: 'her husband remaining in Edinburgh for five–six years'; mentioning that he'd called himself James – 'Jas. Quinn – until he died'. The family provided Owen's Newington address, and his false identity was rumbled – but three years too late to ask him to support his estranged wife. The Inspector assessed Mary to be of 'weak intellect', perhaps because of her illiteracy, or because she was visibly distracted.

In the system, the applicant (on this occasion, formally Mary) first had to agree that all her dependants were written to, partly to verify the statements their mother had made, partly to ensure that no-one in the family was trying to evade their responsibilities. If the family could provide financial support, the Parochial Board would not. All of Mary's children with known whereabouts are listed: four of them, Thomas, Augustine, James, Patrick, have 'contracts at Melrose Asylum to support'. Thomas and Augustine were both living in lodgings at Bowden Moor, near the asylum, Dingleton Hospital. None of the four brothers were hospital inmates, so these are labouring contracts, but not generating money to spare for their mother's medical needs. The hospital was expanding and two extensive wings were built between 1900 and 1910, with new wards for women and men, and modern facilities which reflected the values of the hospital's liberal leaders, who were prominent advocates of new methods of treating mental illness. Patrick was also a bricklayer on the project, a train journey down the Waverley line from his Edinburgh home, although his daughter decades later remembered living in Bowden. For James it was a five-mile hike down the road from his home at Melrose near Galashiels, a manageable round trip, though he could bed down with his brothers some nights. On large building projects, and in the mines, weekly boarding on site was the norm for those who had miles to walk to work. Bessie ('Elizabeth') is reported to be in domestic service in Keswick, out of reach. Mary, unemployed, now 'keeps house', and Peter earns 20 shillings (£1) per week as a Singer's polisher. This was a good wage at the time, but not enough to support them all and pay for medical treatment. Bessie was clearly not sending money home. Mary's application was approved.

23 Scotland and France
Other Brothers: Roads Taken and Roads Home

Finding Augustine was an early research breakthrough for me: the first of Bessie's siblings to be brought back to life beyond raw census data. On my first trip to Galashiels in May 2017, I rang the doorbell of the Borders Family History Society (BFHS) on Overhaugh Street. BHFS is a magnet for family-history hunters from across the world, the Scottish and Irish–Scottish diaspora. Two volunteers made me coffee and offered help. I showed them the names of Bessie and her siblings – with no expectations, but nervous anyway. Christine studied my list of lost relatives, and when she got to the bottom she stopped, repeating to herself 'Augustine Quinn, Augustine Quinn … that name rings a bell'. She called across to a fellow volunteer, 'Elma, does the name Augustine Quinn mean anything to you?' Elma did recall that six months earlier an elderly man had walked into the Centre. He had just helped to clear out the attic of a friend who'd died, and he found a First World War Honourable Discharge Certificate. It was Augustine's, issued when he was discharged from the army in 1919. Mice had nibbled one corner, but the cardboard was otherwise intact, and the rusty-red Britannia image has hardly faded. Augustine served as a driver in the Army Service Corps (the 'Royal' prefix was attached from 1918) from the outbreak of war in 1914 until he was wounded and 'disabled' in 1918. After he left the battlefields of France, he was officially stationed at Greenock, but lived with his brother Patrick in a tenement block, 27 Stewart Terrace in Gorgie, Edinburgh, another regular refuge for Tom. The initial discovery of the Discharge Certificate had caught the BFHS volunteers' imaginations, so they'd done some digging on the Scotland's People website and published an article in their magazine, appealing for more information. None was offered, and Augustine's connection to the cleared house couldn't be found. My visit a few months later was pure coincidence: a lesson in family-history research. Prepare for surprises, keep furrowing, meet a dead end, and, if you're lucky, someone will point out a hidden track to follow.

441340 Pvt Augustine Quinn
Royal Army Service Corps
Served with honour and was disabled in the Great War.
Honourably discharged on 25th June 1919
George R.I.

Figure 30: Augustine's Army Discharge Certificate, 1919

Augustine emerged as a lively and determined character who set up an independent life, alone at 13 when his family left Galashiels, although Arthur and James could have kept an eye on him. Augustine followed in his father's footsteps: apart from his war service, he broke stones for years until he became too weak to work at all. Augustine did not complete the 1901 census, but in 1904 he was working in the Borders as a stonebreaker with James, Patrick-Peter, and Tom, building an ambitious extension to the Dingleton Hospital (Melrose Asylum), sheltering Tom in his room nearby at St Boswells, Bowden Moor. In 1905 he was still living there, still working on the site. In 1906, the hospital building finished, Augustine changed tack, working as a storekeeper, living with the Dalglish family at Ettrickbridge, near Selkirk. By June 1906 he was breaking stones again, at Yarrow Braes, the hillsides a few miles from Selkirk which inspired romantic and pastoral poems of love and longing for the Borders by Scott and Burns and Wordsworth. It must have been on Yarrow Water and the Tweed that Augustine learned the art of covert fishing for salmon, grayling, and trout, pursuits for which he was famous.

Augustine attested for the army in 1912, before the great 1914 rush to volunteer, then joined the 2nd battalion of the King's Own Scottish Borderers (KOSB). His regimental number was 23325 and his rank was

Private, from first to last. His medical examination was probably brief and limited, and he probably claimed to be younger than he was. And although the upper age limit was high, many thousands claimed to be younger as well as older than they were. Recruiting officers, desperate to enlist half-way healthy soldiers, winked them through without birth certificates. Army numbers were tiny by comparison with other European countries before 1914. But from boy soldiers to middle-aged men, well over 900,000 from Great Britain and its colonies were dead by 1918, and over two million wounded – from a force of six million men.

Augustine survived and earned his victory medal for more than four years' service in the KOSB. Still formally attached to the regiment, he served throughout as a driver in the Army Service Corps (ASC). He served in the Horse Transport section, as his service number indicates: T/441340. This was still the largest element of the ASC, as we know from the millions of slaughtered horses: motorised transport was still in its infancy. Augustine's ASC company served both the KOSB and the King's Own Yorkshire Light Infantry (KOYLI). 'Lines of Communication' was its function and it was dangerous work, but in the army's hierarchy of respect the ASC was disparagingly known as 'Ally Sloper's Cavalry', after a famously shifty, bungling cartoon character. Horse-drawn and mechanical transport vehicles moved in and out of the action, bringing meat, bread, water, ammunition, and equipment to 'forward dumps'. The sections were constantly in danger along their 'long long trail a-winding'. Often in the line of fire, horse-drawn loads would be driven from ports and depots to the front line, drivers sleeping in camps, dumps, and trenches.[67]

In the thick of the action from 1914, Augustine was wounded during the Battle of Passchendaele in Flanders in 1917, not for the first time. In his diary, one KOSB officer says of his subordinates: 'I don't think any men of any regiment would have gone to certain death the way ours did. They all knew when they went over that this would happen and not a man flinched so far as I could see. To command such men is an honour of which few among us are worthy.'[68] A junior officer was as likely as the men to go 'over the top', although working-class non-commissioned soldiers lost their lives in far greater numbers than officers. Ever-speedier promotions through non-commissioned officer ranks, sometimes in a matter of weeks, as James Quinn, Patrick's son, experienced, tell a grisly story.[69]

Augustine met Annie Innes in Edinburgh. She was the daughter of a carter from Pitsligo, Aberdeenshire: James Innes and his wife Jane Yeats Mowat. She worked in domestic service, a few houses down from the Catholic Working Boys' home where his childhood companion Arthur George lived. Augustine and Annie married on 31st October 1918, just before the Armistice, at the All Saints Scottish Episcopal (Anglo-Catholic) church in Edinburgh – a compromise between their two faiths. He was still in the army, but he recorded his work as 'bricklayer': disabled, unfit, not yet discharged, but free to work. Augustine stated his age as 31 (he was 34), and Annie was 28.

Augustine had been sent home from the front for good after sustaining 'aggravated' wounds in the left arm and left leg, and suffering from bronchitis which was 'attributable' to his service. Infectious diseases were rife in the war, influenza, trench fever, and typhoid among them. More soldiers died from disease than from wounds. Augustine was judged 30 per cent disabled and entitled to 8 shillings and 3 pence a week ('8/3d' – a little over £4) from June 1919. What's more, he was entitled to an additional allowance of 2 shillings a week for one child born before July 1919. Who was this child? Annie Innes had been a domestic servant when she met Augustine. In 1917, still in service, she gave birth to a boy, William Lennox Duncannon Innes, at Edinburgh Royal Maternity Hospital. No father on the record – just 'illegitimate'. Annie continued working as a domestic servant, now at 39 Lauriston Place in Edinburgh, and as she couldn't keep the baby there, he'd be with her parents in Pitsligo. William Lennox was probably conceived on a spell of home leave, but whether or not Augustine was the biological father, he brought up William, soon registered as Quinn, as his legitimate son, from his army discharge to the end of his life.

By the time Augustine married Annie, his parents were both dead, so far as he knew. His brother Tom was dead, and Bessie was beyond reach, in London, according to Patrick's family grapevine. Most of his wartime friends were lost or permanently disabled, including his nephew Jimmy Quinn, who'd lost a leg. Other comrades were shell-shocked: never again the people they once were.

After Augustine was fully discharged from the army in London with his pension settled, he, Annie, and William Lennox lodged with his brother James and his wife in Melrose. The security and support would have been comforting as he rebuilt his life. Augustine had gone it alone for many years, and hadn't lived with the family since they left Galashiels, but seems to have kept his whereabouts known to James, holding their Edinburgh and Clydebank family at a distance.

In 1919, Annie and Augustine settled at Halliburton Place. The rent was £7 and 13 shillings a year (about £350 in today's purchasing power). We can be confident it was a good deal, because Annie turned out to have a good head for money. She kept them afloat and did well later in life as a widowed mother. Number 273 was on the same side of the street as Augustine's childhood home. He evoked his best childhood years when he wrote 'gardener' next to the entry about his father on their marriage certificate. In 1920, Augustine and Annie had a second child: Elizabeth – another 'Bessie' Quinn – who also became a woollen weaver in the Galashiels mills. Elizabeth married William Herning, a local cabinet-maker; she lived until 2001, and her descendants still live in Selkirk.

Augustine never moved from Halliburton Place. He worked as a stonebreaker, quarryman, and occasional bricklayer until his health gave out. He had one more decade to live. According to family memories, he always brought healthy food to the table from the fields, woods, and landed estates around Gala, famous in family memory as a 'prodigious poacher' of hares and rabbits, his skills no doubt learned from Owen, along with stealth fishing. Poaching was a risky practice. It was still a serious crime, but essential to the livelihood and wellbeing of the rural poor, especially if any surplus caught could be sold. Augustine had an adventurous, courageous streak, ready for whatever was needed to keep body and soul together. Rooted in the Borders, he kept the habits of a country boy all his life.[70]

From 1927, Augustine suffered repeated episodes of TB, until, in April 1930, he was diagnosed with 'advanced tuberculosis'. He was admitted to East Fortune Sanatorium in Athelstaneford – less than three miles from Brownrigg farm in East Lothian, where his mother and the young Lyons family had worked as farm labourers when they first arrived in Scotland.

Getting back to Gala was always Augustine's strongest impulse: he came home once from the Sanatorium, but he was readmitted towards the end of July, and after 92 more days he died there, on 30th October 1930, of 'pulmonary tuberculosis'. He was 46. Annie lived on at Halliburton Place with their children, upgrading to a house which cost her £12 a year— nearly twice the rent of No. 273. As well as her army widow's pension, it seems she had other earnings, and a talent for managing money.

James Quinn and Arthur George: family bonds

The life of James, brother and friend to Arthur and Augustine, is nearly a happy-ever-after story. He was childless, but that may have been a choice: not an unusual reaction to an upbringing in a big, poor family. And his wife suffered, possibly for years, from a neural, or nerve-related, condition. By choice or not, he lived a quiet life after a tumultuous childhood and a succession of upheavals.

James, Mary and Owen's fourth child, was born on August 4th 1870 at Comelybank Terrace, beside the woollen mill. He started work as a mill-piecer, advancing to become a tweed finisher. Later he became a qualified bricklayer – the skilled and better-paid trade which enticed several of the Quinn boys and thousands more away from factory work and stonebreaking. The lure was an apprenticeship, outdoor work, more independence, and reasonable payment by results on a sure-fire succession of contracts. When Owen and Mary's Galashiels life was in freefall, James was working on one of myriad building sites in Newington, the expanding neighbourhood on Edinburgh's south side, where he scouted for cheap lodgings for the family. James and his sisters had looked after their ailing brother, Arthur, while he and his son lived in Galashiels. When Arthur died in 1898, James held the Newington family together. He then witnessed the end of his parents' married life, as his mother and Bessie moved to Clydebank. When Owen died, it was undoubtedly James who persuaded his younger brother Peter to take in the last of the Mowat Place family: their sister Mary and the children Owen and Arthur George. James, it seems, was a dutiful, good-willed character, who, at 31, shed his burden after years of worry.

A homebird, like Augustine, James returned to the Borders whenever there was work. By 1903, he'd found bricklaying work near

Melrose, rented a room at Darnick, a nearby village, and fallen in love with a neighbour: Mary, the daughter of Irish immigrants, Patrick and Mary (yes, another Mary) Rehill. This Mary, his beloved, was working as a 'mother's help'. Her father Patrick Rehill and brother James Rehill were road surfacemen. Their family lived at 84 Sprouston Cottages, Newtown St Boswells. Not as remote or rural as it sounds, this was a new suburb built outside an ancient rural village in the 1860s to house railway and road workers. For the inhabitants of the old village, the new settlement was a mixed blessing, bringing an Irish community of railway workers and their families to that part of the Borders for the first time. Sprouston Cottages was nicknamed 'Cordy Raw', lampooning the railwaymen's signature workwear and pointing to the arrival of a rough breed of strangers. But the new Sprouston Station was also welcome to farmers and residents, taking live animals to the Newton St Boswells Auction 'Mart', as well as whisking passengers through the Borders, along the Tweed, and up to Edinburgh. Goods and passenger services ran until 1969, when Sprouston Station and the railway line were closed following the 'Beeching' cuts, along with 2,363 stations and 5,000 miles of track across Britain: over 10,000 workers lost their jobs.

James Quinn and Mary Rehill both still attended Mass, and in 1903 their local priest, Father Rooney, married them at the church of Our Lady and St. Andrew, nearly forty years after the wedding of Owen and Mary there. James and Mary were both 33 – late for her, but normal for the Quinns and for Irish bachelors with few means to set up home in anything more ambitious than a room as a lodger. These two found a red-brick dwelling in Sprouston Cottages, with three windows – one more room than James had ever known – and their own garden. They had a regular income in a quiet place, looking out to the Eildon Hills.

Soon afterwards, they set off for their one great adventure: sailing to America. At least that is what their mother told the Poor Law inspectors in June 1904. Whether they intended to emigrate permanently, or just to work in America for a time, or even try to find James's eldest brother Owen, they were back in Edinburgh by 1905, living in lodgings with Mrs Masterton at 51 Earl Grey Street. James was bricklaying again. But by 1911 they'd flown back like homing pigeons, settling at 81 Sprouston Cottages, next door to Mary's parents and James Rehill. On the census that year, James's father-in-law Patrick Rehill was 83, his wife Mary 78, and they had been married for 54 years. Nothing else in the Quinn story was as calm or uneventful as these 'ordinary lives'.

Away from the storms of the older Quinns' separation and the chaos of life in Edinburgh and Clydebank, Bessie's brother James and his wife lived together for decades, tending to her fragile health, among their own people, near to the countryside along the Tweed. The only move they made after America was to a house further down the same street: number 15. They both died there: Mary on 30th July 1934, of 'neural incompetence', which could be one of numerous conditions, mental and physical, and possibly a stroke. James died of stomach cancer less than a week later. Each was too ill to look after the other, and it seems they had an agonising final year. They were both in their sixties, but on the record their ages had accrued a four-year discrepancy since they married – most likely because Mary's brother James Rehill, present at both deaths, wasn't sure what to report, or how old they were. Would it have mattered? Precision on the public record was smudged so often by human error. The point was to do the necessary as quickly as possible. There were funerals to organise. Doctors, too, could be cavalier, vague or inaccurate about causes of death, especially faced with unfamiliar symptoms at a time when medicine was rapidly advancing. Some paid little attention to the family-background columns on death certificates.

James Quinn chose to be closer to his new family's way of life and stick to the familiar, though his own family ties remained strong. Someone in the family must have kept in contact with Arthur George and smoothed the way for his eventual return to Galashiels once he was no longer an institutionalised 'boy', but an adult in need of care. How else but with his uncles' support would Arthur George, in his late teens or early twenties, return to Galashiels between 1911 and the outbreak of war in 1914? Once he was over-age for the boys' home, it appears most likely that James stepped in. Only he and Augustine still lived in the Borders, and Augustine, at the latest from August 1914, was on active service, and from 1912 in barracks. Arthur George's life was not viable without support, nor could he have made his own decision to leave an Edinburgh institution and set off for the Borders with no knowledge of how to organise his life. Through his long life, he never lived independently. The Catholic Church, which ran the Edinburgh home, could have helped to relocate him, but only with family support. James, probably his formal next of kin, either took Arthur George in at Newtown St Boswells – they had the luxury of a spare bedroom – or they found him somewhere nearby, possibly at Dingleton Hospital or one of its community-based homes. At the least, they'd have offered him a square meal from time to time. James's official records speak of someone who lived out his life with generosity, loyalty, realism, and good grace.

His nephew was finally home in a deep sense, in the Borders, reconnected with family: James and Mary Rehill, Augustine, and the descendants of Maggie Tocher. The actions which enabled Arthur George to return are evidence of a viable family network and human sympathy, counter-currents against the divisive, alienating consequences of interventions by the State system, offering 'relief' for poverty in ways which undermined and destroyed the social and emotional resources of families.

Arthur George lived in Galashiels for over 50 years, most of them in the former Combination Poorhouse on Kirkbrae, designed by James Campbell Walker in 1859–60 in the style of a large manor house in landscaped grounds with views of the Eildon Hills. In 1930 it was renamed 'Windyknowe Public Assistance Institution', associated with Dingleton Hospital, and accommodated people of all ages with conditions like Arthur George's. At the latest when Mary and James fell sick in the early 1930s, 'Windyknowe' was the obvious place for him to live. He'd come full-circle to the old Poorhouse, where he had stayed with his father Arthur in the late 1890s. In 1950, Windyknowe was renamed the Eildon View Home, and Arthur George went on living there for the rest of his life. Now it is a privately owned care home for the elderly. The Kirkbrae Poorhouse's successor institutions were long associated with Dingleton Hospital. There are uncanny connections: Arthur George's uncles James, Augustine, Patrick, and Thomas had building contracts there in 1904, the year that he was sent to Girvan to live in Isabella McLean's attic.

Nothing is written about how Arthur George managed financially or medically, under the care of the Selkirkshire authorities, nor how he passed his time. Did he earn a livelihood, or just keep busy with in-house occupations? Dingleton hospital had had a national reputation as an innovative and progressive institution, and from the later decades of the 19th century it was respected for unusually humane and integrative treatment of people with mental-health problems and disabilities, including supported residence outside the hospital walls and freedom of movement for hospital inmates.

Arthur George died in 1965. He was 73, outliving James and Mary Rehill-Quinn by thirty years. Perhaps James Rehill still related to him after they died. Augustine's family, still living in Galashiels, might have visited him. But the staff and co-residents in his care home would have been his closest companions. He died without family or friends present. The informant, Doctor Walker at Eildon View, confirmed the causes of death as coronary thrombosis and pneumonia.

The records of Arthur George's life make disturbing reading: a person with learning disabilities, possibly also physically disabled, living in an age without human rights or professional advocacy, who probably lived his last three decades with little or no direct family contact. From the age of 12 he lived in institutions, benign or otherwise. Arthur George may have been a good companion to people who crossed his path. And at Windyknowe he was surrounded by others like him who needed care, a community, with social activities, three meals a day and medical attention. Arthur George must have cut a familiar figure in town, perhaps exchanging greetings, or resting in the same library and museum which, in my mind, once kept his almost-mother Bessie and uncle Alex absorbed while he and his cousin Owen played at their feet. With others, he could have reminisced and made some sense of his story: the pain of being wrenched away, and his long journey back to Galashiels. He had witnessed so much change, as the woollen mills which had provided his grandparents' and parents' livelihood closed down one by one. Tall weeds hid huddled lovers and teenagers sharing cigarettes among the abandoned old shells, before they were summarily destroyed and tarmacked over.

It's tempting to hope that Arthur George felt safe and at home within a good-enough regime compared with the cruelty and malpractices recently uncovered in post-war institutions which risk obscuring the ordinary, kind, imperfect best that society provided for many vulnerable people before the passing of disability-discrimination legislation – inadequate as that still is, especially for adults. But Arthur George Tocher-Quinn was a survivor who died in a quiet place that he knew as home, outlasting Bessie's generation of Quinns and many from his own.

Patrick Quinn: lost and found

As I unearthed Quinn after Quinn, Patrick eluded me, rising to the surface only in circumstantial evidence, never substantiated by hard facts. He'd disappeared down a crater, presumed dead, or abroad, possibly having emigrated to the USA or Canada, without a ship's passenger record to prove it. Patrick, Owen and Mary's second son, born in 1866 at Buckholmside, had left Gala after a few years at the mill, and never again appeared on official records – or so it seemed.

After months of fruitless hunting in 'Scotland's People' files and other archives, I gave up on Patrick. Then a clue appeared, on Peter Quinn's 1904 and 1906 applications for poor relief. All the children who might be in a position to support their mother financially were listed, with addresses where known. No Parish support would be forthcoming if waged family members could pay up. And there was Patrick, living at 21a Jamaica Street, a tenement in Edinburgh's New Town. He was married with three children, so couldn't help with their mother's predicament. It was enough to renew my search of censuses and certificates: I'd missed him. The Scotland's People records are that good: no-one just disappears. But still I drew blank after blank and started spending recklessly on the harmless addiction of paying for dud certificates. One day, squinting again through a magnifying glass at the detailed Poor Law inspector's notes, I hovered over the entry for Patrick and noticed it read 'Patrick (Peter)'. How on earth had I overlooked this? I'd assumed the Poor Law inspector hadn't got the family story straight: Peter, of course, lived in Clydebank and his older brother Patrick in Edinburgh. To me, those brackets had simply meant 'according to Clydebank Peter's story'. The penny dropped. Was it possible that Patrick called himself Peter? Within an hour I'd found him and all his family in a sheaf of records. He was 'Peter' Quinn. He'd left Galashiels to work in Edinburgh, still a teenager, and his first home was 27 Balbirnie Place, near the railway lines at Haymarket, where the road bends towards Murrayfield. Next he lived at 28 Wardlaw Place, the address that his brother Tom had supplied at his military attestation in 1898. Patrick was still living there in 1901, now married, and by 1904 he was living in Jamaica Street in Edinburgh's New Town.

Patrick was not estranged from his family, at least not all of them. He, or more likely his wife, was fairly regularly helping out Tom. He travelled across Scotland to work in Renfrewshire as a bricklayer, living in Scotstoun, along the road from the Quinn family at Clydebank. His third child, Barbara, was born there in 1902.

Then Patrick worked on the extension to the Dingleton Hospital at Melrose in the Borders with his brothers Augustine, James, and Tom, living briefly at Bowden Moor before moving the family back to Edinburgh.

Early on in his Edinburgh-based life, Patrick became Peter. This was almost as confusing as unscrambling the legion of Marys. First Peter Lyons, then Peter Quinn, and now Patrick (Peter) Quinn. The second-born Quinn boy will be Patrick-Peter from now on in this book, to distinguish two very different characters. The biblical name Peter, 'petros' meaning 'rock', was suitable for Clydebank Peter. Following the 19th-century influx of Irish Catholic immigrants into Scotland, the name Patrick became popular in honour of Ireland's patron saint, who it is said was born in the fourth century at Old Kilpatrick near Dumbarton. St Patrick's Church, built in the 19th century in Dumbarton, commemorates his birthplace, and his name has been a constant emblem of changing cultural identities among the twists and turns of Scottish and Irish religious hostilities. Catholics in Ireland once thought his name too sacred for common use, but it became popular, and by the mid-nineteenth century Patrick was viewed disparagingly as a Catholic name in Scotland. By contrast, Peter became more cross-cultural, used by Protestants and useful to Catholics wishing to blend more easily into Protestant Scottish life.

Patrick-Peter changed his name, his grandson suggests, after he met his future wife, Ellen Brooks, who lived at Roseburn Place, just round the corner from his rooms. Ellen was a Protestant from an Edinburgh family and it is likely he became Peter, despite its being the birth name of his younger brother: part of his bid to adapt to the identity of her respectable family. And perhaps he just preferred it: after all, he could have called himself anything. None of Patrick-Peter's descendants knew him as anything but Peter.

Ellen ('Nellie') Brooks was born in 1866 at Shornecliff Barracks, Elham, in Kent, the daughter of Adam Brooks, a journeyman tailor, and his wife Helen, née Fairgrieve, both born and brought up in Leith. Adam became a master tailor for the army, attached to the Royal Artillery, and took a decent army pension at 48, on grounds of ill health. Ellen's childhood was spent moving around England, Scotland, and Ireland, wherever her father's work took him: seven siblings were born in three different countries. When Adam died in 1885, Helen was pregnant again, but she and her daughter Barbara found work straightaway as laundresses at Murrayfield House, a large estate nearby. The Brooks children's future was bright enough. One of Ellen's brothers was already a tailor, another apprenticed to an engineer, and both had successful careers in England.

In 1893, when she married 'Peter' Quinn, Ellen had been working for a few years as a cook in a Church of England (sic) school in Edinburgh. Their Church of Scotland wedding was on 30th June. Ellen's mother was present, and her sister Alison was a witness, but there were no Quinns in sight, at least not as witnesses. More curious name changes appear on their marriage certificate. Patrick Quinn now became Peter Queen. His father is 'James Queen', a gardener, a more respectable occupation than stonebreaking, but one which his father Owen had only recently taken up. Patrick-Peter was making a strong new identity for himself. His mother, 'Mary Queen', was now 'née Johnston', not Lyons, so evidently he was in touch with his family enough to know about adopted name changes and Owen's new occupation. Queen, Johnston, and James sound suitably Scottish to fit Patrick-Peter's purpose as he wed a staunch Protestant. The marriage date, 1893, suggests the Quinns' pseudonyms were in use long before the flight from Galashiels to Edinburgh, and they lasted: his father would still be 'James' when Mary met the Poor Board inspector in 1904. Perhaps in 1893 Owen was already using the new name to evade pursuers; or perhaps Patrick-Peter himself had started the 'Johnston' idea, to downplay his Irish identity. Queen could be a simple spelling glitch, but that doesn't account for all the other changes. Adopting a new name to suit the exigencies of the moment was a Quinn habit.

And so many changes on one certificate feel deliberate. By 1901 Patrick-Peter was 'Quinn' again, although in 1902 he was back to Queen. He never reverted to Patrick.

The Brooks family were a cut above the Quinns, so Ellen's Peter, an Irish-Catholic man of no means, must have charmed and sweet-talked his way into her affections, or so his descendants suggest. Ellen spent the rest of their lives together forgiving him for his ill-treatment of her. Marrying Patrick-Peter offered her freedom from the custodial drudgery of domestic service. Independence was the hope and dream for millions of live-in women servants at the turn of the century as they saw more and more women and girls like them dressed up smartly to head for a day's office work and the freedom of evenings spent with friends. Marriage was a different route out.

By her grandson's account, Ellen was 'refined, kind and generous … and the signs that her life had been anything but easy did not show'. His grandson describes 'Peter' Quinn as not a nice person and violent when alcohol got the better of him. Always in work or in search of it, he downed some of his wages before he got home, possibly at Kay's Bar at 39 Jamaica Street in their years at No. 21. Kay's is still a vibrant local after 200 years, still evoking the hard-drinking male world of Victorian pay-days, but fashionable now, a mixture of wine-bar and traditional pub. Patrick-Peter's youngest son, David, recalled preventing his drunken father attacking his mother Ellen with a knife – not, apparently, an isolated incident. David was teetotal all his life, reluctant to talk about his father, and probably the one who made sure that no photograph of him survived.

Patrick-Peter and Ellen had four children: James, 'Jimmy' (1894–1951); Ellen May, 'Nellie' (1897–1994); Barbara, 'Babbie' (1902–1980); and David (1907–1985). Ellen May was the Quinn family scribe, the only one among Bessie's siblings and their offspring that I've found, apart from my own father. She carried the family's memories, seeing the best in everyone, writing, preserving photographs. Thank you, Ellen May. She is the only person I've come across who remembers meeting Bessie. She recalled being a young child in Clydebank in 1902, when Patrick-Peter and family lived at Scotstoun Place. She remembered a ship launching on the Clyde, and 'very good-looking' aunts': Mary and Bessie Quinn are the only possible candidates. She also remembered knowing both James and Augustine Quinn – perhaps from Bowden Moor or Edinburgh. In 1914, Ellen May's elder brother Jimmy, an apprentice engineer with a lively social life and good prospects, volunteered for army service. Ellen May 'did well at school', went on to night school to learn shorthand, typing, and bookkeeping, winning prizes for her essays, and joined McVitie and Price's biscuit factory in Edinburgh – not on the shop floor like her cousins, but in the office. In 1917 she left for London to support the war effort, working at the Staines munitions factory, one of about 800, making brass artillery shell casings on a lathe. She married and lived all her adult life in Penge, south London, working her way up at Barclays Bank's City of London and St John's Wood offices. Her daughter, Rosemary, lived until 2020. Like millions of women, she was forced to give up her job when she married. 'Nellie' May lived near my parents' 1960s home in Anerley. If only they had met, I would know if she ever visited Bessie in Hampstead Garden Suburb. She became a Londoner, spoke like one, and never returned to live in Scotland.[71]

Figure 31: Ellen 'Nellie' May Quinn

Figure 32: James Quinn of the Royal Scots 9th Battalion: the kilted 'Dandy Ninths'

'Jimmy', the eldest son of Patrick-Peter and Ellen, was born in 1894. He volunteered at 19 years old, joining the Royal Scots regiment, the 'Dandy Ninths', so called because of their Hunting Stewart tartan kilts, jaunty caps, badges, and pins. Starting as a Private, he survived two years of the worst trench warfare, a brave, gentle spirit, withstanding hellish trench life with humour. He was promoted to Corporal, and finally Sergeant in 1916 soon before he was badly wounded, losing a leg at the Somme the same year. After the war Jimmy married a girl from Walkerburn, the first home of his grandmother Mary Lyons in the Borders. In the mid-1930s, seeing another world war looming, he emigrated to South Africa, determined his two sons would not endure his experiences. Jimmy was loved and revered among his branch of the Quinns. In the 1930s, he wrote a memoir of the war in the form of long letters laced with wry wit and rich Edinburgh dialect, addressed to a fellow-soldier and friend of his youth in Edinburgh. Ellen May lodged the memoir at the Imperial War Museum, and it was quoted in a recent history of the 9th Regiment.[72] It's said that Ellen May visited him in South Africa, but came home early, distraught at the racism, poverty, and inequality she witnessed. Jimmy returned to Scotland in 1951, hauling himself uncomplaining round Galashiels and Walkerburn with his wooden leg. He said his goodbyes, and died unexpectedly on his journey home to Johannesburg. The significance of his visit was known only to his younger brother David, who'd driven him round the old places. But David 'had to have the past wrung out of him', especially on the subject of his father, Patrick-Peter. He preferred to look forward. A bus and lorry driver, known for his dry wit, he supported his mother Ellen, and, to the point of self-sacrifice, made sure his son's education would be a springboard to a good life.

Patrick-Peter was one of the Quinn siblings' longest survivors, still working as a bricklayer when his final illness took hold. He died in July 1928, aged 62, of TB and bronchial pneumonia at the Craiglockhart Sanatorium in Edinburgh. He and Ellen were still 'usually resident' at 27 Stewart Terrace in south-west Edinburgh. She was with him at the sanatorium when he died. He's a Quinn again on the record; Owen is Owen, and Mary is restored to 'née Lyons'. Ellen May recalled that her mother gave her husband a fine send-off, despite everything: black-plumed horses pulled a grand hearse all the way to Dalry, the once-imposing but now dilapidated cemetery, known for its trees and wildlife, where he is buried under an engraved headstone. Ellen lived until 1950, keeping a watchful eye on her daughter 'Babbie', the baby niece Bessie knew in Clydebank. Stone-deaf from the age of 13, Babbie was roughly treated by the man she married in middle-age. For decades, the Quinn–Brooks family hugged their corner of Edinburgh, south-west of Haymarket, along Gorgie Road, close to Dalry, Murrayfield, and the Heart of Midlothian football stadium.[73]

The Craiglockhart sanatorium where Patrick-Peter died is a significant emblem of an era scarred by public-health disasters as well as war. TB sanatoria were created in early 1900s. Social and health reformers heralded them as the best chance of keeping TB sufferers isolated and the disease in check. Specialist institutions, they were also part of the wider movement to promote the benefits of fresh air, wholesome nutrition, and outdoor holidays for the poor in the countryside or by the sea. Some sanatoria were single-purpose, such as East Fortune, where Augustine died. Others began as Poorhouse infirmaries, for example at Dumbarton and Craiglockhart, which had been built in 1867–9 on the same piece of land. The Craiglockhart sanatorium was developed from a mid-19th century hydropathy centre. 'Water cures' were becoming fashionable among middle-class sufferers for treating certain diseases, including 'consumption' and undiagnosed physical frailty, From 1877, the Craiglockhart hydropathy centre offered a brutal form of shock therapy, based on alternate applications of cold and hot water, aimed at producing a bodily 'crisis' which flushed out impurities, creating pus and profuse sweats, all washed away by cold plunges. Hydropathy belonged to the faddish end of experimentation with cures for TB, a middle-class version of the 19th-century belief in combining bodily purification, cleanliness, and fresh air to heal the bodies, minds, and morals of the working class.

Craiglockhart became famous from 1916 to 1918 as a specialist psychiatric military hospital where officers, including Wilfred Owen and Siegfried Sassoon, were among 1,700-plus patients who were treated for First World War trauma and post-traumatic stress: 'shell-shock', as it was popularly known. Other ranks, soldiers like Jimmy Quinn, were treated elsewhere, if at all. Wilfred Owen thought it shabby and melancholy, a 'decayed Hydro'. Sassoon called it Dottyville. It was said that the memories of fallen fellow soldiers were all too easily evoked in the gloom. The Craiglockhart story was brilliantly re-interpreted in Pat Barker's 1990s trilogy, *Regeneration.* When Patrick-Peter died there, TB was still taking its toll on the poor as well as veterans of the First World War. Sanatoria did not disappear until the 1950s, after antibiotic treatments were widely introduced in the early years of the National Health Service.

24 Radnor Park and Kirkcudbrightshire 1904–1906: Granny Quinn and Her Daughter Mary

Arthur George and his grandmother were not the only Quinns whose lives became unsustainable within the family. On 2nd May 1905, Father Denis Scannell, the Clydebank parish priest, made an application to the Poor Board for medical relief (today's sickness benefit) on behalf of Bessie's elder sister Mary. Now 32, she'd been working in a factory, probably Singer's, but had been unemployed for 11 weeks with no income. Father Scannell calculated that she'd been living in Clydebank with her brother for six years, so, as the 1901 census shows, in the years when Owen was alive, his daughter Mary must have split her time and support between the estranged households in Edinburgh and Glasgow. Father Scannell reported his fears that Peter was 'going to remove (his) mother and the applicant to Edinburgh', which would have overwhelmed both of his frail female parishioners. Perhaps Peter and his brothers argued over where their mother and sister should live, because without Bessie he could no longer cope. Patrick, the only Quinn in Edinburgh in 1905, was unlikely to offer his mother and sister a welcome, despite Ellen's generous spirit. It seems as though Mary's relationship with Peter was tense, and she cooked up a convincing plea for change which reflected badly on him. Alternatively, Peter colluded with a story against himself because they all wanted the same thing: for mother and daughter to move out of Victoria Street. Whatever the truth, the two women's preferences would be irrelevant to the Poor Board's decisions, if not to Peter.

The Inspector noted as usual who should receive formal written notification of the application, requesting information about their resources, with reassurances that they would be told the outcome. The Board already knew Peter's exact income. James was in America, but Bessie and Augustine were among the siblings written to: two singleton Quinns who might pay up. It's not clear that the Parish Board's requests reached either of them – one in England, the other on the Borders, each trying to keep their own head above water. In this game of cat and mouse, the 1905 application for sister Mary's medical relief was approved, but subsequently withdrawn again. Perhaps help had been forthcoming from Bessie or a brother.

There was relief for Peter though. His mother and sister were moved out soon afterwards to live together at 14 Salisbury Place on the edge of Radnor Park, an area of cheap tenement housing built to accommodate Singer's burgeoning workforce. A massive complex of tenements housing Singer employees was built in the 1880s in Radnor Park. The new buildings were nicknamed Holy City, as the flat roofs were said to resemble Jerusalem, though for some the name reflected the numbers of Irish Catholics living there. Holy City is gone, destroyed in the Clydebank blitz, replaced by post-war houses with gardens.

Their street, up the hill from Dalmuir Station, looked out over the tangle of intersecting railway lines. Mary was designated her mother's 'housekeeper' – 'carer' in today's language. The two women made another application on 10th June and this time, just a few weeks later, an 'enrolment', the derisory sum of three shillings a week, was approved on the grounds of daughter Mary's deteriorating medical condition: 'phthisis'. The Parish Board relented, but the delayed arrangement was short-lived. Mary Quinn lost her elder daughter on 26th July 1905 after a seven-month struggle with TB. She'd been in no condition to care for her mother when they moved in. That decision had been too late, and unworkable. Mary's 'housekeeper' role was a fig-leaf to dress up unforgiving practices. Her TB would have been spotted the first time by an Inspector, who must have witnessed many cases. To the Parochial Board, medical relief was a necessary but unwelcome cost chalked up to the disease's stampede through the urban poor.

Peter was in attendance at his sister's death, once again mourning one minute, wondering what to do the next. He decided that Owen, now a qualified painter and decorator, would take care of his grandmother at Radnor Park, and watch out for her wellbeing. Some months passed. Tom's sporadic visits to sleep on their floor at Radnor Park made independent life more difficult, but he knew better than to ask Peter for a bed: he might refer him to the Parish.

In January 1906, Peter did make another application for poor relief, this time for his mother. As usual, the addresses and circumstances of family members were checked out before the Parochial Board considered the case. It seems no-one could offer any money. On one side of the large double-spread sheets, the inspector's report is painstakingly detailed. By contrast, the one-word decisions in the far column offer no explanation: 'Refused' or 'Approved'. In January 1906 James was back from America, lodging with his wife at 51 Earl Grey Street, Edinburgh, with a resident landlady. Patrick was still at 21 Jamaica Street, New Town, with Ellen and their three children, working as a bricklayer. Peter had moved from 1 Victoria Street to 7 Second Avenue, lodging with the Walker family in a Singer-owned house. Bessie was still a cook in England. The family had not a penny more to put towards their mother's keep than the year before. After relief was refused by the Board, Owen continued to live with Granny, still working as a painter at Singer's. Mary's infirmity and need for support are put down to 'age' and 'family not supporting'. That January, her only identified ailment was 'age'. Reading the cold and contradictory record, I felt indignant on Peter's behalf, especially as a brief note at the bottom of the page records that he 'pays regularly'. By now, he'd surely let himself believe he might turn hope into reality: Susan Boyle was now his girl-next-door on Second Avenue. The door to independence was being slammed in his face again, but the couple were renewing plans to live together. By summer, Susan was pregnant. Peter must have made promises to her and prayed he could keep them. Every extra penny was going on looking after his mother. Tom was sleeping at Radnor Park off and on: demanding, dependent, unemployed, sick, penniless – his head no doubt still full of fantasies. And a new worry gnawed at Peter: no-one else may have noticed, but young Owen was laid up more often, missing days and losing wages under Singer's uncompromising regime. Peter was aware of the fumes from the paint and varnish in the workshop. The situation at Radnor Park had been patched up, but it couldn't last.

On 27th June 1906, Peter made a last – desperate? – application to the Old Kirkpatrick Parish Board. Mary was now judged to be suffering from 'insanity', a dramatic decline from purely age-related weakness, in just five months. No symptoms are described, and it's unclear if this is a new condition, or a suggested diagnosis made by the family and accepted by the Inspector. The list of Mary's missing, migrated, destitute, or sick adult children was set out again, and for the first time Mary's first-born, Owen, is declared 'dead'. 'Patrick (Peter)' is still in Jamaica Street. Bessie, recorded as 'Elizabeth', is working as a cook, this time in Yorkshire. Either Peter misinformed the Inspector about her whereabouts, or Bessie misinformed him. Peter was clearly desperate to shed responsibility for his mother, Owen, and Tom. If any of them passed money along to Mary, it would be squandered on Tom's drinking habit. She wouldn't notice. Peter's actions were protective: of young Owen and of others. Let Bessie start her new life, free of all of them. Give Augustine a crack at freedom, let James find his foothold in Edinburgh. Seemingly, Peter spared them: who knows if the addresses were correct, or if they ever replied? The record confirms Tom as a bricklayer, but 'presently idle with mother'. The status quo was untenable.

The Quinns' dismal circumstances were defined by mental-health diagnoses which, despite the absence of a doctor's examination (none was carried out), still carried consequences. The verdict on Tom illustrates the systemic moral superiority towards those deemed improvident: he belonged to the undeserving poor. A doctor would quickly have seen that he was too ill to work and mentally unstable, with a tenuous hold on reality. However, help for the poor was attached to tightly knotted strings: unemployment alone was no qualification for help: only illness counted, its severity judged subjectively by administrators rather than medical experts. People like Tom must be starved into work, so as not to encourage others. If help under the Poor Law was granted, recipients were preferably sent away from the temptations of the city. Working family members must prove that their straightened circumstances exempted them from their duty to support ailing relatives. No wonder people changed their name or hid behind the vaguest addresses: Bessie Quinn, Keswick.

I take pity on Peter. The shame of thousands of Irish immigrant families forced to swallow the bitter medicine meted out by censorious Parochial Boards now visited his tribe. He carried the weight of the family's mortification, sometimes under suspicion or blamed by both officials and family, despite taking in a succession of people in need. A quiet, respectable life still eluded him. He had hollowed out his own means, depleted his energies, and reached the end of his tether. The

Quinn family was humiliated on public record, despite holding their lives together over decades of hard-fought independence.

Peter's defeat turned out to be his salvation. At a price. In the absence of anyone else to help her out, Mary Quinn's case was clear. Implausibly quickly, she was judged to have deteriorated from old and worn out to insane and unable to live alone. But as a Singer lodger on Second Avenue, Peter shared one room; and Mary could no longer live only with Owen. They had stumbled to the edge of a fast-eroding cliff. In accordance with the Poor Law's common option of 'outdoor relief', in the summer of 1906 Mary was boarded out. In that year, one-sixth of those classified 'insane' in Scotland were boarded out, mostly in rural districts, where 'removed from the bustle of everyday life, they could live a quiet, orderly life, with nothing to excite them'. She was placed nearly 100 miles away in Kirkcudbrightshire, a county now integrated into Dumfries and Galloway. Her host, Mrs Isabella Milne, was registered as keeper of a residence for Poor Law patients at a cost to the Parochial Board of seven shillings a week – cheap compared with the average charge of 12 shillings in an asylum.[74] Peter must have escorted her by train and cart (a long journey with several changes), to her internment in a place not of the family's choosing, the tiny remote village of Kirkpatrick Durham, a few miles from Castle Douglas. About 500 people live in the village today; it has shrunk since it flourished from the late 18th century as a new centre of the handloom weaving industry, attracting Irish settlers. In her youth, Mary would have had plenty of skills to offer in Kirkpatrick Durham. At 60, her fate was to live there until further notice, with no-one she knew. What, if any, medical treatment, pastoral care, or emotional support Mary received for her mental condition, or how she occupied her time, is not known. Precious little, probably, although she was kept well fed and probably had domestic duties. Whether Peter, Patrick-Peter, James, Augustine, young Owen, Arthur George, or Bessie visited her is a blank sheet. Who knew she was still alive? Mary Lyons Quinn was far from Clydebank, from Galashiels, from Nungate, from Girvan – and a long, remembered journey over land and sea from Sligo.

I had not expected to be writing that my great-grandmother, Mary Lyons, lived for years in a Poor Law institution, old and worn down, but mentally suffering perhaps from nothing more strange, or threatening to herself and others, than forgetfulness or the early onset of some kind of dementia, which didn't gallop, although it may gradually have taken a stronger grip than it had by 1906. That seems to be the truth of it. I hope Mrs Milne and her successor Jane Walker, an Irish-born Clydebank woman, ran a benign house, that Mary was not locked up, the 'mad woman in the attic'; that she had someone to talk to and a view of green fields and flowing water from her window. There's more to Mary's story, later.

25 Clydebank, Govan, and the Road to Nowhere 1904–1909: Poor Tom

Peter finally married Susanna Boyle, 'Susan', his fellow-worker at the Singer Factory, a few months after his mother's departure. Father Scannell, the priest who had taken up the cause of Peter's sister Mary with the Parochial Board, married them on 11th February 1907 at the first-ever Catholic church in Clydebank – Our Holy Redeemer – built in 1889. Peter was 31, Susan was 23. There is no sign of Bessie or any other Quinn at the wedding. Peter's friend James O'Rourke was his witness. It's fanciful to imagine Bessie would come up from England: her working life and the expense would have ruled it out. And Bessie's life had changed dramatically: she had her own plans on her mind.

By 1907 Susan was a skilled machinist, trialling finished sewing machines as they emerged from the Wood Department, and then promoted to a supervisory job. Susan's parents, John and Charlotte, were Irish-born agricultural workers, but the Boyles became a thoroughgoing Singer family, moving to Kilbowie by 1890, when her father became a night-watchman. By 1891, their eldest daughter started at Singer's, her brother was a nickel-plater, and her sisters were all to become French polishers. It's not hard to work out where Peter and Susan met.

Peter and Susan's married life began eventfully. They went to live at 7 Pattison Street in Dalmuir, a few yards from the railway station. Their tenement has gone, and a post-war block sits in its place between the remaining Victorian tenements: Number 7 may have been a casualty of the Clydebank blitz, along with other nearby tenements. One series of dilemmas had been resolved, for better or worse, but now Peter faced more challenges. His son James was born in May, three months after they set up house. After all the waiting, they still had good reason to be cautious. Before the baby was born, Tom appeared at Pattison Street and they took him in. His life had descended from chaotic to calamitous. He was homeless and sick. The pull towards Clydebank may have been half-unconscious, the habit of a son who'd always gone back to his mother for the comfort and refuge of unconditional welcome, or, as the authorities termed unemployment, 'to idle with her' in a warm nest. She was no longer there, and he was lost.

From Pattison Street, Thomas Quinn sought admission to the Dumbarton Combination Poorhouse for medical relief while suffering an acute TB episode. An old hand at Poor Law processes, Peter would have nudged him into applying. He had Susan and James as well as himself to protect. Before he turned up, Tom had spent a run of nights in the Govan Poorhouse, and the application to Dumbarton was approved. He was sent the short distance from Dalmuir by train on 11th April at the expense of the Parish, probably in pain and distress. But treatments that Poorhouse patients received had little effect. They were more likely to make things worse. The records show that Tom would have shared sleeping quarters with several others, although the minutes of Poor Board meetings the same year acknowledge that big dormitories spread the disease faster. The Board confirmed their intention to provide phthisis patients with separate rooms, but they were in no hurry to take the steps that would improve the survival chances of people in their care. Once Tom survived his immediate health crisis, perhaps he worked in the gardens, one of the activities that kept inmates productive and in fresh air, before he was discharged.[75]

Figure 33: Dumbarton Combination Poorhouse, Townend Road (image 1966)

Tom's spell in the Dumbarton Poorhouse was a brief respite from his prolonged descent into homelessness, destitution, disease, and confusion. Soon homeless again, on 10th October 1907 he struggled to describe his recent movements to the Inspector or to remember where he'd spent recent nights. It seems Tom's main solace and rapid undoing was alcohol and, always likely to latch on to the latest trends, cigarettes. Smoking was growing ever more popular and, unknown to Tom, aggravating his impending fate. At this point there was another claim pending on Old Kilpatrick from the Govan Poorhouse for Thomas Quinn – so he must have been re-admitted there meanwhile. He had been in 'his present house', Peter's place, for just one night. And over the previous three months, he'd been in and out of the 'Clydebank Model', which means he'd sporadically had work and enough money for a bed.

Model Lodging Houses were two notches up from the Poorhouse, one up from common lodging houses, which offered a refuge for working people as well as the unemployed homeless. 'Models' were created to provide cheap accommodation for casual and day labourers and those migrating between jobs and cities without a bed for the night. Patrick McGill's *Children of the Dead End*, which first appeared in 1914, describes navvies' spells of living in the 'Model'. McGill, a Donegal man known as the 'Navvy Poet', knew all about them first-hand. Models provided dormitory beds for single labouring men. There were also Models for women: street sex workers, labourers, and street-sellers were among those who used them. Similar accommodation was provided by charities, including the Salvation Army. In 1916, Beardmore's opened the Benbow Hotel in Dalmuir for casual dockyard labourers without local homes. Entry to the Model was on a first-come, first-served basis. They were usually overcrowded and unhygienic, though the Salvation Army tried to raise standards in Clydebank when they arrived in 1893 in the hope of tackling disease and addiction as well as homelessness. Their hall still exists, near the Co-operative store in the centre of town. Those workers who could not afford the Model or were turned away lived in tents around the Clydebank area: partly to avoid a means test and protect the small wages they earned from apprenticeships or low-paid work, and partly because the Model was often full.[76]

In October 1907, Old Kilpatrick Parish's plan for Tom changed again. He was to be boarded out 'in the country', like Arthur George and his mother. The move was routine practice, designed to improve health as well as to remove young men from the moral dangers of Glasgow life: drink, rough-sleeping, women, and 'idling'. Perhaps the decision to send him away worked out for a time. But Tom was a restless soul and hard to contain. By autumn 1909, as nights grew cold, the dyed-in-the-wool city boy was back in the Dumbarton Poorhouse – filthy, exhausted, and desperately ill. On 8th November 1909, as night fell, he died there of 'Phthisis Pulmonalis'. There is no record of how long he'd been suffering, and nobody there who could testify: McCullom, Governor of the Poorhouse, who informed the authorities, would not have known. It would have been years, not months, although he'd been declared healthy enough for army service in 1898. For once, Tom's brother Peter was absent at a family member's death. Perhaps he didn't know where Tom was, or he'd given up on his wayward brother.

Perhaps Tom didn't want them to fetch Peter, if it was allowed, or he was too fevered to summon his wits. I doubt Peter organised Thomas's burial: he could scarcely afford it. His family life had taken root and he now had two children to raise. He could have been counting his luck, watching his own health, and clutching the bit of happiness he'd retrieved from his family's collapse. Without Peter's help, Tom will have been buried in a pauper's grave.

Peter, Susan, and the last Owen Quinn

Thomas was not the only Quinn whom Peter and Susan looked after when they first married. When his nephew Owen left school, Peter had helped to find him an apprenticeship in the Singer's paint shop and in 1906 took him in at Kilbowie Street after his grandmother Mary left Radnor Park, leaving him homeless. Owen moved in with Peter and Susan when they married, but his health, too, deteriorated. Episodes of TB intensified and he grew weaker. With Owen, 'Phthisis Pulmonalis', which had killed so many of the Quinn and Lyons families, continued into a third generation. Owen died at 7 Pattison Street on 1st December 1907; the only deathbed visitor was probably Father Scannell. Owen was 18. Peter's presence at the death of his siblings – and now his nephew – was a grim ritual: a brother-priest with a litany of comfort, followed by the official duties. Besides grief and resignation, the toll of death and dementia and the disappearance of Bessie must have left Peter anxious. He'd have understood the causes of TB by then. The facts of the bacillus were widely known, and he'd have learned enough from doctors, newspapers, information circulated by Singer's, and health reformers' anti-spitting campaigns.

When Peter signed Owen's death certificate, he confirmed that his nephew's mother, Alice Butler, and his father Owen Quinn, a 'general labourer', were both dead. Was Peter so sure about the fate of his brother Owen, the dead boy's father? Or did he simply believe he'd died – not in Scotland or England, as far as records go (unless he changed his name), but in America or another continent. Dead or alive, the oldest Quinn brother was long lost to his family in Scotland, oblivious to the blight that had now killed the baby he'd left with his mother nearly twenty years earlier. Another thought: which of the 'Owen Quinns' – the dead boy's father or grandfather – was Peter actually referring to when he recorded 'Owen' as dead, under the 'Father' column on the 18-year-old's death certificate? His grandparents Mary and Owen had been his only parents since babyhood. And Owen's father, Peter's brother, was not a 'general labourer', as Peter wrote on the death certificate. Unlike his grandfather Owen, the young man's disappeared father was a railway plate-layer and mason. He was still 'missing', perhaps still alive.

Regrets must sometimes have engulfed Peter in those years, like a fast-moving sea-squall darkening a sunny day. They would have caught him unawares, polishing-cloth in hand in Singer's wood workshop – as if his dilemmas had been hibernating and woken up with a start. His stomach may have turned when he thought of the two mentally afflicted ones, exiled by the Poor Law. He might repeatedly have relived what happened, but it was cold comfort that there was nothing different he could have done, that he could not have known in advance what the Poor Board would decide, and that he was powerless to change anything now. Susan may have urged him to put the past behind him, or offered to accompany him to visit his mother or Arthur George. Perhaps they did. What is certain is that Peter would always have known their whereabouts: he was the applicant, and the Parochial

Board kept tabs on cases until they no longer paid out and the file was closed. That was not yet the case.

Two generations on from his grandparents' arrival in Scotland, the images of the youngest Owen's short life create a distorted reflection of the whole family's history – so much of which was shared with other working-class Irish Catholic communities. His grandparents' hopeless outlook as malnourished young people in Ireland and their inevitable emigration were followed by years of relative stability in Galashiels, as they built a life and survived – at times even thrived – in a close-knit community. For families like theirs, it was a matter of pride that all their children grew to adulthood and that the family had held together through periods of acute adversity. It had taken immense effort to make decisions, resist victimhood, and shape their lives, innocent of the price to be exacted. They were still unaware of it when they began to be buffeted by misfortune and breakouts of the hidden diseases that lurked invisibly around them.

When Mary and Owen's family succumbed to acute pressure at the end of a long economic depression and fell into deeper poverty, they still tried to hold on, clutching at loose strands blowing away on the wind. As for millions of Scottish and Irish miners, factory workers, shipyard labourers, and farm workers, ill health ultimately determined the extent of their downfall. The sickness that befell them was bewildering: they couldn't know how it began, or that it was aggravated by the hazards inherent in their successful survival: by the inhalation of deadly fibres and living and working conditions which laid their bodies bare to attack. If they had understood, they could still have done nothing about it.

Did they experience their living conditions in good times as 'cramped', 'unsanitary', 'squalid', or slums, to use a few terms used by liberal social superiors from the mid-century onwards, and by some historians to this day? Or was it simply their home, how people like them lived? They were oblivious to the perils of sleeping together in small spaces, their breath, saliva, catarrh, and phlegm mingling every night of their childhood years as they huddled and snuffled, packed tight for warmth in shared beds. Those conditions were normal, their dangers seen only in hindsight. The mills offered regular wages but sealed a Faustian pact with powerless people. A price was exacted from those with no choice but to live in factory housing, and work on until they were fighting for breath, their bodies shaken by pain and exhaustion. TB consigned its victims to horrible, untimely deaths. The way of life which gave them food, shelter, stability, and hope also caused their demise. Doctors were unaffordable until, occasionally, close to the end, or to confirm death. They could only prescribe the impossible: rest, fresh air, and time off work. The youngest Owen had avoided the hazards of the woollen mill, only to be exposed to toxic paint-fumes and lead-white. TB destroyed him on the cusp of adulthood, just as it had struck Peter Lyons in Nungate in 1868, nearly forty years earlier.

Apart from Owen, the eldest of the Quinn siblings, only Bessie dared to follow a track across the border into an unknown country. Scarred by loss, she would try to outwit the fate of women like her: an early grave via overwork, exhaustion, and sickness, or a longer life dependent on family and the Poor Law. This intelligent drudge was about to find out where a different track would lead her.

PART THREE

somewhere I have never travelled, gladly beyond
any experience, your eyes have their silence:
in your most frail gesture are things which enclose me

e e cummings
(from 'somewhere i have never travelled', in *ViVa,* 1931; reissued by Liveright, 1997)

26 Cumberland
1904: A New Life

Bessie left Clydebank in January 1904. She made a beeline for Keswick. Perhaps she'd been tipped off about available work there, but perhaps it was more than that. Legend had it that John Ruskin had passed through Galashiels more than once and flattered the Borders people with his talk of 'The Singing Country'. In any event, John Ruskin was famous, not least in Scotland. Bessie might have discovered him in the church or town library. If so, she would know that Ruskin's creative genius was alive and well in Cumberland. Before he died in 1900 at Brantwood, overlooking Coniston Water, new schemes had been launched in Ruskin's name in Keswick. Unemployed men were learning to make useful, beautiful objects: jugs, vases, trays, and kettles from beaten copper. Unemployed women were being taught ornamental embroidery and how to edge linen objects with his 'Greek' lace patterns. Bessie headed for England to earn her keep and help Peter, but chose a place where she might also seek out craftspeople.

Bessie and Peter would have been practical about her departure. He must have given her money – who else could have provided the train ticket and money to survive while she found her feet? In the tableaux I'm visualising, she said her goodbyes to the Clydebank family. She picked up Arthur George for the last time, folded her arms round his heavy frame, her cheek against his, and glanced at his puzzled face. I can't imagine she brought herself to explain her departure, but, like a cat, the boy must have sensed disturbance and loss. She kissed her mother's forehead, hugged her sister and nephew Owen, and gripped her calico bag. Peter closed the door behind them, and they walked down the tenement stairs and along the canal bank towards Clydebank Station. Peter promised Bessie her paid-up sewing machine once she settled, and handed her a purse with coins to last her a week. He fished out of his pocket a small brown-paper parcel, tied up with sewing-machine silks, handing it to her as the train left. Inside she found a muffler and gloves: dark brown, serviceable, indestructible: Peter, through and through. Not what she aspired to wear in her daydreams, but her hands were frozen and the gloves fitted. She unpicked the label from the Clydebank Co-operative Store. Bessie blinked away tears and slid the folded paper and thread into her pocket. She stepped down at Charing Cross in Glasgow, wove through morning crowds to Central Station, and caught the Carlisle train, squeezing herself into a few inches of slatted bench, craning her neck to see Lanarkshire's factories give way to rolling green fields, then bare rounded hills and streams. She'd no book for company. She clutched her bag close, opening it only to unwrap her plum-jam piece. A few hours later, she boarded a train to Penrith and then a local train on to Keswick. Her body ached from sitting still, and her high spirits evaporated. She wasn't much afraid, but guilt rushed in: she'd fled, abandoned Arthur George. She tried to rally: she was sure to be back anyway and she should make the most of this adventure. She owed her new beginning to Peter, and she'd try to succeed. When she saw him again, perhaps he'd have a place to call home. He was nearly 30, and she believed Susan offered him a good life. The Singer Company too, though they were so hard-nosed it was as easy as shattering glass on a stone floor to fall foul of them. She couldn't see an end to his troubles yet. The Quinns' misfortunes had ground him down, made him irritable and impatient. Bessie underestimated her brother. And herself.

From Keswick Station, Bessie would have walked to the middle of town. I see her sitting on her bag beside the River Greta, exhausted, cold, and hungry. Across the river, nestling among a row of cottages, she'd have spotted one which she might have heard of: 'Porch Cottage'. When she saw bundles of flax lying out beside the river, she knew she was in hand-spinning, linen country. Her mother's ancestors' way of surviving. Flax and hemp were traditionally retted: soaked in still or slow-moving water to remove cellulose, the stems scutched to remove straw and woody parts. Within an hour of arriving in Keswick, Bessie could have found what she'd come for. If she could first find work, any work, she could learn how to make clothes to sell.[77]

At some point Bessie summoned up the courage to meet the people behind the new Keswick Linen Industry. She'd discover that it began in 1883, making lace which realised John Ruskin's ideas and teachings. His friend Albert Fleming first put them into practice, reviving old spinning and weaving techniques in the Lake District and establishing lace-making, using patterns that Ruskin had found in Italian churches.

Their purpose was to help unemployed people to find useful, sustainable, creative work. Marion Twelves, a teacher and housekeeper to Albert Fleming, migrated north from Hertfordshire with him to establish the first Ruskin workshop on Elterwater, near Skelwith Bridge in the Langdale Valley. She learned to scutch and ret flax to prepare it for spinning into linen yarn, and to use the spinning wheel, passing her knowledge on to women in need of a new source of livelihood. The spinning wheels were made by local carpenters, and the spinners, once they were proficient, took wheels home, spun yarn, and were paid for the work they sold. Weaving initiatives followed, and by 1884 the Elterwater workshop was flourishing, led first by Marion Twelves and later by local working-class women who became highly skilled spinners, weavers, and needlewomen. Marion Twelves also transformed Ruskin's ideas for lace making into a practical technique, first known as 'Greek Lace'; then, once Ruskin had given his blessing, re-named Ruskin Lace and successfully marketed.

Figure 34: Marion Twelves, at her spinning wheel, Porch Cottage, Keswick

In 1889, Marion Twelves left her assistant, a local working woman, to take over the running of Elterwater. Elizabeth Pepper's skills were outstanding and eventually led to an invitation from Queen Alexandra to teach her to spin at Sandringham. Marion Twelves moved to Keswick to join the Keswick School of Industrial Arts (KSIA) and work with Edith Rawnsley, wife of Hardwicke Rawnsley, a social activist and Vicar of Crosthwaite Church. She set up shop in an old woollen mill, later moving to Porch Cottage, adding 'Ruskin Cottage', next door. Twelves was undeviating in her purist adherence to Ruskinian principles, delighted that he had officially granted permission for the Ruskin name to be used in her workshops. He even visited Porch Cottage with his close friend James Reddie Anderson, a Glasgow lawyer and poet, who lived near Crosthwaite Vicarage with his wife Emilie, whose cousin Sarah was secretary to John Ruskin. Marion Twelves was at the heart of this circle of creative, socially engaged activists. Hardwicke and Edith Rawnsley had set up the KSIA in 1884 in the middle of a worldwide depression which lasted from 1873 until the mid-1890s, the same crisis that hit the Galashiels woollen industry. But in Britain farming was hit hardest of all, not least in rural Cumberland. Poverty and hardship among unemployed agricultural workers and their families was caused by cheap imported food, and low grain prices accelerated the growing exodus to towns and cities. Mechanisation was fast reducing demand for agricultural labour. Cumberland farm workers were particularly hard hit because the small size of farms, and the large number of smallholdings with tiny numbers of employees, made it difficult to join the agricultural labourers' unions formed in the 1870s and resurgent again from the 1890s, or participate in their action.

Keswick had long been associated with poets, painters, countryside explorers, ramblers, and trippers from industrial towns. But the Keswick that Bessie experienced in the winter of 1904 was a small, grey, rain-sodden town on the northern shore of Derwentwater only slowly recovering from the depression. It was surrounded by subsistence farms grazing sheep on the hillsides. Local mines fed local manufacturing, but every type of trade and business had been affected by the slump. Rough woollen goods and edge tools were manufactured in Keswick, and Banks's factory made six million lead pencils a year.

The lead came from local mines where graphite, copper, and slate were dug out of the mountainside. For most working people in Keswick and surrounding villages or on the land, the romantic associations of the Lake District with Wordsworth, Coleridge, and Southey, and the stream of artists and wealthy beauty-searching travellers, were as far from their lives as the stars on a clear night. Rich and poor intersected only in places where travellers met local hosts: people who owned or worked in hostels, inns, hotels, grand houses, middle-class villas, refreshment rooms, libraries, and shops; on railways, carts, carriages, and boats; and at church events. In their own time, working people fended for themselves, with their own organisations: pubs, clubs, Friendly Societies, night schools, chapels, churches, and temperance organisations.

The KSIA was trying to build bridges between these separate worlds. The initiatives of the Arts and Crafts movement, including the KSIA, were partly social and economic, partly aesthetic, spiritual, and health-related. Their impulse was to create new kinds of work without the gross inequalities and excessive de-skilling of the new worlds of industry and urbanisation, and to foster simplicity: the chance to earn a livelihood close to nature, plying a useful skill. The movement saw itself promoting modernity, but through the revival of ancient crafts, invigorated by innovative designs which combined practicality with beauty. In Keswick, evening classes for unemployed adults were offered in woodwork and metalwork, including making jewellery, later extending to textiles to attract more rural women. The Rawnsleys' aims at the KSIA differed from those of Marion Twelves, for whom Ruskin's ideas, rooted in traditional methods, came first. Benefits to people would follow from adhering to Ruskinian ideals. And for many of the women she worked with so exactingly, benefits did come. For Edith and Hardwicke Rawnsley's enterprise, the primary purpose was to help unemployed people out of poverty by learning to make objects they could sell – starting with Ruskin's ideas, but embracing the ideas of followers. William Morris, his fellow thinker-activists, and makers of Arts and Crafts designed buildings, furniture, wallpaper, tapestries, utensils, and much more, inspiring the KSIA. They were admired for their pursuit of social reform through agitation as well as art, for the social innovation of making objects which were both beautiful and useful, and for opening the countryside to everyone. The Rawnsleys sought reform with searing intensity: bringing together moral awareness and social action to create a better world.

Figure 35: Canon Hardwicke Rawnsley in 1907, the year he conducted Bessie and Cecil's wedding at Crosthwaite Church, Keswick

Figure 36: Edith Rawnsley, artist and co-founder, KSIA

Ruskin was the seer, the originator, and guide on which associated movements were based. He was also autocratic. William Morris blended a Ruskinian vision with democratic political beliefs in practice: art, poetry, making things and encouraging others to make things: the Rawnsleys, Marion Twelves, and a host of artists and designers, including Walter Crane; Edmund and Dorothea Hunter; Godfrey Blount and the Peasant Arts Society; and the Yeats sisters. For all of them, it was making things that changed lives. Morris's followers did not all share his socialism, but they were fellow radicals in their rejection of industrial capitalist values. They sought a just society with thriving creative communities which brought nature, countryside, and traditional skills into a fast-urbanising nation. Blending work with pleasure was the key to art and a fulfilled life.[78]

Within ten years, more than 100 men and many local women were attending classes in Crosthwaite. KSIA work was exhibited nationally, winning prizes for copperware and decorative silver metalwork. The popularity of the products enabled the Rawnsleys to raise money for a new headquarters, which opened in 1894. Walter Crane, Holman Hunt, and G. F. Watts were among their artist supporters. During the 1890s, the town became celebrated as a centre for arts and crafts, led by women as much as men.

Edith Rawnsley's character was more reserved than Hardwicke's, but she was a dedicated activist, still vigorous and beautiful. They lived out their dreams for others, walking long distances through the Lakes, as well as undertaking adventurous journeys *à deux* across Europe, Egypt, and America. Edith was a talented water-colourist, and her art can still be seen in Keswick's museum and on designs for KSIA metalwork. Hardwicke was a parson, poet, and social reformer who fought a very public campaign for the restoration and extension of public footbaths in the Lake District countryside, unafraid to trespass across privately owned land. His reforming spirit also had a conservationist, conservative side. He joined Ruskin in opposing the extension of the railways through Cumberland, which he feared would despoil the countryside, in particular the Newlands Valley, along which a new line was planned to carry away slate from the Honister mines. It would have seemed strange to Bessie Quinn that they wanted people like her and her brothers, who went everywhere by train and worked on the railways, to benefit from fresh air and exercise, yet abhorred the idea of railways to bring them there: how else would they come? Unlike Rawnsley, who fought and won his battle for public footpaths, Ruskin stayed aloof from the reality of working people roaming the fells – 'I don't want to let them see Helvellyn while they're drunk' – or coming too close at all, even the ones realising his vision. Bessie no doubt had the measure of the gulf between the classes. Yet these contradictions propelled Rawnsley into action, and in 1895, again influenced by Ruskin, he founded the National Trust with two like-minded social reformers, Octavia Hill and Robert Hunter.[79]

The wider goals of movements that the Rawnsleys and their associates espoused from the 1880s acted as a magnet for women. Some who learned new, liberating skills in the KSIA became suffragists and suffragettes, or joined campaigns to sweep away repressive Victorian values which had blocked their paths into the public world. A series of Acts were passed which began to change women's status and rights. In 1884, married women could own their own property for the first time (Married Women's Property Act); a series of divorce-law reforms began in 1857, and the Contagious Diseases Act was repealed in 1888. These Acts were passed after campaigns led by women who withstood sustained, ferocious opposition. From the 1870s women attended extra-mural lectures and degree courses and took degree examinations in subjects including medicine – like Ellen Brook's sister – but were not allowed to graduate formally until 1920.[80] They could be elected to local School Boards and campaign to choose when to have children. Freedoms that women sought included joining organisations like the KSIA, taking office jobs, opening a bank account; and recreations like cycling or hiking through the countryside with groups of strangers. By 1904 these changes were there for Bessie to observe or take part in.

Bessie's life was steeped in textile making. Professional experts told me that the three surviving children's smocks – and photos of others – made by Bessie strongly suggest the Ruskinian method. In Keswick, that meant the KSIA or Porch Cottage.[81] Her surviving work achieves what Ruskin called 'the beautiful imperfection' of hand-spinning. Her inheritance was spinning and weaving wool and linen: she'd learned sewing from her mother, and weaving at the mill. At Porch Cottage she could add entirely new skills. The importance of the Borders in the Scottish woollen industry would not have been lost on Marion Twelves. She would have taught Bessie more, and entrusted her with pieces of cloth to embellish, Greek lace borders on linen, drawn-thread work and embroidery in the distinctive Ruskinian decorative style, which workshop women sold to help earn a livelihood. It's likely that Bessie became one of Marion Twelves's 'outworkers'. Untouched by the depression, wealthy customers from across the country had money to spend on beautiful things.

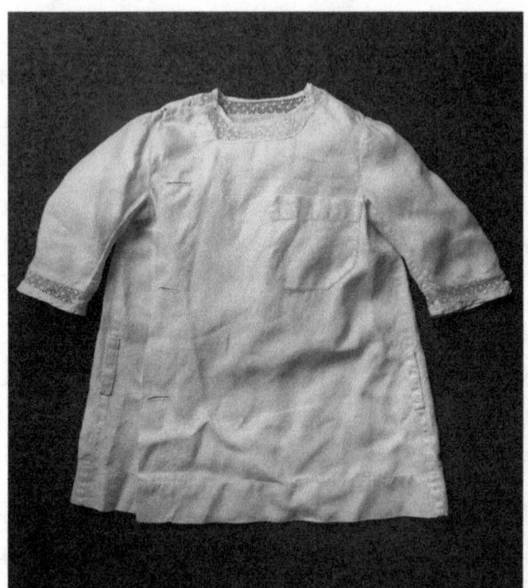

Figure 37: One of Bessie's Ruskinian-lace edged linen smocks; others, modeled by her sons

By the time Bessie arrived in Keswick, Marion Twelves' Ruskin Linen Industry had broken its alliance with the Rawnsleys' KSIA and become part of the 'Guild of St George' which Ruskin had founded in 1871 to realise the potential of workmen and labourers. For Marion Twelves, honing individuals' craft skills to the height of Ruskinian perfection remained the be-all and end-all, causing continued tension with the Rawnsleys' ambition to alleviate poverty and engage more people, even at the expense of Ruskinian standards. Twelves's textiles created a sensation. Yet she could compromise, bringing in many unemployed women, not all of whom reached the standards of Elizabeth Pepper, mother of five and wife of a slate-worker, who'd become the manager at Elterwater. Bessie would have fitted in well. She knew about unemployment and poverty. The KSIA went on teaching crafts at any level, Edith Rawnsley managing the textile side. Both organisations made household goods and personal articles – clothing, tablecloths, and domestic linen. Demand continued to outstrip supply.

Bessie would have picked up letters from the Post Office, and from April 1904 at the latest, she'd have replied, as a requirement of the Parish Board. It would have been clear to Bessie by then that Peter was addressing deepening troubles, and that there was a lot he hadn't told her before she left. The linen workshops offered a future way of earning money to send home, but that would take time, and there were outgoings to meet now. Outworkers paid towards the cost of materials in the Ruskin Linen Industry, though expenses over and above 5 shillings (25p) were met by the Ruskinian Guild of St George. It would be impossible to make a living from sales of work as a single woman: although most trainees were unemployed, many were labourers' wives with other sources of family income.

Bessie had to find work in Keswick before Peter's purse was empty. But Keswick was her lucky place. She must have found a cheap, out-of-season room in a lodging house, because by June 1904 she's on record working as a cook. This could have been in the kitchen of a refreshment room, hotel, or private house. There were tourist lodgings on every corner: the Skiddaw Temperance Hotel on Main Street, grand lakeside hotels, and smaller lodging houses like Greenhow's Hotel. An alternative was domestic service, even with Edith Rawnsley or her neighbour Emilie Reddie Anderson. If either were prospective employers, Bessie could impress as a cook, maker and mender of clothes, and cleaner. The Rawnsleys' network was an unusually strong and like-minded set of liberally inclined people, likely to have found Bessie's skills and demeanour attractive. She could have fitted in Porch Cottage on days or evenings off. Her association with Porch Cottage would have attracted them further. Bessie met the philanthropic mood to help young women to better themselves. She had the makings of 'a project', adding to a long history of well-disposed middle-class people taking up and promoting working-class individuals judged as exceptional, often dropping them back into obscurity and poverty as quickly as they'd been adopted. Robert Burns and John Clare are famous examples.

27 Keswick
1904–1906: Significant Strangers

The Rawnsleys may have been kindness personified but still have seemed intimidating to their protégées, including Bessie. Born in 1845, Edith Rawnsley was almost the same age as Bessie's mother, but the difference in their physical appearance alone must have been shocking. The smooth-skinned, radiant 59-year-old, her thick hair piled up on her head, had been spared the ravages that child rearing, grinding hard work, and poverty had wreaked on Mary Quinn's face, body, and mind. Edith had energy to match the determination to do her best by those she felt responsible for. That much she and Mary had in common as fellow human beings.

Nineteenth-century life was not only stratified along social-class lines but segregated too. Before she arrived in Keswick, Bessie had rarely if ever talked with a middle-class person, apart from priests, factory managers, school teachers, library volunteers, and possibly the occasional doctor. In Keswick, apart from customers for worked linen, Marion Twelves, the Rawnsleys, and their circle were the first middle-class English people she'd ever have related to with any degree of mutuality. One or more of these strangers became acquaintances, helping Bessie to develop the confidence to keep her life moving forward. What Edith gleaned from Bessie when they first met may have been enough to want to encourage her into the KSIA fold. Bessie may not have disclosed much, but appeared exotically attractive compared with local working girls: equally poor, but poised and independent, with a musical Scottish voice. It seems the Rawnsleys and their networks helped Bessie to carve out her future.

'Sponsors', 'significant others', 'transformational figures' are among the terms social historians have used to explore ways in which changes in life chances came about for working-class people, both women and men, in the 19th and early 20th centuries. In a world where millions dreamed of a better world, actually bringing it about required rare luck as well as determined action, often in the teeth of family opposition, Often it took the form of a chance meeting with a complete stranger, or a conversation with a political ally or trade-union activist, Sunday

School or literacy teacher, or benefactor whose belief in you nurtured self-belief. Sometimes negative encounters and relationships fuelled the fire to prove yourself against all odds. Some felt compelled to fight for greater justice beyond the self, on behalf of 'people like us'. Motivations varied, but change was invariably a social as well as individual process. Somebody turned up at a critical point, and a spark was ignited by a favourable wind.[82]

Bessie was no exception. In Keswick, she tapped a rich seam of initiatives for working-class people leading comparable lives – one difference being her Irish–Scottish outsider status. A crucial agent of change for Bessie was Thomas Arthur (T.A.) Leonard, Hardwicke Rawnsley's fellow reformer and friend. Leonard was a Congregationalist minister in Nelson and Colne when he founded the Co-operative Holiday Association (CHA) in the 1890s. His mission was to provide holidays for children and young workers from industrial towns in Lancashire and Yorkshire who'd never experienced fresh country air, the physical and spiritual benefits of which were a growing obsession among those dedicated to replacing the horrors of city slums with healthier places to live, work, and play.

Figure 38: T.A Leonard, founder of the Co-operative Holiday Association

When Bessie arrived in Keswick, the CHA, together with the National Home Reading Union (NHRU), already ran outdoor holiday bases in Keswick, in a group of houses in Stanger Street and at Greenhow's Hotel on Main Street. Rawnsley, a shareholder in Leonard's enterprise, regularly hosted the CHA's holiday parties at Crosthwaite, with lectures on Wordsworth, Ruskin, Coleridge, and others. Early in 1904, Leonard –'TA' to his associates – was planning a radical addition to his holiday schemes. Near the village of Stair in the Newlands Valley, south-west of Crosthwaite towards Borrowdale, he had discovered an ideal location for a new Co-operative 'guest house'. This was a disused and dilapidated woollen mill beside a beck, most recently used to prepare lead for the pencil industry. When Leonard visited the site with CHA committee members and hoped-for supporters, it was a wet, dark day, and most of them were emphatically against buying this ruin. Leonard's stubborn persistence won the day, and on 3rd June 1904 he bought the lease for £1,270 from Hogarth, the owner, and then acquired the mill cottages behind it from Mary Vickers, then owner of the Keswick pencil factory. 'TA' was typically confident he could carry out all the repairs and adaptations needed and set up the Newlands Guest House as a Co-operative holiday centre the following year. The Co-operative Union in Manchester had already drafted the rules and regulations for the centre, which was to provide walking holidays for workers and single people who were willing and able to take strenuous hikes up and down Blencathra, Skiddaw, and Catbells, or walk the wooded pathways round Derwentwater. They would eat, drink, sing, and bathe in the river and its pools – both sexes together, in the modern way. If the plan came off, there would be work at Newlands too for skilled labourers and domestic staff, who would automatically be members of the association.[83]

At some point in her first Keswick year, Bessie became aware of this scheme. Weeks after she arrived in Keswick and some months before T. A. Leonard arrived, another figure in the network of reformers visited the town. In March 1904, Hardwicke Rawnsley invited Ebenezer Howard to speak at a public meeting in Crosthwaite Parish Rooms. He was to lecture about his Garden City ideas and report on progress towards building a healthy, harmonious new community on green fields at Letchworth, Hertfordshire. Howard was a strong supporter of the National Trust and also the KSIA, in which the artist Walter Crane had interested him. Crafts were to be central to life and work in Letchworth and Welwyn Garden City. Rawnsley and Howard knew each other well as social campaigners motivated to alleviate the miserable state of city housing, especially in London. Both had strong connections to Toynbee Hall, founded by another radical vicar, Canon Samuel Barnett, and the energetic Henrietta Barnett, who had also started a holiday scheme for slum-dwelling city children. They shared core beliefs: healthier, less class-divided communities for millions of people living in disease-ridden crowded housing, where working hours were long, jobs were precarious, and holidays unknown. Even with the arrival of railways, the majority of town and city dwellers were shut out from the natural world for lack of time and money. Reformers did not all see eye to eye about opening up the countryside, but Howard regarded railways as essential to the success of a community built in the country.

Figure 39: Ebenezer Howard in his fifties, the time of his Keswick Lecture

Hardwicke and Edith Rawnsley undoubtedly read Howard's *Tomorrow – A Peaceful Path to Real Reform* when it was published in 1898. It was the blueprint for realising his long-held dream to banish the horrors of slum living by creating an environment which brought together the best features of town and country. His big idea and its visualisation, *The Three Magnets*, quickly caught on. The money was raised in less than five years and building work began at Letchworth. Homes, workplaces, social and outdoor facilities were laid out in walking distance of each other, and a railway halt was in place as the first inhabitants arrived.

How did Howard do it? In terms of social standing, Rawnsley and his fellow campaigners lived in a different world from him. Ebenezer Howard had little schooling and hardly a penny to his name beyond what he earned as a shorthand writer. To his well-heeled, influential supporters, most of them associates from Oxbridge days, he was the 'humble man', a London pastry-cook's son and cranky inventor. But Howard's dream gave shape to their ambitions. What is more, he was an intriguing character, always on the road promoting his ideas, drawing on lessons learned from youthful years in Chicago, knowledgeable about land reform in theory and practice. He worked non-stop, not only to raise money from lectures to promote Garden Cities, but to put enough food on the table of his long-suffering family, teaching evening classes for the Co-operative Union on top of his day job as a parliamentary stenographer with Hansard. Howard's frail but determined wife Lizzie – his active partner in the Garden City movement and a very effective fund-raiser – had to raise her four children on scant rations.

'Ben', as everyone called Ebenezer Howard, was a cheerful, generous man, driven by his dream, making light of setbacks and conflicts. Although sharp-tongued commentators, including socialist supporters and financial backers like H. G. Wells and George Bernard Shaw, talked publicly about this 'simple' man, rather dull as a conversationalist, they remained his friends. As long as they put up money and found other donors, what did their comments matter? He had other abilities which justified his confident expectation of success. When he climbed on to a stage and began to speak, audiences witnessed his metamorphosis into a mesmerising and irresistibly persuasive speaker, pale blue eyes barely blinking. His reputation grew among liberal politicians, Fabians, the London literati, and the charitably minded, including philanthropic aristocrats. Above all he was supported by socialists – especially the Independent Labour Party (ILP), to which he belonged, and by pacifists and internationalists who sought peace through co-operation and mutual understanding. His Garden City idea caught on. Young architects and artists, especially within the Arts and Crafts movement, made their names on projects he had inspired. Plans for smaller settlements around the country – and abroad – were on the drawing board.

Ebenezer Howard's talk that March evening in Keswick was reported in the local paper and kindled enthusiasm for a Garden Village in Keswick. The town had a serious housing problem, too many back-to-back slum dwellings with such bad ventilation that medical officers had been raising alarm for twenty years, so his ideas fell on fertile ground. Land above Stanger Street was identified for the Garden Village scheme, near the spot where Porch Cottage women washed and dried linen on the Greta River. It was to be co-operatively owned and run. The prime movers were Mr Crossley, the Secretary of the Co-partnership Tenants Housing Association, and Anthony Wilson of Braithwaite. Six years later, Greta Hamlet was complete, with communal green space and allotments which still remain, as do some co-operative principles attaching to ownership.[84]

It is likely that Bessie attended Ebenezer Howard's talk: she met him somewhere, some time, in Keswick before 1905, or I doubt I'd have this history to write. Bessie may have been encouraged to attend, with some of the KSIA women. Liberating women from drudgery through co-operative, shared domestic facilities was central to Howard's ideas of Garden City life. It's possible of course that Bessie was cooking for Edith: it was her reported occupation. If she met Ebenezer at the Vicarage later that evening, she could have answered questions about life in Glasgow tenements, Edinburgh back-to-backs, and the cottages with allotments beside the Galashiels woollen-mills. Ebenezer Howard gave talks in Scotland in these years, he knew what to ask, and Bessie had the knowledge. When he left Crosthwaite that night, he'd have walked across town to stay with his cousin Catherine

Howard, travelling back to London in the morning in time for a lecture that evening.

Among Bessie's new acquaintances, the talk was always about the need for change. In the life she'd left behind, change was unwanted, generally for the worse, causing distress and dividing people. Other words she'd have overheard now were reform, progress, alleviating poverty, public health, hygiene, the curse of city life, outdoor pursuits for all, better wages. For all their statistics, social research, home visits, and pitying phrases – poor diet; overcrowding; cramped insanitary dwellings; unhealthy living conditions; rough manners; oversized families; simple people; the masses; moral danger – most reformers had little idea of, or interest in, how people like the Quinns saw themselves, the daily choices they faced, their agency or lack of it. Working-class people, the poor, were the subjects of constant investigations conducted by middle-class observers like Henry Mayhew, and Maud Pember Reeves. Among them, M. E. Loane, a Portsmouth district nurse turned forensic chronicler, came closest to reality by attentively watching and listening. Perceptive acceptance emanates from her books, despite some judgemental language.[85]

In her interactions with the Keswick circle, Bessie must have put bemusemenet and annoyance at sweeping assumptions and lofty attitudes to the back of her mind, straightened her apron and kept her head down. She had never been more alone, although she'd have seen that Ebenezer Howard was different and had more than an inkling of the complicated, compromising realities of life in poverty. She must have been homesick and felt her exile status; but also relieved and exhilarated, tasting the strangeness and freedom of solitude. It seems she hadn't the slightest desire to go home.

The energy for change at the turn of the 19th and 20th centuries marked a moment in history when the promise of a new life, even for all, seemed possible, and not only to middle-class social reformers. Working-class people were acting for themselves in unprecedented numbers, in new ways – as Bessie knew from women in the Keswick workshops and the Clydeside shipyards and factories where her brothers had worked. New trade unions, general unions for unskilled as well as skilled labourers, recruited millions of workers. Training for office work opened up jobs to women clerks as typewriters replaced pen and ink, offering alternatives to domestic service or factory work. Working women joined the middle-class 'New Women' to demand radical change, above all the vote.

Denied much if any schooling, millions of men had pursued literacy and learning independently during the 19th century, flocking to adult schools, mutual-improvement groups, mechanics institutes, and reading rooms, before free elementary education was established in 1890 in England, nearly two decades after Scotland (though not yet for Catholics). Until the late 19th century, for the many women who joined them, independent learning was harder: an often clandestine, after-dark activity. Bessie benefited from a fundamental social change in which it became acceptable for women to be out alone, not for shopping but for personal purposes, or to go to the office.[86]

As Bessie's life in Keswick unfolded, women were demanding the right to vote and go to university; Irish nationalists demanded Home Rule and in some instances total independence from Britain. The labour movement was strengthening, and Keir Hardie, the Lanarkshire miner, became its first MP in 1892 as the parliamentary Labour Party was gradually established. New Life socialism meant not only abolishing poverty but also practising new cultural, religious, artistic, sexual, and social freedoms. From 1905 a reforming Liberal government supported urban planning and introduced free school meals. Women like Bessie could benefit from a dynamic mood for change. Her next steps suggest she had decided to engage.

28 Keswick and the Newlands Valley 1905–1906: A Working-Class 'New Woman'

Keswick was alive with activities in which women like Bessie could participate, run by, as well as for, working people. Along with May Day parades there were organised rambles, cycle and motorcycle rallies, women's suffrage protests, and concerts and dances in the community hall. There was a hunger for literacy, learning and getting together with a purpose, usually the promotion of temperance. Co-operative societies ran lectures, the National Home Reading Union (NHRU) ran reading circles, and the Oddfellows Hall, part of the Manchester Unity Friendly Society, offered education and theatre performances. The Skiddaw Temperance Hotel dominated the high street. Today the temperance movement has vanished: the Hall is now the Oddfellows Arms, and the hotel is plain 'Skiddaw'.

The Lamplugh Friendly Society and the Free Gardeners Friendly Society were both for men only. If Bessie earned more than she spent, some money could have gone to Peter through the post office. Female Friendly Societies were in their infancy. The Girls' Friendly Society was founded in 1875 by philanthropists for 'unblemished' working women who subscribed as members. Help included food, social gatherings, finding jobs, emigration, Homes of Rest, and cheap accommodation, all provided within a tight moral framework. In 1901, there were 40,000 members, and it was active in coastal west Cumberland.[87]

Religious initiatives flourished, notably the Keswick Convention, which the sometime owner of the pencil factory, a Quaker, co-founded together with the Vicar of St John's (the town's other Anglican church). The Convention brought Anglicans, Quakers, and other non-conformist faiths together, broadening the social profile of worshippers, women as well as men. There was a branch of the Band of Hope, sewing classes, and Pleasant Sunday Afternoons organised by the Brotherhood movement. Temperance formed a bond between self-improvement and social-reform movements, both promoting education, religion, thrift and recreation, and an ethos that encouraged women to participate in public life.

By Spring 1905, Bessie must have been introduced to the charismatic Thomas Arthur (TA) Leonard. Like his friend Ebenezer Howard, Leonard was a Congregationalist, with a similar background, political beliefs, and talent for preaching. He was born in Finsbury, London in 1864, the son of a London clockmaker, but grew up with his mother, who ran a boarding house in Eastbourne after her husband died young. TA first worked as a clerk in a builders' office, but he was spotted as a gifted Sunday School preacher and trained by the Congregational Church. From the early 1890s he was appointed minister at Colne in Lancashire, but – like Ebenezer Howard – also attended Quaker Meetings, a staunch pacifist in the run-up to the First World War. Leonard was a founder member of the Independent Labour Party (ILP) in 1893, sometimes making speeches alongside fellow founder Keir Hardie. In Colne, he began to encourage young workers and children to take healthy country holidays instead of the railway trip to Blackpool or Morecombe – the way 'hardworking mill-folk' normally spent Wakes Weeks. TA took a dim view of this 'thoughtless spending of money', with its 'inane amusement', unhealthily overcrowded lodging houses, precious free days spent devoid of any appreciation of the beauty of being outdoors in the countryside. He considered Blackpool to be bad for the character of mill-workers. His first initiative in 1891 was a Rambling Club, followed by Guild Holidays in Ambleside: '*Wayside Flowers and Wordsworth*'. He believed that an appreciation of nature led to a love of literature, but he was nonetheless amazed that his holidays were such a success, despite the absence of bands, crowds, and shows. Bigger dreams took shape. A Co-operative Holiday Association would be his contribution to wider political actions. He renewed contact with his mentor, Scottish Congregationalist and reformer Canon John Brown Paton, and they plotted a way forward together. At Christmas 1895, TA held a meeting in Rochdale, which included fellow Co-operators. They made links with Rawnsley, who introduced him to Ruskin, now a frail old man living at Brantwood on the shores of Coniston Water. He then persuaded Miss F. N. Pringle of the NHRU to join in.[88] Well-wishers stumbled over each other to lend Leonard money, and he soon assembled the funds to found the Co-operative Holiday Association (CHA). By 1893 he had acquired six buildings in varying states of dereliction, renovated and equipped them as holiday centres. Now the CHA was about to open a centre in the Newlands valley.[89]

Miss Pringle ran the NHRU from home, at The Towers, Portinscale, close to Newlands. The organisation, set up to guide working-class and middle-class people in their reading and cultural pursuits, typified the Victorian middle-class impulse to steer people towards uplifting, wholesome recreational pursuits, away from the frowned-upon sensationalism and vulgarity of mass-circulation papers, magazines, and penny-dreadfuls. If the CHA promoted fresh-air holidays in the hills as an alternative to the temptations of Blackpool, so the NHRU promoted improving literature for the newly literate, who were otherwise prey to dangerous influences. The NHRU was another thread in the warp and weft of social movements which Bessie encountered at Keswick. Pringle had been impressed by Leonard when she first read his sermon on 'The Philosophy of Holidaymaking' in the *Colne & Nelson Times* in 1891, when he started 'The Poor Folks Holiday Fund', the so-called Fresh Air Scheme for which collections were made at his Sunday afternoon services. She attended a critical meeting held at the Manchester YMCA and joined Leonard, Rawnsley, and Dr John Paton on the 'Poor Folks Holiday Committee'. The Towers became a 'poor folks' holiday centre. Today it is 'Derwent Manor', offering self-catering holiday flats, as a fully commercial operation. Further along the Newlands road at Derwentbank, Emily Etherington added a Holiday Fellowship wing to her imposing house, which is still part of the Holiday Fellowship, created by Leonard as an alternative to the CHA. The road to Stair hosted a lasting holiday-movement colony.[90]

On 3rd January 1905 the old mill at Stair officially became the Countrywide Holidays Guest House. The span of holidays was to fit the pattern of an annual half-week or, at most, one-week holiday, apart from Wakes Weeks and Fair Fortnight in Scotland. Leave was virtually all unpaid, including Christmas Day, but gradually extended to one week plus public holidays, and then two weeks, although in Great Britain a legal requirement for employers to provide paid leave lagged behind several other European countries. The types of CHA holidaymaker quickly expanded to include office workers and middle-class people who couldn't afford holidays in boarding houses. It was this upward social drift that led Leonard to split the CHA and create a new organisation which fulfilled his original mission. Newlands became part of his new Holiday Fellowship.[91]

Bessie's brother Peter was the only person she'd ever known to benefit from a paid holiday: at first, a day trip from Clydebank 'doon the watter' and along the Ayrshire coast was a popular option. Her parents would have been open-mouthed at the idea. As children she and her siblings had one or two Holy Days of Obligation free – going to Mass, with the rest of the day off school. There was no paid time for leisure in the Quinns' lives.

As I picture it, by Spring 1905 Bessie joined a group visiting the conversion underway at the mill. In March 2017 I drove there from Keswick, a quicker journey than by horse-drawn cart, but little else seemed changed. I crossed the bridge by the pencil factory and past Portinscale, then took the narrow road (already metalled in Bessie's days), down Derwentwater's west shore towards Buttermere and Grange-in-Borrowdale. The Newlands Beck was swollen after heavy winter rains – nothing compared with the winter of 1904–5, which saw 18 inches of snow before Christmas; but swirling waters cut the banks and tumbled over the stony bed. Catkins shook. Wood anemones and primroses were in bud along the banks. The sun lit up watery meadows with streaks of silver. At Stair hamlet, I turned down the mill's steep-sloping driveway, through bare trees. In 1905, the shabby old building was covered in scaffolding. During the months of refurbishment, Leonard must have asked Bessie if she'd come and work as a cook when the Guest House opened in late summer: a full-time job with free board and accommodation in the cottages behind the main house. All staff would be full members of the Association, as guests were. I see a wary smile, her 'yes'.

At this point, Bessie must have learned to ride a bike. If she was to take the job on offer, cycling and the stamina for long walks were essential to get to and from Keswick and Stair. She'd already have seen early bicycle models as a girl in the late 1880s, at Boyd's depot on Market Street in Galashiels, lined up alongside tricycles, tandems, and, a few years later, pedal-started, petrol-driven motorbikes. James Boyd was Secretary and Treasurer of the Gala Cycling Club, which wasn't the only one in town. But there would have been no money for such

Figure 40: Newlands Guest House – the Old Mill, Stair, 1907

luxuries in her Scottish childhood then, or now. Perhaps someone in Keswick gave her a bicycle. However she came by it, it is likely to have been the 1898 'Raleigh 12' ladies' bike, made in Nottingham by the world-leading bicycle innovator. Bessie could easily have learned to ride on paths through the flat meadows between the town and the lake, where the town carter's horses grazed when they were not carrying passengers from the station to the tourist hotels and, soon, down to the Newlands holiday centre. The space is now known as Hope Park. After a day or two's practice, skirts hoisted up, elbows and shins grazed, and perhaps accompanied by her friend Jeannie Rayson (who will reappear in the story), she could have pedalled down beside the lake as far as the new sculpture dedicated to John Ruskin at Friars Crag. Rawnsley had organised it in October 1900, the year of Ruskin's death. It stands on a few square yards of land, the first site in the Lake District to be bought by the National Trust. Ruskin loved Keswick, calling it 'almost too beautiful to live in'. The monument, made of slate from a mine near Newlands, stands at a viewpoint across Derwentwater, past St Herbert's Island towards Catbells.

Cycling and cycling clubs were a feature of the age, offering cheap transport and healthy exercise for all. Women like Bessie increasingly took to the saddle for Sunday afternoon outings. Temperance organisations like the Band of Hope, adult schools, and Pleasant Sunday Afternoons promoted cycling. Cycling was becoming an emblem of progress for women, and wheeling round Keswick was a sign that Bessie was embracing modern ideas. She would have known that some people frowned on cycling for women as unbecoming, and in some people's eyes downright socialist. 'Fellowship through cycling' was indeed part of the culture of socialist organisations like the Clarion Club, which started in Manchester in the 1890s and spread out from its strongholds in northern towns like Bolton and Leonard's Colne. Riding a bike was connected with other efforts to throw off Victorian constraints on women. For supporters of the women's suffrage movement, cycling emblemised the struggle for emancipation and independence. If Bessie was racing – or labouring – up and down the lower fells, skirts billowing behind her, it was evidence of how far she had come since leaving Scotland behind.[92]

Figure 41: Women cyclists' outing, 1900s

Cycling went with temperance, and it seems likely that both were part of Bessie's Keswick life, a reaction to her family's downfall. My father remembered how, a decade later, Bessie taught her own small children to ride bikes. And that both his parents leaned towards temperance, as well as vegetarianism. Alcohol had accelerated the deaths of men in her family and community. Drink doubtless reduced her father's resistance to bronchitis and wreaked havoc not only on wild ones like Tom, but on the families of hard-working and hard-drinking brothers like Patrick-Peter. Alcohol-fuelled violence simmered close to the surface, and many in the next generation recoiled from it.

Any church-inspired temperance organisations which Bessie joined were Protestant. There were Band of Hope branches in Keswick and Stair which met on Sundays at 3pm, as they did everywhere. At the Band of Hope, Bessie could have made Protestant friends with a background nearer to hers. It was part of a vast national web of groups, mostly affiliated to churches and chapels, which worked for temperance and the moral and educational benefit of 'the poor'. I found Band of Hope reports and notices in 1900s issues of the Crosthwaite Parish Magazine. Since its beginnings in the 1840s, it grew steadily, and from the late 1880s spread like wildfire. By 1897, there were over 3 million members.

The language and rites of 'non-Catholics' would have been alien to Bessie at first, but there was no Catholic church in Keswick then, no Mass, nor a priest to tell of the sorry events she heard about from Peter: her mother's condition and the removal of Arthur George. It would have been hard to admit to the formidable Anglicans that she owed her education to priests and nuns. She'd have overheard prejudices, seen the shadows which clouded friendly faces when Catholicism was mentioned. Things were going well, and what good would come of disclosure? She probably felt herself drifting away, observing her faith like a distant friend disappearing down the far end of the street.[93]

It wasn't that Bessie had to lie outright, or stretch the truth very far, to make new acquaintances who would help her without urging her to reveal much about her past. Her Borders accent and elegant good looks may have helped her integrate more easily than if she had been a Lancashire mill-girl or Cumberland farm-worker. If she had been less discreet, her life story would have been passed down very differently in my family. She was not the only sibling who kept quiet, about whom very little was known – even among Quinns. Middle-class reformers would have been intrigued by Bessie as a self-improving young women. They were preoccupied by hopes and dreams for women like her, but not so curious about the life of a particular one. The Keswick group weren't social investigators, scooping up the stories of the poor for detailed social statistics. They were doers.

Working-class autobiographies from the 19th and 20th centuries accentuate a reluctance to expose experiences and feelings to interested 'superiors'. The privacy of poor families was so often invaded, and silence was a defence against misunderstanding, disapproval, and hectoring. Combined with the lack of middle-class interest, it is unsurprising that the details of so many lives are hidden or homogenised. Plenty was known by servants about middle-class women, who would have been astonished to know what women like Bessie observed and knew about them. Servants were present in rooms where private conversations happened, or when unhappiness spilled over. As they didn't count as fellow humans, they saw and heard anger and exasperation at the actions of domineering men; anxiety and gloom deaden bright, earnest faces; bodies sag under the weight of duty, and self-belief crumple, shoulders hunch and the sound of weeping muffled by the handkerchief that a good servant had at the ready. Bessie might have felt consoled that she and they shared something. But it was not mutual understanding. They could never know the world inside 20 Mowat Place, or understand what a hard fall it was from Halliburton Place. She might have concluded: they think all our 'slums' are the same; they think we are all alike, while they, their homes, their pains and pleasures are unique. The story of Bessie's broken family and its characters would be too alien, and the differing fortunes of large numbers of differing characters couldn't be conjugated into the simplified language used by her patrons about the world of indistinguishable others.

Bessie's life now depended on where she was going, not where she came from. She had a lifetime of practice at keeping quiet, to put up a solid front. In Keswick, people seemed to like this young woman from elsewhere. It was enough to accept some help to nurture her new life and stay politely independent, even charming when required. She wasn't going to broadcast her story. If, some nights, she re-lived her good fortune, on others anxious memories and fear were inescapable. Her mother, Arthur George, and Peter haunted her, and she grieved for her father and brothers. In summer 1905, she received Peter's news of her sister Mary: *In the midst of life we are in death*, a chant of her childhood. In the still-unfamiliar quiet of Keswick life, she flew in her imagination over the Cumberland mountains to the green and yellow Borders, the scene of her whole life before she was wrenched away to the strangeness of cities, then back to the gorse bushes flowering beside Derwentwater. The connection was comforting.

Bessie had no-one with whom to share the worries or regrets behind her mask of politeness. She'd never seen Owen again after moving to Clydebank with her mother five years ago. She hadn't been home to Scotland. She didn't want to, but guilt still clung on. In the daytime, she took comfort in the practicalities of her enjoyable, promising present. Little by little, Bessie must have steeled her heart against reports of her mother's declining state of mind and body. Perhaps she still went to the post office in Keswick to send home small amounts of money, pick up Peter's letters and read what she dreaded, though he expected nothing of her. In summer 1905 Bessie's life was about to change again, and the distance between them grew.[94]

29 Stair: The Newlands Guest House
1905: Jolly Holidays: 'All for one and one for all'

Bessie was well qualified for her new job. She'd fed her family, from working men to new-born babes, for much of her life. Since arriving in Keswick, 'cook' had been her occupation, in a Keswick refreshment room or one of her benefactor's houses. In summer 1905 Newlands Guest House opened its doors to holiday-makers, and it seems Bessie worked there from the start, chopping piles of vegetables in a white starched apron, sleeves rolled up to the elbow. In summer 1906, 'cook' was still her officially recorded occupation. It seems she'd been at the Guest House at least a year before her life changed again.

T. A. Leonard wrote how 'we converted the drab, dirty old mill into a place of sweetness and light. The old wheel was sold for a good sum and a larder took its place, and so was created the best-loved of all our centres'. At Newlands today, the serving hatch between kitchen, larder, and dining room, where Bessie and her fellow kitchen workers would have served the food, is exactly where it was in 1905: the spot where the mill-wheel once turned. The communal dining room is also in exactly the same place. From day one, staff lived in the row of cottages behind the mill. The Co-operative Holiday Association had paid Mary Vickers and her sister, the mill's former owners, and their successors, £15 6s a year to use them, part of the overall deal that Leonard struck. A year or two later, when they began to take families, the cottages became married guests' quarters.

Newlands fast became the cornerstone of the residential, outward-bound holiday movement, the model that other centres adopted. In its early years, just as TA wanted, it was for 'poor folks', but also for low-waged clerks and others who could not afford holidays: young to middle-aged men and women. Holiday-makers came from towns and cities, with regular groups from Manchester, Leeds, and smaller industrial towns in Lancashire and Yorkshire. Bursaries helped those who otherwise couldn't afford to come. A Newlands holiday cost just over £1 a week (22 shillings and 6 pence). Guests arrived at Keswick Station, their bags often sent in advance.

Figure 42: Mr Pape's waggon taking Newlands holiday-makers to Keswick Station

They were met by Mr Pape, the local carter. Resident holiday-makers climbed aboard his two-horse wagonette to greet newcomers, then wave them off again at the end of the week, packed tightly for the few miles to and from Stair. Once at Newlands, they made up their beds, dubbined their boots, and got to know the house rules, meal times, and duties, including the rota for preparing vegetables and sandwiches for lunch, waiting at table, cleaning, and washing up. Hot water was scarce, so the hardiest ones washed in the ice-cold beck that flowed beside the mill, swelling after rains to a gushing river. By contrast, the drying room was a furnace – essential for getting walkers' sodden clothes and squelchy boots ready for the next day's hike.

Staff such as Bessie kept everything going, even though the CHA ethos intended them to be indistinguishable from guests. Comprehensive rules were drawn up for male and female guests:

> Don't bring luggage you can't lift with one hand: there are no men servants at Newlands. Bathing in Newlands Beck is mixed, full

> costumes are worn and undressing and dressing is done in the house; bicycles will be found very useful …. and motor cycles and sidecars can be had at a small charge. Bring bath towel and drinking horn, Rucksack or satchel and strong nailed boots – guests wearing shoes will not be allowed to join the mountain climbs: this will be enforced. Quiet between 11.30 pm and 6.30 am: the days are long and hard and we need plenty of sleep.

Guests were woken promptly at 7.15, and breakfast was served at 8 o'clock. There were sandwiches at 1 pm, whether at the Guest House or out on the fells; tea at 4.30, indoors or out; and dinner was dished up at 7 pm. Every night, there was cocoa or soup at 9.30, followed by a roll call; bed by 10; lights-out and quiet at 11.30 prompt, although it was hard to quieten down the Guest House by that time. These were 'jolly holidays', in the words of guests. Men who slept on the ground floor complained of the noise of 'girls' talking overhead. There were reports of larking about, practical jokes and booby-traps laid in the dormitories. Men against women and women against men, giving as good as they got.[95]

Rules and routines were the framework for the glorious freedom of putting on hobnail boots, hitching up long skirts with girdles so they bulged like pantaloons, and tying bonnets or scarves inelegantly under the chin. Men wore breeches, braces, and long socks under their boots. They set off on ambitious trails: nearby Causey Pike, or the six fell-tops of Blencathra, or Catbells, or round the back of Skiddaw, or down to Grange-in-Borrowdale and over Honister Pass as far as Buttermere. Some groups scaled Scafell or Helvellyn. Bikes or cart ride took them to distant starting points. Groups of 20 or more would gather after breakfast, ready to set off in all weathers. When they returned at night, limbs aching, they could plunge into a deep, cold pool or dabble blistered feet, relaxing on the bank before dinner.[96]

Changing arrangements for men and women were separate, but otherwise it was all in together as CHA members, with no social class or gender segregation in this self-consciously emancipated world. Typical of the times, the photographers among them captured the outdoor pursuits: groups perched on bridges, standing under waterfalls, drinking from mountain streams; women with skirts hitched up, struggling up steep slopes; picnic lunches and tea *al fresco* at a Grange-in-Borrowdale café. Some images survive, on the wall and in boxes to leaf through at Newlands Adventure Centre, as it's now called, or in the archives at the Keswick Museum and Art Gallery.

Figure 43: Women dipping in the mill pond, Newlands (1930s)

Figure 44: Up Scafell, 1907

Figure 45: Walkers' tea party al fresco, Newlands Valley

Alcohol was taboo: Leonard's CHA was strictly temperance. But evenings at Newlands were lively, with folk-singing, dressing-up, and recitals in a blend of rooted rural Englishness, inflected with internationalist, modern, and egalitarian sentiments. Anglo-German connections were actively fostered: a sister organisation was founded in Hesse's Taunus hills. On Sundays, some guests walked to Crosthwaite Church to hear Rawnsley preach, or to attend chapel; reflecting links between Quakers and Baptists, there was a Fellowship Hymn Book, published by the Adult School Union and the Brotherhood movement.

Bessie shared a room in the cottages, listening to the mill-stream cascade into the pond. With reasonable working hours, this was undreamed-of freedom, with time to think, read, and brush out her hair unobserved by teasing brothers. She'd stalk round like a cat, marking out the room. It seems Bessie made a good friend at Keswick or Newlands: Jeannie Rayson, who might have spent holidays there. Together they could have mended clothes and made costumes for the festivals and fancy-dress parties which were part of Newlands life, along with maypole dancing and rural jollities. A photo taken outside the cottages shows a group of women dressed as milkmaids: guests or staff, or both. None of them is Bessie.

Bessie and her fellow cooks, cleaners, and housekeeping staff must have crept round exhausted to the cottages for a shorter night's rest than the guests. It was almost, but not quite, one community. There's no way of knowing how much if any walking or hiking Bessie could take part in, given her shifts. She was fit enough for it all: she'd walked miles every day for as long as she could remember, like her parents before her. And in years to come, she's remembered as a keen walker, babes in arms, undaunted by mountain paths on adventurous holidays. She was formally a member of the Newlands community, and the status must have been satisfying. Time off for more than an odd day's walking or cycling was probably more elusive. She'd never had a holiday and may have envied the high-spirits of people like her, free to enjoy the vacation that she was toiling to provide.

Figure 46: Hikers resting on Grange Bridge, Borrowdale

30 Newlands Guest House 1905 or 1906: A Meeting

This chapter swings between fact, speculation, and imagination. I will try to make their boundaries visible in this reconstruction of the historically known encounter between two people at Newlands in late 1905 or, less likely, early in 1906, when romance blossomed between Bessie Quinn and Arthur Cecil Howard, and led to their marriage. My evidence is the theatre of their meeting; my father's memories of his parents; his half-sister Betty's memories of my grandfather, and my own memories of him; the handful of photos and letters between Ebenezer and Lizzie Howard about their son. Nothing enables me to say definitively: this is precisely how it happened. I can only extrapolate.

My account embroiders undeniable facts: that they met; where they met – at Stair; approximately when they met; that they fell in love (subsequent reports suggest a passionately devoted couple); that they married and had children; and how, at their happiest, they continued to do the things together that each of them had enjoyed before they met; that their relationship still moved those who survived them. When strangers become acquainted and fall for each other, they are often without attentive witnesses. So it was for Bessie and Cecil. Readers can take the version offered, reject it, add to it – or create their own.

At some point between Newlands' opening in autumn 1905 and early spring 1906, Bessie, with her fellow cooks and kitchen workers, was dishing up dinner at the dining-room servery. It could have been a steak and kidney suet pudding with savoy cabbage and mashed potatoes, or a beef stew with dumplings: one of the hearty canteen meals typically on offer to holiday-makers after strenuous mountain hikes. Given the ethos of the CHA, and the beliefs of some guests, vegetarian food would have been a staple on the menu. A crowd of walkers gathered in the dining room before 7 o'clock. September and October were busy months at Newlands, and after a winter lull it was teeming with guests again from March. Walkers hastily washed, brushed up, and changed after their long day. Some had climbed Blencathra's peaks, and when they got back a few of the hardiest men and women had taken a dip in the pool. There was a hubbub as tales of the day were exchanged.

At the back of the dining room, a tall, slight man stood on his own, leaning against the wall. Obviously not part of a group, nor a walker: he was over-smart for Newlands in a brand-new, wool-and-leather motorcycling outfit. Not that cycling gear was anything unusual in itself: motorcycles and bikes could be hired by holiday-makers at Newlands. He had light-brown wavy hair parted in the middle, and pale blue eyes. And hung back as the noisy queue jostled towards the hatch. Eventually, the servers beckoned the straggler to move forward. When it was finally his turn, he was tongue-tied, but eventually managed to ask if there was a vegetarian dish. There was.

Figure 47: Arthur Cecil Howard in his twenties

Figure 48: The Dining Room, Newlands 1907

Vegetarianism was on the increase, an integral part of the new social movements. The Co-operative Holiday Association was no exception. Vegetarianism was already well established as a cause and a way of life, not just a fad on the margins of society. Over the course of the 19th century it had become interwoven with social movements since early converts like Percy Bysshe Shelley, who denounced meat production in 1812 as a reason for food shortages among society's poorest people. The Vegetarian Society was established in 1847 after the Chartist movement for universal suffrage adopted the cause in the 1830s. By the 1890s, the vegetarian movement held international congresses, and publications like *The Vegetarian* set an ambitious tone, promoting recipes for banquets as well as daily living, to help banish the criticism that vegetarian food was limited and tasteless. Among vegetarian social reformers Bessie knew, or came to know of, were Ebenezer Howard (mostly vegetarian), Annie Besant, Edward Carpenter, and George Bernard Shaw. Isaac Pitman, whose shorthand system was controversial when Howard adopted it as a clerk in 1870s Chicago, was a Swedenborgian – a religious radical – and Vice President of the Vegetarian Society. Howard, a Congregationalist, also embraced spiritualism, which promoted vegetarianism. Ruskin abhorred 'hurting any living creature needlessly' and the killing of animals, declaring he would 'strive to save and comfort all gentle life, and guard and perfect all natural beauty, upon the earth'. Late in life, he wrote wryly to his doctor that he was 'impressed by the arguments of vegetarians.... My diet consists chiefly of green peas, gooseberries, melons, cucumbers and wedding cake'. This was a time when Ruskin was overwhelmingly dependent on opium – his 'tonic'. Vegetarianism was never just about food: it was a dimension of social reform. Bessie, as we've seen, grew up on a diet consisting of far more vegetables and dairy produce than meat – and her parents even more so.[97]

Menus of the many vegetarian restaurants that sprouted up in English and Scottish cities in the 1880s would have been partly reflected in the Newlands canteen: pulses, vegetables, grain, eggs, and macaroni, cooked with a liberal use of herbs.

Bessie guessed that the motorcyclist in the dining room was not from a northern city. His unaccustomed twang may have reminded her of someone, but she struggled to make the connection. He murmured his thanks, took a seat in the corner, and looked up gingerly at the boisterous crowd. The next morning Bessie saw him walking purposefully across the cobbled yard towards the stables near the cottages, where the 'for hire' motorcycles were sheltered. The one he wheeled out looked different, like a heavy bicycle, with chain and pedals. She'd seen them around Keswick's market place, where the motorcycle rallies were held. He leapt on to it and pedalled hard until it whirred, wheezed, stuttered up the drive, and swerved left into the lane towards Grange.

Figure 49: Motorcycling pioneers at a Keswick rally

This was where Bessie and Arthur Cecil Howard – Cecil to everyone – met. As our research progressed, my father (Geoffrey Howard) became unshakably convinced of it, with good reason. His aunt Kathleen Daisy ('Kitty'), Cecil's sister, confirmed it irrefutably. Cecil's father Ebenezer ('Ben') would have told the family about his Crosthwaite lecture when he returned home to his wife Lizzie and family at Stamford Hill. He'd have enthused, as was his way, about the beauty of Derwentwater, the motorbikes, the forward-looking town, and people even proposing to build a garden village. Ebenezer loved travel, and liked a holiday, writing cheerful letters to Lizzie from far-off places.[98] Catherine Howard, Ebenezer's cousin, whom Cecil and Kitty called 'Aunt', had impressed the family with her paintings of Cumberland's landscape. A single woman and semi-professional painter, she'd lodge in Keswick for weeks on end, wandering in the hills and around the lakeshore with easel and palette, dressed in loose clothes and visiting Keswick refreshment rooms with Bohemian artist friends from her row of Hampstead studios. Kathleen Daisy sometimes painted alongside her carefree aunt. 'Ben' sought out cousin Catherine's company: a kindred spirit who'd talk to anybody and come home to London full of stories. The Howard family would have known that Leonard's Co-operative Holiday Association was to open a Guest House not far from Crosthwaite Vicarage. Any Howard would be welcome there. Kathleen Daisy was adventurous, but would her brother Cecil dare to take a trip on his own? A more vulnerable, cautious soul, his struggle to converse with people puzzled his gregarious father.

Lizzie Howard, née Bills, had died the year before, on 7th November. For years, Cecil had witnessed his mother's illnesses, staying close to her especially during his father's long absences. His childhood was full of love, play, and sport, but his mood would swing between hope, anxiety, and foreboding. Lizzie had supported the Garden City campaign tirelessly, but also urged her husband into (doomed) efforts to patent and sell his machines abroad, to add a little to the family's breadline budget. Cecil had one bold streak, which helped him now. His passion for motorcycles offered him a way of leaving London behind and riding into the countryside. He was often dog-tired from his walk to work and back. His wrists and arms ached from long days writing in the courts. When the family moved to Letchworth in 1905, Cecil took lodgings close to work, at 60 Chancery Lane, but he was often dispirited and prey to anxiety. He would feel listless, half-paralysed, and struggle to keep attending the courts each morning. When he couldn't ride his motorbike, playing or watching cricket was his other release, at the Oval or Lords, preferably with his father, listening to his anecdotes of the legendary W. G. Grace. According to my Dad, his father and grandfather watched the unorthodox Australian batsman Victor Trumper score an unforgettable century at Lords in the Ashes 1899 tour, when Cecil was 15. Cricket was a bond between fathers and sons across two generations, through good and bad times.[99]

Figure 50: Lizzie Howard, Ebenezer's wife, Cecil's mother, Garden City advocate

Cecil was crushed by the death of his mother. His parents' correspondence suggests that she and Cecil were wrapped up in each other: confiding, mutually dependent. He clung to his mother like a sweet pea to a trellis, and any self-confidence she nurtured in him seems to have died with her. Lizzie died in London weeks before she and Ben could move into their new house at Letchworth, and she was buried in the churchyard at St Mary's, the ancient parish church on Letchworth Lane. It was a bittersweet occasion as a crowd of public figures mingled and paid homage to the pivotal role 'Mrs Howard' had played in the Garden City movement. That winter, Cecil found it difficult to shake off the bleakness in his soul as he grieved with his sisters Kathleen Daisy, Edith, and Marjory. Edith's grief was angry: she later publicly expressed her resentment that her father had left their mother to cope in impossibly straightened circumstances, although she never questioned the love between them and became a lifelong guardian of Ebenezer's reputation, keeping his work in the public eye, tetchily challenging every minor mistake and misconception in published articles and correspondence. She was proud of her father, but distress over his neglect of her mother's health and the family's wellbeing lingered. For decades, Lizzie had scraped food together for the table. Ebenezer was a well-intentioned but hopeless provider, his tunnel-vision of garden cities blocking out the need to put meals on the table. Lizzie loved him, but her final exasperated letters to him border on despair: he was not, she wrote, a person suited to married life. [100]

Cecil decided to visit Catherine while she was painting in the Lake District with Kathleen Daisy, assembled his motorbike and set off, probably well before the winter of 1905–6. According to family memory, the two women painted landscapes from their base in a hired caravan, an emblem of pioneering new forms of leisure: eccentric before they became mainstream. Edith Howard and her husband were fellow enthusiasts, and in the 1920s, when their money ran out, even lived in a caravan before being charitably rehoused, as a Howard daughter, in a Welwyn Garden City bungalow. Camping and caravanning in farmers' fields and orchards took off in the early 20th century, associated with the growing popularity of cycling and hiking. As with bikes, the trend started in the 1880s, and by 1907 the 'Camping and Caravanning Club' attracted nearly 1,000 members, drawn by a romantic association with Romanis and Travellers, the lure of a Bohemian lifestyle, and living in simple structures close to nature – even for just a few days a year.

Bessie was better equipped than Cecil to follow up a chance meeting. In Keswick, she hadn't lost time making friends, summoning the courage to meet strangers in a place where she was the outsider. She must have been intrigued enough to take the initiative with the disappearingly shy man in motorcycling gear, who looked at her with childlike trust as if he had recognised a familiar.

The next evening, Bessie was ready to offer Cecil a vegetarian meal: let's say a lentil cutlet, with carrots, turnips, and baked potatoes. For dessert, rice pudding with raspberry jam (she was later famous for that). She wove her way among the tables as he finished his meal in the corner of the fast-emptying dining room. She was clearing dishes, wiping tables, and putting out cutlery for breakfast. She noticed his long, delicate fingers, unlike the Quinn men's or her own reddened, scarred hands, which she tucked under her apron. The hard swellings on his fingertips told her who this man reminded her of. She said nothing, but stood beside him, asked after his day, and introduced herself. He got to his feet, chair scraping, and said his name was Cecil Howard. When she finished her work he was still there, studying a map. She sat down. Why not, she was off duty and she was as much a CHA member as he was? He had no airs and graces, yet it was clear he'd never done a hard day's work. At Newlands, the clerks and teachers stood out among the mill-workers, and there were still occasions, here, when the best-intentioned people made their sense of superiority plain in small gestures and words, consciously or not.

Bessie made the connection to Ebenezer. She'd liked his father's lecture on the Garden City project, she said: her brother Alex had dreamed of a world like that and she'd seen a similar little settlement back in Scotstoun. Public meetings were not his favourite pastime, Cecil said, though he'd been to more than a few. She told him about the KSIA, the National Trust, Porch Cottage, and the Band of Hope. He told her he'd ridden to Seatoller, sat on the Bridge at Grange, and walked across the fields to his sister's caravan, where they'd had tea. Tomorrow he planned to go up and over Honister Pass, towards Buttermere and back. Over the next few evenings, their conversations became a habit. They wandered outdoors and down to the Beck and agreed it would be nice, should he ever come back, if Bessie showed him Rawnsley's memorial to John Ruskin at Friars Crag.

What did Cecil notice about her? She was even thinner than he was. Her eyes were greenish-blue and slightly hooded. A slight smile twitched at the corners of her mouth when she spoke, which was disconcerting. Did she find him comical? She was friendly, but her faultless courtesy also felt like a guard and seemed to discourage questions. He noticed that she spoke in a soft low voice with a Scottish accent, which to the end of his life he still heard as if she were turned towards him, confiding. He astonished himself that he'd done so much talking and learned next to nothing about her. His curiosity took him aback.

Was Bessie determined to be the author of her own obscurity? Or did she panic, not sure how to present herself when she felt there might be a lot at stake?

She had felt awkward talking about herself with people like the Rawnsleys, Marion Twelves, and Keswick friends: she stuck to Galashiels, the place where she was born and brought up. People were interested, and it was a way of dodging personal questions. What would she say if Cecil asked more about her life? What, if anything, should she say about her parents? As their walks around Newlands lengthened, she decided: her mother and father were Irish, and her father had been a 'contractor' in Scotland until he died. 'Contractor' was a term she'd heard used to describe the people building Newlands. And her brothers had carried out contracts on building sites like the Dingleton Hospital. It had a ring to it and could mean a lot of things. If pressed further, she knew how to change tack or make her excuses. She must have felt pleased with her ingenuity.

The next thing to tell this sweet stranger and anyone else was that she was an orphan, with siblings who had died, which was partly true. The Quinns had emigrated to escape hunger, and they'd built a good life in Galashiels. She was reluctant to mention the Catholic Church to him, not least because lies, which in her childhood she'd regularly purged at confession, were accumulating on her conscience. And her new acquaintances belonged to a still-bewildering array of Protestant organisations. It crossed her mind that her story would be hard to change: but she might never see him again, and it wouldn't matter. She felt a stab of guilt towards the memory of her father and mother, her two dead brothers and sister Mary. But her pain and prayers belonged to her: why share them with someone she hardly knew?

She didn't need to worry. The next time they sat down, side by side again, looking straight ahead, Cecil sensed not to ask questions in response to this briefly worded, information and didn't draw her back from a swerve into a new subject. At the mention of her orphanhood, though, he took her hand, turned towards her and wiped tears from his eyes with the back of his hand. She soon insisted it was his turn, and he astonished himself: once he started his story, it poured out, with only occasional prompts or queries.

Cecil's mother had died just before his 22nd birthday, which characteristically she would have made a fuss of. She was admired by many, but understood by few. Like his father Ebenezer, he was sceptical about the Christianity that had kept Lizzie so resolute and hopeful. For him, this life was what there was, and without Lizzie it had lost its purpose. Social change drove his father's life, but Cecil had felt the consequences and preferred a quiet life. His older sisters Edith and Kathleen Daisy (Kitty) were gregarious and talented, hoping to marry and build their lives elsewhere. He adored Kitty, his artistic, funny sister – but she was not one to stop and mope. He had spent the weeks after Lizzie's death moving mechanically through each day. At Ebenezer's typically practical suggestion, he took up woodwork, helped by his father's craftsmen friends, and found that making and decorating useful things was comforting.

His father's grief seemed inaccessible – displaced into frantic Garden City activity. After the funeral, Ben was taken for a long walk with an associate to mourn. After that, his loss was locked up, invisible for ever. He slipped in and out of the family house, running full-pelt to catch buses and trains, charging up and down between Stamford Hill and the Letchworth building site. His sister Tamar Annie helped out. He inspected the works, sat in meetings, lectured, and wrote. Eventually, Ebenezer noticed his son's distress and bought him a Bradbury motorbike on the never-never, a glorified motorised bicycle, made by a sewing-machine manufacturer and barely more powerful. Cecil was machine-mad and liked to travel: that much he and his father had in common. Ben suggested a trip north to dispel his gloom with Catherine. And here he was.

After he'd left school, Cecil had been a clerk at Martins Bank for three years before he left to join 'The Exploration Company', a city firm which dealt with the sale of mines: the 1890s had seen a flurry of gold discoveries, and gold shares boomed. A lot of money was won and lost across continents, from Coolgardie to Mysore to the Klondike. Cecil's salary was paltry, but he was trusted to travel to Genoa and other European cities to prepare the paperwork for brokered sales: he was good on detail and honest to a tee, dismayed by the sharp practices he witnessed. So he learned shorthand, proved adept at his father's skill, and started work in the bankruptcy courts. This wasn't well paid either, as he knew only too well, but it was a reliable income. He was far better suited to regulated court procedures than to hard-nosed business.

In September 1905, with holiday money saved, addresses in his pocket, kitted-out in cycling gear by Ben, and with Lizzie's leather hold-all strapped to the motorbike, Cecil wove his way out of London. The trip would be his memorial to his mother's determined spirit. The ride north was exhilarating. Outdoors, seeing and smelling the changing landscape for as long as the light lasted, sparks of new energy spurred him on, and the wind on his face brushed away wisps of grief and anxiety. Invading memories of the airless curtained room, sounds of sickness, and chattering funeral crowds fell away into the verges of long whitening grass. He chugged along miles of minor roads, stopping in small towns to find a room, a simple dinner, a beer, and petrol from one of the bicycle or motor workshops springing up everywhere – petrol stations were a thing of the future. One night he stayed in Nuneaton, avoiding the Newdigate Arms where Lizzie had grown up in a struggling family, plagued by her alcoholic father, whose collapses left his children serving behind the bar to keep the business going.

Cecil, the timid boy and mother's companion, was the most unlikely hero of this *Boy's Own* adventure. He may have seen the funny side: motorbikes and cars were already becoming primary symbols of a 20th-century manliness that he certainly did not embody. But he shared the obsession of the age with machinery: his uncles were photographers and Remington typewriter salesmen; his father was a mechanical inventor; his sisters and aunts rejoiced in sewing machines, typewriters, bikes, and caravans. Machines opened up new prospects for work, independence, leisure, learning, and creativity for women and men.

After three days, Cecil arrived at Keswick and rode on to Newlands, where Ben had arranged a room. Cecil was not brimming with confidence as he walked through the front door, but he was ready to keep going with his adventure. All this Cecil told to Bessie Quinn, who didn't seem to tire of listening.

Cecil returned to Newlands in March or April 1906 for a few days, this time by train and Mr Pape's wagon. Bessie must have known he was coming. He joined the hill-walking groups and after dinner they sat at the edge of a high-spirited crowd making music and singing. Bessie, intent on her independent life, enjoying the recognition of her skills at Porch Cottage, and exhilarated by her new circle of acquaintances, was falling in love. She'd never met a man who talked about feelings and wept so easily, whether happy or sad or both at once.

Bessie loosened the strings of secrecy which she'd drawn round her previous life, becoming less reticent each day. She'd had six months to weave a well-rehearsed story together and needed Cecil to hear it. He inspired trust. It had been easy when they met to talk enthusiastically about Newlands and her new freedom, leaving her family story wrapped in evasive generalities: what would it serve to parade her past and her people when she could sense the possibility of a different future? But her whole life until a year ago stalked round her mind unbidden until she was sure it was luridly visible to him anyway. She feared he would shrink away from a Poor Law supplicant, mill-girl and biscuit-factory worker with red hands and poor teeth. But the urge to confess grew stronger, vying with a determination to stay in control.

Alex was the first brother she told Cecil about. Then she drew some cameos from her childhood, stories that didn't lead to anywhere awkward or arouse alarm. She could weave a tale and remain true to herself, even to her family. She sometimes changed the subject: how she longed to see London. Their talk petered out into silent pauses. If Cecil wondered how to react, or whether something about Bessie was not quite as it seemed, he didn't let on. After he left again for London, she began to fear the consequences of revealing her past and wondered whether he'd approve of her newfound love of independence. Her family's problems would be familiar to him in theory, from his father's cause and his mother's work at the Hoxton Christian mission. They had things in common: loneliness in company, the loss of beloved people, and endless struggles to pay the rent. Affection, hope, and longing alternated in Bessie, and then another shadow: would it matter that she was a few years older than him?

Back at home, Cecil wrote letters – short, still non-committal, but warm. She felt he knew her, even though he did not. If and when Bessie was ill in bed at Newlands, fears must have invaded, as they do, to threaten good fortune. She'd seen the love between Owen and Alice, between Arthur and Jane. She wanted to live. Other fears loomed, but she thought of gentle, ladylike Ellen Quinn, who stuck by wild Patrick-Peter, though he'd never change his ways. Would Cecil's family accept her, or so disapprove that he would spurn her?

The answer came. In late spring or early summer 1906, Cecil rode back to Newlands on his motorbike. There was a side-car attached to it: a woven basket on wheels. Bessie asked for an afternoon off. They rode into Keswick and walked across the meadows to Friars Crag. Taking each other's hands, they followed the path that led to the rocky outcrop and sat by the memorial to John Ruskin.

Figure 51: From Ruskin's Memorial, Friars Crag over Derwentwater to Catbells

Now Bessie knew she was loved in return, and awkwardness melted as they looked across Derwentwater to the green pincushion of St Herbert's Island and to Catbells on the west shore, Stair hidden among the slopes. Yellow flowers smothered a huge gorse bush: bending down to catch its coconut scent, their heads knocked together: awkwardness returned. In Scotland, she told him, they called the gorse 'whin', and the Borders hillsides were dotted with it. There was a farmhouse near Galashiels called The Whin, where her father had lived when he was young. He used to say kissing's not in season when gorse is not in bloom, After a while, they clambered down to skim pebbles across the lake. They were as skilled as each other: another of my father's memories. Gleeful, with wet, bedraggled hems and shivering, he asked her to marry him and she agreed. They began to plan their life together before they reached town. They could have drunk hot chocolate in a hikers' steamy refreshment room, wandered down Main Street and peered into a jeweller's window. Cecil bought a plain wedding ring and a thin gold neck-chain. For now, their secret would be hidden under Bessie's blouses. These were her first pieces of jewellery, perhaps the only ones she ever owned. Nothing was passed down the generations.

When Bessie revealed a little more about her past, Cecil was captivated, though probably less interested in the left-behind Quinns. As she'd guessed, he was nervous about how her story would be received by his family, friends, and illustrious supporters, including the socialists. He felt ashamed, but he'd lived his life with the difference between idealistic aspirations and the ability to actually connect with people seen as lower class. He saw class-consciousness every day at the bankruptcy court. His quiet rejection of it came from his father, who was allergic to the pervasive, casual snobbery of his associates. Cecil hoped fervently that Bessie would be welcomed for what she was, which would be easier without her life story. He didn't want to see her patronised. So when she asked him to keep secret for ever all she'd told him of her childhood and family, he agreed without a murmur. Only Ebenezer, Kathleen Daisy, and Catherine Howard would know, or guess, more. At Friars Crag, they shook hands on their pledge. At Newlands they held on to each other, and then Cecil watched her window until the light went out.

31 Keswick, London, Letchworth, Cornwall
Catherine Howard: Emancipated Eccentric

Before he left Cumberland for London, Cecil took Bessie to meet his Aunt Catherine Howard. According to family memories, and her surviving paintings, Catherine was a regular visitor to Derwentwater, sometimes joined by Kathleen Daisy. She painted from her makeshift studio, a rented caravan. It was pitched in a hollow below Catbells, near Littletown Farm to the west of the lake, a manageable bicycle ride from Newlands.

Catherine was close to her older cousin 'Ben', admired his wife Lizzie, adored Letchworth, and wholeheartedly supported the Garden City ideal. She embraced new causes energetically, gathered friends, made people laugh, and aspired to be a 'new woman', vote and wear what she wanted. With a verve unquenched after long years cooped up in the family home, she struck out on her own and quickly found her feet in an unconventional community. She and Kathleen Daisy were the family members whom Cecil would trust to befriend Bessie.

Through Catherine, Bessie encountered a new dimension of Keswick – the mountain outpost of Letchworth's creative eccentricity, where women artists were casting off their corsets, living more freely and comfortably with their bodies, and taking their future into their own hands. In some ways, Bessie was oddly well equipped to mingle with such self-consciously modern women. Victorian prudery scarcely registered in a crowded working-class household. She was used to living cheek-by-jowl with men and boys, although there were unwritten codes that guarded their accepted levels of modesty. With the changing cast of brothers and nephews who'd been dependent on her for meals, clean clothes, baths, and bottom-wiping, and their parents sleeping close by, exposure to bodily functions in confined spaces was normal: not a talking point.

Catherine Howard was a Londoner, living in a row of studio cottages designed for artists in Hampstead. She wore the latest loose-fitting clothes from Jaeger, popular among bohemians, pacifists, and socialists, the 'New Lifers' who were moving into Letchworth and also seen wandering the Lakeland fells. Years before the 'gasper girls' of the

1920s with their 'Lucky Strikes', Catherine smoked cigarettes – to the horror of respectable acquaintances. But she'd laugh it off: the right to smoke was part of women's emancipation. She supported the suffragists, scoffing at the stifling attitudes she was discarding. She carried on living her own way, which included shared reading with Ben (Tolstoy has been suggested) and espousing his pacifism. She would fit seamlessly into the early Letchworth community.

Cecil's eldest sister Kathleen Daisy liked to paint alongside her aunt, staying close by, or parked in a horse-drawn Gypsy caravan. Kathleen Daisy paid her dues to the Caravan Club – or its predecessors. They were sometimes joined by Kathleen Daisy's lover Charles Compton Rawlinson, another painter and caravan enthusiast. For the two women, it was their perfect base for painting landscapes. It has also been suggested that Kathleen may have joined the Ruskin Linen workshops in Keswick.

Catherine was a friend and older sister figure for Bessie. As escapees from family, they were kindred spirits, and though neither of them may have disclosed their deepest confidences, they would have kept each other's secrets. Catherine was committed to art, and her circle of artist friends included the architect and artist Barry Parker, the designer of Letchworth Garden City. In the first years of the 20th century, the Parkers lived nearby at Baldock in Hertfordshire and had been longstanding friends of Lizzie Howard, Ebenezer's wife. It was Lizzie who had successfully pressed the case for Barry Parker to become the first Garden City's architect, with Raymond Unwin. Despite fierce opposition, Lizzie's choice won over Ebenezer's preference for a different London-based firm. She had known Parker and Unwin's earlier work in Buxton, Derbyshire and was well acquainted with the Parker brothers, all of whom were committed to the Movement. Barry's brother Stanley had trained at Manchester School of Art with Letchworth artist William Ratcliffe, and taught at the innovative Bedales School in Hampshire. Roger, the third brother, would become Letchworth's first urban farmer with his partner Frank Storr.

Catherine Howard's early life exemplified the severe social restrictions placed on girls and women until the late 19th century. Leaving home was impossible for almost any reason other than marriage in an aspirational lower-middle class family like hers. In her youth, respectability was the enemy of female independence. She was born in Fairlight Villas, Hackney in 1865, the child of Ebenezer Howard's paternal uncle, John Branney Howard. Her mother died young. Born in 1808, John Branney had become a London tailor and draper and built up a good living. Catherine and Ebenezer were first cousins who knew each other from childhood days in London. 'Ben' was 15 years her senior, and she'd heard him fizzing with ideas, demonstrating a series of inventions before he sailed to America in 1870 when she was five. When he returned to London, their friendship blossomed. Unusually, Catherine was still at school at the age of 16, living with her family at 205 Amherst Road, near Hackney Downs. Her father was long retired, living with his second wife, affluent enough to employ a servant and to declare himself in the 1881 census as a man of 'independent means'.

All Catherine had ever wanted to do was paint for a living, but ten years later she was still at home, a frustrated 26-year-old free spirit with aged parents and no declared occupation. Her elder sister, Fanny, had fewer inhibitions and greater strength of purpose: she moved out and trained as a concert pianist, with some success. A niece's letter mentions that she inherited the small attaché case in which Fanny stashed the sandwiches which kept her going between public performances.[101] Drawing and painting staved off Catherine's days of boredom, but not her sense of being left behind as opportunities for women began to open up. Painting trips to the Lake District began her long-drawn-out release from confinement. Catherine's father was no tyrant. His need for care was the justification for refusing the unthinkable: that his daughter would live alone as a single woman. She internalised her parents' needs: held by kindness, passively accepting the social power that restricted her freedom, she was a Victorian victim of 'repressive tolerance' – until, in her late 20s, Catherine found her courage, packed her bags, and moved to her own home, supported, reluctantly or not, by subsidies from John Branney's carefully accumulated capital.

By 1901, Catherine Howard was a full-time artist selling her work: a single woman living the bohemian life in a Hampstead artists' colony. The Mall Studios were tucked away in an alleyway off Tasker Road. Artists lived in each of the eight cottages, some alone, some with family, others with friends. Walter Sickert and others in the Camden Town Group lived or visited there, and possibly also Harold Gilman, William Ratcliffe, Stanley Parker, and Spencer Gore, several of whom joined Letchworth's early artistic community. Long after Catherine left Hampstead, Barbara Hepworth was based at Mall Studios, first with her sculptor husband John Skeaping, then with Ben Nicholson – to be followed briefly at No. 2 by Henry Moore. Catherine lived and painted at No. 4 with another painter, Mabel Parminter. Watercolour was her medium. Among her neighbours was Eva Roos, a successful illustrator of children's books, including Kingsley's *Water Babies* and Ellen Wood's 1860s sensational best-selling novel of middle-class morality, *East Lynne*, which was still going strong 40 years later. Roos's husband was the American painter Simon Vedder. Another neighbour, John Scott, became a Royal Academician.

In her newly liberated life, Catherine visited 'Ben' and Lizzie in Stamford Hill. She was close to both of them and took their daughter Kathleen Daisy, 15 years younger, under her wing. In the early 1900s, as Letchworth was being built, Catherine met its architect, Barry Parker, the missionary who inspired Garden City settlements in Brazil, Portugal, Italy, Germany, and South Africa. From 1905, Letchworth's socially progressive, libertarian, and artistic pioneers began to move in alongside working-class Londoners. Catherine began to spend time in the new community, interested in its modernity and in the artists and craftspeople flocking there. She befriended Barry's brother Roger, a secret she shared with no-one at first. He was 15 years younger, living with his mother at Baldock, where Catherine was a welcome guest. Roger confided in her: it's likely he was in a gay relationship. Bisexuality and cohabitation outside marriage were strong elements of 'New Lifer' beliefs and experimental ways of life, including in the Hampstead artists' enclave and the new Garden City.

Roger Parker and Frank Storr began farming together as tenants at Manor Farm, Norton in the Letchworth Grange area. Sometimes called 'Old Manor Farm', it was made up of barns and outbuildings dating back to the 17th century. Catherine was a regular visitor and is said to have painted the farm. She would doubtless have engaged with craftspeople setting up in the town, discussing textiles at the St Edmundsbury silk-weaving workshop with Dorothea and Edmund

Hunter, and watching George Adams making replica Indian sandals. Edward Carpenter, prominent socialist and early proponent of sexual freedoms, straight and gay, had invented the sandals, and Adams had been his lover and business partner at their communal experiment near Sheffield, taking the workshop with him to Letchworth. Sandals signalled freedom, lampooned as the badge of 'cranks', unsettling critics like George Orwell. In his attacks on Letchworth he also denounced its dreary 'high minded women' as 'bluebottles descending on a dead cat'.[102]

After a few years Frank Storr left for Canada for unknown reasons. Roger bought 'Old Manor' Farm.[103] In 1909, it was 'radically modernized' by Barry Parker and co-designer of Letchworth, Raymond Unwin. Their improvements, which reflected Letchworth's – and Catherine and Roger's – eccentric lifestyle, included 'open-air bed-space' on a balcony at the rear and a badminton court. In 1912, the farm was sketched and painted by William Ratcliffe, family friend and one of the Camden Town artists who came to live in Letchworth. Ratcliffe stayed on for decades, a well-liked citizen, but less successful than most of his peers, always painting but selling little. He struggled with poverty throughout his life.[104]

Roger and Catherine appear as a couple in the 1911 census, living on the farm with a woman art-teacher, and married for less than a year. According to Barry Parker's widow Mabel, in her beautiful 1960s memoir, Roger and Catherine married in 1910, and held perpetual open house, welcoming an endless stream of visitors, including Catherine's artist friends. Of all the 'in-laws', she was Mabel's favourite: 'infinitely kind, warm-hearted, sensitive, self-less, hospitable and welcoming on all occasions … She made us all so happy at "The Grange"' (as she called the farm). A good friend for Bessie, adrift from her own family, to have. Catherine took courses in dairy farming and became a skilled farmer. She delivered calves, made butter, and lavished love on her ducks. Her only dislike, wrote Mabel Parker, was hens, despite their plentiful eggs. She brought art into farming, hanging her paintings in the cow-shed above the milking stalls, and she swore the cows enriched their milk by gazing at them.[105]

Figure 52: Manor Farm, Norton, Letchworth Grange, William Ratcliffe's 1912 painting of Roger Parker and Catherine Howard's farm. The figures could be Catherine and Roger, with family or friends.

Catherine gradually abandoned her ambition to be a professional painter when she and Roger left Letchworth for south-west Cornwall in 1921 and bought farmland and a house called Penharvon above the Helford river. Several Mall Studio neighbours were later associated with the Newlyn School. Barbara Hepworth arrived in Cornwall in 1939, late in Catherine's life. Perhaps they met: art and artists remained part of her Cornwall life. Bessie and Cecil would have visited early in their Hampstead Garden Suburb days, arriving by motorbike and side-car. Catherine and Bessie were friends who had taken charge of their lives against the odds and guarded old secrets behind new public identities.

According to Mabel Parker, Roger and Catherine 'mothered the village', drawing her family into their Helford circle like 'a magnet'. In the late 1920s, Barry designed Tree Tops, a modern house on Roger and Catherine's land. It was a holiday home, but mostly let out to make ends meet or to make friends happy. Like Ebenezer's family, none of the Parkers had enough money to finance their taste for adventure. They had to work hard, day by day and contract by contract.

Alongside their dairy herds and ducks, Catherine and Roger grew violets for the London market. Violet-farming in Britain disappeared long ago, but the little purple flowers were a long-lasting 19th-century obsession, encouraged by Queen Victoria's passion for their highly perfumed petals. The popularity of violets lingered on through the first half of the 20th century: when I was a child in suburban Manchester in the 1950s, small bunches of violets, tied with raffia and wrapped in a large leaf, sat in small tin buckets on the florist's counter. Violets were also grown to flavour sweets like Parma Violets and shortbread, and crystallised for cake decorations. They were picked, tied, packed, and carried on the overnight flower train from Penzance to Paddington every night, along with primroses, snowdrops, Solomon's Seal, narcissi, and bluebells, and driven to Covent Garden market by five in the morning for the start of trading. The 'flower train' ran until the 1990s, when railways were privatised and Cornish blooms were sent up by lorry instead. By then, the popularity of tiny scented flowers had faded. Big bright blooms flown in from overseas eclipsed them in a global market for lavish bouquets and long-stemmed glamour. Violets persist in gardens and in the wild, where they refuse to disappear.[106]

Cornish flowers are linked to this story not only because Catherine was Bessie and Cecil's friend. The violet trade was a colourful example of the practical social movements that Bessie encountered. On the streets of London, violets were sold by flower girls: orphans and children disabled in factory accidents, for whom this was another means of earning a living. To alleviate their distress, John Groom, a silver engraver and Sunday School teacher, founded the 'Watercress and Flower Girls' Christian Mission' in 1866. A schoolroom, soup kitchen, and flower factory followed in the 1870s. 'John Groom's Crippleage' was housed at his Sekforde Street buildings in east London, a place where homeless flower sellers could live, work, and learn to make artificial blooms, which were growing in popularity. Like T. A. Leonard's and Henrietta Barnett's fresh-air holiday movements, Groom created orphanages for blind and disabled children in the 1890s at Clacton-on-Sea, where they could recuperate and train for the Clerkenwell works or for domestic service. The orphanages expanded to 250 beds and became a seaside holiday centre for children and Mission staff. The belief in fresh air as a vital remedy for society's ills runs through this story, energising diverse social, educational, and public-health initiatives.

The sense of Catherine Howard living her life through love, friendship, and easy laughter feels as tangible now as it must have been to Bessie. Catherine and Roger were an unusual couple, companions brought together by idiosyncratic creativity and a wish to live off the land. Close, but, who knows, perhaps not sexual partners? One day in early July 1939, when they had been together for 30 years and were still farming, Catherine and Roger went to stay with friends at Yellam Farm near Okehampton in Devon. The following day they got married by licence at the Register Office in town. Catherine was 73 and Roger was 58. Why then, and why by licence, a quicker, less public process than public banns? What was the hurry, and why keep so quiet about it? Perhaps because to the rest of the world they were married already, although if they'd thought about it, none of their friends would remember attending their wedding in Letchworth. Was Catherine ailing? Probably not. Although she died less than three years later, it was acute pneumonia that killed her. War was looming, and they would not have been immune to universal fear and uncertainty, not least as it would put paid to the violet business. Catherine might have had a health scare, perhaps the onset of a degenerative disease, which made them think again about their lives, to avoid leaving any legal complications. It's unlikely they married for inheritance reasons. When Catherine died at Penharvon in 1942, aged 76, she left Roger the princely sum of £174.11 (about £17,000 today). Her father had lived to be 97, and his independent means had been whittled away over decades. Roger admitted to being 'retired' when Catherine died. Without her spirit and companionship, it seems he lost the heart to carry on farming. Catherine and Roger had tolerated the assumption that they were married: whatever their beliefs, it made for a quiet life. Their silence protected them from the scandal-focused moral disapproval of the age, gossip, and tiresome questions.

Catherine and Roger's relationship seems to have been both a mutual convenience and a companionable friendship. Her reasons for keeping her story to herself feel different from Bessie's. They illustrate the limitations to the loosening of the tight moral straight-jacket passed down from the Victorian age, including in 'New Life', loose-clothed, free-love-influenced Letchworth, and especially for women, who bore the weight of the social conformity which still exerted its relentless pressure, even on *'Lebenskünstler'* like Roger and Catherine, artists of a freer life. Roger Parker died in 1969, aged 87. He never remarried and was living alone when he died. Penharvon is demolished, though 'Tree Tops' survives. Another legacy flourishes: clusters of violets flowering beside nearby lanes.

32 Letchworth and Keswick 1906–1907: Four Weddings

This chapter elaborates recorded facts to reconstruct Bessie's introduction to the Howard family in Letchworth Garden City, working the loose threads into stories of how events unfolded.

On the long ride to London in Spring 1906, Cecil would have rehearsed telling Ebenezer about his engagement to Bessie, mentally batting away the family's probing questions. He had no qualms about the likely responses of his father or Kathleen Daisy. Kitty was a firm friend: she'd know already. Her wedding to the charming Charles Compton Rawlinson was to take place in Letchworth in the coming August, and Cecil wanted Bessie to accompany him as a guest. At Cecil's lodgings in Chancery Lane, his father told him other news. Edith Mary intended to marry Frederick Berry, a young man with prospects in the silk trade, doing an obligatory stint as a commercial traveller, with his eye on promotion. A big wedding was planned. Cecil might have felt outshone by his sisters, and the thought of bringing Bessie to meet confident, suave Frederick – and both bridegrooms' socially ambitious families – was uncomfortable.

Cecil clearly hardened his resolve to share nothing about Bessie with his family beyond the pared-down narrative which they'd agreed on: just enough to explain her Scottish accent and her presence in Keswick. His father would have cheerfully told the world all he'd gleaned about Bessie, her family, and Galashiels childhood; but Cecil knew the world would let him down. He didn't want to confront anyone: his wish, always, was to evade conflict and stay in the background. For her own reasons, Bessie wanted exactly the same.

Cecil feared that in the social circle that Bessie was entering, her family's poverty, Catholicism, and Irishness, as well as her factory-girl, domestic-servant status, would obscure everything else about her. Her poise and courtesy would be found pleasantly surprising in someone of her background. Edith's hauteur and antennae for social status typified ways in which progressive thinking in the abstract had hardly begun to dissipate middle-class prejudices in real life. Generosity, kindness, and philanthropy, even socialism, were ideas generated by their own class to benefit the poor. Cecil, as he is remembered, and Ebenezer himself would have been exasperated by the social contortions and twisted language of condescension. Cecil admired the rebarbative energy and intelligence that his diminutive sister Edith invested in both her parents' work, promoting their reputations and more than once saving her father from foolish ideas. But there was a flipside to her dissenting Protestant views and her support for social reform. She prized the Howards' hard-won social position. For one thing, it gave the sisters freedom to live, work, and learn as modern women, following in the footsteps of their Aunt Annie, Ebenezer's sister, who took her suburban train to a city office every day. Equally, Edith's marriage would ratchet up the Howards' standing in middle-class circles, progressive and otherwise, into which she and Kitty were both marrying. Kathleen Daisy teetered close to the edge of social respectability, provided for precariously by her troubled husband, and propped up by Ebenezer. Cecil remained anxious about his working-class bride, and missed his mother's lack of hypocrisy, always standing up for Christian values in the face of prejudice.

Cecil's was a world of fears. But Bessie was surely much more self-confident by now. She wasn't looking for social convention or higher social status. She would have believed, rightly, that the Howards' upwardly mobile journey into the middle class, however short of money they were compared with others in their circle, was a trifling step up compared with her giant leap from Ladhope to Letchworth. For her, Ebenezer may have been the son of a City of London pastry-cook, but he'd long moved freely in a privileged social milieu and was now an internationally respected figure, on dining terms with the Prime Minister. His daughter Edith might have liberal theories and champion Garden Cities, but she didn't dwell on her own family's 'humble origins'. In later life she even sought evidence of blood-links to aristocratic Howards. Why would Bessie offer grist to this fantasy mill? Looking forward was Ebenezer Howard's way. It was hers, too.

Kathleen Daisy (Kitty)

Bessie made her first journey to the south of England to attend Kathleen Daisy's wedding on 2nd August 1906. Unfortunately, Letchworth's first newspaper had already folded, and the second one didn't appear until 1907, so there's no press report. Bessie would have taken trouble with her home-sewn outfit: linen and Ruskin lace. A hat was *de rigueur*, but a much simpler model than the extravaganzas worn by Cecil's mother Lizzie: Cecil would have shown her photographs. Fashion dictated that it would perch on top of her head, pinned in place or tied with a length of silk under her chin, possibly with net and ribbon trimmings, under which her long hair was swept up each side of a middle parting, and tucked in. She'd have been met by Cecil at Letchworth's new railway halt and driven in a horse-drawn cart to Mrs Crouch's cottage in Letchworth Lane, where Lizzie and Ebenezer had always lodged while they watched the building of 'First Garden City'. Mrs Crouch looked after Lizzie and Ebenezer well. Years later, on his deathbed in 1928, when Mrs Crouch was old, widowed, poverty-stricken, and facing eviction, Ebenezer bought her a life-long tenancy at the cottage. He didn't have the money, of course, but his friend and political ally Frederick Osborn stepped in, not for the first time.[107]

Figure 53: Letchworth Railway Halt, 1912. F. Spencer Gore (1878-1914)

Kitty's wedding may have presented an ideal occasion to introduce Bessie to his family, but if it was nerve-wracking for Cecil, how daunting was it for Bessie? She was resolute, but hardly brazen. Cecil's nervousness was infectious, and anxiety about walking into this unknown family's celebration might have drowned out the pleasure of anticipating her latest adventure: travelling alone through London. Ebenezer's political, literary, and aristocratic well-wishers would have turned out in numbers, including some whom Bessie might have seen in Keswick. For Ebenezer, every occasion brought the possibility of new financial and political support for the Garden City movement. Catherine Howard would have escorted Bessie, and the sight of Kathleen Daisy would be reassuring. Mrs Crouch, who always attended Howard events in Letchworth, was another comforting presence. But Bessie had made bolder life changes than anyone in her prospective family, Ebenezer and Catherine apart. She was an independent woman who had joined in Keswick's febrile community life wholeheartedly. Bessie would recognise the confident social ease of the wedding guests, and the airs and graces of the Rawlinsons and Berrys. While Charles's father described himself as a 'gentleman', his son wanted to be an artist and craftsman, attaching himself to Catherine Howard's Keswick circle as an artistic waif and stray. He especially looked up to art nouveau and Arts and Crafts artist Walter Crane, children's book illustrator, socialist, co-operator, and Letchworth *aficionado.* His respectable stock-broking family had other plans. Once Charles was married, he was dragged under, his dream of an artistic life dying in a stuffy city office. At the time of his marriage he was already described as a 'secretary'; at other times 'private secretary': euphemistic catch-all phrases, like Owen Quinn's 'contractor'. Charles was a clerk. It was, my father insisted, a miserable mismatch of person to role, and 'no wonder that Charles turned to a slug or more of whisky to gather Dutch courage'. Bessie soon understood that the family's cheerful masks hid layers of discontent.[108]

There is no evidence that Bessie had attended a wedding before, with or without a party, in Galashiels, Edinburgh, or Clydebank. Kathleen Daisy's reception may seem simple compared with celebrations now, but at the turn of the 19th and 20th centuries, weddings involving more than close family or just a couple and their witnesses were unknown to Quinns, and fairly novel to people like the Howards. If there was a party, it was generally held at home. This wedding was ambitious for its time, foreshadowing the lavish late-20th-

century reinvention of imagined traditions: a country-house reception and mingling on the lawn – but with a vegetarian menu and soft drinks.

The ceremony itself was genuinely traditional, held at St Mary's, the 12th-century Anglican parish church where Lizzie Howard had been buried in the tiny graveyard less than two years earlier. Bessie's first impression of southern England must have been richly coloured: a summer wedding in a quintessentially rural setting on a hot summer's day. The reception was in the gardens of a Jacobean manor house, Letchworth Hall, turned into a hotel as part of the Garden City. It stood at the edge of the new, nine-hole golf course which replaced a deer park. Outdoor recreation for the people was top of the Garden City wish-list. Today, the hotel survives as a conference venue, still hosting weddings and exuding the faded charm of grander days.

Imagine Bessie walking into the socially assured gathering, alongside Cecil, and under discreet scrutiny. He was much loved. To the end of his life, his modesty and shyness disarmed people and brought out protective instincts, especially in women. As far as anyone knew, he'd never courted anyone before, so surprise fuelled murmured gossip that he'd found this 'girl' on adventures north. He stayed close to Bessie and she was welcomed, but they probably left before she could be drawn into searching conversations. At dawn the next day Cecil would have met Mrs Crouch's cart at Letchworth station halt, and they took the train to London. When Spencer 'Freddy' Gore (friend of the socialist artist Harold Gilman, a Letchworth pioneer) painted the railway halt in summer 1912, it looked much as it did the day after Kitty's wedding. The couple walked from King's Cross to Euston and embraced under the station's massive arch. Cecil headed for the courts, and Bessie found a third-class carriage on the train north, sat down, bewildered and exhausted, and dabbed grit from her watery eyes until she sank into a doze. For two days, she'd felt her way towards an unfamiliar future.

Edith

When Bessie attended Edith Howard's wedding on 20th March the following year, her presence was on public record, reported in the *Citizen,* Letchworth's second local paper. By now, it was public knowledge that she and Cecil would marry before the year was out, encouraging inquisitive guests to ask more openly about her Keswick life, her Scottish childhood, and her Irish name.

This ceremony was an exemplar of Letchworth's alternative, modern Englishness. It brimmed with 'firsts': the first wedding to be held at the Free Church Hall, Letchworth's first new church. There would soon be several more. Perhaps steered by Ebenezer, Edith chose a Congregationalist service. The first reception to be held at 'Mother's Hall', which over thirty years later was still how Cecil and Edith referred to 'The Mrs Howard Memorial Hall' on Norton Way. It was Letchworth's first public building, created in Lizzie's honour with an Arts and Crafts design by Barry Parker, and opened in early 1906. Lizzie was more present in the Garden City after her death than in her lifetime: it was the place she'd dreamed of, and she'd worn herself threadbare to bring it to life. Her burial in the old churchyard was followed immediately by the family's move from London to Letchworth, where, within three years, two of her daughters were married. It was, as her children believed, as much Lizzie's place as anyone's. Her drive to create the town had fuelled their hopes and haunted their long sorrow. In 1906 Bessie would already have seen the Hall dedicated to the mother-in-law she would never meet but always live with. She knew Cecil was drawn to the strong spirit of Lizzie that he felt in her, both women more self-possessed than he could comprehend.

Figure 54: 'Mother's Hall', Letchworth's first public building, opened 1906

At Edith's wedding, swathes of wild flowers and bunches of primroses expressed Letchworth's oppositional, nature-loving Englishness. Simplicity trumped artifice in 'First Garden City' forms of modernity, with its socially mixed population and radical, free-spirited people: artists, craftspeople, suffragists, and intellectuals living alongside working-class Londoners. Arts and Crafts houses, from small cottages to grand villas, clustered on wide streets with plenty of new and ancient trees and green verges. Life was for living together, outdoors, in parks, with communal allotments to promote self-sufficiency.[109] The town's activities at the time resemble Keswick's: rural festivals, maypole dancing, the Simple Life Hotel (complete with food-reform restaurant and health-food store), a temperance pub (The Skittles), and Co-op stores. New churches and halls were built early on: Theosophist, Spiritualist, and a Free Church, as well as the Quaker Meeting House, Howgills. Raymond Unwin, one of Letchworth's architects, a 'New Life' socialist and Labour Church supporter, believed in a strong spiritual dimension to building better communities.[110] New Life socialism found expression in the ILP branch, with its pacifist and internationalist ethic.[111] Letchworth became a home to Quakers and suffragists, like Annie Jane Lawrence; the Suffragettes Annie Kenney and Millicent Price came to live there. Letchworth symbolised communal living, and, for some, sexual freedom, of whatever orientation. Ebenezer was not always approving of new-lifers. His first priority was to provide a better life for working-class people, and when he met Millie Price and her children rambling 'over the Common, hatless and stockingless', he 'begged them to desist'. They would give 'the garden city a bad name as a home for cranks', and discourage new residents. The likes of George Orwell had got to him.[112]

A number of small factories and works were established, including textile workshops and the sandal-factory. J. M. Dent moved his Temple Press there, disturbing the peace with his tempestuous, energetic presence and grievously bad spelling for a publisher. From 1906, he launched Dent's famous Everyman's Library books in Letchworth, publishing 152 titles in the first year alone.[113]

The write-up of Edith's wedding in the *Citizen* spared no detail: it was attended by 'many guests', including Letchworth's founders, managers, and benefactors: a deceptively simple occasion, half wellcorseted, French-derived elegance, half loose-clad Letchworth. Edith's outfit was white silk with Parisian embroidery; she had three bridesmaids, who all carried bouquets of (out-of-season) roses: creamy-white Niphetos and the fragrant yellow French climber, Maréchal Niel. The complete wedding-gift list offers an insight into the times and tastes of Letchworth as well as Edwardian Britain's contrasting cultures. Edith's political seriousness and attachment to the Garden City movement was reflected in gifts beyond the usual array of linen, silver, and bone china. One Garden City luminary, Harold Craske, Secretary of First Garden City Limited, presented her with a set of John Ruskin's complete works. Others gave poetry books, including works by Browning and Coleridge. Copper, the metal favoured by Arts and Crafts designers, was prominent. Dutch, Armenian, French, and Japanese gifts featured alongside modern English designs. Religious differences were expressed: Edith was close to Lizzie's birth family, the Bills's, and Lizzie's mother, cousins, and friends attended the wedding. A Miss Stabb presented the couple with an inscribed Bible celebrating the first wedding at the Free Church. Lizzie's efforts to convert the Howard family to her stringent version of Christianity lived on.

As an unmarried couple, Cecil and Bessie gave separate gifts, and Bessie opted for practical modernity: 'Fire proof china', the guest list in the *Citizen* revealed. She was a professional cook, and aware of newly invented ceramics. Pyrex was only a few years away, with its revolutionary fire-proof glass. She'd have been reassured to see Mrs Crouch, present again that day, giving the couple a plain breadboard and knife. Edith's wedding reflected her contradictory and competing social impulses.

Ebenezer

Five days after Edith's wedding, on 25th March 1907, far from Letchworth, 'Ben' Howard married Edith Annie Hayward, a 42-year-old farmer's daughter, in her home village of Sleaford, Lincolnshire, where she was resident. All his children were horrified. Edith, in protest, promptly changed her name to Editha, for life.

Bessie

The marriage banns for Cecil and Bessie were published and read throughout August 1907 at St Kentigern's Church, Crosthwaite. The couple would have visited Canon Rawnsley for spiritual preparation. Edith Rawnsley would help them with practically everything else – she took her role seriously. Ebenezer placed a notice in the Letchworth *Citizen:* his son Arthur Cecil Howard was to marry Bessie Quinn, 'only daughter of Owen Quinn, deceased'. True, up to a point. Bessie's father and sister Mary were both dead. 'Only surviving daughter' would have been more accurate, but might have led to wondering and whispering. Neither banns nor notices mention Mary: mothers, dead or alive, were not recorded on English marriage certificates. No questions asked, no discomforting ghosts revealed. So began the legend of our little orphan Bessie.

Bessie had friends in Keswick to help her prepare her wedding. One was Jean (Jeannie) Rayson, invited to be a witness. The two must have met when working linen, or at Newlands, or in an organisation like the Band of Hope at Crosthwaite or Stair. Records show Jeannie was an Assistant Schoolteacher a few years older than Bessie. Teaching was not a middle-class profession, and Jeannie, whose brother was an agricultural labourer, would have started as a pupil teacher after leaving school. She and Bessie had both been at school for six or seven years. That year, Jeannie was working at the Church of England National School in Ivegill, a hamlet south of Carlisle, reached by an unmade road. Her mother kept the shop and Post Office in the tiny remote settlement, where now traffic roars past on the M6. Jeannie remained an Assistant Teacher for many years afterwards, a single woman living with her brother Herbert Rayson in Carlisle.

Perhaps in possession of her own sewing machine by now, Bessie would have made her own outfit after hours. The dress would have been simple and incorporated Ruskin lace. At Porch Cottage, she could have picked up slubby linen remnants in natural colours – the only acceptable tones – cream or fawn, and trimmings of silk and crêpe de chine. Bessie could have made the lace at Porch Cottage: Guild of St George roses and a simple veil dotted with Ruskin roses. Under the soft falls of her frock were loose underclothes. Her well-worn light boots would do. On the day, she would tie her hair back with a mother-of-pearl clasp decorated with late violets and give Cecil a bunch for his button-hole. He was clean-shaven as always, among the long moustaches and beards of guests, wearing the everyday suit he wore to the courts, a white shirt with a small round collar, and a soft silk cravat. His black ankle boots were almost identical to Bessie's.

On the afternoon of Thursday 5th September 1907, Bessie and Cecil were married at St Kentigern's. Bessie declared herself to be 26; Cecil, 25. In fact, he was 24 until November that year; she was already 28. Like many couples, they plotted their harmless fib, perhaps sitting by Friars Crag, intended perhaps to present more conventional age differences to the world and divert attention from such different life-stories. Quite possibly she'd never told Cecil her age, which would account for later records he signed. The witnesses to their marriage were Ebenezer Howard (there was no sign of his new wife), Kathleen Daisy's husband Charles Compton Rawlinson, and Jeannie Rayson. An account of the day by Kathleen Daisy was discovered in a letter a lifetime later. Charles would have been happy to be back in Cumberland, released from floundering in his stock-broker's office. Jeannie Rayson was Bessie's witness, a new woman friend in the absence of her family. But she could hold her own. Catherine Howard would have come, perhaps with Roger Parker. My father inherited from Cecil a watercolour of Derwentwater by Catherine. It could have been her wedding present.

Afterwards, guests took part in a wedding party, probably a high tea. According to a letter from his Aunt Kitty to my father nearly 50 years after the event, a 'happy' wedding party was held at the newly opened Friar's Café. It was 'the first party they'd given'. Where was it? Keswick in 1907 was chock-full of hotels, boarding houses, refreshment rooms, and cafés. References to Friars are still prominent in Keswick's tourist branding. They stem from the Anglo-Saxon hermit, St Herbert of Derwentwater, who lived and died on the island named after him. 'Refreshment rooms' had started in 19th-century railway stations across the country: think institutional white cups and saucers, and *Brief Encounter*. After sifting through the lists and small advertisements in Kelly's 1906 and 1910 directories, and no 'Friars Café' listed, I'm convinced the café that Kathleen Daisy remembered was part of Friars Hotel (which boasted a café), listed as owned by John and Sophia Greenhow. Kitty wrote that the family was 'friendly with the owners'. John Greenhow was born and bred in Keswick and a joiner by trade. For several years before Newlands opened,

Greenhow's Hotel had taken groups of Co-operative Holiday Association guests, and Greenhow had a close association with T. A. Leonard and the Rawnsleys. With these connections, he and Sophia were likely to have hosted the wedding party. Greenhow's was on the corner of Penrith Road and Station Road, opposite the entrance to Upper Fitz Park, where the Keswick Museum and Art Gallery – a fine Arts and Crafts building – stands. Today, the building is 36 Station Street, an agent for Cumbrian holiday cottages.[114]

If Cecil spoke at his wedding, it would have been in character: brief and tearfully romantic. Ebenezer or Charles Compton Rawlinson would have proposed a toast, with glasses of non-alcoholic beverages – though not all the guests would have declined a glass of whisky if offered, especially Charles. Sherry and port were other Edwardian wedding favourites.[115] At dusk, guests could have strolled across the water meadows on the north shore of Derwentwater – now Hope Park – as far as Friars Crag, shivered in the north wind, and looked over yellow gorse bushes across the water to Catbells. 1907 had been one of the coldest, wettest summers for years. According to Kitty's letter, Cecil and Bessie spent the next nights in Newlands' married quarters, then travelled by motorbike and side-car to Devon, where they missed their beloved, 'bracing' Cumberland among soggy moors and south-westerly downpours.[116]

It is highly unlikely that any of Bessie's brothers attended her wedding. The previous years had seen the demise or disappearance of one sibling after another, as well as the death of her father. Owen, Arthur, Alexander, and Mary were gone. Tom was wandering homeless between Edinburgh and Glasgow, and would any of the working men who struggled along – Patrick-Peter, James, Peter, or Augustine – venture south of the border to attend the wedding of their far-away little sister to an English stranger? They did know that she'd made a good match: in her nineties, Nellie Quinn, Bessie's niece, remembered from 'family talk' that 'one of them had made an excellent marriage, but I have no idea to whom'.[117] Peter would have sent Bessie news of his own wedding to Susan Boyle in February, the progress of their baby James, and the fact that they were sheltering young Owen and Tom. If any Quinns were in Keswick that day, it could only have been Peter.

33 Kirkpatrick Durham, Kirkcudbrightshire
Mary Lyons Quinn

One Scottish story remains to be told. Regardless of her absence from Bessie's marriage documents, or any subsequent reference to her anywhere, her mother Mary Lyons Quinn was very much alive in September 1907. I have already told how in June 1906 Mary was sent to Mrs Milne's boarding house in Kirkcudbrightshire under Kilpatrick Parish Board's outdoor relief system, on grounds of 'insanity'. There, for the first time in her life, Mary slept alone in a room. Apart from her journey from Brownrigg across the Lammermuir Hills to Walkerburn, she had never been away from family. She was not judged mad enough to be committed to an asylum: not in 1906, nor at any point in her life. She would have been increasingly forgetful, anxious, and eccentric. Unused to solitude, living among strangers, she must have been trapped inside the slow-creeping fog that her life's inconsolable losses had brought in. There's no evidence of a fast-advancing, character-altering dementia, like Alzheimer's, which scrambled her memory and use of language.

Keswick was 82 miles from the village of Kirkpatrick Durham, where Mary lived in 1907. She would surely still have recognised her surviving daughter, last seen in early 1904. But a visit to her, even accompanied, was unthinkable: forbidden even if it was practicable. Even for a fit and healthy person it was a long and circuitous journey to Keswick and back, with stops and changes on trains and carts. Geographically, Kirkcudbrightshire was out on a limb. And for Mary, Bessie's new milieu was on a different planet. Mary Quinn could not have mingled with easy-mannered middle-class English strangers in a country she'd never visited. It was tough enough for Bessie, despite inheriting Mary's inner strength. There is no sign that Mary ever left Kirkpatrick Durham, let alone crossed the border into England. Though it is possible that Bessie, or more likely one of her brothers, Peter or James, visited their mother.

Imagine Mary Lyons, the tough survivor from Heapstown, Sligo. She and her younger siblings had walked across lowland Scotland to labour in the East Lothian fields. This is the young woman who struck out for the Borders, found a factory job, sang as she walked with other girls to the mill; who could spin, weave, and sew; who became the mother of ten babies, all of whom she fed and raised into adulthood, then took in two orphaned grandchildren. In her late fifties, overwhelmed, she'd left her husband and his mounting troubles. She'd finally lost heart, or acceded to her son Peter's decision to take her to safety with him in Clydebank. Her luck did not turn: two more children, Alex and her daughter Mary, were lost within two years, before the Parish Board stripped her of a lifetime's independence. In exile, she was reduced to a category: 'insanity'.

It is more likely that Mary suffered depression, grief, loneliness, and a lack of emotional support. She was the victim of a common misdiagnosis made in ignorance of the external factors that had contributed to her decline. Heartbreak must have been the catalyst of mental breakdown: extreme emotional distress, which compounded the chronic exhaustion of a lifetime's hard labour. Mary could have suffered a trauma-induced depression and anxiety, in which confusion, loss of memory, slipping-sliding timeframes, and constant weeping mingled as symptoms. All this seems more appropriate to her state of being than a diagnosis of 'insanity'. Mad perhaps – mad with bewildering loss – and grieving without emotional and psychological support to help her recover. Mary's independent life was born of malnutrition and sickness in Ireland. Her children's deaths and her own displacement would have sent her reeling back in time, a formidable character disappearing into the depths of her early experience.

In December 1907, 18 months after she was sent away, came the death of Owen, the grandchild she'd reared from babyhood, who looked after her during her last months at Radnor Park. 1907 was an eventful year for the Quinn family. Perhaps Mary was not fully aware of these deaths, every one linked to lung disease. However, the Boarding-house Keeper's accountability to the Parish Board for those in her charge, and Peter's role as the linchpin of a family bound to report changes in their circumstances, make it likely that Mary was informed of family events. She would have known little if anything about Augustine's First World War service; or that her grandson Jimmy, who'd visited his 'Granny Quinn' in Clydebank as a child, served two years at the front in the Royals Scots regiment before he was badly wounded at the Battle of the Somme. She was spared some of the anxiety and mental breakdown among mothers of soldiers in the King's Own Scottish Borderers lost in France, mothers she knew from Haddington and Galashiels.[118] She might have learned of Bessie's happy London life – and her death – if Bessie had not broken the terms of the Poor Law and cut her ties with the family.

Mary is recorded on the census, living at Kirkpatrick Durham in 1911 with Jane Walker, an Irish-born woman from Dumbarton known to the Poor Law officials in Old Kilpatrick. In 1911, Jane Walker had moved away from Clydebank with her son Alexander, aged 12, to become a 'Boarding House Keeper', taking over from Mrs Milne, Mary's first landlady. The house had four rooms in total and accommodated two boarders. Mary was one, now classed as a 'lunatic'. Agnes Wilson was the other, a 67-year-old 'totally blind' woman, also from Dumbarton. Mrs Milne meanwhile had moved her Poor Law Boarding House establishment to a larger house, where, with her son, she set up an 'imbecile home' for adult male 'lunatics' down the road in Crocketford. The documents point to a handover of her Kirkpatrick Durham house to Jane Walker. Mary continued to live there.

How were her days filled for 16 years – 5,840 days – in outdoor relief? Mary, a skilled woman, could still possibly have stitched, spun, or cooked. More likely, while she had the strength, she was required to scrub, dust, peel 'tatties', and change bed linen – as she always had. She couldn't read or write. But if she could access memories, at least she and Jane Walker could swap stories of their childhoods in Ireland.

Mary's death was not caused by a medically assessed mental illness. She died on 26th October 1922, aged 78, after a seven-day bout of bronchitis. She was recorded as the widow of Owen Quinn, his status elevated to 'mason': that information could have come from the Old Kilpatrick Parish Board, or Jane Walker's memories of the Quinn family. No Quinn ever described Owen as a mason. Either Jane or the Parish Board inspector informed Peter, so the family certainly knew of her death, and it is just possible that Peter, James, or Augustine attended her funeral. She was buried in a common grave in the kirkyard of the Church of Scotland at Kirkpatrick Durham. Mary Quinn lived her last 16 years in a village about the size of Heapstown, the Sligo townland where she was born and lived for most of her first 16.

Mary was the last link to her branches of Irish-born Quinn and Lyons relatives in Ireland, a country which by 1922 was radically changed. That year, the Irish Free State came into being in the midst of civil war, and Michael Collins was assassinated as a traitor by fellow nationalists for his leading part in creating a hated compromise with the British. Mary's own place in Ireland's history became even more invisible in the same year. She died four months after the Dublin Public Records Office was burned down on 30th June 1922, during the 'Battle of Dublin'. Explosives were detonated in the Four Courts Building during an exchange of fire between the Irish Republican Army and the British, destroying many of the records held there, including possibly hers and Owen's. The War of Independence and the Civil War (1921–1923) were brutal new chapters in Anglo–Irish relations.

Eight years after Mary Quinn's death, mental-health institutions and terminology relating to mental conditions changed across Britain. The Mental Treatment Act (1930) provided free voluntary treatment for psychiatric conditions, and access to outpatient clinics. The term 'asylum' was replaced with 'mental hospital', and 'lunatic' was replaced by 'person of unsound mind'. Also in 1930, Poor Law unions and workhouses, including those in Scotland, were abolished following the Local Government Act (1929). Poorhouses became hospitals, or 'public assistance institutions', operating under local councils.

Two decades after their Poor Law applications, Mary and her grandson Arthur George might not have been so hastily incarcerated simply for being poor, different, and vulnerable, their Catholic beliefs and practices ignored in the decision taking of the Poor Law system and its heavy-handed, punitive solutions for dealing with people in need. Tom might have had a gentler end in a TB sanatorium, like two of his brothers who died later of the same cause, even if he'd have struggled to stay put for long even in a benign institution.

The Poor Law changes after the First World War reflected the gradual shift in attitudes and public policy over the next three decades which laid some of the ground for the Welfare State established by the Labour government in the late 1940s. The economic slump of the early

1920s led to the abandonment of the rule that unemployed people were not entitled to poor relief. The Poor Law Emergency Powers (Scotland) Act of 1921 recognised 'ordinary' as well as 'able-bodied' applicants. Tom would have fitted both categories. The Quinns were among millions who had suffered the humiliations of the Poor Law. The Mitchell Library holds records for over a million applications from Glasgow, and west along the Clyde, with a disproportionate number of Irish people among those who suffered the ignominy, the culture of shame, the punishment of poverty, and the stigmatising of mental frailty and illness.

34 London: Hampstead Garden Suburb
1907: At Home Alone

Bessie and Cecil spent their honeymoon in Devon getting soaked. They'd have walked all day, bent against winds and horizontal rain. When they arrived in London, the plaster was still wet on the cottage that Ebenezer Howard had arranged for them to move into – on Asmuns Hill, one of the first streets to be built in Hampstead Garden Suburb. Their home was designed by Letchworth's architects, Barry Parker and Raymond Unwin. The pioneering settlement in north-west London was designed to bring the best of the country to the city, a mirror-image of Letchworth's vision, and initially with similar social ambitions. Working-class and middle-class people would live together in progressive harmony. Ebenezer was the inspiration behind the Suburb, which was taken forward with zeal by the prominent social reformers Henrietta and Samuel Barnett, and designed by Raymond Unwin, as committed as ever to architecture which reflected the simple life, meeting the real needs of its occupants.[119]

Figure 55: Living on a building site: Hampstead 'model village' under construction,1908

Among the first residents of the Suburb, Cecil and Bessie would have seen architects' plans and ploughed their way across the muddy site. Until it was ready they lived above a shop, 19a St James Parade, Muswell Hill. For the first time in her life Bessie had money and time to spend beyond her wildest imaginings. Turning over a pile of ephemera in the Carlisle archives, I came across a handwritten postcard from Bessie to the Keswick School of Industrial Arts, dated 21st October, 1907 at 7.15 am. It was Monday morning, so Cecil must have left for work and she was alone, probably spending wedding-present money. She was after a 'copper spirit-Kettle' with jug and sugar bowl, 'about 42/-s' (shillings: over £2 or £230 today). She'd have known the design, or seen it in a Keswick display.

> I should very much like to have one or two sent on app. I remember seeing one I liked very much on a visit. It was a little squat-shaped one. If you have got such a one, I should like it sent on. Hoping you will send them as soon as possible, and oblig, yours truly, B. Howard.

The couple would have received cheques from Howard family and friends – a common wedding gift, according to newspaper write-ups. Enough money for Bessie to bring talismanic objects from her Keswick world, if not from Scotland. She made out her order in the slightly grand and impatient tone of a visitor, not a worker. The kettle was squared-off top and bottom. It survives, along with the spirit burner, jug, and sugar bowl: useful, beautiful objects, true to Arts and Crafts principles. They were once well used, dropped on a hard floor a few times by the look of it, but since Bessie's death they have served only as ornaments.

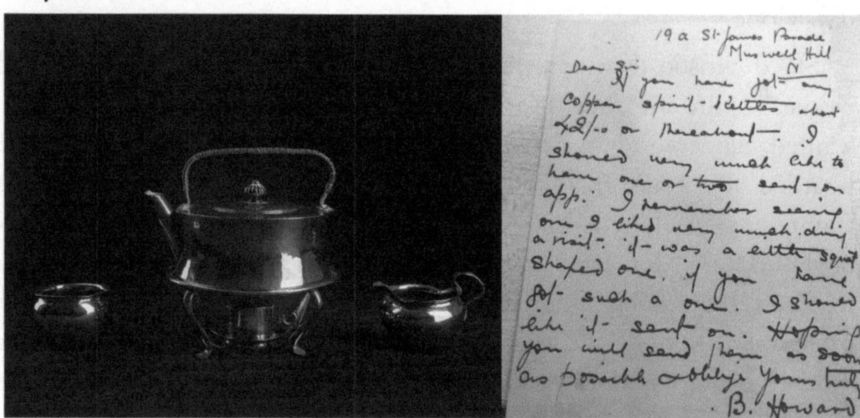

19a St James Parade
Muswell Hill

Dear Sir
If you have got any copper spirit-kettles about £2/-0 or thereabout. I should very much like to have one or two sent on app. I remember seeing one I liked very much during a visit. It was a little squat shaped one. If you have got such a one. I should like it sent on. Hoping you will send them as soon as possible & oblige Yours truly
B. Howard

Figure 56: KSIA Copper Kettle set and Bessie's handwritten order.
So Dad's trademark 'd' upstrokes copied hers.

Later that autumn, Bessie and Cecil moved into 22 Asmuns Hill, a semi-detached Arts and Crafts cottage with a garden front and back. A gate at the bottom of the back garden led to a communal tennis court and allotments. Their house had a sitting room, kitchen, indoor bathroom, and three bedrooms. Five rooms, each with a window, for two people: two rooms was the maximum the twelve Quinns had ever known. There was gas for cooking, electric light, and coal to heat the kitchen range. Cecil left each morning for the Bankruptcy Court from Golders Green, the terminus of the Northern line; a 1908 railway poster by an unknown artist depicts the planned new suburb, with tree-lined avenues and an idyllic lifestyle among leafy open spaces.

For the first time in her life Bessie was alone all day, responsible for no-one except herself, with little to do except housework – light for her – and shopping. She must have looked around her new environment and absorbed the unaccustomed quiet, broken only by birdsong and building work, with long hours alone to take in where she was and who she now had become. The eeriness of a silent house in an unknown place was unlike the inner retreats from the noise and demands of others, a life spent among the clamour and clutter of family, the din of the mill and the biscuit factory, non-stop talk at Porch Cottage, or staff flying about the Newlands servery, shouting above rowdy guests and handing out balm for blisters. But however homesick and confused she might be, strong love and cold clarity told her she never wanted to go back. Here's how I imagine one of her first days alone.

She'd chosen this man, this life, and this place. She could spin and weave her life into her desired pattern and tell her story any way she wanted. Since she had decided next to nothing in her life before she boarded the train from Clydebank, this freedom must have been frightening and lonely. Like other women used to sharing small spaces or bound by domestic service, she was supposed to be enjoying freedom, but anxiety, guilt, and her family's fate stalked her. However often she ushered them out, they returned, especially thoughts of her mother, living who knows where or how. Cooped up in Clydebank, the liberty Bessie had craved was not meant to feel like this.[120]

Over the coming weeks Bessie must have steadied herself, following the ghost of her resilient father through the back door into the garden, where the lumpy London clay, gluey from November downpours, was strewn with stones and builders' rubble. Listlessly she picked up a few clods, and threw stones into a paint-bespattered bucket. She sat on the kitchen step, and a blackbird arrived: company which sparked a current of energy. She stood up, picked out a spade from a shiny line of garden tools, another wedding present. Sleeves rolled up, she dug with a determination which belonged to her mother. Over the following days, she marked out borders with the stones and hoed some rows to sow seeds. The blackbird continued its subdued winter song from the chimney-tops. She remembered the stories of her parents leaving Ireland for a new country, penniless and hungry, and how blackbirds, rowans, and whin bushes were their links across borders, between past and present. When it was nearly dark, the bird's song turned to anxious chatter, then stillness. Bessie slumped on to a wooden bench, another wedding present. Indoors, she'd take a bath, get dressed, and hurry down to Temple Fortune Lane to buy the ingredients for high tea when Cecil returned from work.

Step by step, plant by plant, Bessie settled herself, feeding the bouncing blackbirds and robins. From scraps of builders' hardwood, Cecil carved a bird-table – another of my father's insistent memories – until, as I imagine it, she was confident enough to help neighbours to plant a joint hawthorn hedge and start digging on the shared allotments. She was easing herself to the edge of the growing band of residents and their social activities, holding back a little, always wary of conversations which might get out of hand.

The confidence that Bessie had developed through her Keswick acquaintances, above all 'Ben' (who was now her only father), equipped her, just about, for encounters with the leading lights of the Suburb: Henrietta Barnett, who surged through the suburb's muddy streets like a galleon in full sail; Raymond Unwin, architect of the Suburb, eloquently pouring out socialist ideals; and even her forceful sister-in-law Editha. Henrietta and Samuel Barnett were friends of Canon Rawnsley and Octavia Hill. Ebenezer knew them well: they shared a belief in 'practicable socialism'. Like John Groom, Henrietta Barnett had started a holiday scheme for slum children from London's East End.[121] Bessie was in familiar territory, although the metropolitan style, the unconscious *hauteur* of the Hampstead people, must have been more intimidating than the sociability of her Keswick benefactors. But she had her mother's courage and she could discuss almost everything with 'Kitty' – Kathleen Daisy, living just across the road at 7, Asmuns Hill and expecting her first child. Kitty knew a lot about Bessie and could confide in her about unhappy Charles. Bessie was more wary of Editha and her urbane husband. They lived a few streets away, mingling easily with the Suburb's grandees and delegations of VIPs from home and abroad, royalty included.

At weekends, Cecil and Bessie took day trips on the motorbike and sidecar. The Bradbury had been replaced by a twin-cylinder BAT. At Wayland's Smithy on the Ridgeway they picnicked in fields near the Uffington White Horse. In the summer swifts screamed and dived above the rooftops of tiny Berkshire villages, reminding Bessie of Galashiels. In May 2017, I watched them free-wheeling above the rooftops of Halliburton Place. On the Ridgeway, Cecil might point out Neolithic long barrows and stone circles. There's a battered postcard from a later trip that he took to Wayland's Smithy, long after Bessie, with who knows what thoughts of past pleasures in his mind.

Figure 57: The Maypole Dancing at the top of Asmuns Hill 1909

35 Hampstead Garden Suburb 1909–1919: Modern Mother

In February 1909, Bessie gave birth to her first child at Asmuns Hill. They called my father Cecil Geoffrey: no Quinn roots were exposed by such a stoutly Welsh–Norman name. When their second boy was born in 1911, Bessie must have felt bolder about her identity: they called him Donald Gordon. All his life, his daughter Julie has told me, Donald loved Scotland, proud of his 'Scottish side'. He bought Gordon Highlanders' tartan kilts for his daughters from Lochcarron, or another of the dwindling number of Borders mills in the 1950s. From the late 1930s, Donald was a builder of suburban strip housing that he was convinced honoured Ebenezer's Garden City vision. He wanted to buy a holiday house in Scotland and was disappointed when his wife persuaded him to buy an apartment on the French Riviera instead. Gently accommodating like his father, he agreed.[122]

Bessie was no newcomer to bringing up boys: she'd wiped her little brothers' noses every day of their lives, as well as child-mothering baby nephews Owen and Arthur George. As right-hand helper to her exhausted mother, she'd kept the small children washed, well clothed, and out in the fresh air, eking out Owen's subsistence wages, searching out cheap cuts of meat and vegetables to keep them healthy. She'd become a professional cook. In London, she learned about the new ideas and practices of motherhood and baby-rearing influential in progressive social circles. Now she embraced innovative educational methods for kindergarten toddlers. Sewing was second-nature to her, and she had time to apply her Ruskinian lace-making skills. She was a cyclist and hill walker. Bringing up her own babies in a house with three bedrooms, hot running water, and a steady income: what could be so difficult about that? She had time to wheel them in a single high-wheeled pram round the Suburb, down to Temple Fortune Lane and into the newly public Hampstead Heath Extension. In her curiosity to explore modern life and motherhood, it grew easier to swat intrusions of guilt back to the past where they came from – and mostly stayed put.

This chapter draws on conversations with my father and the memoir he wrote while we were searching for Bessie. In his account, her young family had a whale of a childhood: all ups and no downs.[123] Only the sunny glow of love was allowed into his remembered utopia, perched on his beautiful mother's lap, or sitting on the floury kitchen table while she made pastry – or her unequalled rice pudding with raspberry jam. They had sweets galore: Dad's love of liquorice allsorts, and Duncan's Walnut Whips (invented in Edinburgh in 1910), lasted a lifetime. For Bessie, were these treats reminders of the Newington factories? The only inconsolable moments of my Dad's remembered childhood were the ones that became funny stories, like the time he was playing catch with his Walnut Whip on a visit to the local bank with Cecil: tossing it too high, he scored an own-goal into the bowl of a high-hanging lampshade. He was devastated by the irretrievable loss, he told my sister Ros.

According to Dad, both his parents taught their sons to read before they started school. They learned to sew, and watched Cecil at his carpentry – making tea-trays and pot stands, carved with Arts and Crafts motifs. They built model aircraft with wood and oiled silk. Dad's gardening skill goes back to the Suburb: his fuschias, roses, sweet peas, and domes of primroses always burgeoned under green fingers in his fine-sifted compost. Bessie encouraged them to draw, study nature, and ride a bike, perching them on hers when they were barely tall enough to sit on the saddle. The four of them played tennis on the Suburb's communal courts, Cecil fired up his sons with his love of cricket, and they'd all take off to the Oval with a picnic and scorecards to update with stubby pencils. Grandfather Ben would join them. In winter, they watched Tottenham Hotspur, never *Spurs*, a lifelong allegiance. He'd intone the full name, then, volume turned up, roll out the 1921 first-team line-up like a list poem. All these memories earthed potent experiences

Even school was beautiful. Progressive educational ideas were mainstream in Hampstead Garden Suburb, as they were in Letchworth. Bessie chose the local Montessori School, based on a pioneering and innovative educational philosophy which, like many initiatives of the time, amounted to a social movement. Montessori's child-centred pedagogy was one of several in Britain and Europe which challenged

19th-century educational methods. The pedagogy of Pestalozzi was followed by the theories of Froebel, Margaret Macmillan, and Maria Montessori, whose first school, the '*casa dei bambini*', opened in 1907 in the slums of Rome. Born in 1870, she became Italy's first qualified woman doctor. Montessori was interested in how poor children could best learn, including children with learning difficulties and disabilities or undiagnosed conditions similar to those now understood as the autism spectrum. Arthur George Quinn could no doubt have benefited. Montessori's call to 'follow the child' promoted independent learning and self-discovery: beautiful objects, colours, and diverse textures were used to inspire creativity. My father wrote of handicrafts, drawing, and music – failing at the piano lessons he shared with 'a much more receptive girl'. Resenting the praise showered on 'Esther', he describes deliberately spoiling their duets to annoy her – letting slip a spiteful, jealous side to the blissful years. No reprimand or punishment was recalled. But these moments of temper and the mood of the garden photos suggest a childhood with ordinary frustrations, anger, and disappointments.

Montessori's curriculum was a long way from Galashiels RC elementary school, but not so far from Froebel's teachings, adopted by Galashiels's philanthropic Sime sisters, whose well-publicised new methods at their kindergarten, Bessie may have known about. Montessori's ideas also reflected the practical and imaginative creativity that she encountered in Keswick.

Bessie's attachment to Montessori indicates again that she did not simply or suddenly transform herself from a girl from a poor Irish family with only a basic education into a progressive middle-class London mother. The mutation evolved over time in changing circumstances; her character, personality, and upbringing fed a confidence strong enough to charge the reinvention of her identity and her adaptation to a different social class. The powerful catalyst for Bessie, as for others, was decisive intervention by influential actors. Someone or some people in her family, school, or church, or the cultural institutions of Galashiels, affirmed her intelligence and promise in an act of recognition. Keswick was a place where seeds would drop on fertile ground and sprout, watered by love, skill, and the belief that they would bear fruit.

After Montessori, Bessie's children went to the school founded by Henrietta Barnett in 1911 'for girls and little boys' to offer a good, progressive education to children from poor families. The increasing gentrification of the Suburb gradually skewed Barnett's original goal towards middle-class children. But Dad remembered the Henrietta Barnett School as a socially mixed, creative place, where boys and girls played together at a time when gender-separated playgrounds were the norm. Drama was central to the curriculum, and he also remembered playing the Carpenter in *The Walrus and the Carpenter* and, used to getting what he wanted from doting parents, protested his outrage loudly on stage when the Walrus (played by never-to-be-forgotten Arthur Draper) stole his lines. Paradise had its stormy moments.

As the First World War ended, the boys' education became more mainstream. Geoffrey was sent to University College School for boys in Hampstead (UCS). He had thrived at sport, especially gym and netball, with an adored female teacher at Henrietta Barnett. At UCS it was all-male athletics, rigorous physical training, and competitive sports. Donald shied away from all that. In a rather patronising recollection, Dad writes that his little brother 'struggled' and 'never read a book', preferring to stay close to his mother. Donald emerges as more introspective, physically less co-ordinated, and intimidated by school regimes. His daughter's sense of her father's childhood was about a boy growing up in the warm glow of his mother's affection, in the shadow of his outgoing, charming, but powerfully competitive elder brother.

The family's adventurous holidays surfaced repeatedly in Dad's memory pool. Perhaps he caught Bessie's excitement at the idea of a holiday, an unknown element of life before she arrived in Keswick and met the early-20th-century surge of both mainstream and radical tourism. Before then, the occasional Catholic Holy Day of Obligation (attending Mass as the 'obligation') or watching pleasure boats on the Clyde would have been her only sense of free time. For working-class people in the 1900s, going away on holiday was still a novelty. As Britain industrialised, time off work (unpaid) was granted only when factories were closed during Wakes Weeks – or, in Scotland, Trades Fortnight. These weeks had grown from ancient, less regulated patterns of agricultural labour, when the observation of a saint's day stretched into 'St Monday', days off to recover from drinking and festive revels. Access to the railways made day trips and short holidays accessible to many more people. Seaside resorts for wealthier people had been growing out of fishing villages all around the coast for decades. And from the mid-19th century Glasgow workers sailed out 'doon the watter' to Rothesay or Bute, or down the Ayrshire coast to places like Girvan. Scottish workers also travelled further afield to Blackpool, for longer breaks and in large numbers. In Bessie's childhood, hundreds of Gala mill workers headed for Blackpool in Trades Fortnight each year – at least those who could afford it. Families like the Quinns did not have money or time for far-flung trips.

However, travel was no longer only for the rich to explore Europe, or the extended spells of seaside convalescence beloved by Victorians, such as Dickens and Darwin – including Cecil's mother Lizzie, who spent long weeks at Hastings, sometimes with her son, to rebuild her strength and restore her spirits. Ebenezer and Lizzie had honeymooned in style in 1879 in Paris, at the Hôtel du Parc, near Montparnasse, and Ebenezer now enjoyed solo trips to the south of France, Holland, and other countries, tagging days of leisure on to Garden City lectures. Days and weekends in Blackpool were hugely popular with working-class people, including sea-bathing, believed to have beneficial physic qualities. But the Howard family, Bessie included, belonged to different holiday movements, including the Co-operative Holiday Association and the Youth Hostel movement, whose aims were to lure people away from the raucous drinking and gambling cultures of seaside towns to breathe fresh air amid wild mountain and coastal scenery: walking, cycling, caravanning, staying in farmhouses and all-in lodgings where landladies provided meals – forerunners of Bed and Breakfast and package holidays.

Attached to Cecil's modest motorcycle was a hooded, basket-weave side-car for three, open at the front with a pram-handled detachable hood. The side-car kept out the sun, although not hard rain or spattering mud. No clutch, no gears, no kick-starter: the bike and side-car had to be push-started with passengers and luggage already aboard. But in Bessie's childhood walking ten miles and more each day was routine, and she took easily to the motorbike and outdoor holidays.

Their first holidays with the boys were in Folkestone, and among Dad's earliest memories were expeditions there on a 'much-loved red rowing boat'.

Emboldened, they returned to the Lake District. Their romantic natures drew them back to Derwentwater. For one summer holiday in the Lakes in 1912, the BAT motorcycle – known as 'The Brute' – was reassembled and the side-car attached. Geoffrey was three and Donald an 18-month-old toddler. They set off up the Great North Road, the A1, on a journey of more than 300 miles. There were several stops for picnics, peeing, and petrol, and at least one overnight stay. In Pontefract the bike broke down and they stayed overnight at an inn while a blacksmith repaired it. At Stair, they'd stay in the cottages for married guests where Bessie and Cecil spent their wedding night. Revisiting the site in the 1990s evoked a faint sense of recognition for Dad: 'This is how it must have been'. Newlands was the ideal base for exploring Borrowdale and over to Buttermere and Crummock Water. In the first of two vivid memories of this paradisiacal time, Cecil was running up Honister Pass, pushing the motorbike beside him to the top, engine switched off. It was barely powerful enough for such a steep climb for one rider, let alone three passengers. It was a hot day and Bessie followed Cecil slowly, carrying Donald, holding Geoffrey's hand as they trudged uphill step by small step until they reached the top of the Pass and looked down over the slate mine towards Gatesgarth Farm, the two long lakes beyond, and the path to Haystacks. In his second memory, Donald lost his dummy (at the time, a brand-new invention for ultra-modern families, known as a 'child comforter'). They were paddling happily, skimming stones on the shore of Buttermere. Then, an inconsolable child: the trauma of an essential 'transitional' object sunk for ever in deep black water. It wasn't Dad's loss. But Donald's howls must have captured all his parents' sympathy for this memory-splinter to be so deeply wedged under his older brother's skin.

Perhaps holidays in the Lakes proved too ambitious, and by 1913 the looming mood of war inhibited long journeys. The next family trips were beach holidays at Heacham in north Norfolk. Their isolated lodging, Beach Farm, still perched on the cliff when I visited with Dad and Mum in the 1990s, but now surrounded by a caravan park. He wept at the sight of it. Wherever Cecil and Bessie went, they rode by motorbike to places which fed their romantic longing. In Dad's memory at least. Looking west from Heacham over The Wash, they could watch the sun go down over the sea. A short walk away, the Linn Chilvers nurseries were already growing fields of French lavender. After the holiday came the practicalities: in autumn the motorbike was dismantled, the parts wrapped in newspaper and stashed away in scattered wardrobes and trunks until the following spring, when the next adventure beckoned.

A Christmas outing to see J. M. Barrie's *Peter Pan* on stage became Dad's metaphor for life before and after Bessie: delight mixed with terror. It's not clear from his memoir if this was one special treat or an annual ritual, but the play was central to Dad's myth. Re-telling the story in his eighties, he took the part of himself, enacting the childlike expressions of an entranced child. It was both grotesque and strangely moving to witness him become the engrossed, playful, then terrified child, hands over mouth, eyes dancing: 'If you believe in fairies, clap your hands!' In his account, the two brothers engaged wholesale with the dramatic rollercoaster of Peter Pan: 'Up on our feet with enthusiasm, then tears as Tinkerbell's light faded, quickly dashed away as she brightly shone again', and Captain Hook's shouts of 'Somebody put out the light!'.

This was no amateur Garden Suburb production, but a top West End performance at the New Theatre. Gerald du Maurier was Captain Hook, and the young Irish actor and local Hampstead girl Unity Moore played Peter Pan. She performed the role in 1915 and 1916; even in wartime Bessie and Cecil were ambitious for their children's cultural life. Du Maurier, who lived in Hampstead all his life, was well known for his collaborations with J. M. Barrie and had played Captain Hook at its first-ever performance in 1904, at the Duke of York's Theatre. By 1915–6, he was an old hand at Hook and world-famous, with a cigarette named after him. Unity Moore would soon find fame as another little boy: 'Jo the Crossing Sweeper', in the 1918 film based on Dickens's *Bleak House*. The other Hampstead Garden Suburb branches of the family joined their theatre parties. West End theatre, as well as local amateur dramatics, had been part of their childhoods with

Ebenezer and Lizzie, and Cecil's passion for the stage never abated, though it was later cut out of his life completely.

'Grandfather Ebenezer' was undoubtedly with them at the play, if he was in London between lecture tours. He was lonely, but would not let it show – always the cheerful companion to his grandsons. By 1910, his second marriage was, according to his biographer, 'virtually in ruins', worse even than his children had predicted in 1907, when every one of them expressed distress and anger that their mother's memory had been traduced by their father's misalliance. In 1910, Ebenezer spoke to the London Spiritualist Alliance of a past event when he had betrayed a 'dear friend', purging himself by this 'confession' to a trusted audience. The suggestion is that the 'dear friend', who had freely forgiven him, was Lizzie. His children's visceral dislike for Edith née Hayward never abated, and she returned their hostility redoubled in wanton acts of meanness and cruelty towards Ebenezer as he grew old and infirm, including serving raw liver for supper to this long-standing vegetarian, forcing him to sleep on a couch and banning his children from the house. Edith Howard's mental instability had quickly become apparent, and soon after their marriage the couple separated, the first of several splits lasting years, during one of which she lived in a caravan. She was committed several times to mental hospitals. She took a strong dislike to Letchworth, her later home in Welwyn, and the Garden Cities idea in general. 'Ben' took flight from his unhappiness and hers into the easy company of Bessie and his son, side-stepping his second daughter's continuing resentment: she was still determinedly 'Editha'. Dad's memory is of regular visits by his 'one grandparent', who was a nimble 59 when Geoffrey was born. Separated from his wife for the whole of the war, the boys' grandfather was a vital part of that idyllic time, 'interested in everything and everyone'. My father remembered how fit and slim-built he was: in his late sixties the two boys couldn't overtake him as they ran to catch the bus down Finchley Road. Ben may have had few close friends, but he brought associates to visit Cecil and Bessie. One of my father's most vivid recollections was walking up Asmuns Hill holding hands with his grandfather on one side and George Bernard Shaw on the other, and Editha's daughter Meg remembered sitting on his knee, with a signed copy of *The Adventures of the Black Girl in Her Search for God* which, Shaw joked, would make them rich one day.[124] Was it Shaw, or perhaps H. G. Wells, another political ally, having tea in the garden that afternoon? Or Romney Green, Arts and Crafts furniture maker and fellow ILP member; or Frederick Osborn, pragmatic fellow Garden Cities activist; or Raymond Unwin, a neighbour at Wyldes Farm? Like Cecil, Unwin was seconded to the Ministry of Munitions during the war to plan Garden Village-style settlements around the explosives factories at Gretna and Eastriggs – south of the Borders.

It's possible that Peter Quinn came to see his sister, perhaps tagging a visit on to a Singer employees' trip to London. Peter and James were the only Quinns likely to come to London, although Ellen, Patrick-Peter's wife, would have visited her daughter after 1917, when her daughter Ellen May (Nellie) moved to London to work at the Staines munitions factory. Bessie knew her from Clydebank days, when Patrick-Peter's family lived in Scotstoun. Nellie later recalled looking up to her aunts Bessie and Mary as a child. They could have become friends as adults, but there's no evidence of it.

When war was declared in August 1914, little changed for the family in the Suburb, although young men began to disappear into the armed forces. In Letchworth, conscientious objectors kept the faith among socialist and Quaker residents, but the mood of most pacifists changed to reluctant support, as it did in most ILP branches. Ebenezer, who had long declared himself a 'man of peace at any price', slowly and reluctantly changed his mind. In the first two weeks of the war he had made flamboyant anti-war declarations, including writing and printing a leaflet addressed to the 'Working Men of Germany', urging them to lay down their arms: they were being duped by their leaders. He planned an air-drop from a plane to fly over Germany (with himself on board) until his enthusiasm was jumped on by Shaw, Wells, and others, whose scribbled notes told him to drop his wild idea and get on with his practical, useful work.[125] He threatened to close the Mrs Howard Memorial Hall in Letchworth when its war-supporting managers banned conscientious objectors from meeting there. The momentum of war gathered pace, and Letchworth's light engineering facilities were commandeered for an armaments plant, owned by Belgian refugees and staffed by Belgian workers. A Zeppelin raid was made in retribution.

Anti-German propaganda intensified, and images of 'the brutal Hun' took hold. Children like my father experienced storybook versions: one neighbour in the Suburb, a single woman, was ostracised for owning a dachshund. The plight of Belgium's children and refugees captured public sympathy, and stories like Angusine Jeanne McGregor's 'Mrs Bunny's Refugee' enjoyed wide circulation.[126] Although technically Cecil could have enlisted – the upper age was 41 – he was sent to the Ministry of Munitions in Northumberland Avenue. Cecil's civilian role, if not his focus on armaments, was in keeping with the spirit of his father, Ebenezer continued to work for peace and help conscientious objectors forced into hiding, including Frederick Osborn.

Cecil worked directly for the Minister for Munitions in the Liberal-led coalition: first for Lloyd George, and then, after he became Prime Minister, for Winston Churchill. Cecil, my father insisted, thought that Lloyd George made a far greater contribution to the war effort as Minister than anyone else in government: if an order came through for 50,000 shells, he would double it, building stocks of armaments essential for a long war, despite predictions that it would be over in months. Cecil, a shorthand speed-wizard, enjoyed working as private secretary to Lloyd George, but not for Churchill, who showed little regard for his subordinates' dignity and sensibility. He was morally offended when subjected to Churchill's habit of summoning staff to take dictation as he lounged in his bath, smoking a cigar. My father's inherited admiration for Lloyd George lasted a lifetime. It is claimed that 'Lloyd George Knew my Father', which became a soldiers' marching song (to the tune of 'Onward Christian Soldiers'), was an oblique *nudge-nudge wink-wink* at the Welsh Wizard's womanising. It was one of Dad's favourites on long car journeys. I had no idea how well Grandpa knew him.

During the war years, unless there was a late summons from a Minister, Cecil came home to Asmuns Hill each evening like clockwork. Family life changed little, apart from a number of air-raid alerts, when wardens rode the streets on bicycles, blowing whistles and shouting 'Take cover', then 'All clear' when it was over. The war that Bessie and the boys experienced illustrates the vast gulf between soldiers at the front and their families at home. Holidays continued, closer to home: Herne Bay, Broadstairs, Cromer, Hunstanton – and Heacham, the runaway favourite. Dad recalled: 'the thrill of … picking up luncheon baskets at Norwich or taking a fork in the road at Melton Constable to ride across toward the Wash don't diminish with age … nor approaching any of those places with magic Norfolk names, the memory of wriggling on a cushion, alongside the motorcycle, peering out into dusty country roads through seemingly endless fields red with poppies, then catching a first glimpse of the sea'.

Figure 58: Family Outing, Herne Bay pier, 1920s – photo by Bessie

Although air raids were few, they were spectacular. Dad recalled his fear as Zeppelins came by night: long, slender, slow-moving, noisy silver 'cigars', sought out at night by weaving searchlights and targeted by anti-aircraft guns. There were stories of the first one to be shot down in 1916 at Cuffley, near Hatfield, bursting into a huge ball of fire to great cheers, despite the crew's horrible death in the hydrogen furnace. Later, there were daylight dramas as airships were shot down by planes, and a British bomber crashed over Hendon, not far from the De Havilland aircraft factory at Edgware.[127]

There is another mood in Dad's memoir. At Henrietta Barnett School, his 'first but very remote love' was 'the athletic and beautiful Miss Adams who taught gym and netball', followed by a sequence of adored women teachers. As if all the women he encountered were bathed in Bessie's reflected light. Curiously shame-faced memories follow, of 'childish explorations with the girls next door in the woods at the bottom of the garden'. For those times, the Garden Suburb children had unusual freedom to play unsupervised around the Suburb, run in and out of each others' houses, up to the Hampstead Heath extension, or clamber on the pergola at Golders Hill. The land-reformers' motto, 'Life, love and liberty', extended to the new child-rearing philosophy. Unlike Donald, Geoffrey was at the centre of things, bossing the group of cousins and friends. There's a slightly prurient tone to his descriptions of games of Doctors and Nurses and crushes on teachers – not the routine stuff of reminiscence. Or perhaps it's a daughter seeing hints of a parent's sexuality, however long ago, which is always uncomfortable.

Spoken memories that Dad omitted from his written memoir feel odder, because of the fate of Geoffrey and Donald's cousin and constant playmate, Derwent Rawlinson. 'Derry' was Kathleen Daisy's eldest child, a year older than Geoffrey. Dad wrote that Derry was 'a worry' for his mother because he'd wander away and go missing for hours. Fascinated by the Underground, he took off alone from Golders Green on the 'Hampstead Railway' (soon the Northern Line) down to the District and Metropolitan railways in central London (a kind of inner circle before the Circle Line), where he could curl up and go round and round London while a hunt got underway.

In other respects too, Derry's behaviour caused alarm. In today's professional characterisation of emotional and behavioural difficulties, he might be judged 'inappropriately sexualised' for a pre-adolescent. He was physically big for his age and had 'learning difficulties'. Like Bessie's Arthur George, once he was diagnosed, he would have been labelled 'feeble-minded', or 'mentally deficient', which then often pointed to 'congenital mental weakness'. My father remembered Derry hugging girls too tightly; and he thought it might have been more intrusive than that: girls were frightened of him. Aged 15, Derry was permanently removed from home and out of the lives of his cousins, by now living in Letchworth. He was admitted to Bigod's Hall, Dunmow in Essex in 1923, where he stayed until 1929. Dad's memoir refers only to the lure of the Underground as a 'dangerous obsession', and to Derry's sudden disappearance. He spoke regretfully about Derry being sent to an asylum, 'pretty sure' he had died there (Derry's much younger brother, Tony Rawlinson, was his informant). But when it came to writing, 'the details escape the memory'. Identifying with his aunt, my father wrote that Derry was a 'terrible problem' for Kathleen Daisy: a distressing trauma for the extended family in the Suburb, but most of all for Bessie. As Kathleen Daisy's friend and confidante, she carried hidden knowledge of the fates of her own nephew and her mother, held indefinitely under the Poor Law on grounds of feeble-mindedness and insanity.

The waters closed over Derry's story. But records reveal that after Bigod's Hall he was sent to Hill End Asylum in Hertfordshire until 1934, 'under certificate': compulsorily detained. From there, he was discharged on 11th December 1934, 'not improved', and, reported as without property, he was sent the following day to a new 'colony for mental defectives' next door to Hill End. Soon, many Hill End patients with learning difficulties and disabilities were being transferred to Cell Barnes Mental Hospital at St Albans. Charles Derwent, institutionalised from his teenage years, spent the rest of his life there. The institution aspired to offer a freer, more social way of life for the mentally ill. But in none of the documents I've seen do family names appear as correspondents, visitors, or informants. He died at Cell Barnes in 1985. Kathleen Daisy was 97 when she died in 1977, living nearby in Welwyn Garden City, but I'm unaware of any connections Derry had to his mother's family before or after her death. His death certificate was signed by officials. The parallels with Arthur George Quinn and Dingleton Hospital are striking: two examples of the age of institutionalisation, from which beliefs and practices for adults with mental-health issues very slowly evolved, until the radical policy of 'Care in the Community' arrived in the 1980s, when mental hospitals were closed and their resident patients dispersed with wretchedly, sometimes fatally, inadequate support, as public spending drained away.

36 Hampstead Garden Suburb
1919: 'We Had Not Known Illness'

In the golden remembered years, nobody at Asmuns Hill was ever sick: my father was certain of it. Good health was the primary purpose of the Garden City movement, an essential ingredient of family contentment. One photograph shows Bessie clutching a handkerchief, but in Dad's memory runny noses, sore throats, and even the more serious childhood infections could not disfigure the innocent beauty of his early life.

On 11th November 1918 the catastrophic war ended, but the celebratory mood across Britain was short lived. Although 1919 was a boom year for some, for most it was a year of fear and disillusionment. Soldiers returned to an unwelcoming world with little prospect of a better life in an indifferent country hit by the costs of war. Anger at continued poverty, inequality, and poor housing – where were the Homes for Heroes? – and industrial unrest were fuelled by the 1917 Russian revolution. Growing numbers of working-class people and their allies were drawn to socialism. That year saw 34 million strike days and protests in towns and cities, including a race riot in Glasgow. Britain in late 1918–19 was a tinderbox, and under it a smouldering fire began to spread, turning remaining energies and hopes from peace into collective anxiety and gloom.

The disease they called Spanish Flu had arrived in early 1918. Although there was no certain origin, Russia and China were initially suspected. A military barracks in Kansas, USA is now agreed to be the most likely source. And of the three countries, the USA was by far the worst hit. China contained the disease. Spain bore the stigma of its origin largely because the disease was widely reported there, early in 1918: as a neutral country in the war, it was not subject to media restrictions. In fact the Flu arrived in Britain via Spain with a shipload of infected passengers, who travelled on home by train. In May 1918, the first cases were reported in Glasgow; by June, London was affected and the highly contagious disease fanned out across the country. A massive, lethal, second wave broke in August 1918, spreading quickly and lasting well into winter. A third wave ran from January to May

1919. The pandemic penetrated every corner of the world and killed between 25 and 100 million people. Estimates now converge at circa 50 million deaths world-wide.[128]

Spanish Flu claimed its first famous victims in autumn 1918. The Prime Minister, Lloyd George, only just survived after collapsing on a visit to Manchester in September. The Viennese artist Egon Schiele died in October, and the poet Apollinaire in Paris in November. In Britain, actions and directives were undertaken and issued mainly at the local level, and Flu was not mentioned in Parliament until October 1918. Cases were not notifiable to authorities until the spring of 1919. Some 'social distancing' and closures of schools and other institutions took place, but cinemas stayed open, their windows opened before a performance to air the auditorium. Postmen and post-office workers wore masks. A muted response was met by apathy and some hostility to policies associated with the war. Other countries took more stringent action. In Britain, coffins piled up on streets awaited a multitude of corpses, but too few: bodies lay unburied for days. In London's streets, blackout curtains indicated afflicted houses. All in all, 228,000 people died in Britain in 1918–1919, after the last wave ebbed away over the second summer. Small eddies still swirled over the next few months. The London boroughs near Hendon all suffered deaths among both rich and poor: but not alike. The poorer boroughs lost by far the greatest numbers. The family at 22 Asmuns Hill survived without a snivel.

Spanish Flu was a constantly changing virus, 'whole zoos' of micro-organisms with familiar flu symptoms: headache, shivering, dry cough, sudden spiralling fever, muscular aches, dizziness, loss of sleep. But the patient, constantly wet and clammy, also suffered diarrhoea, gastro-intestinal pain, sore throat and head cold, nose-bleeds and a fall in blood pressure. Often, as the final blow, pneumonia developed. The signs of a fatal infection were ghoulish: heliotrope cyanosis turned sufferers purple, lilac, and red, with an ashen tint on the arms and chest. Some patients experienced neither pain nor distress, but gradually sank. But witnesses found it horrible to see many others who were conscious and had no idea they were dying. It was said that they would brighten up as they were near to death and show a spirited desire to live. Others would fight against suffocation and collapse, acutely aware of their fate. Their consciousness of the truth was dreadful to witness.[129]

When Bessie fell ill, influenza in London had subsided to very few cases. Spanish Flu dates range from 1918 to 1920 because there was a last small outbreak from January to March 1920. She and her family had survived 18 months of the epidemic, no doubt as conscious and fearful as everyone else. She may now have felt that what was happening to her was inevitable. Every cough that lingered after a cold might lead to something threatening, possibly even a symptom of the old disease which had never erupted. But she had always been careful, especially since joining the healthy-life enthusiasts in Keswick: a nutritious diet, cycling, walking, and avoiding large crowds were all second nature now. No wonder she loved mountain and seaside holidays. As she fell ill, there were good reasons to be confident of a quick recovery, even though her respiratory symptoms were severe. She no longer lived, or worked, in a polluted place too close to others to ward off infections, and it was nearly 15 years since she'd stood face to face with her family's nemesis and watched Alex die. The Spanish Flu had been all but over for months, and it was surely not endemic.

There is no reason to conclude that Bessie was not suffering complications of influenza, although to catch it as it disappeared in December 1919 was particularly unlucky, and statistically unlikely. She was at the upper age limit of those most likely to die. More young people, counter-intuitively, died of this virus: those aged 20–40 were the most severely affected: many victims were under 30. One still-current explanation was the lack of exposure to similar flu viruses in people born after 1889. Many born previously, like Bessie, had immunity from the great Russian Flu pandemic of 1889–92. If that is true, why did a healthy 40-year-old contract flu and pneumonia, the common final cause of Spanish Flu deaths?

Of course, other lethal diseases and susceptibilities circulated every year. Bronchitis had killed Bessie's father. The old Quinn enemy may have been lurking. However slight or dormant, perhaps tuberculosis inhabited her body: a 'prior medical condition'. She had been intimately exposed to infection from 1898 to 1903, and to its breeding grounds since childhood. Links between flu (including Spanish Flu) and TB have been found in medical trials.[130] Those with TB in their system were more likely to die of Spanish Flu and other strains of influenza. Bessie's death is likely to have been caused by more than 'Spanish Flu'. For the future, the relationship was positively reversed: Spanish Flu reduced the level of TB in the population, as it wiped out many younger people who might, like Bessie, have succumbed later in life or passed it to their children. It's cold comfort to conclude that if she was carrying TB, she'd have remained more susceptible than most healthy 40- or 50-year-olds to seasonal influenzas. Was a chronic health threat one reason for her – and Cecil's – silence about her past? She was probably never destined to live to a great old age.

Disease struck Bessie in early December 1919. After two weeks of manageable infection, her symptoms intensified and she struggled to breathe. Doctors could do nothing. On 15th December she died of pneumonia and heart failure. Her two boys lay awake in the room next to her: 'We had not known illness in the house, so the terrible manifestation of serious illness, as she struggled with pneumonia... and then silence, whilst we lay in wonder in our bedroom next door, are as real in old age as they were in boyhood'. The children were confused by what they'd heard and confused again by the silence that followed. Their father was too stricken to tell them their mother had died. So their grandfather Ebenezer sat down on the bed where they'd huddled together and broke the news. 'He was consoling, sympathetic and loving, but the devastation and loss were an awesome shock despite the signs, which we thought were just … illness, not death.' At 10 and 8, neither Geoffrey nor Donald could grasp the finality of death, nor the unending loss about to sink their lives into years of disarray. They simply felt the absence of 'mother'. There was another frightening absence: the distracted strangeness of their father. Their loving, energetic father had folded, like a crumpled rag doll, looking the other way. They longed for his arms round them, his smile, but he could not turn round.

The funeral took place on 19th December, four days after Bessie's death. Her children were not allowed to attend. My father insisted that both the dumbstruck boys wanted to be there, or at least did not want to be left behind at home. They knew what was happening – their grandfather Ebenezer had explained it – and already dreaded that they had lost more than their mother. In Dad's memory, the two stood holding hands looking towards the crematorium and knew that their mother was not coming home. Their father was still a stranger. Cecil, tears washing over papery cheeks, brought her remains home in an urn, placed them shaking on the mantelpiece, and never spoke of her again. His sons internalised the silence and the symbolism of their mother's transformation into a bloodless spirit, with no history and no future. The loss of his mother was my father's founding myth and warped the contours of his emotional life until his memory finally urged him to find her, to understand her, and enjoy her presence again after so long.

37 London and Letchworth
1934: Return to Golders Green

When I enquired about Bessie Howard's funeral at Golders Green crematorium, staff searched for the record and found nothing. This unsettling news reopened questions about her legend and the frailty of memory. Forced to wonder if she was buried elsewhere, even in the nearest Catholic churchyard, I found my energy slumping at a setback which threatened to upend my narrative. I lost momentum and for a while I felt like turning my back on the whole project. Now I'd become the petulant child. But a few weeks later another email arrived, from another staff member at the crematorium. Thinking it was an invoice for the fruitless search, I didn't rush to open it. When I did, I read that they had taken another look in the record book and found the entry for 19th December 1919 for Bessie Howard, written in such a faint and exaggerated copperplate hand that it had been easily missed and took time to decipher. It was confirmed that her ashes had been taken away after cremation. Normal practice in 1919, when there was no Garden of Remembrance, and the practice of scattering ashes was unheard of. The trouble that the two women had taken, unasked, rescued me from the doldrums.

There was more. My correspondents added that there was a second entry. On 29th August 1934, 15 years after Bessie's death, an unnamed person had returned to the cemetery and dispersed her ashes in the Garden of Remembrance. Who else but Cecil could that 'someone' be? The return of the ashes took place a week before what would have been Bessie and Cecil's 27th wedding anniversary, on 5th September. Not a memorable date as far as we know, but it could have been the anniversary of their first meeting in Cumberland. For unknown reasons it was a good time for Cecil to do something significant, to send a final message to his great love. Did anyone go with him? Perhaps it's significant that Cecil's return to Golders Green took place nine months before my father and Donald were both planning to marry. In their twenties, they had found themselves in happier places than they could have dreamed of in their embattled teenage years. I can't banish altogether the possibility that my father was with Cecil that August Wednesday, but it's much more likely to have been Donald, who was closer to his father and would not have found the occasion awkward or mawkish. For neither of them was there ever a standoffish distance between love and sentimentality. Donald would have felt the necessity of the mission and probably enjoyed duping his stepmother, the woman Cecil had married two years after Bessie died. As the owner of his own business, Donald was a freer agent than Dad, whose time was regimented as a nine-to-five clerk at Martins Bank. On this surreal and undoubtedly secret journey, Cecil must have carefully tucked the urn with Bessie's ashes into a bag, caught a train from Bickley to London Bridge and then along his old Northern Line commuting route to Golders Green. Did Cecil revisit 22 Asmuns Hill at the same time? Dad told me in 2001 that he himself had never returned there since 1919 and, despite the instances of selective memory-sharing, this rings true. No telling events blocked the long view over his shoulder to his lost mother's house.

After her death, profound shock, my father wrote, had led Cecil to make 'hasty decisions and not very well-considered actions', particularly the immediate clearing of the Asmuns Hill house and removal of his boys from 'the environment which Mother had created'. Another explanation is possible: did Bessie ask him to keep her secrets and hold the Quinn family at bay after her death, leaving no trace? Cecil sent the children to live with Ebenezer in Letchworth, while he disposed of 'almost every single thing, all the reminders (of) his love, and the happiness she radiated .... By the time he turned the key to their home for the last time, everything had disappeared. Peter Pan had told us of "The Lost Boys": now in reality we were.' Dad was 'bitterly upset' to leave his Hampstead Garden Suburb school. There had once been talk of a progressive boarding school, but Bessie had opposed it. Dad was sure she wanted her boys at home. In any case, boarding school was utterly alien to anything in her own childhood experience, unless it was a Poor Law establishment.

The boys moved into Ebenezer's tiny flat at Homesgarth, a block designed for communal living, with shared dining room and utilities. Cecil came up to Letchworth at weekends. In early 1920, both boys started as weekly boarders at Arundale, a Theosophist co-educational school in Letchworth (later merged with St Christopher's School, which still maintains some of the original liberal ethos). The Arundale curriculum offered more arts and crafts than academic subjects, with an emphasis on outdoor life, sports, personal freedom – and a vegetarian diet. They were both reportedly happy, still growing up in the spirit of Bessie's beliefs. They later had to have extra maths and English tuition to win places at conventional schools: Geoffrey at Alleyne's in Stevenage, Donald back to Hampstead Garden Suburb for the school week, to attend University College School, living under Aunt Editha's protective wing at Temple Fortune Hill: she and Fred moved into ever-grander houses (one boasting a billiard room) as long as Fred's fortunes prospered.

Figure 59: Geoffrey and Donald on Cecil's motor-tricycle by Homesgarth, Letchworth, Ebenezer Howard's communal flat, 1921

Dad's memoir gets more cheerful, but all was not well in London during the working week. Anxieties and fatigue plagued his father, who couldn't afford to maintain the Letchworth and London households on his earnings. The Bankruptcy Court's working day was long: shorthand records taken during the day were dictated to a typist on the same evening. The final version had to be perfect by the next morning, down to the last comma. The first physical sign of Cecil cracking was an attack of acute 'neuritis', or writer's cramp, which prevented him working for most of 1920. Ebenezer Howard bailed out his son, although he himself was fully occupied: Welwyn Garden City was being built, and he still kept his 'eyes on, but hands off' Letchworth.

He had no money to give Cecil, but took his place in the court, still a crack shorthand writer at 70. He successfully held his son's job open.

According to Dad's memoir, throughout 1920 Cecil was 'a distraught and unhappy man probably on the verge of bankruptcy, in poor health both physically and mentally, with two young children and no fixed home'. In this precarious state, he re-established contact with a woman who'd been a clerk at the Ministry of Munitions in the last years of the war. One evening at a London theatre, a year and half after Bessie's death, Geoffrey and Donald were introduced to a stranger: 'This is your new mother'. The moment was traumatic for both boys, though they never blamed their father. In Dad's view, his father was still in love with the memory of Bessie, his grief distorting his capacity to care for his bewildered children or the courage to act on his own misgivings. Cecil tried to withdraw his proposal, but failed. And the marriage brought misery, as he dreaded it would.

Of Bessie's two sons, Donald probably suffered most, struggling at school and the main target of his stepmother's hostility at home. Dad was more adept at appeasing and evading Bessie's successor, though later vocal in his loathing of her. There are echoes of Ebenezer's disastrous second marriage in Cecil's fate. Like the poor malleable woodcutter of fairy tales, he seems to have been too weak to thwart his new wife's will and help his struggling children.

Dad's half-sister Betty believed that the presence of Bessie's ashes in an urn in her parents' home was the most likely cause of a long, unexplained, unresolved conflict which she knew festered between her mother and Cecil. It hung heavily over her childhood. If so, it is surprising that his second wife tolerated Bessie's mortal presence for so long. It's even remotely possible that she herself 'stole' the urn and took it back to Golders Green: she was unbalanced enough. But it's highly unlikely, and she could have disposed of the ashes much more easily.[131] There were many causes of discontent and distress between the couple, but Cecil's intolerable, unspoken preoccupation was Bessie. The visit to Golders Green may have been his attempt to heal his trauma for the sake of the present, miserable though it was. Was it a laying-to-rest, or a re-engagement with unfinished business, when Cecil revisited the scene of his loss, ceremonially taking leave of Bessie in the Garden of Remembrance and making a new written record? Behind his feelings, silence still surrounded the woman who was mourned so long after her death, obsessively preserved in mind and matter.

Without Bessie's or her family's own life stories, however, there could be no finality for Cecil or his sons. That history came too late for them all. Decades later, Bessie did wander back, a puzzling but comforting presence who demanded her first child's attention. Even later, her Irish family in Scotland also reappeared.

POSTSCRIPT: A LONG AFTERWARDS

Washboards and mangles are on my father's mind.
In conversation he will return to the soaked linen
of his childhood – its labour-intensiveness –
as though these shirts and sheets, ready for the line,
floated behind my head in a basin together

and he could reach across and bring them in
amazed how they come up white again and again
after all these years – the marriage and the 'money-grubbing',
the household overrun by lunatic women
putting one thing after another through the wringer.

Leontia Flynn
('Mangles', in *These Days*, Jonathan Cape, 2004)

One spring day in 2001, I took my father to London to visit his childhood home for the first time since Bessie died there, 82 years earlier. By not preparing him, I hoped to clear space for his memories to flow. It wasn't until we turned off Temple Fortune Lane that he realised where we were. He gasped, his hands covering his face, shook his head, and slowly smiled.

Happily, the world before The Fall was still Paradise. On a sunny afternoon, the cherry trees were blossoming and the house was exactly as he remembered. We walked down Asmuns Hill and turned into Wilmington Road, where his father Cecil would whistle to signal that he was home from the Inns of Court. His waiting boys would run to meet him on the corner, and all three would chatter their way home to the supper their mother had already laid out.

No-one answered the door, so we peered through the wooden side-gate into the garden and wandered round to the community allotments at the back. Dad stooped suddenly to pick up a soggy tennis ball, turning it round and round in the palm of his hand with his thumb. Tears meandered down his cheeks. Once upon a time the allotments had been tennis courts where his father first taught him his characteristic blend of hard low balls and drop shots. The courts became allotments during the First World War. We stayed barely an hour on Asmuns Hill, but when he returned there in his mind, fresh memory-shoots poked through what had once been unyielding ground.

My father's mother had always been present: the fairy-tale orphan of my childhood, a silhouette flimsier than the paper dolls I cut out from my own mother's dressmaking pattern covers. Rootless Bessie hovered in daydreams, the unearthly one among grandparents, maiden aunts, and uncles. Huguenot clockmakers, wholesalers, teachers, and a Scottish bookseller on my mother's side; social reformers, tenant farmers, pastry-cooks, typists, and shorthand-writers on my father's. Some doughty and serious; others playful and kindly. Londoners, all. Their photos, letters, and postal orders could be touched; visits enjoyed or endured, life histories told.

There was nothing solid about Bessie, just dawn mist hanging above the land where real people lived. Orphanhood has been called a 'narrative intensifier', a symbol of pathos which evokes 'poverty, vulnerability and sadness'.[132] But for me as a child, contemplating

Bessie was not about placing her socially, identifying a poor, lost family and its legacy. Her orphan self lent a romantic otherness to life, and I savoured her distracting image.

Our grandmother left not a scrap of paper from which to reconstruct a plausible life story, although there was a liturgy to our legend: she was a 'simple Irish girl'. Her birth family was non-existent. She was a domestic servant, or was it a barmaid? She worked, maybe, in Grange-over-Sands in Lancashire and met Cecil Howard, somehow, somewhere. The only facts were her marriage, motherhood, and death. She'd slipped into my family, made it joyful, and left a wasteland of misery as she vanished back into obscurity. Her husband, my grandfather, fell to pieces, a fragile vessel irreparably damaged. But her character, childhood experience, the balance of darkness and light in her life, her silent secrets and her own family's noises-off were hard to prise from their historical hiding places, even now with a sheaf of official records on my desk.

My girlhood fantasies about Bessie were pinholes to peer through at her stage-set. She was grown-up and enviably independent. Black-haired and rosy-cheeked, she was dressed in a white apron and cap, sweeping dirt into a metal dustpan in the bay window of a light, airy Victorian villa overlooking the sea. In the alternative narrative, she was gliding round a dim-lit bar, a bright figure in sharp relief, moving back and forth between guests – smudgy as figures in an impressionist interior. It was easy to imagine her in Grange. We lived in a Manchester suburb, so the north Lancashire coast and the Lake District were destinations for childhood outings and teenage Youth Hostelling holidays. I never dreamed of Bessie doing the dirty work, the stereotypical Irish drudge at the bottom of a rigid hierarchy of household servants, slopping-out pots and black-leading grates. She was clean and graceful. Two fantasies were in play: one was Bessie's rags-to-riches story; the other, my own debut role as film star/heroine. Our Lancashire Cinderella was rescued by an improbable prince – shy, sweet-natured old Grandpa – and lived happily for twelve more years.

In the 1990s, when we began to look for Bessie, Dad volunteered little more about his relationship with his mother. Of course he'd have had at most seven years of retrievable memories of her, and surely more goes missing when a trauma splits childhood and adolescent life into two halves. I counted his stories on the fingers of two hands, highlights of the years of maternal affection and apple pie. In ordinary circumstances a child might not remember much about being ten. His circumstances weren't ordinary: a childhood, seemingly secure, free, and happy by the standards of any time or place, cut short by her death, a boy swept out to sea by his father's desperate attempts at flight and forgetting.

Dad knew his mother was a working-class Irish woman, but would never have used that language. 'Simple Irish girl' was safer than an awkwardly flesh-and-blood historical being. His phrase kept the door to an uncomfortable shift of identity firmly locked. In our joint quest to discover his mother's true origins, he was ambivalent as well as eager, longing for and dreading what he would find. He identified unshakably (occasionally, mockingly distancing himself) with all he'd achieved in the conservative world of international cricket and with his brother's success as a well-regarded, well-to-do house-builder, driving to lunch at the golf club behind the wheel of his Jaguar. Social class mattered to my father. Our middle-class family may have been perennially hard-up and often in such serious debt that my father had to take his begging bowl to the bank manager, but we kept up the lifestyle we couldn't afford on his vanishingly small salary. Mum tried to 'economise' from time to time: margarine instead of butter. But her efforts at frugality, apart from making all our clothes, never lasted long. Dad's snobbishness towards working-class people, including his prospective son-in-law, sat uneasily with pride in the 'humble' origins of Ebenezer Howard's family and his own liberal sympathies. He voted for Attlee in 1945, and in 1963 was outraged that 60 per cent of Manchester's housing had no bathrooms. Dad battled (successfully) to move Old Trafford's Irish painter and decorator Jimmy up the council's housing list and to get staff higher wages. As the Secretary of Lancashire County Cricket Club, a manager and companion of men – cricketers and craftsmen – he loved and was loved back. When Aunt Editha suggested there were Howard ancestors far grander than the offspring of London pastry-cooks, he scoffed at efforts to find the aristocrat born the 'wrong side of the blanket', while enjoying himself with the rich, famous, and well-connected of his sporting world.[133]

The patterns of Dad's fatherhood were complex, too. He hugged his daughters, worked late, brought home bags of sweets, antiques, and old cars; he told a good shaggy-dog story and liked a practical joke. He cried easily at news of tragedies and others' grief. Long absences – as captain of an RAF rescue launch in wartime, then six-month tours as England cricket manager – were bridged by stacks of loving, story-laden airmail letters. His close Indian and Pakistani friends gave our lives a rich international dimension unusual in 1950s England. Homecomings were intensely anticipated, flamboyant, gift-laden re-entries into family life. Cakes iced in MCC colours and new outfits for all. Joy and peace were often short-lived. He could be visibly pained by children's eager enjoyment, especially of food, and especially at Christmas, the cruel season of his mother's death. He forgot birthdays, including our Mum's – his wife Nora. He bristled as he tidied our heaps of clutter, well taught by a mother who grew up in cramped spaces. If he wasn't tending runner beans, mending cars, nodding off, or on the phone to his father, it was probably Sunday lunchtime and trouble loomed.

Dad took out his uncontrollable feelings on my eldest sister, goading her as a teenager until she exploded. Something drove him to destroy our mettlesome, self-reliant female ecology. Mum looked on distressed, her meal ruined, but stayed quiet. Was he unconsciously testing love, hoping for forgiveness for his own outrageous behaviour while he forced his daughter to apologise repeatedly for her 'temperamental' outbursts of rage? Who was the parent, and who the child? And why pick on his most beloved daughter? I can see from photos of Bessie that my sister was the grandchild who most resembled her. The steep straight forehead, fine pointed nose, chiselled ankles, and long fingers: did his daughter reignite the dormant fury of an abandoned boy? Did she also evoke Bessie's presence more deeply than looks? Was he daring her to abandon him, too, a shy but annoyingly strong-willed young woman, pulling away from his grand plans to marry her into cricketing stardom? Her working-class artist husband was to be patronisingly admired for his creative skills, but his family were disdainfully caricatured. Fatherhood was fraught while Bessie stirred under the skin, shifting down the generations. His limpet attachment to my sister lasted until he died.

When my father began to unblock slow-trickling memories of his mother, he was losing the wife who'd looked after him for 60 years with love and patience as well as wry detachment. After my mother died in 1995, time travel occupied lonely days. Newer recollections began to bubble up through the mud, mostly from the miserable years after Bessie died. In the words of W. H. Auden: *Rummaging into this living the poet fetches/The images out that hurt and connect.* In the nightmare of toxic teenage years with a loathed step-mother, the keys to the casket containing the chequered, imperfect, all-too-human story of the first ten were lost. Living with abandonment without exploring it, enduring pain, and getting on with life appropriated his energy. Neither he nor his brother Donald were able to revisit their trauma.[134] When the past re-emerged in old age, Dad regressed. He cursed his stepmother and as he struck such sharply painful seams of memory he let out a groan, also his expression of self-reproach ('You fool!') and disbelief at other people's incompetence. With the obliviousness to convention of a seven-year-old, he'd sometimes swing between charm, kindness, and telling well-meaning strangers to 'shut up', or commenting audibly on people's appearances. Surrounded by young grandchildren, loving praise, pride and laughter could turn with bewildering suddenness to sharp rebuke and even attempts to end boisterous games or guzzling pleasure in Granny's fine food.

In Dad's memoir, Bessie the person remained cloaked in an adoring son's praise. Beyond her mother-ness, he struggled to grasp her human presence or sense the changing textures and emotional weather of her life. He was searching for a whole living person, but through the eyes and sensibilities of an abandoned child. The woman who was Bessie until 1919, who had fashioned a new life from the clay of a childhood in poverty, and could have grown in new ways, came to a standstill. She was a lost mother, with neither a past nor future self to be loved, appreciated, or deplored by her children.

While some memories were shadowy and elusive, others were crystal-clear, like facts from a period TV documentary. Facts were Dad's hard currency, lined up as neatly as his rows of garden tools, or the carefully labelled fruit-pastille tins where he stored bits and bobs, oases of orderliness in the messy reality of our family's lives. His bookshelves were lined with encyclopedias, thesauruses, and dictionaries. 'Did (or Didn't) You Know…?' was a conversation staple. Google would have been his heaven. He loved biographies, especially of people he knew as a child: G. B. Shaw, H. G. Wells, and his grandfather, Ebenezer. He declaimed poems learned by heart, particularly by Tennyson, and more often after my mother died: *Oh for the touch of a vanished hand/ and the sound of a voice that is still.* Whose hand?

Searching for Bessie with Dad was as reckless as scrambling willingly through a thick thorn hedge. Memory, the tool of his emotional digging, led him into contested territory, ugly as well as lyrical. He did not welcome alternative interpretations, holding his ground as the authoritative parent of his childhood. He explored events and feelings by the infinite re-telling of episodes and mental images, rather than free association or locating memories in their social–historical context. When conversations cut too near the bone, I struggled to join in the theatre of his unresolved losses and myths and hold my tongue. Mutual irritation sometimes erupted, dissolved by retreat and quick apologies. The pattern was familiar: exasperated quarrels had always been part of our spiky love, resilient, righteous, but ultimately forgiving.

Satisfaction at new findings was followed by doubt. 'That's just speculation, you're guessing'….'I'm afraid we won't find out more'….'We still know so very little…'. Dad needed to talk, wanted help and companionship, but didn't want anyone to know more about his mother than he did. New evidence coexisted with old myths until he died, when the elastic which held them together finally perished. Despite recovered memories and new information, his frozen-outside-time story was the cherished remnant he held on to, sometimes stronger than evidence. Residual grief 'hibernated in his dreams'. The past could never be 'come to terms with', just grappled with, consciously and unconsciously, transformed into a restless quest to reinvent the future.[135]

While I contextualised Bessie's story in cultural history and social class, made connections, and reconstructed events, Dad resisted weaving facts and memories into speculative historical narratives. But we had little to go on, and between us sought ways to thicken the gruel. Family history was a slow slog before on-line access to official records opened the floodgates of genealogical research in the early 21st

century. Dad's love of letter-writing helped. Satisfying replies began to drop on the mat, starting with Bessie's marriage and death certificates (but never a plausible birth certificate). Archivists and librarians offered pointers and evidence, mostly circumstantial, which supported or challenged myths. We looked again at the handful of artefacts attributed to Bessie, surviving relics of her uncanny presence. We explored the meaning of findings, and took a trip to Keswick, wandering around Bessie's and Cecil's places: Newlands, Grange in Borrowdale – not Grange-over-Sands.

Was Bessie Catholic? Dad was reluctant to concede she might have been, though he had followed my mother's wartime conversion to Catholicism and gone along with his four daughters' Irish convent education. Late in life, he followed my mother back from religion towards atheism – as far as agnosticism, with an upward glance at the established church. Despite drawing a blank among Scottish records, he became increasingly fixated on Scotland as Bessie's birthplace, as if a deep, wordless memory had floated to the surface. Scottishness favoured Protestantism. When he was growing up, anti-Irish prejudice was virulent. And in 1950s Manchester, with its big Irish population, 'Rooms to Let' notices still read 'No blacks, no dogs, no Irish'. Yet we lived among working-class Catholics of Irish origin, in our mixed community of town, church, and school.

If Bessie was not Scottish, Dad argued, why was his brother named Donald Gordon and always loved Scotland, kitting out his girls in tartan kilts and reciting Burns – *My Love is Like a Red Red Rose* – at family weddings? But Donald had died in 1984 after a life spent turning loss into easier, more comfortable ways of loving. Was Dad recovering long-forgotten conversations, plucking an old fiddle, hearing his mother's Borders lilt in corners of his mind? He'd remembered the taste of her puddings. Slowly, other senses were waking up. Were Geoffrey and Donald her little boys – or wee bairns – crying or greetin'? Did she speak the 'yow and mei' of the Borders? If I'd asked him more questions, I could hear her better now.

As Dad grew preoccupied with death, his impatience and opinions softened. In his last weeks he was as loving and cheerful as I'd known him, singing funeral hymns as he snipped off lavender heads. He was collaborating on a book about his life.[136] We left Bessie there. My regrets came later. If only… I'd taken time off work to study the censuses. If only… He could have known so much more about his mother.

Dad held something back from me to the last. Soon before he died, he handed me Kitty's letter with vital new facts about Bessie and Cecil's wedding in Keswick, confirmation of her Newlands life and their honeymoon. 'Just found ….'. A moment's murderous fury – now you've really done it! – and I realised he was handing over. Forgive, and go on. Hard work, yes, but it was his gift.

The night Dad died, in November 2002, I was in Edinburgh at a conference in the Caley – the Royal Caledonian, a grand old railway hotel. Irish navvies and stonebreakers had built the hotel; Irish surfacemen maintained the railways. He was right: his mother and her family were in Scotland all along. I hope he's listening to their life-stories – he's the silent ghost now. I'm not sure he'd like all he read, but I do know he'd make sure the whole world knew about the Quinns.

Notes and Resources

---

[1] For the Crematorium Society (founded 1874) and the design of Golders Green crematorium and its social significance, see Arnold, C. (2007) *Necropolis: London and its Dead*, Pocket Books, pp. 233-235; 243-5.

[2] For accounts of industrial Galashiels, the wool industry, and living conditions in the mid 19th century, see Hall, R. (1898) *The History of Galashiels*; limited circulation; on CD/PDF from Hawick Heritage Hub; and Moffat, A. (2002) *The Borders: A History of the Borders from Earliest Times*, Selkirk Deerpark Press, pp. 314; 358-360.

[3] Vaughan, G. (2019) 'The Distinctiveness of Catholic Schooling in the West of Scotland before the Education (Scotland) Act, 1918', Ch. 3 in McKinney, S. and McClusky, R. (eds) (2019) *A History of Catholic Education and Schooling in Scotland: New Perspectives,* Palgrave Macmillan.

[4] Carter, A. (1975) 'The History and Development of the Library Services of Galashiels and Selkirkshire, Including the Social and Economic Factors Influencing that Development', University of Strathclyde, MA Thesis, p. 126.

[5] Moffat (2002) (see note 2).

[6] McGahern, J. (2005) *A Memoir*, Faber and Faber, p.1.

[7] Clarkson, L. A. and Crawford M. E. (2001) *Feast and Famine: Food and Nutrition in Ireland 1500–1920,* Oxford University Press, pp. 77-80; 88-9;102-108; 133; links to disease, pp. 241-243.

[8] Collins, B. 'Origins of Irish Immigrations to Scotland in the 19th and 20th century' in Devine, T. M. (ed) (1991) *Irish Immigrants and Scottish Society in the 19th and 20th Centuries. Proceedings of the Scottish Historical Studies Seminar,* University of Strathclyde 1989–90, Edinburgh, John Donald, pp. 1-19.

[9] O'Grada, C. (1988) *The Great Irish Famine.* Dublin, Gill & McMillan, pp. 41-2; 50.

[10] Tóibín, C. and Ferriter, D. (2001) *The Irish Famine: A Documentary,* New York: Thomas Dunne Books, p. 31.

[11] Tóibín, C. (2003) *Lady Gregory's Toothbrush*, London, Picador. The title refers to a letter from Lady Gregory to W. B. Yeats in 1909, following riots at the Abbey Theatre's production of Synge's *Playboy of the Western World*, in which she referred to 'the old battle' between those who use toothbrushes and those who don't.

[12] Tóibín, C. and Ferriter, D., see note 10; pp. 24-7; p. 32.

[13] Tóibín, C. and Ferriter, D., see note 10; pp.14; 24-27.

[14] Farningham, M. (1907) *A Working Woman's Life. An Autobiography*, London, James Clarke & Co. Quoted in Howard, U. (2012) *Literacy and the Practice of Writing in the 19th Century: a Strange Blossoming of Spirit*, Leicester, NIACE, pp. 94, 214.

[15] MacAtasney, G. (2014) *The Dead Buried by the Dying: The Great Famine in Leitrim,* Sallins, Kildare, Merrion, pp. 5-8; Poor Law: pp. 42-3.

[16] Burrowes, J. (2004) *Irish: The Remarkable Saga of a Nation and a City*, Edinburgh, Mainstream Publishing, Ch.5.

[17] Devine, T. M. (2008) 'The Great Irish Famine and Scottish History' in Mitchell, M. J. (2008) *New Perspectives on The Irish in Scotland*, Edinburgh, John Donald, pp. 20-31.

[18] Burrowes, J., see note 16; pp.17-45 tell the full story of the 'Londonderry disaster'.

[19] Taylor, I. C. (1970) 'The Court and Cellar Dwelling: the 18th Century Origins of the Liverpool Slum', The Historic Society of Lancashire and Cheshire, No.122, p. 59; Harrison, J. (2018) 'The Origin, Development and Decline of Back-to-Back Houses in Leeds 1787–1937', *Industrial Archeology Review,* Vol 39/2, pp.101-116; Hunt, T. (2019) *Building Jerusalem: The Rise and Fall of the Victorian City,* Penguin, pp.107-8; pp.248-51; p.293.

[20] 'Reports of the Medical Officer of the Privy Council and Local Government 1866-7': Leeds; Harrison, J. (2017) 'The Origin, Development and Decline of Back-to-back Houses in Leeds 1787-1937', *Industrial Archaeology Review* 39:2, pp. 101-116.

[21] Collins, B, 'Origins of Irish Immigrations to Scotland in the 19th and 20th Century' in Devine, T. M. (ed) (1991), see note 8.

[22] Lobban, R. D. (1971) 'The Irish Community in Greenock in the Nineteenth Century', *Journal of Irish Geography* Vol 6 (3), pp.270-281.

[23] Barber, M. (1840) 'Five Score and Ten: A True Narrative of the Long Life and Many Hardships of M Barber, taken down from her own dictation.' Crewkerne, Penny & Makeig.

[24] McGill, P. (1914) In Chapter 10 of *Children of the Dead End: The Autobiography of a Navvy,* published by Herbert Jenkins, McGill writes of his journey across Ireland en route to Derry Pier 'with the rest of the potato squad'. Later chapters describe navvy life.

[25] Quoted in Vaughan, G. (2019) 'The Distinctiveness of Catholic Schooling in the West of Scotland before the Education (Scotland) Act, 1918', Ch. 3 in McKinney, S. J. and McClusky, R. (eds) (see note 3). On debates about the Catholic Church's influence and networks, see also Mitchell, M. J. (2008) 'Despised by Scottish Workers and Controlled by the Church?', Ch. 1 in

Mitchell (2008) – see note 17; and Walker, W. M. (1972) 'Irish Immigrants in Scotland: their Priests, Politics and Parochial Life', *The Historical Journal*, Vol 15/4, pp. 649, 667; Ferguson, F. and McConnel, J. (2009) *Ireland and Scotland in the 19th Century*, Portland, Four Courts Press. In the same volume, see O'Reilly, A. (2009) on community-generated associations, Irish (Hibernian) Friendly Societies, ties to Ireland, and associational life: 'All Irishmen of Good Character: the Hibernian Story of Glasgow, 1792–1824', pp. 147-159; and on attitudes and policies towards poverty in Irish immigrant communities, see Gray, P., 'Thomas Chalmers and Irish Poverty', pp. 93-107.

[26] Lobban, R. D., see note 22.

[27] Martine, J. (1883) *Reminiscences of the Royal Burgh of Haddington and Old East Lothian Agriculturalists*, Edinburgh and Glasgow, John Menzies; on 'The Nungate', see pp. 86-96 and on Hardgate, pp. 60-69; and see p. 206 on 'wretched and ragged children' 'rioting and swearing'.

[28] Haddington History Society (2016) 'Memories of Haddington's Nungate & Afternoon Tea', www.johngraycentre.org.

[29] Pearson, S. and Mitchell, B., *Blood on the Thistle: The Heartbreaking Story of the Cranston Family and their Sacrifice in the Great War*, John Blake Publishing, Part 1: 'The Sands'.

[30] Campbell, R. H. (1966) 'Diet in Scotland', quoted in Mintz, Sidney W. (1985) *Sweetness and Power: the Place of Sugar in Modern History*, Penguin, p.127.

[31] Moffat, A. (2017) *The Hidden Ways: Scotland's Forgotten Roads*, Edinburgh, Canongate, p.207.

[32] Hall, R. (1898) *The History of Galashiels*; limited circulation now on CD/PDF from Hawick Heritage Hub. For Borders railways, see Moffat, A (2002) *The Borders: a History of the Borders from Earliest Times*, Selkirk, Deerpark Press, pp. 358-360; Lawson, Margaret C. (1997) *Forgotten Families of Galashiels; Guid auld Galashiels*, Galashiels, M. C. Lawson.

[33] Hall, R., see note 32.

[34] Interview with Jared Squirrel, Borders Family History Society, Heritage Hub, Hawick, 17/5/2017.

[35] Devine, T. M. (ed) (1991) *Irish Immigrants and Scottish Society in the 19th and 20th Century: Proceedings of the Scottish Historical Studies Seminar, University of Strathclyde 1989–90*, Edinburgh, John Donald.

[36] Tóibín, C. and Ferriter, D., p. 27 (see note 10).

[37] McKinney, S. J. and McClusky, R. (eds) (2019) *A History of Catholic Education and Schooling in Scotland: New Perspectives*, Palgrave Macmillan; Walker, W. M. (1972) (see note 25).

[38] Rose, J. (2001) *The Intellectual Life of the British Working Classes*, Yale University Press, pp.16-18; 59-61.

[39] Vincent, D. (1989) *Literacy and Popular Culture: England 1750–1914*, Cambridge, CUP, pp.29-32 ; Howard, U., pp. 8; 92-3: see note 14.

[40] Frost, G.(2008) *Living in Sin: Cohabiting as Husband and Wife in 19th Century England,* Manchester University Press. See also, Project by the Centre for the History of Medicine, University of Glasgow (undated) *The Scottish Way of Birth and Death 1855–1939.*

[41] Parliamentary Papers, February 1837, parliamentary election in Gala and Walkerburn. https://hansard.parliament.uk/Commons/1837-02-03/debates/7764d826-fd66-488a-a4c6787a6751b7e3/FictitiousVotes(Scotland).

[42] McCluskey, R., 'Catholic Education Beyond the School. Sodalities and Public Lectures', Ch. 7 in McKinney S. J. and McCluskey, R. (see note 3).

[43] See Trevor-Roper, H. 'The Invention of Tradition: the Highland Tradition of Scotland' in Hobsbawm, E. and Ranger, T. (1983) *The Invention of Tradition,* Cambridge, CUP, pp. 23-28; Moffat, A. (2002) *The Borders. A History of the Borders from Earliest Times*, Selkirk, Deerpark Press, pp.347-8.

[44] *Haddingtonshire Courier*: Justice of the Peace column, 11/10/1887, 'Sudden Death' report: 9/3/1877.

[45] M. K. Ashby (1961) *Joseph Ashby of Tysoe 1859–1919: A Study of English Village Life,* Cambridge, CUP, quoted in Willes, M. (2015) *The Gardens of the British Working Class*, Yale University Press pp.122-3; Willes, M., *op. cit.*, pp.132-133.

[46] W. W. Knox, 'Health in Scotland' in *A History of the Scottish People, 1840–1940,* SCRAN. https://www.scran.ac.uk/scotland/pdf/SP2_3Health.pdf.

[47] Clayton, P. and Rowbotham, J. (2008) 'An Unsuitable and Degraded Diet? Part 2: Realities of the mid-Victorian Diet', *Journal of the Royal Society of Medicine* 9/2008 101(9), 452-462; Mintz (see note 30) argues (pp.127-130) that the use of bread, sugar, and jam increased when women went out to work and had less time to prepare raw ingredients.

[48] Vaughan, G., see note 3.

[49] McCluskey, R., see note 42.

[50] Carter, A., see note 4.

[51] Pooley, Sian (2013) 'Parenthood, Child-rearing and Fertility in England 1850–1914', *The History of the Family* 18/1, pp. 83-106; Spence, N. (2008) 'The Long-Term Consequences of Childbearing: The Physical and Psychological Well-being of Mothers in Later Life', *Res-Aging*, Sage, 30(6), pp.722-751.

---

52 Melrose Parish Board records, 1871–1874, 1875–1883, 1st edition, Scottish Borders Archives and Local History Centre/Borders Family History Society; Lothian Health Services Archive, University of Edinburgh. Dingleton Records 1881: GD30: 38/3; 41/1; 47/1; 58/3: Elizabeth Quinn case.

53 Willes, M., pp.188-189, see note 45.

54 Esbester, M. (2020) 'Railway Work, Life and Death', *Journal of Labour History* 119, pp.209-226; see also https://www.railwaysmuseum.org.uk/objects-and-stories/navvies; Working-class movement library: https://www.wcml.org.uk/our-collections/working-lives/railway-unions/

55 Hall, R. (1898), see note 32.

56 Works consulted on TB in the 19th century include Bynum, Helen (2012) *Spitting Blood, The History of Tuberculosis*, Oxford: OUP; Spence, D. P. S. et al. (1993) 'Tuberculosis and Poverty', *BMJ*, Vol. 307, pp.759-761; Daniel, Thomas M. (2006) *The History of Tuberculosis in Respiratory Medicine*, Elsevier; Kelly, Susan (2009) 'Cures for TB in Ireland' in Ferguson, F. and McConnell, J. (eds) *Ireland and Scotland in the 19th Century*, Portland, Four Courts Press, pp. 125-130, describes traditional TB remedies in Leitrim; http://www.kumc.edu/wwi/index-of-essays/tuberculosis.html, University of Kansas School of Medicine.

57 Hamilton, A. R. C. (2010) *Halcyon Days of Singer and Other Stories*, West Dunbartonshire Libraries and Museums. p.34; Singer Staff magazines and ephemera at Libraries and Cultural Services, W. Dunbartonshire Council.

58 Works consulted on the 1911 Singer Strike and wider Clydeside activism: Craig, Maggie (2018) *When the Clyde Ran Red: A Social History of Red Clydeside*, Edinburgh, Birlinn; Glasgow History Workshop (1989) *The Singer Strike, Clydebank 1911;* Middlemas, K. (1965) *The Clydesiders: A Left-wing Struggle for Parliamentary Power*, London, Hutchinson.

59 Loane, M. E. (1908) *From Their Point of View*, Bibliobazaar (1998), Ch. 6 'The Working Class Father', pp. 144-156.

60 Vincent, D. (1989), see note 39; Rose, J. (2001), see note 38; and Howard, U. (2012), see note 14.

61 Examples of Singer hire-purchase agreements and related material at West Dunbartonshire Libraries and Cultural Services, Council Archives, Dumbarton and Clydebank Central Library.

62 Ellen May Quinn, MS Memoir, 1980s, David Quinn, family papers.

63 City of Glasgow Heritage and Design (2005) *Scotstoun Conservation Area Appraisal*; Williamson, E., Higgs, M., and Riches, A. (1990) *Glasgow (The Buildings of Scotland)*, Penguin/National Trust for Scotland, pp. 381-389.

[64] See, for example, Pennington, C.L. (1979), 'Mortality and Medical Care in 19th Century Glasgow', *Medical History* 23, pp. 443-450; McFarlane, N.M. (1990) 'Tuberculosis in Scotland 1870-1960', PhD Thesis, University of Glasgow, confirms 8,000 deaths in Scotland annually, the majority aged 15–40.

[65] Interview (2018) with Nerys Tunnicliffe, Mitchell Library archivist.

[66] Gammons, J. and Munro, P., *Borders Poor Law Records, Melrose Parish 1871–74; 1875–1883*, Borders Family History Society/Scottish Borders Archive and Local History Centre, first edition (undated).

[67] For accounts of the ASC, soldiers' experiences, and attitudes towards it, see Baker. C., 'The Long, Long Trail. Researching the Soldiers of the British Army in the Great War of 1914–1918' at https://www.longlongtrail.co.uk; and Stewart, Herbert A. (2015) *Ally Sloper's Cavalry. From Mons to Loos with the Army Service Corps during the First World War*, Oakpast; pp. 377-381 in Moffat, A. (2002) (see note 2) tell the story of another Borderer's ASC experience.

[68] War Diaries: 2nd Battalion KOSB and KOYLI, Somme, November 1914, National Archives, Kew.

[69] Quinn, J. (1934) 'Memories of the 1914–1918 War, 9th Royal Scots', MS, Imperial War Museum, London.

[70] Menzies Herning. great-grandson, on family memories of Augustine Quinn.

[71] David Quinn, grandson of Patrick, comment and correspondence with UH 2020; and Ellen May Quinn, manuscript memoir, family collection.

[72] Quinn, J., see note 69, and Gilhooley, N. (2019) *A History of the 9th (Highlanders) Royal Scots – the Dandy Ninths*, Barnsley, Pen and Sword.

[73] Quinn, David, see note 71.

[74] Gammons, J. and Munro, P., see note 66.

[75] Dumbarton Combination Poorhouse (1900-1909) Minute Books, West Dunbartonshire: Libraries and Cultural Services. Records of admissions and other records with names between 1900 and 1922 are missing.

[76] Works consulted on Model and Common Lodging Houses: O'Neill, J. (2015) *The Secret World of the Victorian Lodging House*, Barnsley, Pen and Sword; McGill, P. (1914), see note 24; Laidlaw, Stuart I. A. (1956) *Glasgow Common Lodging Houses and the People Living in Them,* Glasgow Corporation, Glasgow Caledonian University, pp. 22-31; Glasgow Caledonian University, https://www.theglasgowstory.com/story/?id=TGSD0.

[77] Works consulted on John Ruskin's textile ideas and design: Prickett, E. (1985) *Ruskin Lace and Linen Work*, Dover Publications; Hallam, S. E. (2004)

John Ruskin and the Lakeland Arts Revival 1880–1920, Merton Priory Press; Eagles, Stuart (2010) *After Ruskin: The Social and Political Legacies of a Victorian Prophet 1870–1920*, Oxford: OUP. For an illustrated history of the Keswick School of Industrial Arts, its place in the Arts and Crafts movement and relationship to the Ruskin Linen Industry, see Bruce, I. (2001) *The Loving Eye and Skilful Hand*, Carlisle, Bookcase.

78 McCarthy, F. (2014) *Anarchy and Beauty: William Morris and His Legacy 1860–1960*, London, National Portrait Gallery: exhibition and book, which explores his impact on Rawnsley, Howard, Carpenter, Crane, the Barnetts, and others relevant to this book.

79 See Clayton, P., Cowell, B., and Griffiths, V. (2020) *The Three Founders of the National Trust*, Pavilion Books; Rawnsley, Eleanor (1923) *Canon Rawnsley: an Account of his Life*.

80 Quinn, Ellen May, memoir, see note 71.

81 Advice on Bessie Quinn's linen work given by Louise Pullen, Archivist, Ruskin Collection, Guild of St George Collection, Sheffield Museum, and Rachel Dickinson, Manchester Metropolitan University and Ruskin's Guild of St George.

82 Brandt, D. (1998) (1) 'Sponsors of Literacy', *College Composition and Communication* 49/2, pp. 165-185; (2) *Literacy in American Lives*, Cambridge, CUP, pp. 105-145.

83 Newlands Guest House Association: Shareholders' Meeting, Manchester, 1904 with the Cooperative Union; Leonard, T. A. (1934) *Adventures in Holiday Making*, Holiday Fellowship, pp. 19-36, 51-55, 120,135-6; Hope, D. G. (2017) *The Legacy of Thomas Arthur Leonard, Founder of Cooperative and Communal Holidays and Father of the Open Air Holiday Movement*, Cambridge, Scholars Publishing; Ridley, R. 'TA Leonard: Adventures in Holiday Making: a Political Approach to Leisure', typescript, Newlands Adventure Centre, Stair, Cumbria.

84 English Lakes Visitor and *Keswick Guardian*, 19 March 1904; Bott, G. (1994) *Keswick: The Story of a Lake District Town*, Cumbria County Library/Chaplins of Keswick Booksellers, describes the making of the Keswick Garden Village, pp. 154-55; Beevers, R. (1988) *The Garden City Utopia: Ebenezer Howard, A Critical Biography*, Basingstoke: Macmillan, analysises his public achievement and personal life. Howard's correspondence is at Hertfordshire Archives and Local Studies Centre and includes material on his brother, Harry Caswell, a founder-member of the ILP, attending its inaugural meeting in Bradford in 1893 shortly before his tragic death.

[85] Loane, M. *The Queen's Poor*, London, Middlesex University Press (1998); Cohen, S., (1997) 'The Life and Works of M Loane', M Phil Thesis, University of Middlesex.

[86] See Vincent, D. (2020) *A History of Solitude*, Cambridge, Polity Press, pp. 56, 93, on emerging new freedoms of girls and young women, including working-class girls.

[87] Harrison, B. (1973) 'The Girls' Friendly Society', *Past and Present* Vol. 61/1 pp. 107-138. There was a branch of the Society in Galashiels, advertised in the local almanac.

[88] Leonard, T. A., see note 83.

[89] *Comradeship*, Magazine of the CHA, then Holiday Fellowship: 1907-12 Vols 1-6, National Cooperative Archive, Holyoake House, Manchester.

[90] Snape, Robert (2002) 'The National Home Reading Union 1889–1930', *Journal of Victorian Culture*, 7 (1), pp. 86-110.

[91] *Comradeship*, see note 89.

[92] *Resources on Cycling History*, Nottingham Industrial Museum; Crosthwaite Parish Magazine, Carlisle Central Library; Pye, D. (2004) *Fellowship is Life: The Story of the Clarion Club*, Bolton, Clarion Publishing; Prynn, D. (1972) 'The Clarion Clubs, Rambling and the Holiday Association in GB since the 1890s', *Journal of Contemporary History* Vol 11, pp. 66-75.

[93] Bott, G., see note 84, re Catholic worship in Keswick from 1920, pp.133-4.

[94] McGee, Gary B. and Thompson, Andrew S. (2006) 'Lines of Credit, Debts of Obligation: Migrant Remittances to Britain, c.1875–1913', *Economic History Review* 59/3, pp.539-577; Vincent, D. (2015) *I Hope I Don't Intrude: Privacy and its Dilemmas in 19th Century Britain*, Oxford, OUP, pp. 190-8.

[95] Leonard, T. A., see note 83.

[96] *Comradeship* magazine, see note 89.

[97] Gregory, J. (2008) *Of Victorians and Vegetarians*, London, Tauris; Spencer, Colin (2014) *Vegetarianism, a History*, London, Grub Street. John Ruskin's 'animal rights' stance was expressed in a creed for adherents of his Guild of St George in 1875: *Fors Clavigera*, Vol 5, letter 58.

[98] F. J. Osborn Archive, Hertfordshire Archives and Local Studies (HALS): correspondence Ebenezer and Lizzie Howard.

[99] Howard, C. G. (1990s) Unpublished memoir, family collection.

[100] Beevers, R., pp. 106-7, see note 84.

---

[101] Letter from Margaret Ann Passingham, daughter of Edith Howard, to a cousin, George Howard. 1984, family collection.

[102] Garden City Collection Study Centre (GCCSC) Letchworth, Exhibition 2018: Women in Letchworth, https://www.letchworth.com/blog/women-in-letchworth-special-exhibition; Vicky Axell, quoted in Maev Kennedy (2017) *The Guardian* 4/12/2016; Beevers, R., pp. 120-122, see note 84.

[103] Known also as Norton Grange Farm, dating back to the 17th century.

[104] See *William Ratcliffe - 150 years*. YouTube illustrated lecture, Ros Allwood, Cultural Services Manager, North Hertfordshire Museum. November 2020.

[105] Parker, Mabel, undated manuscript held at GCCSC, Letchworth.

[106] Zambra, G. L. (1950) *Violets for Garden and Market*, London, Collingridge. For a fictional account, see Gaynor, Hazel (2015) *A Memory of Violets*. London, William Morris.

[107] HALS, DE/FJO/IS/A. FJ Osborn: deathbed interview with EH, 1/4/1928.

[108] Howard, C. G., see note 99.

[109] Small Cottages Exhibition 1905. Young Arts and Crafts architects later became prominent, cutting their teeth on 95 Garden City competitions, including, for example, William Curtis Green. Details and drawings held at GCCSC, Letchworth.

[110] Swenarton, M. (1989) 'Raymond Unwin: The Education of an Urbanist' in *Artisans and Architects: The Ruskinian Tradition in Architectural Thought*, pp. 126-166, gives a full picture of the links between social movements in the period and the centrality of 'new life' and 'simple life' principles to Garden City design.

[111] Yeo, S. (2018) *A Usable Past. Vol 2, New Life: the Religion of Socialism in Britain 1883–1896. Alternatives to State Socialism*, Brighton, Edward Everett Root.

[112] Price, M. 'This World's Festival': Suffragette Millie Price's unpublished autobiography, London, Women's Library. Annie Kenney of the WSPU was also a Letchworth resident and wrote *Memories of a Militant* (1924) there; reprinted 2015 by Facsimile.

[113] Letchworth Local History Research Group (2021) *Industrial Letchworth: The First Garden City 1903–1920,* University of Hertfordshire Press.

[114] Rawlinson, Kathleen Daisy, letter (1960) to her nephew Geoffrey Howard. Family collection.

[115] Hands, T. (2018) *Drinking in Victorian and Edwardian Britain: Beyond the Spectre of the Drunkard*, Palgrave Macmillan.

[116] Rawlinson, Kathleen Daisy, letter, see note 114.

[117] Ellen May Quinn, see note 71.

[118] Pearson, S. and Mitchell, B. (2014), see note 29.

[119] Miller, M. (1995) *Hampstead Garden Suburb*, HGS Trust, Chalford Publishing; Swenarton, M. (1989), see note 110.

[120] See e.g. Noakes, D. (1980) *Faded Rainbow: Our Married Years*, Brighton, Queen's Park Books, p.1.

[121] Creedon, Alison (2006) 'A Benevolent Tyrant? The Principles and Practices of Henrietta Barnett (1851–1936), Social Reformer and Founder of Hampstead Garden Suburb', *Women's History Review* 11:2 pp. 231-252.

[122] Thanks to Julie Rudkin for memories of her father, Donald Gordon Howard.

[123] Howard C. G., see note 99.

[124] Dick Passingham, Margaret (Meg) Howard's son, shared the memories of Editha's life in the Suburb and Welwyn Garden City.

[125] Documents held at GCCSC Letchworth.

[126] McGregor, A. J. (1915) *Mrs Bunny's Refugee*, Glasgow, Blackie. Thanks to my sisters Frances Pilston and Joy Howard for unearthing the book, much read in our childhood by Scottish children's writer and illustrator Angusine Jeanne McGregor (1881–1961).

[127] Atkin, J. (2016) *Hampstead Garden Suburb during the Great War*, HGS Archive Trust, pp. 40-41.

[128] Work on Spanish Flu consulted: BBC 2 (2018) 'The Flu that Killed 50 Million', https://www.bbc.co.uk/programmes/b0blmn5l; Honigsbaum, Mark (2009) *Living with ENZA, the Forgotten Story of Britain and the Great Flu Pandemic*, London, Macmillan; Johnson, Niall J. (2006) *Britain and the 1918–1919 Influenza Pandemic: A Dark Episode*, Routledge; Spinney, Laura (2018) *Pale Rider: the Spanish Flu of 1918 and How it Changed the World*, Vintage Digital.

[129] Johnson, N.J. See note 128, sets out in detail the Flu symptoms, statistics and policy measures: pp.1-67; 78-81; 18-121.

[130] Oei, W. and Nishiura, H. (2012) 'The Relationship between Tuberculosis and Death during the Influenza (H1N1) Pandemic', *Computational and Mathematical Models in Medicine.*

131 Interviews with Betty Rowlands, née Howard, and correspondence with Dorothy Jenner, 2010–2019.

132 Sampson, F. (2018) *In Search of Mary Shelley, The Girl Who Wrote Frankenstein*, pp.87-88, London, Profile Books.

133 In 'Family Romances', *Penguin Freud Reader* (2006), ed. Adam Phillips, pp. 422-426, Freud writes of a child's 'longing for the happy times gone by'… 'when his father seemed to him the strongest and most distinguished of men, and his mother the dearest and loveliest of women', interpreting an adult's later belief that she/he belongs to 'grander personages'.

134 Freud's concept of 'Nachträglichkeit' (carrying loss in the unconscious until memory later creates the trauma), for example in 'On Mourning and Melancholia', felt relevant to the Howard children's delayed mourning of their mother.

135 Grass, Günter, 'A life in writing', interview, *The Guardian*, 1.11.2010.

136 Chalke, S. (2001) *Geoffrey Howard: At the Heart of English Cricket*, Bath, Fairfield Books.

Index

A

Adam, William, 55
Adams, George, 259
ages
- changed at marriage, 273
- changed deliberately, 41, 42, 47, 60
- changed in relief application, 91
- inconsistent in documents, 41, 182
- marriage, 181

agriculture
- Ireland, 26, 28–30, 30–37
- Letchworth Grange, 256, 258, 259–261
- Scotland, 71

alcohol. *see also* temperance
- abuse, 71, 137, 196, 201
- cause of death, 86–87, 231–232
- distilleries, 58
- Dutch courage, 267
- escape from realities, 122, 126, 150
- Newlands Guest House, 239
- public houses, 23

allotments, 82, 93, 283, 310
America, 33, 39, 71, 116–117, 181
Anderson, Emilie Reddie, 217
Anderson, James Reddie, 211
Athelstaneford, 50
Auden, W. H., 314

B

Baillie, Mrs, 170
Ballantyne, Henry, 65, 66, 77
Band of Hope, 231, 232
Barber, Mary, 52
Barnett, Henrietta, 9, 221, 280, 283, 288, 295
Barnett, Samuel, 221, 280
Barrie, J. M., 291, 304
Bell, Tom, 143
Berry, Edith. *see* Howard, Edith (Editha) (later Berry)
Berry, Frederick, 264, 305
bicycles, 104, 229–231, 289
Bills, Eliza Ann. *see* Howard, Lizzie
biscuit manufacture, 130–131, 149
Bloom, John, 261
Borders Family History Society, 175
Bowland House, 74, 76–78
Boyle, Susan. *see* Quinn, Susan (nee Boyle)
Brodine, Karen, 25
bronchitis
- Augustine Quinn, 178
- common illness, 99
- Mary Quinn (b 1844), 277
- Owen Quinn (b ca 1831), 23, 92, 149–152

Brooks, Ellen. *see* Quinn, Ellen (nee Brooks)
Brownrigg Farm, 59–61
Burns, Robert, 67, 217, 316
Butler, Peter, 113

C

cameras. *see* photography
cancer, 182
Catholic Church
- catholicism among Irish migrants, 16, 36
- Clydebank, 153, 199
- confirmation, 100
- converts, 80, 316
- cultural hub, 23, 68, 72, 79–80
- dangers of requesting relief, 92
- discretion about background, 249

dressing for church, 39
Edinburgh, 113, 127
education, 68, 71, 73, 95–97
Galashiels, 22, 23
Haddington, 50
holy days, 288
illegitimacy, 75–76, 113
Keswick, 232
libraries, 23, 79, 80, 98
marriage between faiths, 178, 186, 187
Nungate, 56
pay rates of catholic and protestant workers, 143
prejudice, 45, 48–49, 56–57, 163, 232
priests connecting families, 84
Relief Acts, 79, 80
Roman Catholic Home for Working Boys, 171–172, 178
schools in Galashiels, 21–22, 80
sports, 113
support for migrants, 53

cemeteries
burial, 191
common graves, 133, 151
cremations as alternative to, 2
learning to read from graves, 38
Kirkpatrick Durham, Kirkcudbrightshire, 277
Mount Vernon, Edinburgh, 133, 151
recording of families, 38

census returns
attitudes of enumerators, 14, 27, 100
inconsistencies, 41, 47, 100
showing migration, 27

Charles, Patrick, 74

childbirth
complications, 114
effect on health, 93–94, 105–107
Mary Quinn, 74, 75–76, 78, 82–83, 91

children
attending funerals, 2–3, 85, 301–302
care of those with learning difficulties, 166–172, 182–185, 287, 297
child mortality, 83
death of mothers, 115–116, 118–119
disabled, 261
gardening work, 110
literacy tasks for family, 120, 125
mill work, 81, 101–102
playing with parents, 159
work to support families, 99–100

cigarettes, 137, 256
Clare, John, 217
Clarion cycling club, 231
Clifford, James, 44, 46, 47–48
clothing. *see also* sewing
children, 21–22
holidays, 237
home sewn, 7
mending, 21, 70
of migrants, 52–53
in photographs, 7, 10
social events, 62
weddings, 266, 272–273
working class in Ireland, 38–39

Clydebank, 140–141, 153, 199
Comelybank woollen mill
description, 14, 68, 81–82
tied housing, 19–20, 81, 93, 122, 126

Connel, Mary, 74
Connolly, James, 113, 145
consumption. *see* Tuberculosis
Co-operative Holidays Association
formation, 219–220, 227–229, 274
Newlands, 220, 228, 229–230, 235–240, 290, 317
vegetarianism, 243

co-operative societies, 66, 94, 141, 162, 209, 226, 270
Co-operative Union, 220
Corry, Father James Henry, 74, 75, 97
court cases, 87–89
Crane, Walter, 214, 221, 267
cremations, 2, 3, 301–304
cricket, 147, 246, 286, 312, 313
Crouch, Mrs, 266, 267, 271
Cummings, e. e., 207
Cummings, James, 58
cycling, 104, 229–231, 289. *see also* motorcycles

D

De Valera, Eamon, 32
deaths. *see also* individuals
  attitudes to, 2–3
  caused by alcohol, 86–87
  child mortality, 83, 94, 95
  coroners investigations, 86–87
  deaths of mothers, 115–116
  during famine, 31, 35, 39
  following childbirth, 114
  migrants, 52–53
Dent, J. M., 270
dentistry, 94
Devany, Martin, 44, 46
Dingleton Hospital, 68, 173–174, 176, 183–184, 186, 297
du Maurier, Gerald, 291
Dumbarton Parish authorities, 116–117

E

Edinburgh
  biscuit manufacture, 130–131, 189
  Mount Vernon Cemetery, 133, 151
  Roman Catholic Home for Working Boys, 171–172, 178
education. *see also* individuals; literacy
  adult self education, 73, 220–221, 223, 225
  apprenticeships, 73, 97, 123–124, 143
  boarding schools, 304
  Catholic schools, 21–22, 68, 71, 73, 80, 95–97
  Catholics in Protestant schools, 22
  curriculum, 97–98, 99
  early years, 286–288
  educational materials, 21
  Hampstead Garden Suburb, 288
  industrial schools, 172
  Ireland, 72, 97
  Mechanics Institutes, 99
  Scottish system, 95–96
  short schooling, 71
  supported by employers, 147–148
  suppression of Gaelic, 41, 72–73
  teaching profession, 272
  training in skills, 208, 210–217, 256
elections, 69, 78
Elterwater workshop, 210–211
Episcopal Church in Scotland, 78

F

famine, 15, 20, 26–29, 30–37, 38, 41
Farningham, Marianne, 38
Fenighty, Mary, 47
Fleming, Albert, 209–210
Fleming, Alexander, 114
flowers, 261
Flynn, Leontia, 309
food
  cooking by children, 22–23
  diet in Ireland, 28–30
  effect on health, 28–30, 154
  growing food, 93, 110
  motherless infants, 115–116

nourishment in illness, 92
in poverty, 15
sugar, 54, 95, 130–131
vegetarian, 241–244, 248
wedding parties, 273
working class diet, 20, 95
French Revolution, 68
friendly societies
activities, 226
alternatives to, 147
for better-off workers, 45, 47
Catholic communities, 79
funerals
Alexander Quinn, 164
Arthur Quinn, 133
Bessie Quinn, 2
children attending, 2–3, 85, 301–302
mass graves in famine, 15, 35, 37
Myles Lyons, 87
Patrick (Peter) Quinn, 191
Peter Lyons, 85
Quinn family graves, 191, 202
Quinn family in common graves, 133, 151, 277
women attending, 85, 87

G

Galashiels
Catholic Church, 74, 79–80
description, 14, 19–20, 104
Irish community, 67, 72
political culture, 69
gambling, 71
Garden Cities. *see also* Hampstead Garden Suburb; Letchworth Garden City; Welwyn Garden City
development, 266, 270
early examples, 163
Keswick scheme, 223
lecture in Keswick, 220–223
Lizzie Howard, 222, 247, 256, 269
outdoor recreation, 268
railways, 221, 266, 268
supporters, 9, 221, 266, 267, 270
gardening
allotments, 82, 93, 283, 310
Hampstead Garden Suburb, 282–283, 286
photographs of gardens, 7–11
work, 94–95, 109–111
George, Lloyd, 294, 299
Girvan, 170–171
Glasgow, 123–124
Gore, 'Freddy' Spencer, 266
Gramsci, Antonio, 17
Great Famine in Ireland, 15
Greenhow, John, 273–274
Gregory, Sir William, 34
Griffiths Valuation, 37

H

Haddington, 55–56
Hampstead Garden Suburb, 7–11
archive records, 12
children's association, 13
construction, 280
death of Bessie Quinn, 2, 3
gardening, 282–3, 286
housing, 280, 281–282
Howard family home, 7–8, 280–284, 285
photographs, 4–5
sports, 12, 282, 310
Trust, 12
Hannon, Canon Edward J., 113
Harrison, Elizabeth, 9
Harrison, Frederick, 9
Hawick, 68, 70
Hayward, Edith Annie (later Howard), 271, 273, 292
health. *see also* mental health
ageing, 154
child mill workers, 94, 99–100, 101–102
cigarettes, 137, 256

cost of treatment, 114
difficulties of diagnosis, 119
effect of diet, 28–30, 154
effects of childbirth, 93–94, 105–107
herbs, 111, 150
influenza epidemic, 298–301
overcrowding, 103, 134
prevention of accidents, 143, 148
Hegarty, Michael, 44, 46
Hepworth, Barbara, 258
Herning, William, 179
Hill, Octavia, 215
Hogan, Anthony, 46, 47
holidays
Bessie and Cecil Howard, 280, 284, 288–291, 295
camping and caravanning, 247, 256, 289
Co-operative Holidays Association, 219–220, 227–229
health benefits, 136, 227–228, 289
Holiday Fellowship, 228, 229–230, 235–240
holiday homes, 285
Howard family, 8
slum children, 283
unpaid, 104, 288
working class, 288–289
Hope-Scott, Charlotte, 22, 23, 80, 98
Hope-Scott, Robert, 22, 23, 80, 98
housework, 21, 22-24, 71, 102, 158, 162, 174
housing
Bowland House, 76–78
evictions, 34
during famine, 32
Hampstead Garden Suburb, 280, 281–282
healthier up hill, 108
heating, 92
Leeds, 44–47
legislation, 46
lodgers, 46, 47, 48, 90
Newington, 128–130
Nungate, 56
overcrowding, 103, 134
tied at Walkerburn, 65–66
tied to Comelybank Mill, 19–20, 81, 93, 122, 126
tied to Singer Sewing Machine factory, 167, 194
Howard, Bessie. *see* Quinn Bessie (b 1879, later Howard)
Howard, Betty, 306
Howard, Catherine
art, 255–258, 260
death, 262
Derwentwater, 223–224, 245, 247, 255
description, 255–256, 260
Garden Cities, 255, 258
relationship with Bessie Quinn, 255, 256, 260, 273
relationship with Ebenezer Howard, 257, 258
relationship with Roger Parker, 258–263
Howard, (Arthur) Cecil
birth of sons, 286
carpentry, 11, 286
death of Bessie Quinn, 2, 3, 301–302, 305–306
death of Lizzie Howard, 245–247, 250, 251
description, 241–244, 245–246, 248
discretion about Bessie Quinn, 4, 264–265
education of sons, 286
holidays, 280, 284, 288–291, 295
interest in machines, 251–252
interest in photography, 9
introducing Bessie Quinn to family, 264–271

marriage, 271–274, 317
meeting Bessie Quinn, 241–254
motorcycling holidays, 244, 245–246, 250, 251, 284
motorcycling maintenance, 8
motorcycling with sidecar, 3, 253, 289–291, 305
move to Letchworth, 304
relationship with sons, 310
second marriage, 306
war work, 11, 294
wedding anniversary, 9
work, 250–251, 282, 305–306
Howard, Donald Gordon (b 1911)
birth, 285
character, 285, 313
death of Bessie Quinn, 3, 301–302, 303–304, 314
description, 10
education, 288, 296, 304–305
love of Scotland, 285, 316
photographed with Bessie Quinn, 6–10
relationship with brother, 290
second marriage of father, 306
Howard, Ebenezer
character, 266
death of Bessie Quinn, 301, 303–304
death of Lizzie Howard, 245–246, 250
description, 12, 222–223, 265, 292
Garden Cities, 8, 220–223, 256, 280, 305–306
lecture in Keswick, 220–223, 245
living in Letchworth Garden City, 3
marriage of Bessie Quinn and Cecil Howard, 3, 272, 273, 274
marriage of Kathleen Daisy Howard, 266, 267
meeting of Bessie Quinn and Cecil Howard, 241
peace work, 293–294
relationship with Bessie Quinn, 283
relationship with Catherine Howard, 257, 258
second marriage, 271, 292
spiritualism, 8, 292
sports, 246, 286
support for Cecil Howard, 304, 305–306
theatre, 292
travelling, 8, 11, 245, 289
vegetarianism, 243, 292
visits to Bessie and Cecil Howard, 292
Howard, Edith (nee Hayward), 271, 273, 292
Howard, Edith (Editha) (later Berry)
camping and caravanning, 247
death of Lizzie Howard, 247
description, 250, 265
marriage, 264, 268–271
second marriage of Ebenezer Howard, 271
support for Donald Howard, 305
Howard, Eliza Ann (nee Bills). *see* Howard, Lizzie
Howard, Fanny, 257
Howard, Frances, 313
Howard, (Cecil) Geoffrey (b 1909)
character, 287, 312–313
cricket, 246, 286, 312, 313
death, 317
death of Bessie Quinn, 3, 301–302, 303–304, 313
description, 10
education, 288, 295–296, 304–305
marriage, 63, 303, 313, 314
memories of Bessie Quinn, 3, 13, 14, 160, 231, 310–317

memories of childhood, 287–291, 295–297, 304–306, 310–312
memories of first world war, 294–295
memories of parents, 241, 245
photographed with Bessie Quinn, 6–10
relationship with brother, 290
relationship with Ebenezer Howard, 315
research about Bessie Quinn, 310–317
second marriage of father, 306
visit to Hampstead Garden Suburb, 310
work, 313

Howard, Harry Caswell, 9
Howard, John Branney, 257
Howard, Kathleen (Kitty) Daisy (later Rawlinson)
Derwentwater, 255
description, 250, 265
marriage, 265–268
marriage of Bessie Quinn and Cecil Howard, 273–274, 317
relationship with Bessie Quinn, 284
son Derwent Rawlinson, 296–297
visits to relatives, 9, 247

Howard, Lizzie (Eliza Ann) (nee Bills)
death, 245–236, 250, 268
description, 266
Garden Cities, 222, 247, 256, 269
letters from Ebenezer Howard, 8, 11, 241
memorial hall, 269, 293
relationship with Cecil Howard, 245–247, 250, 269

Howard, Nora (nee LePlastrier), 63, 303, 313, 314, 316
Howard, Rosalind, 286
Hunter, Robert, 215

I

illegitimacy
attitude of Catholic Church, 75–76, 113
followed by marriage, 75–76, 119, 178, 195, 199

illiteracy. *see* literacy
immigration. *see* migrants
Independent Labour Party, 223, 227, 270, 293
Industrial Workers of Great Britain, 145, 147
influenza epidemic, 298–301
Innes, Annie, 178–179
Innes, William Lennox Duncannon, 178–179
Ireland. *see also* migrants
British industry dependence, 54
flax, 29–30, 70
Great Famine, 15, 20, 26–29, 30–37, 38, 41
Irish language, 36, 37, 41, 56–57, 72–73, 154
land ownership, 29
linen, 29–30, 48–49, 70, 85
prejudice, 19, 36, 53–54, 146, 316
prejudice against Catholic Irish, 45, 48–49, 56–57, 163, 232
songs, 61

Irish communities
Galashiels, 67, 72, 79–80
Glasgow, 124
languages, 57, 61, 75
Newington, 130
political societies, 79
Scotland, 96
social events, 62

J

Johnston(e), Mary. *see* Quinn, Mary (b 1844, nee Lyons)

K

Keswick
description, 211–212
Garden City scheme, 223
Greta Hamlet, 237
Keswick School of Industrial Arts, 4, 211–217, 221, 281
leisure activities, 226, 228, 255
linen, 209–210, 216–217, 256
pencil factory, 211–212, 220
Porch Cottage, 209–211, 215–216, 272
religious groups, 226
wedding of Bessie Quinn and Cecil Howard, 273–274
Kirkpatrick Durham, Kirkcudbrightshire, 195, 197, 275–277
Knox, John, 55
Koch, Robert, 135

L

Labour Party, 225, 239, 278
lace making, 68, 208, 209, 210, 216, 266, 272, 285
Ladhope, 93, 102–103
Ladhope Inn, 23, 74
Langfier, R. W., 6
Leeds, 44–47
Leonard, Thomas Arthur, 219–220, 227–229, 235, 274
Letchworth Garden City
crafts, 258–259, 270
development, 256, 258, 270, 305–306
farm, 256, 258–261
Howard family home, 246
public buildings, 268, 269, 293
railway, 266, 268
libraries
Catholic Church, 23, 79, 80, 98
Clydebank, 143
public libraries, 99, 104
lighting, 93, 103
linen
Ireland, 29–30, 48–49, 70, 85
Keswick, 209–210, 216–217, 256
Scotland, 54, 85–86
Lines, Mary. *see* Mary Quinn (b 1844 nee Lyons)
literacy
attitudes of officials, 26
children, 125
children responsible in families, 120, 125, 158–159
effect on official documents, 41
handwriting, 98
illiteracy limiting documentation, 16
little stigma for illiteracy, 72
recording stories, 37, 52
signing official documents, 74, 79
useful in changing names, 150
Lloyd, Marie, 9
London Metropolitan Archive, 12
Lyons, Betsy (nee Commons), 37, 42
Lyons, Bridget (b ca 1876), 89, 90
Lyons, Bridget (Betsy)
agricultural work, 55, 59–61
caring for Peter Lyons, 64, 84–85
character, 60
court case, 63, 87–89, 90
death of Myles Lyons, 86–87
migration from Ireland with siblings, 50–52
relationship with Myles Lyons, 64, 84, 85
Lyons, James, 37, 85
Lyons, John, 86, 88, 89
Lyons, Katie, 90
Lyons, Mary Ann, 86
Lyons, Mary (b 1844 later Quinn). *see* Quinn, Mary (b 1844, nee Lyons)
Lyons, Miles snr, 86

Lyons, Myles
  death, 86–87
  Haddington, 55
  relationship with Bridget Lyons, 64, 84, 85
  witness in court case, 88
Lyons, Myles jnr, 90
Lyons, Peter
  agricultural work, 55, 59–61
  dependence on Bridget Lyons, 64, 84–85
  health, 61, 84–85
  migration from Ireland with siblings, 50–52
Lyons, Peter (son of Bridget), 86, 89, 90

M

MacLean, Isabella, 169–170
Manchester School of Art, 256
Mancini, Romeo, 18
marriage. *see also* individuals
  age at marriage, 181, 199
  cohabitation, 258–263
  elaborate ceremonies, 265–274
  between faiths, 178, 186, 187
  gifts, 271, 273, 281, 283
  marriage breakdown, 137–138, 139, 292
  pregnancy followed by, 75–76, 119, 178, 195, 199
Maxwell-Scott, Joseph Constable, 101
Maxwell-Scott, Mary Monica, 101
McGahern, John, 28
McGill, Patrick, 71, 201
McNulty, Alice, 113
McNulty-Butler, Alice, 100, 112–114, 115–116
Mechanics Institutes, 73, 99, 143
Melrose Asylum, 173, 176
Melrose Parochial Board, 91–92, 92
mental health
  ageing, 154
  care of those with learning difficulties, 166–172, 182–185, 287, 297
  Derwent Rawlinson, 296–297
  Dingleton Hospital, 68, 173–174, 176, 183–184, 186, 297
  Edith Howard (nee Hayward), 292
  institutions, 107, 197–198, 277
  Mary Quinn, 195–198, 275–277
  pregnancy and childbirth, 105–107
  treatment, 278, 296–297
Middlemass Biscuit works, 130–131, 149
migrants
  alliegance of children to new home, 125
  America, 116–117
  assisted emigration schemes, 43
  changing accents, 91, 316
  costs of migration, 51
  dangers of migration, 43, 52–53
  health dangers, 135
  homesickness, 61
  Irish building British infrastructure, 17, 39, 45, 48–49, 64, 71
  lack of documentation, 16
  lack of records of stories, 18
  learning languages, 73
  leaving famine, 30, 33, 35, 36, 39–40
  memories of home, 71, 84, 277
  moving towards family or friends, 48, 55
  orphans, 47
  priests connecting families, 84
  repatriation, 47, 51
  routes of migration, 39–40, 42–44, 50–52, 60, 86
  seasonal migration, 49
  support for, 53
  violence, 71

military service, 137, 148, 155–156, 175–178, 187, 277–278
Milne, Isabella, 197–198, 275, 277
mining, 47–48
Montessori schools, 286–288
Moore, Unity, 291
Moran, John and Catherine, 44, 46
Morris, William, 212, 214
motorcycling, 104, 243. *see also* cycling; Howard, (Arthur) Cecil
Muir, John, 55

N

names
  changed in protest, 271
  changing, 19, 38, 185–187
  effect of literacy, 19, 150
  importance, 19, 26
  importance in empathy, 38
  official records, 19, 26, 27, 130, 150–151
  religious identity of names, 91, 187
  use of names within families, 38, 79, 285
National Home Reading Union, 220, 226, 227
National Trust, 215, 221, 230
Newlands Guest House, 220, 228, 229–230, 235–240, 290, 317
Newman, John Henry, 80
Nixon, James, 38–39
North Berwick Law, 61
Nungate, 56–57

O

O'Rourke, James, 199
orphans
  death of mothers, 115–116, 118–119
  migrants, 47, 50
  orphanages, 261
Orwell, George, 259, 270
Osborn, Frederick, 266, 294

P

Paine, Tom, 68
Palmerston, Lord, 40, 43
Parker, Barry, 256, 258, 259, 260, 269
Parker, Mabel, 260
Parker, Roger, 256, 258–263, 273
Parker, Stanley, 256, 258
Pasteur, Louis, 135
Paterson, Thomas, 98
Paton, Canon John Brown, 227
Peel, Robert, 32
Peter Pan, 291, 304
photography, 6–13
phthisis. *see* tuberculosis
Pilkington, Frederick Thomas, 65
pneumonia, 94, 99, 184, 191, 301
police, 88, 89, 90
political reform, 69
Polloxfen, William, 42–43
Poor Law
  applications for relief, 91–92, 93, 167–173, 193–194, 278–279
  boarding house, 277
  institutions, 197–198, 200–202
  records, 42, 279
  reform, 278–279
  underlying purpose, 33–34, 170
poorhouses
  care of illness, 132, 136, 167, 168, 191, 200–202
  Dumbarton Combination Poorhouse, 200–202
  Ireland, 29, 33, 34
  used as form of relief, 92
  Windyknowe Public Assistance Institution, 183–184
Porch Cottage, 209–211, 215–216, 272
poverty
  cause of marriage breakdown, 139
  deserving and undeserving poor, 196

downward spiral, 122
economic downturn, 125–126
effect on children, 15
effect on health, 134–135
flower sellers, 261
Irish famine, 30–37
lack of gendered space for poor, 15, 19
meaning of poverty, 18
modern, 140
relief, 78, 91–92, 93, 167–173, 193–194
Samuel Smiles, 55
prejudice
anti-Catholic, 232
anti-Catholic Irish workers, 45, 48–49, 56–57, 163
anti-Irish, 19, 36, 53–54, 146, 316
less anti-Irish feeling in Glasgow, 72
less towards Protestant Irish, 72
pay rates of catholic and protestant workers, 143
towards travellers and roma, 56–57
Pringle, Miss F. N., 227, 228
public houses, 23
pyloric stenosis, 119

Q

Quakers, 39, 53, 226
Queen, Patrick. *see* Quinn, Patrick (later Peter) (b 1866)
Quinn family
application for relief, 116–117
belief in education, 95–96
catholicism, 100
characteristics, 11, 62–63
description, 17
downward spiral, 122, 204
finances, 124–127, 159
housing, 19, 153
importance of child earnings, 100, 105
migration from Ireland, 20
move to Edinburgh, 126–127, 128
moving house, 93–94, 108–109
Quinn surname, 26
survival of children, 94
tuberculosis, 133, 204, 300-301
Quinn, Alexander (b 1876)
apprenticeship at Singer's, 123–124, 141
birth, 20, 92
health, 108, 110, 124, 163–165
leaving home, 120, 121
mill work, 105
relationship with Bessie Quinn, 139, 160–161
shipyard work, 11, 124, 144–145, 164
Quinn, Arthur, 26, 37
Quinn, Arthur (b 1868)
birth, 20, 84
burial, 133
caring for nephews, 116, 118
caring for son, 132
confirmation, 101
Edinburgh, 128
health, 85, 110, 119–120, 128, 132–133
marriage, 118–119
move to Edinburgh, 132
son cared for by Mary Quinn, 120
work in woollen mill, 100
Quinn, Arthur George (b 1892)
adulthood, 182–185
authority care, 166–172
birth, 119, 120
cared for by relatives, 120–121, 149, 167–168, 208
death, 184
death of mother, 119
development difficulties, 120, 153
Edinburgh, 128, 132
education, 132, 153, 287

work, 170, 172
Quinn, Augustine (b 1884)
birth, 20, 93, 105
caring for nephews, 120
construction work, 136–137, 152, 173, 179
health, 178, 179–180
marriage, 178–179
military service, 175–178
poaching, 166–167, 179
staying with James Quinn, 179
stone-breaking work, 176
support for Thomas Quinn, 166–167
support for William Innes, 178–179
Quinn, Barbara (b 1902), 163, 188
Quinn, Bessie (b 1879, later Howard)
ashes, 3–4, 302, 303, 306
birth, 14, 20, 92
caring for nephews, 116, 120–121, 159–160, 208
catholicism, 316
character, 159, 160–161
childhood, 91, 158
confirmation, 101
contact with family, 233–234, 274, 277
cycling, 229–231, 240, 285
death, 2–4, 13, 291, 301
description, 4–5, 7–9, 163, 218, 248–249, 313, 316
discretion about background, 232–234, 249–250, 252, 254, 264–265, 272, 282
domestic service in Keswick, 174
dreams of leaving home, 156–157, 161
early life, 14–16, 19
education, 21–23, 126, 158, 287–288
education of sons, 285–288
funeral, 301–303
gardening, 282–283
holidays, 280, 284, 288–291, 295
housework, 21, 22–24, 158, 162
importance of siblings, 14, 15
influenza epidemic, 300–301
interest in change, 224
introduction to Howard family, 264–271
Keswick School of Industrial Arts, 4, 215, 221
learning to sew, 21, 121, 209, 215–216
lecture by Ebenezer Howard, 223–224, 248
leisure time, 23, 121, 280–281
literacy tasks for family, 120, 125, 158–159
marriage, 271–274, 317
married life, 280–284
meeting Cecil Howard, 241–254
mill work, 24, 126, 158
motherhood, 10, 160, 285–286
move to Clydebank, 137–138, 139, 141
move to Keswick, 164–165, 208
photographs, 4, 6–13, 109
protestant friends, 232
reading, 160, 161
relationship with Alexander Quinn, 139, 160–161, 164
relationship with Catherine Howard, 255, 256, 260
relationship with Ebenezer Howard, 283
relationship with father, 159
relationship with Howard family, 271
relationship with Kathleen Daisy Howard, 284
relationship with mother, 110, 120–122, 139
relationship with siblings, 121

relationship with Thomas Quinn, 156
Ruskin lace, 68, 216, 266, 272, 285
sending money to support family, 167
sewing, 4, 7, 272, 285
sewing as home work, 70, 110, 121, 162–163
Singer sewing machine, 162–163, 208–209
sponsors in Keswick, 218–225, 227–229, 255
temperance movement, 231–232
textile work, 215–216
travelling to London, 267
tuberculosis exposure, 300–301
understanding of family finances, 159
use of libraries, 23
wedding anniversary, 9
work as a cook, 217, 229, 235–244, 248, 317
Quinn, David (b 1907), 188, 191
Quinn, Elizabeth (b 1920), 179
Quinn, Elizabeth (possible relative), 106–107
Quinn, Ellen May (b 1897)
birth, 188
education and work, 189
memories of Bessie Quinn, 188–189, 293
memories of shipbuilding, 11, 163
visiting South Africa, 190–191
work in London, 293
Quinn, Ellen (nee Brooks), 163, 186–189, 215, 293
Quinn, James (b 1870)
birth, 20, 91
construction work, 152, 173, 180
death, 182
Edinburgh, 127
Galashiels, 151
marriage, 151, 181–182
mill work, 105, 180
move to America and return, 181–182, 195
railway work, 151
responsibility for family, 180
signing death certificate of Arthur Quinn, 133
support for Arthur George Quinn, 166–172, 182–183
support for family, 149, 179
support for Thomas Quinn, 137, 153
Quinn, James (b 1907), 199
Quinn, James (Jimmy) (b 1894)
birth, 188
emigration to South Africa and return, 190–191
injured in First World War, 148, 178, 277
military service, 155, 189, 190, 276–277
visiting relatives, 163
Quinn, Jane (nee Tocher), 118–119
Quinn, Mary (b 1844, nee Lyons)
age inconsistency, 41
ageing, 121, 154
agricultural work, 55, 59–61, 75
alternative birth surnames, 91, 92, 130, 150
application for relief, 91–92, 173, 194–197
cared for by daughter Mary, 193–194
caring for grandsons, 112, 115–116, 120
courtship and marriage, 74–77
death, 277
death of son Arthur Quinn, 133
description, 275–276
domestic service, 74, 77
effects of childbirth, 93–94, 105–106

health, 110, 154, 173–174
illness and death of Peter Lyons, 84–85
Irish origins, 20, 26, 27, 42
Kirkpatrick Durham, Kirkcudbrightshire, 195, 197, 275–277
meeting Owen Quinn, 62–63, 65
mental health, 194–198, 275–277
migration from Ireland, 27, 50–52
mill work, 66
move to Clydebank, 137–138, 139, 141
move to Galashiels, 81
move to Walkerburn, 64–66
pregnancy and childbirth, 74, 75–76, 78, 82–83
separation from Owen Quinn, 137–138, 139, 149, 173
sewing at home, 22, 70, 82, 102
Quinn, Mary (b 1872)
application for relief, 193–194
birth, 20, 91
biscuit manufacture, 130
caring for father, 149
caring for nephews, 116, 139, 149
confirmation, 101
description, 163
domestic service, 153
health, 24, 121–122, 193–194
housework, 102, 174
mill work, 22, 105
Quinn, Mary (nee Smith), 26, 37
Quinn, Owen (b ca 1831)
age inconsistency, 41, 91, 92
agricultural work, 48, 74, 75
alcohol, 122, 126, 150
building work, 70–71, 128
burial, 151
courtship and marriage, 74–77
death, 150–151
gardening work, 94–95, 109–111, 122, 125
Haddington, 59
health, 23, 43, 91–92, 138, 139, 149–152
Irish origins, 14, 20, 26–27, 29
Leeds, 44–47
loss of work, 93
meeting Mary Lyons, 62–63, 65
migration from Ireland, 27, 42, 43–44
move to Scotland, 48
relationship with Bessie Quinn, 159
separation from Mary Quinn, 137–138, 149, 173
stone-breaking work, 122
use of name James Quinn, 130, 150, 173
work, 23
work as labourer, 44–47
Quinn, Owen (b 1864)
birth, 20, 79
catholicism, 100–101, 113–114
construction work, 102
Edinburgh, 105, 112–114
marriage, 100, 112–114
mill work, 100
railway work, 105, 112–113
relationship with siblings, 113
report of death, 116–117, 203
son cared for by Mary Quinn, 112, 115–116
supporting family, 91–92
Quinn, Owen (b 1889)
birth and loss of mother, 114–116
cared for by Bessie Quinn, 23
cared for by grandmother, 112
caring for Arthur George Quinn, 149
education, 127
health, 194–197, 202–204
work at Singer's, 153, 163, 195, 202

Quinn, Patrick (later Peter) (b 1866)
alcohol, 166, 188
birth, 20, 82
construction work, 152, 163, 173, 195
death, 191
description, 188
marriage, 186–187
mill work, 100
move to Edinburgh, 105
relationship with family, 113, 151
support for Thomas Quinn, 153, 186
use of name Peter Quinn, 185–187
use of surname Queen, 187
Quinn, Peter. *see* Quinn, Patrick (later Peter) (b 1866)
Quinn, Peter (b 1874)
application for relief, 166–169, 185, 194–197
birth, 20, 91
birth of first child, 195, 199
character, 123
Clydebank, 139
courting Susan Boyle, 146, 151, 154–155, 167, 209
at death of father Owen Quinn, 150–151
leaving home, 120, 121
literacy, 150–151
marriage, 151, 153, 274
mill work, 105
reporting death of brother Owen Quinn, 116
responsibility for family, 151, 153, 157, 163–164, 193–198, 203–204, 276, 277
support for Bessie Quinn, 162–163, 208–209
support for mother, 194–197
support for nephew Owen Quinn, 116, 202–203
support for Thomas Quinn, 202
work at Singer's, 123–124, 141, 146–148, 151, 195
Quinn, Rosemary, 189
Quinn, Susan (nee Boyle)
courting Peter Quinn, 146, 154–155, 167, 209
marriage, 153, 199, 274
pregnancy and childbirth, 195, 199
Quinn, Thomas (b 1881)
alcohol, 137, 196, 201, 232
birth, 20, 92, 105
construction work, 152, 155, 156, 173
dependent on family goodwill, 151–152, 153, 166, 176, 186, 195–196
health, 199–202
military service, 137, 155–156
relationship with nephews, 120
rootless life, 137, 139

R

railways
cost of travel, 52
Cumberland, 209, 214–215
development, 55
employment, 105, 112–113, 151
flowers, 261
Garden Cities, 221, 266, 268
Irish workers in construction, 43, 48, 181
Singer Sewing Machine factory, 141
underground, 296–297
Ratcliffe, William, 259, 260
Rawlinson, Charles Compton, 264, 265–268, 273, 274
Rawlinson, Derwent, 296–297
Rawlinson, Kathleen Daisy. *see* Howard, Kathleen Daisy (later Rawlinson)

Rawnsley, Edith, 211, 212, 213, 214, 217, 218, 222
Rawnsley, Hardwicke, 211, 212, 213, 214, 219, 222, 272
Rayson, Jeannie, 230, 239–240, 272, 273
Rehill, James, 181, 182, 184
Rehill, Mary, 151, 181–182
research
  Borders Family History Society, 175
  census returns, 14
  documentation of families, 16, 27, 37, 41
  documentation of famine, 35–36, 39
  family research, 310–317
  funerals, 303
  Hampstead Garden Suburb, 12
  inconsistencies in records, 41
  London Metropolitan Archive, 12
  sources of information, 12–13, 18, 27
  tracing Irish generations, 15–18
  use of different names, 185
Roman Catholic Home for Working Boys, 171–172, 178
Roneen, Phelim, 38
Rudkin, Julie (nee Howard), ix, 7, 285, 288
Ruskin, John
  Co-operative Holidays Association, 227
  designs, 209–210, 212–213, 272–273, 285
  lace making, 68, 209, 210, 216, 266, 272, 285
  memorial, 230, 248, 253–254
  training in skills, 208, 211, 215–217, 256
  vegetarianism, 243–244
  visit to Galashiels, 68
  writings, 271
Russell, Lord John, 33

S

sanatoriums, 136, 179–180, 191–192
sanitation
  baths, 24, 103
  Galashiels, 20, 24, 68, 82
  Leeds, 45
  Newington, 128
  Walkerburn, 66
Scannell, Father Denis, 193, 199, 202
Scotland
  immigration, 27, 30, 40
  linen, 54, 85–86
  mining, 47
  textile industry, 69–70
  tweed, 65, 66
  wool, 14, 67, 81–82, 125–126
Scott, Walter, 22, 67–69, 80, 101
sewing
  Bessie Quinn learning to sew, 21, 121, 209, 215–216
  sewing as home work, 70, 82, 102, 104
  sewing machines mass production, 104, 123–124
Shaw, George Bernard, 222, 243, 292–293, 315
shipbuilding
  Alexander Quinn, 11, 124, 144–145
  Irish skills, 54
  toy ships as reminder, 11
  trade unions, 143
ships, 42–43
Sickert, Walter, 258
Singer Sewing Machine factory
  catholic and protestant pay rates, 143
  description, 123–124, 141
  employee benefits, 124, 143, 147–148, 162–163, 209
  employment conditions, 146–148, 202–203
  Irish workforce, 142

sewing machines mass production, 141–144
tied housing, 167, 194
trade unions, 124, 145–148
women workers, 143, 146–147, 148, 154–155, 199
Sissay, Lemn, 1
Smiles, Samuel, 55
Socialist Labour Party, 145, 147, 259
songs, 61
South Africa, 190
Southey, Robert, 69
Spanish flu epidemic, 298–301
spiritualism, 8, 292
sports
catholicism, 113
cricket, 147, 246, 286, 312, 313
Edinburgh, 113
Galashiels, 104
Hampstead Garden Suburb, 12, 282, 310
supported by employers, 147–148
St Joseph's Industrial School, 172
Stobie, James, 88–89
Storr, Frank, 256, 259
storytelling
during famine, 36
by migrants, 52, 61
suffrage, 69, 215, 225, 231, 256, 270
sugar, 54, 95, 130–131

T

Taggart, Father, 79
temperance
Co-operative Holidays Association, 239
temperance hotels, 90, 217, 226
temperance movement, 226, 230–232
textile industry
attitudes of mill owners to workers, 78
Galashiels, 67
Irish flax, 26, 29–30
Irish linen, 29–30, 48–49, 70, 85
Leeds, 44
linen in Scotland, 54, 85–86
Scottish borders, 69–70
skills of Irish migrants, 48–49, 70
training in skills, 210–217
tweed, 65, 66
wool in Scotland, 14, 67, 81–82, 125–126
theatre, 291–292, 306
Tocher, George, 118
Tocher, Jane (later Quinn), 118–119
Tocher, Margaret, 118, 120, 132, 167
Tóibín, Colm, 35, 38
toilets
Galashiels, 20
lack of toilets, 23, 103
Leeds, 46
Newington, 130
Walkerburn, 66
toys, 10–11
trade unions
criminalised, 68–69
day labourers and contract workers, 104–105
prejudice against Irish and women, 105
shipyards, 144
Singer Sewing Machine factory, 124, 145–148
transport. *see* cycling; motorcycling; railways
travellers
Nungate as a meeting place, 56–57
Quinn and Lyons names, 26
romanticisation, 247
travelling. *see also* holidays
children, 84

Ebenezer Howard, 8, 11, 245
Geoffrey Howard, 313
women alone, 64–65, 208–209, 267
tuberculosis, 191–192
Alexander Quinn, 163–165, 179–180
Arthur Quinn, 119–120, 132–133
Bessie Quinn's exposure, 300–301
common illness, 94, 99, 133–136, 204, 300–301
Margaret Tocher, 118
Mary Quinn (b 1872), 194
Owen Quinn (b 1889), 202–204
Patrick (Peter) Quinn, 191
Peter Lyons, 84–85
Thomas Quinn, 200–202
Turner, J. M. W., 68
Twelves, Marion, 210–211, 212, 214, 216, 218

U

Unwin, Raymond
Hampstead Garden Suburb architect, 12, 280, 283
Letchworth Garden City architect, 256, 259, 270
war work, 293

V

vegetarianism, 241–244, 248
Vickers, Mary, 220
violence
alcohol, 188, 231–232
among migrants, 71
civil unrest, 68–69
during famine, 31
Nungate, 58–59
political reform, 69
towards those travelling, 64
voices, recording famine, 35

W

Walker, Alexander, 78
Walker, Eliza, 78
Walker, James Campbell, 183
Walker, Jane, 198, 277
Walker, John F, 78
Walker, William, 77
Walker, William Stuart, 78
Walkerburn, 64–67
war
conscientious objectors, 293–294
Hampstead Garden Suburb, 293–295
injuries, 11, 148, 177, 178, 277–278
memoir, 190
memories of first world war, 11-12, 294–295
military service, 137, 148, 155–156, 175–178, 189, 190, 277–278
munitions, 189, 293
shell shock, 192
Watts, G. F., 214
Wells, H. G., 222, 293, 315
Welwyn Garden City, 247, 305
Whealan, Michael, 113
Whitman, Walt, 18
Windyknowe Public Assistance Institution, 183–184
women
Catholic school teachers, 21
constantly working, 71
cycling, 229–231
domestic violence, 188
friendly societies, 226
Garden Cities, 223–224
housework, 21, 71, 158
increasing opportunities, 215, 224–225, 255–257, 265
lack of gendered space for poor, 15, 128
limited options, 121

marriage alternative to domestic service, 188
mixed-sex schools, 21
modern, 255–257, 262–263
recreational opportunities, 215
suffrage, 69, 215, 225, 231, 256, 270
training in skills, 216–217
training of unemployed, 208
travelling alone, 64–65, 208–209, 267
widows, 47–48, 89
workhouses. *see* poorhouses
working class
attitudes of officials, 42
attitudes of other classes, 34, 39
diet, 20
oral memories, 19
power of church and state, 19, 42
voices, 16, 18–19, 233
work-schemes, 30, 31, 35

Y

Yeats, John Butler, 43

BV - #0007 - 130423 - C15 - 234/156/20 - PB - 9781914151330 - Gloss Lamination